Lament-Driven Preaching

Lament-Driven Preaching

Proclaiming Hope amid Suffering

ELIANA AH-RUM KU

Foreword by Paul Scott Wilson

PICKWICK *Publications* · Eugene, Oregon

LAMENT-DRIVEN PREACHING
Proclaiming Hope amid Suffering

Copyright © 2024 Eliana Ah-Rum Ku. All rights reserved. Except for brief quotations in critical publications or reviews, no part of this book may be reproduced in any manner without prior written permission from the publisher. Write: Permissions, Wipf and Stock Publishers, 199 W. 8th Ave., Suite 3, Eugene, OR 97401.

Pickwick Publications
An Imprint of Wipf and Stock Publishers
199 W. 8th Ave., Suite 3
Eugene, OR 97401

www.wipfandstock.com

PAPERBACK ISBN: 978-1-6667-7431-3
HARDCOVER ISBN: 978-1-6667-7432-0
EBOOK ISBN: 978-1-6667-7433-7

Cataloguing-in-Publication data:

Names: Ku, Eliana Ah-Rum [author]. | Wilson, Paul Scott [foreword writer].

Title: Lament-driven preaching : proclaiming hope amid suffering / Eliana Ah-Rum Ku.

Description: Eugene, OR: Pickwick Publications, 2024 | Includes bibliographical references and index.

Identifiers: ISBN 978-1-6667-7431-3 (paperback) | ISBN 978-1-6667-7432-0 (hardcover) | ISBN 978-1-6667-7433-7 (ebook)

Subjects: LCSH: Suffering—Religious aspects. | Laments in the Bible. | Bible.—Lamentations—Criticism, interpretation, etc. | Bible.—Lamentations—Theology. | Pastoral theology.—Korea (South). | Preaching. | Communication | Theology, Practical—Korea (South). | Jesus Christ—Passion. | Paschal triduum—Liturgy.

Classification: BS1535.52 K8 2024 (paperback) | BS1535.52 (ebook)

VERSION NUMBER 02/29/24

Scripture quotations are from New Revised Standard Version Bible (NRSV), copyright © 1989 National Council of the Churches of Christ in the United States of America. Used by permission. All rights reserved worldwide.

To Yesol and Yeyoon

Contents

Foreword by Paul Scott Wilson | ix

Introduction | xiii

1   Lament in the Book of Lamentations | 1

2   Lament as a Reflection of *Han* (한, 恨) and as a Way of *Hanpuri* (한풀이) | 40

3   The Theology of Lamentation(s) in Paschal Triduum Narratives | 80

4   The Role of Lament in Preaching | 126

5   Lament-in-Hope: Lament-Driven Preaching as a New Approach to Proclaiming Hope | 169

Conclusion | 218

Bibliography | 221

Subject Index | 245

Foreword

FEW TOPICS ARE MORE current for our times than lament, and I am honored to introduce this splendid volume on the topic by Eliana Ah-Rum Ku. The quality of public life has slipped in the last decade as politics has become more polarized as families divide over various social issues and as nations seem more inclined towards war. How might Christians best respond to these changes? An important part of our response can be lament.

Recently, an engineering student began to suffer from depression and went to the university health services. He said afterwards, "I didn't know what to expect. I hoped they would just give me things to do, like physical exercises, or books to read, or tell me to make new friends. Instead, the counsellor wanted me to talk about my childhood. At first, I was reluctant." He did not appreciate then what he now knows, personal counselling commonly works best by probing deep into childhood experience. It assumes that present emotions and actions are largely based on what happened to us in the past. A person being counselled recounts past events, often painful ones, and with regular visits over time, gradually comes in touch with thoughts and feelings that may have been repressed or bottled up inside. Someone once described depression as anger and sorrow turned inward—it needs to be expressed. Instead of being subconsciously driven by pain, one learns with counselling to name and channel it in healthy ways.

Lament is similar to that. Dr. Ku argues for the practice of lament in public worship as a way to come to terms with social ills of the past and present. Particularly now, when the world is so broken and hurting, lament is vital. Every week there are things in God's world worthy of tears and lament. The world is not as it should be. People keep perpetrating terrible acts of violence on other people. How can there be healing if we have not named what causes the hurt?

Lament is theological. It is an offering made in prayerful action before God. It is confessional, listing ways we have been hurt and/or contributed to the hurt of others. It is intercessory, asking help for oneself and others in overcoming pain and suffering and in working for justice. It is thanksgiving that anticipates a new future in Christ who even now restores fullness of life.

Lament matters. God is concerned about those who suffer violence and injustice. Their pain is God's pain. Their silence is a place of God's presence. Their lament is God's. Micah 6:8 reads, "What does the Lord require of you but to do justice, and to love kindness, and to walk humbly with your God?" If hope is to be proclaimed, it must take account of the raw realities of the past and not allow them to have the last word. Lament can be a way to prevent the past from happening again.

Dr. Ku is motivated by her own poignant experiences growing up in South Korea. Many Koreans alive today suffered at the hands of occupying forces during World War II, women in particular, and their continued suffering was largely silenced. Under the military dictatorship that ended in 1979, democratization movements were violently suppressed. In 2014, the Sewol ferry sank, tragically killing 304 people, most of them high school students. These events were largely treated with silence from Korean pulpits, though they were traumatic for the Korean people, and silence added to the pain. Churches did not know how to deal with the suffering and grief. Some preachers even blamed victims for lack of faith. An experience of han, or suffering, has become a part of Korean national identity.

While these events are particular to Korea, every country has similar kinds of stories to tell, stories that often have been suppressed by the powers that be. Many of these stories have been deemed too painful to tell, as was the case in North America for indigenous peoples with the forced removal of their children from parents, language, and culture, to residential schools. Government policies of cultural assimilation were often administered by churches. Hundreds of children suffered sexual abuse and/or died without record. Lament is part of a process of listening, acknowledgement, and reconciliation. It can lead, with the help of the Holy Spirit, to restored relationships, and new opportunities for diverse peoples to live in community as God intended.

There can be danger to lament without good news. Dr. Ku argues that lament in the context of Christian worship necessarily leads to hope. Preaching needs both lament and hope to be a full expression of the gospel. On its own, lament names wrongs, acknowledges suffering, expresses human pain (and God's), and calls for justice. Lament is modeled on the Bible, most notably Lamentations and the Psalms. The crucifixion and resurrection of Christ represent an appropriate relationship of lament and hope. Good Friday has a sense of finality, the powers of the world have had their say and death seems to have the last word. Lament does not eventually erase death or diminish it—it brings it into focus. Jesus rising from the dead at Easter similarly does not erase the suffering and loss, as though it never happened, but Christ redeems it. Preaching the resurrection puts the unlimited powers of God's love over against evil and shows the powers of death to be empty. Both Good Friday and Easter are true, and in the tension between the two are rich opportunities of faith.

All of this is part of the excellent vision Dr. Ku presents in an engaging and invitational manner. She provides pastors with practical directions that draw on lament and celebration in African American preaching, and on trouble and grace as discussed in homiletics. Lament can be part of a healing process of which the world is much in need. What a difference would be made if preachers were to walk the preaching path that she charts so skillfully here. A new heaven and a new earth might be a little closer, and preaching might more fully be for the healing of the nations.

PAUL SCOTT WILSON
Professor Emeritus of Homiletics, Emmanuel College, University of Toronto

Introduction

WHY LAMENT

Many preachers consider preaching to be gospel or good news. But a biblical book like Lamentations might challenge that notion, for it ends with despair in the silence of God and it spills over with suffering. Lamentations might therefore even challenge one's definition of a sacred book, or of what constitutes God's word.[1] It might also seem to be a poor resource for providing definitive hope to those who are suffering. However, the voices of those in Lamentations, like believers in today's world, faced incomprehensible and uncontrollable suffering. Whether those whose voices are recorded in Lamentations or who suffer today, people experiencing the power of evil often feel as if they are surrounded not by God's caring presence but God's silence. What can and should preachers say about suffering when to the sufferers God seems to be absent? How can preachers proclaim hope amidst the reality of suffering?

Beginning in late 2019, the coronavirus rapidly spread worldwide. Though not visible to the naked eye, this virus sparked tragic and painful losses in every corner of the human world, to an extent that few people had foreseen. It sparked not only massive loss of health and life, but concomitant economic, political, racial, and mental problems. It led to increased suffering, social injustice, and hatred toward Asians, Blacks, and other minorities, and to increased domestic violence and anxiety, and to a huge loss in learning and socialization, especially among children. In pulpits during the

---

1. Though Lamentations 3 speaks of hope, the third poem returns the theme of suffering at the end. Perhaps this was intended to prompt an evaluation of the theological tradition of Israel and a comparison with the reality experienced. Dobbs-Allsopp, *Lamentations*, 105. Perhaps it is a rhetorical device to emphasize the reality of suffering. Thomas, *Poetry and Theology*, 171–72.

COVID-19 pandemic, preachers struggled to minister to the anger, hopelessness, and disconnectedness many people felt. Specifically, the misinterpretation or insular theological approaches to the relationship between sin and suffering have led to complex and controversial issues. Preachers may also have been tempted to bypass the reality of suffering by proclaiming hope too quickly or by misinterpreting the gap between the reality of suffering and God's promised world. This tendency is not exceptional in more common situations, even in a post-pandemic world.

Incorporating communal lament into preaching may be one way to address human suffering. Lament is principally about dealing with suffering rather than about identifying the cause of suffering, and it resists the attempt to escape quickly from the pain and suffering one is experiencing.[2] So preachers would benefit sufferers by being more intentional in dealing with suffering, specifically by practicing lament as a transitional place between suffering and hope. Suffering and hope represent two poles in theology and preaching. Rather than advocate for one or the other, or trying to find a safe location between the two existing poles, this book seeks to show the value in inhabiting the tension between them.[3] It proposes lament as a way to dwell in the tension between two poles—lament as a way to bridge suffering and hope. It shows preachers how to use lament to generate a space for envisioning hope, without minimizing the reality of suffering.

THE MEANING OF LAMENT

While lament can of course be understood narrowly as a personal or individual attitude and passive image or action and that generally includes weeping, crying, and tears, in ancient Near Eastern society lament was instead used to restore individual and social balance.[4] It was also used in funeral rituals and to establish and remind people of the history of the deceased and of kinship told through generations.[5] In addition, lament was a form of social protest.[6] In biblical traditions, lament expresses desire for God's help, argument with God, resistance to social injustice, acknowledgment

---

2. It does not deny the existence of hope but questions the history of interpretation that silences pain and despair. O'Connor, *Lamentations and the Tears*, 45; Mandolfo, *Daughter Zion Talks Back*, 101; Linafelt, *Surviving Lamentations*, 17–18; Dobbs-Allsopp, *Lamentations*, 121.

3. Rutledge, *Crucifixion*, 33.

4. Cottrill, "Articulate Body," 104.

5. Stears, "Gender and Athenian Death Ritual," 150–51.

6. Lee, "Lamentations and Polemic," 172; Caraveli, "Bitter Wounding," 169–94.

of the power of sin, the opening of apocalyptic horizons, loss, repentance for sin, and so on.[7] These traditions and practices show that lament is more than complaint and that it commonly embraces both suffering and hope. In this sense, the "lament" can be a valuable homiletic resource—indicating something holistic and including extensive meanings.

Lament is an important form and tool in preaching to deal with suffering as a part of Christian gospel, creating a dynamic between suffering and hope. *Lament is the impassioned expression, witness, and personal and/or social protest of those who suffer in the face of evil and injustice, a longing for God's saving presence.* Lament cries out against systems that demean life, particularly the lives of those who have not sinned but suffer because of the systemic sin of others, including of institutions like the church. Though lament can be interpreted in a wide range of ways, here I focus on lament as the voiced and bodily expression of suffering of those who have faith and have been harmed or seen others harmed in ways they have not deserved. Lament in itself can include hopeful elements, since it is a voice or way of naming and protest, not of defeat, and is—generally—offered to God. Generally, because of course we also read about God lamenting, for example as an expression of solidarity with human suffering, including of Jesus Christ's suffering on the cross.

Lament-driven preaching thus involves human lament and divine lament. Such preaching employs lament as a transitional space that holds and bridges suffering and hope and moves between the two. It offers a way to experience genuine hope, for it reminds hearers of God's presence in both experiences. With the help of the Holy Spirit, such preaching reminds us that God is present in the depths of pain, providing constant comfort in societies that are not easily changed, as well as continuous resistance and transformation in Christ's victory over the power of evil and death.[8]

To proclaim hope amid suffering, in this book I encourage preachers to consider embracing lament in their preaching. Our current lack of familiarity with lament is after all not because of our human lack of experience with grief or suffering, but because we, as the church, seem to be uncomfortable with lament. As a result, our church practices often bypass or sidestep suffering, reducing its meaning to isolated moments, like during our confession of sins, funerals, and particular times of the church year, like Holy Week.[9]

---

7. Öhler, "To Mourn," 150–65; O'Connor, *Lamentations and the Tears*; Mandolfo, *Daughter Zion Talks Back*; Parry, *Lamentations*.

8. Kim, "Sewol-ho Disaster and God," 48.

9. Duff, "Recovering Lamentation," 34. See also Bruggemann, *Message of the Psalms*, 52; MaCann, *Theological Introduction to the Book of Psalms*, 85. Mary Catherine Hilkert

In this book I invite you to consider giving lament-driven sermons not only in special seasons, such as Lent, but also on normal Sundays, knowing from experience that lament in preaching evokes in hearers comfort that their suffering and distress are acknowledged and a part of both the community's life and God's life. Such lament-driven sermons can offer believers a way to experience true hope through God's redemptive action amid suffering. As a result, lament in preaching can help to recall the promises of our faithful God without neglecting the realities of suffering.

MAPPING DISCOURSES OF LAMENT

To support the argument that lament is important in preaching for expressing one's suffering and for envisioning genuine hope, I develop multidisciplinary conversations in biblical, cultural, theological, and homiletical fields. I first study theological interpretations and hermeneutical approaches to the Book of Lamentations. As a framework for the basic research, I suggest the importance of Lamentations as a sacred book for preaching and show how, at least from one perspective, the voices in Lamentations argue with God when God seems silent about people's suffering. By exploring the biblical tradition of lament and its various roles and values through the book of Lamentations, I probe how biblical lament expresses and manages suffering. I argue that lament is both a biblical and liturgical language and an action, which God has permitted for expressing suffering in faith and in the search for hope. Specifically, I explore the fifth poem in Lamentations and its language of grief as a counter-testimony and a communal lament.[10] Lament, here, is presented as a tool of resistance against social injustice, as a conversation between survivors about grief and loss, as an emotional and expressive outlet of the oppressed, and as a survival strategy.[11] Lamentations thus functions as a space-holder in the place of pain, a place for offering

---

also mentions, "preachers fail to do justice to the dynamics of the paschal mystery when they move too quickly to exhortations to hope. Where is there room for grief in Christian liturgy?" *Naming Grace*, 118. Elizabeth Achtemeier agrees that people need time to mourn and lament. Achtemeier has only one condition for using lament in worship, which is that lament should occur when we are repenting of our sin. *Preaching Hard Texts*, 145. Leslie C. Allen suggests that guilt is not a major factor in the process of grief, but confession to God and to others is. He says, "The confession of guilt has grace as its goal." *Liturgy of Grief*, 18–19. Preachers are often tempted to succumb to a "forget it" response, known as denial, and to talk or pray "around" the situation by ignoring tension, conflict, and pain. Schlafer, *What Makes This Day Different?*, 133.

10. Brueggemann, *Theology of the Old Testament*, 317–403; Ferris, *Genre of Communal Lament*.

11. O'Connor, *Lamentations and the Tears*; Linafelt, *Surviving Lamentations*.

sympathy, and of preparation for restoration. Because Lamentations presents colliding perspectives, embracing various voices about suffering,[12] I consider the meaning of diversity, of resisting attempts to impose a single and unified theological perspective on suffering and pain.[13]

Through cultural experiences, the second chapter broadly considers various aspects of human lament in the Bible. To identify the role of communal lament in suffering, specifically in relation to public crisis and structural injustice, the chapter draws on the social, cultural, and homiletical practice of communal lament in Korea, and specifically on the concepts of han and hanpuri. In Korean society, the traditional language for expressing suffering is based on the concept of *han*, a deeply internalized feeling of grief experienced by Koreans. *Hanpuri* is an aspect of *han* and refers to the acts of exposing pain, sharing stories of pain, and demanding justice, rather than simply tolerating and alleviating pain.[14] I explore three ways of engaging *hanpuri*: through external social movements, through individual and communal suffering narratives, and through transcendent religious responses. I then consider the various contributions of lament in public places, which lead to the dynamics between *han* and *hanpuri*. I also show how Korean society has cultivated close ties between *han* and *hanpuri*, and uses them as tools for dealing with pain and fostering community resilience. Interestingly, exploring lament through the movement between *han* and *hanpuri* creates a space for Christian dialogue. For that movement incorporates historical consciousness and social justice beyond the realm of personal faith, yet does so without undermining the theological interpretation of sin and repentance. The universality of suffering and the language of lament appear not only through the language of the Bible and the Christian community, they are also a deep part of Korean culture and of society as a whole.

The third chapter addresses the theological value and place of lament, in which suffering and hope exist in tension. It focuses on divine lament a part of God's response to human lament. I envision the theological place of lament as a transitional space where the dynamics of the crucifixion, burial, and resurrection are connected. This chapter first examines the causes and complexity of human lament. Lament arises from the bondage to sin which results in a fallen creation and can lead to eternal death. Lament consequently calls for divine redemptive action. The crucifixion and resurrection are the divine response to human suffering and lament. Another

---

12. Dobbs-Allsopp, *Lamentations*, 116; Parry, *Lamentations*, 103; Thomas, *Poetry and Theology*, 186.

13. Dobbs-Allsopp, *Lamentations*, 22.

14. Park, *Wounded Heart*, 105.

way of saying this is that God's action involves both lament and comfort. I therefore explore the biblical image of Christ's descent into hell and Holy Saturday to depict the dynamic between suffering and hope. I understand this space between the cross and the resurrection as a place of the merged lament of God and humans, rather than as a description of evil or theodicy. Central to this chapter is the assumption that God alone brings a sentence of eternal condemnation to evil. Humans cannot solve the power of evil. Because of God, evil ultimately has no power to separate people from God's faithfulness. Throughout the theological survey of lament presented here, the meaning of δικαιοσύνη functions as both the motivation and agency of God's action. I consider δικαιοσύνη as the Holy Spirit's empowerment of us humans to be able to live in the tension between suffering and hope. In short, God is there and on the move amid suffering.

The fourth chapter then explores recent homiletical rhetorical features, theologies, and practices to see whether and how the homiletical field has (or has not) used lament since the 1950s, and how that use relates to genuine hope. Topics I consider include listeners and human experience, ethical issues related to public crises and social injustice, our relationship to the Holy Spirit, theodicy, and lectionaries, as well as narrative, metaphor/analogy, imagination/image, and tension. Lament has been portrayed as more than merely a complaint or an expression of pain, though it has not been given much attention by homileticians. Nonetheless, some support the practice of lament, emphasizing the dynamics of suffering and hope. They belong to what I call the Trouble-Grace school. I probe what I call the theological and homiletical grammar of Law-Gospel as a previous form of Trouble-Grace, and some related frames which influenced Trouble-Grace. Finally, I establish the value of lament as a transitional space between suffering and hope based on the work of four scholars: Paul Wilson, Luke Powery, Joni Sancken, and Christine Smith. I do so to show how the movement from suffering to hope via lament is theologically and homiletically viable using such polar concept.

The fifth and final chapter suggests practical applications of lament in preaching. I first deliberate how to identify and treat the complexity of suffering, how to use counter-narratives, how to use lament as homiletical rhetoric, how to approach the violence of God and the absence of God in the Bible, and I explore pedagogical aspects of lament. I then consider psychological concerns about suffering, including some pastoral approaches to suffering. Although from a theological perspective there are some limitations to psychology, it can provide preachers a useful vocabulary that acknowledges and addresses the wounds of sufferers. It can help them to discern the elements of lament preaching that respect and embrace suffering in a

Christian community or an individual. Specifically, I suggest eleven features and considerations for lament-driven preaching. I also suggest how lament can connect the two poles (of suffering and hope) and generate a dynamic response, and how communal lament can help listeners in complex and diverse situations of distress. Last of all, I investigate practical implications of lament-driven preaching, including preachers' attitudes as lamenters, the timing of hope in a sermon, a possible missing part of lament-driven preaching, and possibilities for liturgical lament. Lament-driven preaching can help hearers envision the hope of God's future through God's saving action and by bringing hope into the present without losing sight of the very real experience of human suffering. When a sermon carries human lament, people can experience the gap between the reality of suffering and God's promise being filled by divine lament and comfort, and they can find a new cruciform way of living in hope.

1

Lament in the Book of Lamentations

THE BOOK OF LAMENTATIONS was written in part to acknowledge and share the human experience of grief. The voices in Lamentations reveal unbearable pain and loss, and in doing so, place their tears of pain and suffering in the context of faith. The voices of Lamentations also overturn the assumption that pain and suffering are the result of God's will, and that victims are instruments of divine justice.[1] Lamentations has no happy ending. It testifies to the human fear that God will desert us. God's apparent silence during our human suffering prompts us (and the persons whose voices are represented in Lamentations) to resurface memories of many occasions of suffering that have paralyzed us and that remain latent in us. This strong resistance to the faith of triumphalism is also resistance to the silence of God and the denial of the world.[2] Thus, Lamentations gives us an appropriate biblical lens through which to look at suffering.

Since the 1990s, scholars have identified a variety of interpretations of the pain of Lamentations. Criticizing these interpretations, Paul House notes that Lamentations should be interpreted by distinguishing between suffering as the consequence of sin and suffering that is experienced by those who are innocent.[3] However, I disagree with House because the distinction between the sinner and the innocent person is far more complex in its theological implications than suggested by the dichotomic question of whether humans are the cause of suffering.[4] Our discussion of Lamentations will

1. Hughes, *Lament*, 1.
2. For more on the relationship between Bible and triumphalism, see Brueggemann, *Theology of the Old Testament*, 329.
3. House, "Outrageous Demonstrations of Grace," 37.
4. Chapter 3 deals with this issue in detail.

deal with the potential duality within the word *suffering*. I argue that Lamentations' intentional ambiguity allows its poetry to include a wide range of suffering, one that extends beyond the judgment of sin. Therefore, this book does not focus on the distinction between sin and innocence, but on how Lamentations serves the Bible and the church as a language of grief, and ultimately how it has benefited preaching. It draws on literary-theological analysis as a hermeneutic for preaching.

THE HISTORY OF LAMENT

Outside of the biblical tradition of lament, lament is frequently associated with women's polyphonic voices.[5] In ancient cultures, lament was used mainly in funeral rituals and established a history of self or of kinship status, being celebrated through generations.[6] Lament was used to lead souls and to restore individual and social balance.[7] Ancient Greek lament was a form of social protest against the social limitations placed on women and against war, and of grieving for loss.[8] Greek lament allowed women to lament their oppression under patriarchy and that of their community in crisis.[9] These ancient traditions appear in an expanded form in the Bible.

Lament in the Bible

Lament in the Old Testament

Biblical lament includes a direct and concrete naming of the harsh realities of life, praise of God's reign, and maintenance of the motif of resurrection implies a hopeful ending to lament (Ezek 37:11–12).[10] Lamenters *desire God's help and call for God's positive intervention* by reminding God of God's promises (Exod 2:23). Many lament psalms assert the right to argue with God, whose name is to be called on amid suffering (Ps 79; Judg 20:23–28; Joel 1:12). F. W. Dobbs-Allsopp notes that lament provides space to express individual and community anger before God.[11] *Resistance*

---

5. Suter, "Introduction," 3–4.
6. Stears, "Death Becomes Her," 150–51.
7. Tolbert, "Women Cry with Words," 80.
8. Galchinsky, "Lament as Transitional Justice," 261.
9. Rosenberg, "Voice Like Thunder," 32.
10. Galchinsky, "Lament as Transitional Justice," 264.
11. Dobbs-Allsopp, "Tragedy," 53; Westermann, *Lamentations*, 91.

against social injustice is also included in the lament psalms and prophetic literature. Lament unravels *the reality and power of sin*, which has taken people captive, hindering them from readily repenting of or correcting their wrong ways (Jer 13:23; Hos 5:4). Lament as a curse deals with *hatred against enemies and opens apocalyptic horizons* to alleviate conflict.[12] Lament also functions as a *warning of impending death*. Although *woe oracles*, which contain God's reproach (Isa 1:15), can be included in this category,[13] they do not end with expressions of death, but with God's desire for the people to return (Isa 1:16–17). Thus, woe oracles represent the lament of God and the prophets (Jer 9:1; Hos 11:8; Amos 7:2). Lament also became a tradition of the daughters of Israel after the sacrifice of Jephthah's daughter (Judg 11:34–40). The lament in the Old Testament expresses pain, asserts an awareness of suffering, awaits God's resolution with hope, and builds and maintains a state of tension against common theology.[14] By doing so, lament contributes to broadening the range of perceptions of Old Testament theology.[15]

Lament in the New Testament

The New Testament also contains plentiful laments, expressing individual and communal *experiences of death and loss* (Matt 2:18; Mark 16:10; 5:38–39; John 11:31, 33). Lament is encouraged as part of *repenting of sin*, with warnings to the rich who condemn and murder the righteous while they live in luxury and indulgence (Jas 5:5–6). James recommends that one should "lament and mourn and weep" (4:9) for evildoing, contention, murder, jealousy, adultery, pride, conflict, and disputes (4:1–4). The Bible also notes the pain and mourning that results from *the apocalyptic judgment* (Luke 6; Rev 18:9). The Greek word στενάζομεν (we groan, 2 Cor 5:2, 4) is an expression of both mourning and earnest desire to *possess the invisible*.[16] In Romans, all of creation laments as it awaits God's redemption (8:23). Although the eschaton enters the world through resurrection, all creation has *the fate of death* until the full end is reached.[17] The Holy Spirit laments

---

12. Bouer, "Enquiring into the Absence of Lament," 26.
13. Achtemeier, *Preaching Hard Texts*, 48.
14. Brueggemann seems to accept both the merciful God and the abusive God. See Brueggemann, *Theology of the Old Testament*, 359–72; Brueggemann, *Old Testament Theology*, 24, 26.
15. Brueggemann, *Old Testament Theology*, 23.
16. Öhler, "To Mourn," 156.
17. Öhler, "To Mourn," 163.

and intervenes to accomplish that for which the creation pleads.[18] The New Testament also witnesses Jesus' lament (Matt 27:46; Mark 15:34; Luke 19:41; John 11:35), which elicits God's compassion as a faithful reaction to those who are *overwhelmed by destructive power*.[19] Jesus also commends the people who lament for themselves and their children (Luke 23:28) because he sees the suffering of people who live in *the tension of the "already-not yet"* (Luke 13:34–35; 19:44). To cry out (βοώντων) in the context of prayer has the character of communal lament as a *community petition* (Luke 18:7).[20] It is presumed that Luke's community was crying out for personal and community prayer in the context of fighting against their real suffering and persecution.[21] These traditions and practices commonly show that lament is more than a voice of complaint and has been used as an expression, as a witness, and as a protest to deal with suffering and to look for the answer to their grief.

Historical Understanding of Lamentations

The book of Lamentations is set at the time of the destruction of the Jerusalem Temple by the Babylonians in the sixth century BCE. The book is composed of five poems, each of which is based on alphabetic acrostics.[22] Lamentations includes communal lament such as the voices of women who have experienced suffering from radical loss. The poems blend their voices as they sing of the physical pain of war, mental wounds, and spiritual struggles, as well as of the particular suffering a woman experiences through rape, shame, insults, and the death of a child. The voices of Lamentations resonate with the Trail of Tears of aboriginal communities in North America, and the horrors of the Holocaust, 9/11, the Killing Fields of Cambodia, Black Lives Matter, and other sounds of destruction and pain from around the world.

---

18. Öhler, "To Mourn," 164.

19. Hinze, "Ecclesial Impasse," 481.

20. Freed, "Parable of the Judge," 53. See Matt 27:46; Mark 15:34; You, "Spirituality of Prayer," 594.

21. Reid, "Beyond Petty Pursuits," 290.

22. An acrostic poem is "a poem in which the initial letters of each successive line form a word, phrase or pattern." Coogan, "Acrostic," 6. The alphabetic acrostics are widely accepted as symbolizing "a sense of completeness." In Lamentations, "it is a literary form which corresponds to the completeness of grief which is expressed in the poems." Renkema, "Meaning of the Parallel," 379. The last poem does not have alphabetic acrostics, but it has twenty-two lines which are the same number as the letters of the Hebrew alphabet, and echo the power of previous alphabetic acrostics.

Although the ways in which Lamentations have been studied and practiced vary, here I am interested in how churches and scholars have interpreted and practiced Lamentations in relation to pain. The biblical texts are open to multiple interpretations. The stubborn belief in the past interpretations may deny the creative role of present interpreters in their own historical places and may disturb broader conversations.[23] Nonetheless, looking at various interpretations of suffering in Lamentations through history from the perspective of dialogue will provide some meaningful insight into how each context of the Bible has been interpreted and how it will enrich conversations and free it from prejudices of the past or present.

The Patristic and Medieval Periods

Until the Carolingian period in the ninth century, no commentary on Lamentations existed, and only fragmentary references to Lamentations can be found.[24] It wasn't until the twelfth century that commentaries on Lamentations began to be published.[25] In the patristic and medieval periods, suffering in Lamentations was usually interpreted to be caused by Judah's sin and as a way of revealing Jesus Christ, both in prophecy and his crucifixion. Interpretations related to individual, or community sin were prominent during this period. Gregory the Great (540–604) insisted in his pastoral role that the ruin of Jerusalem, as it is described in the fourth poem of the book of Lamentations, was caused by people's diminishing holiness, and mourning that loss is understood as a means of washing away evil.[26] Gregory Nazianzen (329–390) read Lamentations as a book that describes the consequences for unfaithful living.[27] Eusebius of Caesarea (260/265–339/340) applied Lamentations 2:1–2 to the early church in the period of persecution from AD 302–303. He pointed out that the church's suffering is due to its sins, including conflicts among leaders and their irreverence.[28] Lamentations was also interpreted as a warning of the coming doomsday. John Chrysostom (347–407) wrote that the description of the terrible suffering in Lamentations 4 was intended to convince people that there is a

---

23. Roberts, "Introduction," 3.
24. Hogg, "Christian Interpretation of Lamentations," 120.
25. Andrée, *Gilbertus Universalis*, 55–56.
26. Schaff, *Nicene and Post-Nicene Fathers* (hereafter *NPNF*) 2, 12:18b, 60b.
27. *NPNF* 2, 7:272.
28. *NPNF* 2, 1:324.

hell.²⁹ Gilbertus Anglicus (1180–1250) claimed that Lamentations is full of tears foretelling future judgment.³⁰

Origen of Alexandria (184–253) and Jerome of Stridon (347–420) understood Lamentations as a prophetic text that reveals Christ and emphasizes the importance of spiritual interpretations. Many people interpreted Lamentations as making the connection between the prophecy of Christ and the sufferings of Christ.³¹ Irenaeus, the Bishop of Lyon (130–202), and Rufinus of Aquileia (344/345–411) both saw Christ on the cross through the suffering presented in Lamentations.³² Cyril of Jerusalem presented 4:20 as evidence of Christ's suffering in the debate about whether Christ suffered on the cross.³³ Also, in the Middle Ages, Christ was the key for interpreting the Old Testament.³⁴ For instance, the voice of Jesus calling people to stop struggling under the yoke of sin and instead take his easier and lighter yoke upon themselves (Mark 11:29–30) allegedly interprets Lamentations 1:3.³⁵

Some ancient interpreters believed that Lamentations could help in the formation of spiritual life or offered an ethical model. Origen thought Lamentations provided instructions on how to live a devout life.³⁶ For Gregory the Great, Lamentations teaches us how to live while waiting for God's coming kingdom.³⁷ Abbot John Cassian (360–435) considers Lamentations to be useful for spiritual training.³⁸ Jerome used Lamentations to teach monks a lesson about living without greed (3:27–28).³⁹ Quintus Septimius Florens Tertullian (155–240) said that instead of laziness, Christians should pour out their hearts to God in fasting and prayer.⁴⁰ In 1:7, Gilbertus reminded

---

29. *NPNF* 1, 13:358.

30. Andrée, *Gilbertus Universalis*, 287.

31. Andrée, *Gilbertus Universalis*, 114–15.

32. Irenaeus considers Lam 3:30 and 4:20 as the suffering Jesus experienced. See Irenaeus, *Demonstration of the Apostolic Preaching*, 856, 1698; *NPNF* 2, 3:553.

33. *NPNF* 2, 7:84. Lam 4:20 is also used to testify that Christ is the Spirit, in *NPNF* 2, 7:132. See also various interpretation of Nicene Fathers in Wenthe, *Jeremiah, Lamentations*, 299–304.

34. Lubac, *Medieval Exegesis*, 203.

35. Hogg, "Christian Interpretation of Lamentations," 121. Although this can provide fresh and effective insight, it can also minimize the reality of suffering. Hogg, "Christian Interpretation of Lamentations," 122.

36. Trigg, *Origen*, 79.

37. Thomas, "Lamentations in the Patristic Period," 116.

38. *NPNF* 2, 11:493.

39. *NPNF* 2, 6:38, 81.

40. Wenthe, *Jeremiah, Lamentations*, 286.

believers that falling into the hands of an enemy is like falling into the greed, luxury, and joy of the flesh.[41]

Most early interpreters advocate for God's goodness. Clement of Alexandria (150–215) interpreted the sufferings we experience as trials that will ultimately lead us to salvation.[42] St. Ambrose, the Bishop of Milan (340–397), interpreted Lamentations as a book to lead Jerusalem to repentance and salvation, based on 3:31–32.[43] Early interpreters advised us not to complain, and to endure pain because God knows what is good.[44]

Some church fathers used Lamentations to lament on behalf of others, as a demonstration of comfort and empathy. Basil of Caesarea (290/330–379) quoted 2:18 in a letter to Nectarius, mourning for Nectarius' tremendous pain and loss.[45] In a consolatory letter to the Church of Ancyra, Basil sympathized with the grief arising from a great disaster and appealed to the need for lamentations.[46] Theodoret, a Bishop of Cyrus (393–458), urged the community to await the Lord's Day of salvation together (3:25), helping the weak and raising the fallen.[47]

With the hope of Lamentations 3, early church and Medieval interpreters thought they might expunge the dominant language of complaining. Also, hope appears to be future-oriented when believers endure temporary hardships in the present. Church fathers might have proclaimed to the church that God is good and cares for God's people, in order to protect the church from persecution and to rebut heresies.

The Reformation Era

In the Roman Catholic tradition prior to the Reformation, Lamentations played a central role in the liturgy of Holy Week. It was used to convey the voice of Christ's suffering on the way to the cross, to describe the Jews after the fall of Jerusalem, and to mourn one's sins during Holy Week.[48] However, during the sixteenth and seventeenth centuries, interpreting Lamentations

---

41. Andrée, *Gilbertus Universalis*, 209.
42. Wenthe, *Jeremiah, Lamentations*, 275.
43. NPNF 2, 10:333, 351.
44. Wenthe, *Jeremiah, Lamentations*, 287.
45. NPNF 2, 8:114.
46. NPNF 2, 8:133–34.
47. NPNF 2, 3:274.
48. Tyler, *Jeremiah, Lamentations*, lv.

was not only about personal repentance or the suffering of Christ, it also reflected the sufferings of society, of the church, and of souls.[49]

Against the background of the Reformation, not only religious issues but social and political issues were linked together, so it can be said that lament was used to speak justice and to express resistance. When preaching on Lam 4:5, Martin Luther (1483–1546) lamented the lack of true God's words in the church, comparing the pope's words bought by the price of money and soul to "filth."[50] Luther criticized the pope for not preaching the pure gospel, and for being a blind leader and a soul killer and a sinner. He compared Christian faith to spiritual virginity and described the women of Zion and Judah who were raped in Lamentations (5:11) as the churches that were spiritually abused by those who preached like the pope.[51]

There is also an interpretation of Lamentations that makes an overt connection to Christ. Nikolaus Selnecker (1530–92) insisted that we acknowledge God's cross and "the gracious and paternal will of God in everything," whether we experience sickness, poverty, hardship, accidents, or injustice.[52] Because he might have considered our cross (suffering) a definite sign of God's grace through discipline.

The most dominant interpretation of Lamentations has to do with the confession of sin. Arcangela Tarabotti (1604–52) interpreted Lam 1:9 as the souls of those who follow the dirty path of sin which leads to destruction.[53] Hugh Broughton (1549–1612) interpreted 1:11 as saying that sin prevents people from seeing God's warnings and that the Holy Spirit teaches the godly to lament with unspeakable sighs.[54] Daniel Toussain (1541–1602) wrote that in Lamentations God's justice appears in suffering as punishment for sin, and the suffering is a wholesome remedy by which to renew our faith.[55] Peter Martyr Vermigli (1499–1562) understood that it is God's plan for future generations to be punished for the sins of previous generations (5:7).[56]

In addition, the recognition that sin is the cause of suffering manifests itself as an unconditional defense of God and suffering as God's judgment. John Trapp (1601–69) also said that suffering is God's justice.[57] John Donne

---

49. Tyler, *Jeremiah, Lamentation*, 468.
50. Luther, *Lectures on Minor Prophets I*, 183.
51. Luther, *Church Postils I*, 321.
52. Tyler, *Jeremiah, Lamentations*, 490–91.
53. Tyler, *Jeremiah, Lamentations*, 462.
54. Tyler, *Jeremiah, Lamentations*, 464.
55. Tyler, *Jeremiah, Lamentations*, 492.
56. Tyler, *Jeremiah, Lamentations*, 508.
57. Tyler, *Jeremiah, Lamentations*, 466.

(1572–1631) wrote that God gave us something better than we deserve and that we must endure and remain silent about the suffering God sends because the suffering is much less than the suffering we deserve (cf. 3:27).[58] Calvin asked those in grief to restrain their grief because God is in control of everything (even pain), despite admitting himself that his explanation will not be sufficient.[59] Moreover, Calvin argued that God's anger and revenge are beneficial, referring to God as the provider of suffering.[60] Calvin noted that the faithful suffer all kinds of plagues because it is beneficial to be disciplined by God.[61] Calvin even advocated for the cruelty and excessiveness of God's revenge on young children and innocents, saying that God has good reason to punish even young children.[62]

This positive view of God finds hope in Lamentations' admonition of the benefit of confessing sins. Calvin argued that Lamentations shows that hope remains if people seek God through sincere faith and repentance.[63] Johannes Oecolampadius (1482–1531) interpreted the expression of despair as a result of a desire to rush divine intervention (5:22).[64] Calvin argued that verse 22 is not about despair but hope, because it is a plea with a clear conviction of God's grace.[65] Presenting 5:20 as a model of prayer, Calvin claimed that the intention of the petitions that urge God to shorten the times is to allow believers to benefit from God's mercy in times of difficulty.[66]

There are some intriguing interpretations of Lamentations. A Catholic scholar, Guillaume Du Vair (1556–1621) drafted what could be called a liberal translation, and he and Toussain read Lamentations with a greater focus on human emotions and life experiences than theological and literary approaches.[67]

Reformers generally read Lamentations as Nicene and post-Nicene fathers did in terms of sin, confession, and the cross. However, reformers grasped the mode of hope and considered not only the present recovery

---

58. Tyler, *Jeremiah, Lamentations*, 490.
59. Calvin, *Jeremiah and Lamentations*, 381.
60. Calvin, *Jeremiah and Lamentations*, 442.
61. Calvin, *Jeremiah and Lamentations*, 502.
62. Calvin, *Jeremiah and Lamentations*, 365.
63. Calvin, *Jeremiah and Lamentations*, 352. Calvin wrote a considerable amount of commentary on Lamentations in 1563 and laid the cornerstone of historical linguistic research on Lamentations. House, *Lamentations*, 288.
64. Tyler, *Jeremiah, Lamentations*, 513.
65. Tyler, *Jeremiah, Lamentations*, 627.
66. Tyler, *Jeremiah, Lamentations*, 623.
67. Tyler, *Jeremiah, Lamentations*, lvi.

but also future recovery.[68] Though there were negative views of complaint prayers, some thought the prayers could draw the sufferers close to God and they could overcome all temptations.[69] Also, we witness some conflict between traditional views and new views.

Theodicy (1950s to 1980s)

Mainstream interpreters in the 1950s to 1980s were interested in explaining suffering by including it in the relationship between humanity and God.[70] Specially, Interpreters have construed chapter 3 as a way of championing the goodness of God and considering suffering as a means to attain higher moral or divine purposes. Norman Gottwald sought to draw attention to suffering's historical-traditional interpretation in the theological debate over the rules of retaliation and reward, and to find reasons for God's violent behavior.[71] Gottwald considered 3:31–33 to be the theological center of lament, and argued that God's anger is not final and that suffering serves a divine purpose.[72] Brevard Childs claimed that Lamentations built a semantic bridge between the sixth-century historical situation and the language of faith fighting divinity, and has served every successive generation of sufferers.[73] Brevard Childs likewise contended that Lamentations 3 was key to interpreting the entire book of Lamentations because the third poem expresses the plight of Israel's historical condition in the language of faith and appeals to the whole nation to experience the resources of faith witnessed by the representative figures.[74] Paul Re'emi, as a Holocaust survivor, found hints in the theological interpretation of suffering in Lamentations 3, specifically concerning repentance and positive acceptance of suffering as God's choice for a new future of salvation.[75] Re'emi thought that God's intervention in human suffering in Lamentations referred to Christ.[76]

68. Tyler, *Jeremiah, Lamentations*, 622.
69. Tyler, *Jeremiah, Lamentations*, 623.
70. House, "Outrageous Demonstrations of Grace," 27. In the study of the reception history of Lamentations, the theological subjects and the distinction of three periods after the 1950s follows Paul House. House, "Outrageous Demonstrations of Grace," 28–37.
71. Gottwald, *Studies in the Book of Lamentations*, 51.
72. Gottwald, *Studies in the Book of Lamentations*, 53, 98.
73. Childs, *Introduction to the Old Testament*, 596.
74. Childs, *Introduction to the Old Testament*, 595.
75. Re'emi, "Theology of Hope," 109.
76. Re'emi, "Theology of Hope," 99.

Some scholars focus on the expression of suffering in Lamentations. Alan Mintz claimed that the image of Jerusalem as a woman who has been abandoned, raped, and deprived expresses suffering, and that the woman is a living witness of suffering.[77] In addition, the view of sin was slightly changed, for as Mintz says, "One of the great problems of Lamentations as a whole is its elusiveness on the precise nature of the sin for which Israel has been made the subject of such massive retribution."[78] Bertil Albrektson also pointed out the elusiveness of Lamentations as a meaningful tension that has two traditions together: the Zion tradition (the city of God never falls) and the Deuteronomistic theological tradition (when committing a sin, you are punished).[79]

In this period, a theological focus in biblical studies was dominant compared with the previous focus on historical-critical studies, with attention to things like the authorship or time of writing. Though a majority of scholars regarded the suffering in Lamentations to be caused by sins, some scholars tried to accept the strained relationship because of hermeneutic ambiguity, instead of reducing the multiple relationships to a single one. In the 1990s, the focus shifted to the literary meaning of Lamentations and to attempts to change the existing theological framework of how Lamentations was understood.

Suffering Expressed (1990s)

The research by scholars in the 1990s on the theological implications of Lamentations has shown considerable agreement: that Lamentations expressed the pain and suffering accompanying an event to enable persons to endure the unfortunate reality.[80] Claus Westermann suggested that most lament in Lamentations should be understood as lament itself, saying that "the real significance of laments resides in the way they allow the suffering of the afflicted to find expression."[81] Hillers described Lamentations as an expression of the fear and sadness that the person/voice in Lamentations felt, and that it therefore serves the survivors of some disaster. Hillers claimed that although Lamentations is "the expression and strengthening of hope," it does not quickly and easily blow away the current pain.[82] Johan

77. Mintz, "Rhetoric of Lamentations," 3.
78. Mintz, "Rhetoric of Lamentations," 3.
79. Albrektson, *Text*, 33–34.
80. Westermann, *Lamentations*, 78.
81. Westermann, *Lamentations*, 78, 81.
82. Hillers, *Lamentations*, 5.

Renkema pointed out that all of the pre-1990 commentators presupposed that Zion was guilty, and that reducing Lamentations to God's judgment and confession of sins was to underestimate or to deny the complaints in Lamentations.[83] Dobbs-Allsopp argued that lament theology is central to recognizing and accepting the tragic dimension of life.[84] Dobbs-Allsopp admitted that Judah's tragedy is due to its sin, but argued for the importance of the reality of suffering for several reasons: First, sin is rarely mentioned compared to images of pain, which fill every line; second, the exact nature of Judah's sin is not clarified; third, the confession of Israel's disobedience and rebellion that is immediately followed by accusations against Yahweh is intentionally undermined the acknowledgment of sin (3:42–43).[85]

Another important contribution of the 1990s was from scholars who tried to turn their backs on interpretations of Lamentations 3 as a hermeneutical, thematic, and acrostic center.[86] Westermann criticized interpretations that Lamentations 3 is the center of all poems in Lamentations and has a "didactic-paraenetic nature."[87] Dobbs-Allsopp argued that the problem of suffering should not be justified in the name of a higher good, and that such an ethical vision (3:19–39) among the languages of suffering (3:1–18, 44–66) has been swallowed up by human suffering.[88] Renkema understood the third poem not to have a distinct theme from the other four, but rather to be a rhetorical device, positioned among the poems of suffering to reinforce the ongoing tension expressed between continued suffering and the assurance of restoration.[89]

In the late 1990s, studies of the image of women in Lamentations also appeared. Naomi Graetz studied how the unclean image of Zion as a woman influences the way women are perceived. The assaulted woman, the woman as a rape victim, the woman who is insulted, and women's menstruation in the first poem all show clearly the frequency of female abuse by men, and that abuse is justified by the image of a widow who has been abandoned and who is charged with immorality.[90] However, Graetz proposed that women do not need to identify themselves with Zion. Instead, a new perspective should be presented as part of the theology of protest abuses in the past and

---

83. Renkema, *Lamentations*, 60.
84. Dobbs-Allsopp, "Tragedy," 29.
85. Dobbs-Allsopp, "Tragedy," 37–38.
86. Westermann, *Lamentations*, 67.
87. Westermann, *Lamentations*, 72.
88. Dobbs-Allsopp, "Tragedy," 48, 55.
89. Renkema, *Lamentations*, 70.
90. Graetz, "Jerusalem the Widow," 17.

present.[91] In the 1990s, interest in the cause of pain and in Lamentations 3 shifted to an interest in the expression of pain in Lamentations 1 and 2. After the 2000s, more diversified interpretive discussions arose.

Multi-Layered Meaning (2000–)

Since the 2000s, there have been various interpretive attempts, including feminist, psychological, postcolonial, and literary interpretations. In the 2000s, speaking the reality of suffering in Lamentations and its relevance to contemporary affliction assumed significance in the interpretations of Lamentations; Kathleen O'Connor for example noted the narrator as a witness and a comforter. The narrator breaks Zion's isolation, pays attention to her pain, listens to her, participates in her pain and becomes a passionate advocate.[92] O'Connor particularly valued the role of witnesses, arguing that denial of suffering silences the voices of survivors, thwarts passion for justice, reduces hope, and depletes lives.[93] Dobbs-Allsopp also argued that the recovery of grief language and the vocalization of pain experiences delay and reverse the corrosive action of the suffering voice.[94] Since Linafelt saw that Lamentations' theological challenge was directly connected to the reality of suffering, he insists on bringing the language of suffering into a religious language as an expression of truth.[95]

In interpretations of Lamentations before the 1990s, scholars generally had been working on resolving the pain of the other poems with the hope of the third poem. Also, the scholars tried to analyze and resolve suffering with a theological approach in the relationship between sin and judgment. However, what we may call the lost language of pain was rediscovered in the 1990s, and various discussions after the 2000s have attempted to resist a unified view or theology, taking into account the ambiguity of Lamentations in the dynamics between pain and hope.

The reception history of Lamentations captures the precariousness and tensions concerning the reality of suffering and ways in which one/communities comprehends God within this context. However, the precariousness and tensions can give back to the survivors the language of grief destroyed

---

91. Graetz, "Jerusalem the Widow," 24. Graetz interprets Zion not as a real widow but as expressing an existential fear of exile by emphasizing the condition of being "like" the widow. Graetz, "Jerusalem the Widow," 18–19.

92. Graetz, "Jerusalem the Widow," 99.

93. Graetz, "Jerusalem the Widow," 87.

94. Dobbs-Allsopp, *Lamentations*, 33.

95. Linafelt, *Surviving Lamentations*, 4.

by overwhelming pain and can provide a place to restore relationships. This is because lament allows raw voices to injustice, hurt, and anger.[96] Lamentation—as a communal voice in a liturgical setting—can help sufferers to accept their pain and internalize their experiences, and to engage listeners in the experiences of survivors' pain.[97] Thus, Lamentations is the struggles of sufferers who are wrestling with contradictions, resisting easy theology, and wondering if God has forsaken them forever (5:22).[98]

THE SETTING OF LAMENTATIONS 5

Many scholars admit that Lamentations is a well-designed book of poetry and note that it is "full of poetic artifice and convention."[99] It presents rich images and conveys a message through patterns, repetitions, and rhythms.[100]

Genre

As a literary work, Lamentations "draws on previously known works, genres, and literary conventions."[101] There are three genres that are most relevant to Lamentations—the funeral dirge, the lament psalm, and the city lament—although there has not been a clear consensus of their influence on the overall book. Still, most scholars agree that the book of Lamentations is composed of a variety of genres.[102]

Funeral Dirge

The tradition of the funeral dirge, which is present in David's lament for the deaths of Saul and Jonathan (2 Sam 1), can be identified as a distinct genre. This dirge begins with a shriek, *ekh* or *ekhah* in Hebrew, which indicates

---

96. O'Connor, *Lamentations and the Tears*, 101, 128.
97. Dobbs-Allsopp, *Lamentations*, 34–35.
98. Dobbs-Allsopp, *Lamentations*, 115–16.
99. Hillers, *Lamentations*, 3.
100. Hillers, *Lamentations*, 15.
101. Dobbs-Allsopp, *Lamentations*, 6.
102. Ferris, *Genre of Communal Lament*, 101; House, "Outrageous Demonstrations of Grace," 42; O'Connor, *Lamentations and the Tears*, 8–10; Parry, *Lamentations*, 11; Mandolfo, *Daughter Zion Talks Back*, 55; Berlin, *Lamentations*, 22–30; Dobbs-Allsopp, *Lamentations*, 12.

loss and means "how terrible."¹⁰³ In Jewish tradition, laments were called Qînôth, Hebrew for funeral eulogy or dirge.¹⁰⁴ The words 'êkah, qînôth, and Lamentations, which refer to the book of Lamentations, all correspond to the mourning language used at funerals.¹⁰⁵ Typically, the dirge speaks of a good past and a dark present. This contrast clearly reveals a sense of tragedy.¹⁰⁶ The *qinah* meter used in Lamentations is called the 3:2 rhyme and suggests a funeral march with an unbalanced rhythm, which further indicates the influence of the dirge on Lamentations.¹⁰⁷ Though dirges appear in Lamentations 1, 2, and 4, creating an atmosphere of death, in Lamentations 5 the dirge has a slightly different form: that of resignation.¹⁰⁸ Erhard Gerstenberger also argued that the petitionary element at the end of the fifth poem remains vague, probably due to dirge influences.¹⁰⁹ And yet Lamentations exhibits not only the sadness of a dirge but also pleas to and complaints about God.¹¹⁰

Lament Psalm

Lamentations 5 has the most common thematic elements of communal lament psalms: direct address (v. 1), complaint/lament (vv. 2–18), and an appeal for restoration and justice (vv. 19–22), though it does not guarantee future restoration or hope (v. 22).¹¹¹ The fifth poem has customary expressions, such as repeated iterations of "Why?" (v. 20).¹¹² As Tremper Longman, III pointed out, the distinctions between Lamentations and lament

---

103. Allen, *Liturgy of Grief*, 6.

104. Middlemas, *Lamentations*, 2.

105. Middlemas, *Lamentations*, 3.

106. Middlemas, *Lamentations*, 3.

107. Dobbs-Allsopp, *Lamentations*, 5; Allen, *Liturgy of Grief*, 7. However, not all Hebrew literature uses the qinah meter in laments for the dead. For instance, David's lament for Saul and Jonathan is not in qinah meter (2 Sam 1:17–27). Hillers, *Lamentations*, 18–19.

108. Childs, *Introduction to the Old Testament*, 594.

109. Gerstenberger, *Psalms*, 504.

110. Allen, *Liturgy of Grief*, 7.

111. Ferris, *Genre of Communal Lament*, 110–11. Concerning the definition of communal lament, Ferris notes that it is "a composition whose verbal content indicates that it was composed to be used by and/or on behalf of a community to express both complaints, and sorrow and grief over some perceived calamity, physical or cultural, which had befallen or was about to befall them and to appeal to God for deliverance." Ferris, *Genre of Communal Lament*, 10.

112. Dobbs-Allsopp, "Tragedy," 51; Westermann, *Lamentations*, 216.

psalms may not be sharp.[113] However, it is difficult to conclude that the fifth poem contains hallmarks of lament psalms such as a confidence or praise of God, and the clues of hope are easily refuted due to the overwhelming language of suffering throughout Lamentations 5. Lamentations 5 also makes a relatively short appeal and a very long account of the state's suffering when compared to the psalm's communal lament.[114]

City Lament

The city lament that has been identified in Lamentations shares characteristics with elements of Mesopotamian culture and literature.[115] Lamentations 5 contains an image of a fox (v. 18), which also appears in the ruined cities in Mesopotamian literature, and the voices in those cities cry out about the unbearable suffering of the community.[116] Still, Lamentations is different from other city laments because there include no signs of God's return or of the restoration of the city.[117] Instead, Lamentations is closer to the Curse of Agade, which says the city will not be restored (Lam 5:22).[118] Also, the theological functions served by Mesopotamian literature are not the same as those of Lamentations.[119] Besides, although Mesopotamian laments such as *balags* and *er*semmas*—unlike the Mesopotamian City Lament—tend to have no happy endings and focus on the current state of the destroyed temple, Lamentations can be distinguished from those because it has considered the ongoing suffering of the inhabitants rather than the state of the temple.[120]

---

113. Longman, *Jeremiah, Lamentations*, 331.

114. Hillers, *Lamentations*, 162.

115. There are five laments of Sumerian/Babylon cities. Lamentation over the Destruction of Ur, Lamentation over the Destruction of Sumer and Ur; The Nippur Lament, The Eridu Lament, and The Uruk Lament. Walton, *Ancient Israelite Literature*, 160.

116. Cooper, *Curse of Agade*, 63.

117. Dobbs-Allsopp, *Lamentations*, 9.

118. Dobbs-Allsopp, *Lamentations*, 10.

119. Walton, *Ancient Israelite Literature*, 163.

120. Middlemas, *Troubles of Templeless Judah*, 180–81. *Balag* is the congregation's lament poem from the times of old Babylon, New Assyria, New Babylon, and Seleucid. (18 BCE—2 CE) The *balag* and *ersemma* texts are considered to be closer to the text type of Lamentations as they are more prevalent and less historically specific. Longman, *Jeremiah, Lamentations*, 334.

Liturgical Setting

The five poems of Lamentations seem originally to have been intended as communal laments.[121] Jill Anne Middlemas argues that the book of Lamentations contains the liturgical pieces available to Judah in the exile age (cf. 5:18).[122] Lamentations 5 would have been closely related to the spiritual life of the community in the exile and postexilic period. People would have used Lamentations in worship to remember the destruction and loss of Jerusalem.[123] The first-person plural discourses (vv. 1–10, 15–18) come from Jewish worship to collective articulation in social and cultural structure of early Jewish communities. Gerstenberger mentions that "the prevalence of first-person plural speech in liturgical text has its origin in the real participation of congregational assemblies in the cult," a claim he makes based on the studies of Scharbert and Seybold.[124] Allen insists that Lamentations is the script of liturgy for a therapeutic ritual performed in the ruins of the temple (cf. Lam 5:18).[125] Childs emphasizes the liturgical setting of Lamentations, saying this is a hermeneutical issue that makes it different from other Psalters.[126] O'Connor also characterizes Lamentations as central to the people's worship because she thinks it can help those who have unbearable sorrow and doubt.[127] Thus, Lamentations enables the sufferer to retrieve memories of suffering in the liturgical setting of the congregation that have been paralyzed or latent. In doing this retrieval, the afflicted may be moved to resist unjustly imposed power and remember that they longed for life while they were in pain. This may be not only a response to the past, it may also include identification of ongoing suffering. For instance, Lamentations has been read during the Jewish *Tishah B'Av* service to commemorate the destruction of the First and Second Temples.[128] *Tisha B'Av*, however, also includes in lament all kinds of ethnic and personal disasters, not just the destruction of Jerusalem.[129]

To sum up, though it is not necessarily identical to the actual liturgy, Lamentations 5 has the characteristics of a communal lament in a liturgical

---

121. Matter, "Lamentations Commentaries," 138.
122. Middlemas, *Templeless Age*, 35.
123. Gerstenberger, *Psalms*, 505.
124. Gerstenberger, *Psalms*, 502–3.
125. Allen, *Liturgy of Grief*, 8; cf. House, *Lamentations*, 303; Dopps-Allsopp, *Lamentations*, 33–34; Gerstenberger, *Psalms*, 505.
126. Childs, *Introduction to the Old Testament*, 596.
127. O'Connor, *Lamentations and the Tears*, 133.
128. Lee, *Lyrics of Lament*, 160.
129. House, *Lamentations*, 304.

setting that fosters the resilience of a suffering community, and is influenced by a variety of genres including individual funeral dirges, city laments, and lament psalms.[130] Furthermore, because Lamentations focuses relatively little on the details of the Babylonian exile, it renders the stories more imaginative and resonant to various suffering experiences.

Literary Device

The poems in Lamentations exhibit a confluence of assorted images, themes, and concepts. Dobbs-Allsopp notes that this "flood" is appropriately not impeded by some boundaries of the poems, and insists it is not "chaotic."[131] Instead, Lamentations, which structures and creates meaning through various rhetorical devices, is deliberately composed to reflect a state of mind.[132] In particular, the literary tools in the fifth poem create a sense of weakness and helplessness gnawing at the afflicted. As the language of pain, these tools name a feeling of shame, recognize the legitimacy of telling the truth, impart value to the people's grief and complaint, and request that God pay attention to their wounds.[133]

The Structure of Decrescendo

The structure of the fifth poem is that of a decrescendo. It is the shortest poem and does not follow an acrostic and a qinah meter, unlike the other four poems.[134] Instead, it consists of twenty-two lines, the same number as the letters of the alphabet, so that the force of the alphabet lingers. This device suggests order and unity are useful for those facing the destruction of life, and it ties all five poems together.[135] Allen considers that the absence of an acrostic means the end of grief and an embrace of hope, while O'Connor considers the diminished structure to reflect "the depletion of hope and energy."[136] Dobbs-Allsopp notes in the fifth poem that a completely aban-

---

130. Middlemas, *Lamentations*, 12.
131. Dobbs-Allsopp, *Lamentations*, 14.
132. Dobbs-Allsopp, *Lamentations*, 14.
133. Dobbs-Allsopp, *Lamentations*, 143.
134. Acrostic is form that makes sense by connecting the beginning or the final letter of each line, or the first letter of each line in alphabetical order.
135. Dobbs-Allsopp, *Lamentations*, 17–18.
136. Allen, *Liturgy of Grief*, 148; O'Connor, *Lamentations and the Tears*, 71.

doned acrostic informs readers of an impending ending.¹³⁷ Some consider the fifth poem to reflect a gradual decline of pain since the third poem shows hope.¹³⁸ However, the memory of hope (vv. 19–39) leads to a return to lament (vv. 56–66) in Lamentations 3, which means hope fails to alleviate pain in the last poem.¹³⁹ Also, Lamentations creates a container of sadness by using a qinah meter. The qinah meter has a rhythm that disappears in Lamentations 5. The 3:2 qinah pattern appears in Lamentations 1–3 in the form of a triplet of bicola (3x2), a couplet of bicola (2x2) in Lamentations 4, and bicola only (2x1) in Lamentations 5.¹⁴⁰ The acrostic device is open to various interpretations, yet it imposes a sophisticated order on an array of emotional reactions and sporadic outbursts of grief. As Paul Joyce and Diana Lipton point out, the orderly form, both musical and poetic, helps to contain emotions that might otherwise erupt uncontrollably and this act of control through a rhetorical device or form can be understood as a form of resistance.¹⁴¹

Parallelism

There are four types of parallelism in Hebrew poetry: synonymous, synthetic, antithetic, and climactic. The two most prominent types of parallelism in Lamentations are the synonymous and the synthetic.¹⁴² Lamentations 5 has stronger parallelism than the previous four poems.¹⁴³ Lamentations exhibits about 60 percent of parallel lines in 266 lines, but all passages except the three lines in Lamentation 5 have poetic parallelism.¹⁴⁴ Each line is divided into two parts and each second part echoes the first. כאלמנות (v. 3)

137. Dobbs-Allsopp, "Tragedy," 59.
138. Thomas, "Holy Scripture," 5–6.
139. Thomas, "Holy Scripture," 7.
140. Shea, "Qinah Structure," 106. Lamentations follows a qinah meter, and the formal unit is divided into two parts: the first part is a line of the normal half of Hebrew poetry, but the other half is a group of two or more words, which is shorter than the normal line. It has the form of 3+2, 4+3, 4+2, etc. It is called a limping rhythm. This pattern is found in Lamentations 1–4, but Lamentations 5 has a different rhythm but with the same length of cola. Hillers, *Lamentations*, 17–18.
141. Joyce and Lipton, *Lamentations*, 110.
142. Middlemas, *Lamentations*, 20.
143. Hillers, *Lamentations*, 161. "Parallelism may be defined as the repetition of similar or related semantic content or grammatical structure in adjacent lines or verses." Berlin, "Introduction to Hebrew Poetry," 304.
144. Hillers, *Lamentations*, 19. A line here means "a line of Hebrew text as printed in the *Biblia hebraica Stuttgartensia*.

enhances the reversal and suffering motif.¹⁴⁵ The parallelism between בתלת and נשים, collectively points to wider geographical areas including Zion and cities of Judah and broader ages of female including women and maidens affected by the terrible suffering such as rape. This is very comprehensive and wide-ranging violence that refers not only to the rape of women but to the humiliation and shame of the entire society (v. 11).¹⁴⁶ The parallelism also reveals the sufferings of all generations as their voices gather (vv. 11–14), using contrasting words that strengthen the sense of sadness (vv. 15–16).

Repetition

In Lamentations 5, repetition is not prominent although it is essential in Lamentations.¹⁴⁷ The combination of three imperatives of זכר, הביט, and ראה (v. 1) intensifies the desperate plea for God's intervention.¹⁴⁸ The three perfect masculine singular verbs of רדף, נוח, and יגע (5:5) involve the use of repetition to present the experience of oppression (cf. 1:3).¹⁴⁹ חטא shows "the reversal form from honor to shame (5:6, 16)."¹⁵⁰ The repetition of דוה, חשכו, and שמם (5:17 and 18) articulates the desolation of God's place and people.

Imagery

Imagery enriches the meaning of Lamentations.¹⁵¹ Metaphor is outstanding in Lamentations. Even small metaphorical gestures can indicate intuition, inspire pathos, and deepen meaning.¹⁵² Lamentations 5:2–18 uses the language of grief to express the sufferings of war. In the biblical tradition, images of orphans and widows (v. 3) are often used to denote God's wrath

---

145. Thomas, *Poetry and Theology*, 239.
146. Berlin, *Lamentation*, 122.
147. Thomas, *Poetry and Theology*, 83.
148. Thomas, *Poetry and Theology*, 238–39.
149. Thomas, *Poetry and Theology*, 240.
150. Thomas argues that this repetition functions as an intensification of the result of sin, but Dobbs-Allsopp claims the parataxis in Lamentations refutes granting superiority to one perspective. Thomas, *Poetry and Theology*, 238–39; Dobbs-Allsopp, *Lamentations*, 26.
151. Dobbs-Allsopp, *Lamentations*, 15. Imagery encompasses other tropes including metaphor and personification. Thomas, *Poetry and Theology*, 86; Berlin deals with metaphor and simile in imagery. Berlin, "Introduction to Hebrew Poetry," 311.
152. Dobbs-Allsopp, *Lamentations*, 14.

combined with a sense of abandonment (cf. Exod 22:24; Ps 109:9; John 14:18). However, with "like," it may present the idea that the state of the community lies in insecurity.[153] The dominant images remind the reader of the exile and the suffering of people, including disgrace (v. 1), loss of possessions (v. 2), persecution (v. 5), being ruled over (v. 8), being raped (v. 11), hung up (v. 12), disrespected (v. 12), and fallen (v. 13). The anguished cry of the community, "our hearts are sick ... our eyes have grown dim" (v. 17), is vividly depicted through bodily imagery. The imagery of the poem is so vivid and rich that it conveys a sense of urgency to God, prompting God to witness the suffering and intervene to solve it, while also appealing to human witnesses.[154]

Enjambment

Enjambment is widely used in Lamentations, supplementing the lack of legitimate poetic devices.[155] Lamentations 1 to 4 contain various forms of enjambment, of which about 166 to 177 instances occur in the 244 pairs of lines. This enjambment contrasts with the regularity set by acrostic or closed couplets, complementing the influence of *qinah* in Lamentations.[156] Structural decrescendo can also be viewed through enjambment. Enjambment is reduced in Lamentations 3 and 4, and almost disappears in Lamentations 5.[157] Parallel couplets of enjambment in the fifth poem appear in verses 13, 17, and 20, although most of the verses are parallel.[158] In Lamentations, enjambment creates stylistic cohesion, movement, and speed, emphasizes certain parts, and influences the meaning of certain passages.[159] This movement imparts the poem with a sense of direction and an arc of motion.[160] The enjambment assists the poem in seamlessly moving from one point to

153. Allen, *Liturgy of Grief*, 152.

154. Middlemas, *Lamentations*, 30.

155. Thomas explains that enjambment is "the absence of pause or end-stopping at the conclusion of a colon in a verse." Thomas, *Poetry and Theology*, 85. According to Dobbs-Allsopp, the potential meaning of enjambment is generally vague because it is subordinate to the parallel, and is categorized as synthetic or constructive. Dobbs-Allsopp, "Enjambing Line in Lamentations," 220.

156. Dobbs-Allsopp, *On Biblical Poetry*, 137.

157. Dobbs-Allsopp, *Lamentations*, 18.

158. Thomas, *Poetry and Theology*, 19. 5:9–10 is an example of adjunct enjambments with "a prepositional phrase or a temporal adverbial." Dobbs-Allsopp, "Enjambing Line in Lamentations," 225. 5:18 is the verbal enjambment; see 227–28.

159. Thomas, *Poetry and Theology*, 85.

160. Dobbs-Allsopp, *Lamentations*, 19.

the next, without pauses.[161] By urging the reader to follow this movement, it engages the reader in the lament's essence. This rapid movement boldly guides the reader toward the poignant concern of the final verses in the fifth poem, and from there, to the pause of awaiting a divine response.[162]

Lamentations is lyric poetry that lacks a narrative device, so it constructs its meaning through manipulation of language.[163] Lamentations evokes, contemplates, voices, and emits the language of "grief, guilt, forgiveness, anger, compassion, hope, despair, and shame."[164] The literary devices including acrostic, couplet, enjambment, and so on, which are prevalent throughout Lamentations and not only imbue the poem with a formal pattern but lead to an emotional climax.[165] This reduction in repetitive structure in Lamentations 5, coupled with the reduction of intensified emotional potency, lends the poem a raw portrayal of suffering, vividly depicting the excruciating physical pain and the exhaustion from the torrent of tears.[166] And yet this language of suffering does not flood or overwhelm, but is controlled through an acrostic or *qinah* meter, and the emotions resonate with each other and lead readers to feel empathy.[167]

THE SIGNIFICANCE OF TWO PARTS OF LAMENTATIONS 5

The Significance of the Fifth Poem

The key significance of the fifth poem is as a communal voice.[168] House argues that all previous voices join in the one voice of the last poem.[169] The "we" voice appears partially in 3:30–37 and 4:17–20, and then appears as the complete subject of discussion in Lamentations 5.[170] The reality of suffering, which has been gradual beginning in Lamentations 1, is understood, experienced, and testified to be the reader's own, so that the readers can

---

161. Middlemas, *Lamentations*, 22.
162. Middlemas, *Lamentations*, 22.
163. Dobbs-Allsopp, *Lamentations*, 12.
164. Dobbs-Allsopp, *Lamentations*, 14.
165. Dobbs-Allsopp, *Lamentations*, 105.
166. Dobbs-Allsopp, *Lamentations*, 129.
167. Dobbs-Allsopp, *Lamentations*, 14.
168. Hillers, *Lamentations*, 161–62; Berlin, *Lamentations*, 116.
169. House, *Lamentations*, 457.
170. Dobbs-Allsopp, *Lamentations*, 33–34; Rong, *Forgotten and Forsaken*, 41.

find the path toward healing by acquiring and expressing the language of suffering.[171]

Also, Lamentations ends in despair. This may function as resistance against covenantal optimism.[172] God allows the lament and complaint of people (5:2–18), which causes us to reconsider the nature of our relationship with God. Lamentations 5 offers a bifocal understanding of sin (5:7, 16), and resists a single, uniform theological perspective.[173] God seems to allow space for all kinds of suffering, regardless of guilt or innocence. Lamentations, as a whole, has multi-layered voices and meanings. The most important thing, however, is that it does not attempt to resolve the paradoxes prematurely and is willing to accept an honest conflict.[174] The last poem most successfully serves this purpose.

The significance of Lamentations 5 also emerges from an unexpectedly poignant context. Lamentations 5:11 appears to stand as the sole testament to Israelite women enduring rape at the hands of their oppressors (Cf. Zech 14:2), despite Israel adopting certain rape practices from slavery, including the abduction of women as spoils of war (Cf. Num 21; Deut 20), and notwithstanding various direct and indirect accounts of Israelite/Jewish women enduring systemic rape within their own community (Cf. Judg 21; Neh 5:5; 2 Chr 28:10–15).[175] Moreover, Lamentations serves as a fitting platform by which to address the physical and emotional violence inflicted upon women, as it vividly illustrates how women's bodies are unjustly held accountable for failure and loss.[176]

The Significance of Lamentations 5:19–22[177]

The last part of Lamentations plays a critical role in preventing unripe hope in the presence of suffering in the Bible, and in figuring out the pain of today, calling on God's faithful response and genuine hope in the midst of pain. The expressions of faith in verses 19 and 21 stress the woeful situation and desperate plea to God in verses 20 and 22. The confession of God's reign (v. 19) highlights God's silence and humans' sense of abandonment (v. 20). The earnest plea for restoration (v. 21) gives salience to the rejection

171. Dobbs-Allsopp, *Lamentations*, 34.
172. Stern, "Lamentations in Jewish Liturgy," 89.
173. Dobbs-Allsopp, *Lamentations*, 21.
174. Dobbs-Allsopp, *Lamentations*, 31.
175. Gafney, *Womanist Midrash*, 124.
176. Guest, "Hiding behind the Naked Women," 413–48.
177. For more details, refer to Ku, "Resisting Apathy and Amnesia."

of God (v. 22). O'Connor argues that this miserable ending is the best closing, because it tells painful truths about human suffering and does not force hope.[178] Thus, verse 22 can offer a place to mourn.[179] The space is the point at which God's sorrow and silence meet at the end of the torment of human suffering and the manifestation of anger, and a moment of silence where we and God have seen each other but have not yet found resolution. It is just a place of suffering. Nothing is certain. The ambiguous ending of verse 22 suggests a willingness never to choose easy hope. In other words, as long as there is suffering in the land, lament cannot cease. There is nothing one can do but lament in faith if we know Jesus, who laments on the cross, who embraces a long Holy Saturday, and who seeks to accompany human beings and the whole creation in their suffering and the inevitability of death (e.g., Ps 139:7–10). Therefore, despair is not the last word. Lament in the fifth poem is a way of revealing God's inbreaking into our lives and of situating Christian living in the tension between suffering and hope, or the already but not yet. It is an eschatological point of view that does not lose sight of the present life. The last verses may open the door to genuine hope for a faith community in times of suffering.

THE ROLE OF THEOLOGICAL RHETORIC IN LAMENTATIONS

The aim of the theological rhetoric of Lamentations as a communal lament and counter-testimony is to demonstrate a strong sense of suffering through polyphonic voices, while retaining a sense of hope and faith. This voice includes the laments of "the roads to Zion" (1:4) and "rampart and wall" (2:8). The widespread pain expressed in these laments is evident throughout the personified Zion. The powerful mood evoked by the language of pain highlights the urgency for recovery and the hope in God.

Communal Lament

Faith Community

Lamentations 5 invites communal pain, or "our" pain rather than "my" pain. It may let people know and experience the power of truth-telling as resistance and disclosure, the power of naming pain which is able to draw

---

178. O'Connor, *Lamentations and the Tears*, 78–79.
179. Harris and Mandolfo, "Silent God in Lamentations," 142.

newness, and the power of sharing pain which makes the members of a congregation grow in awareness of the abyss and makes them long together urgently for God's response. Lamentations 5 as a communal lament directly addresses (v. 1) long complaints such as those to a political enemy (v. 2), as well as moral, ethical, and spiritual enmity (v. 11), political calamity (vv. 3–6), spiritual calamity (v. 20) and abandonment/isolation (v. 20), shame/humiliation (vv. 11–13), despair/depression (v. 15), danger from enemies (v. 9), physical impairment (v. 17), death (v. 9), and urgent appeals for restoration and saving (vv. 19–22).

There are references to the sins of the ancestors (v. 7) and to one's own transgressions (v. 16), but these statements are often interpreted as perceptions of guilt and divine wrath lacking specificity, rather than as definitive statements.[180] However, they might signify perceptions of the origin of sin within the self (Exod 20:5–6; Jer 31:29–30; Ezek 18:2) and can carry a variety of meanings. Dopps-Allsopp ultimately resists attempts to reconcile the incongruities between these two disparate concepts, and she cautions against reducing the manifold meanings found in the realms of "within" and "beyond" to a single interpretation.[181] Joyce and Lipton deem this a rhetorical strategy whose purpose is to emphasize the depths of helplessness and despair and to comment on the potential for theological narratives seeking to systematize catastrophe, inadvertently fostering self-loathing and animosity when improperly construed.[182] Adele Berlin views it in metaphorical terms. Berlin's focus lies not on whether the speaker feels guilty, but on their enduring state of constant punishment—they suffer from the ongoing experience of destruction.[183] Despite this diversity of interpretations, scholars assert that the fifth poem provides a place for the articulation of human suffering. The justification for the punishment cannot vindicate the extent of devastation and suffering, and the form and genre of the poem take a direction beyond mere retrospective lamentation, moving towards a focus on survival and the embrace of life.[184]

Israel dares to cry out "how overwhelming is the loss, how great the anxiety, how deep the consequent fear."[185] This is a story of condemnation of God who, despite choosing his people, left them in unbearable suffering. It legitimates people's accusations by showing that accusations against God

---

180. Middlemas, *Lamentations*, 54.
181. Dobbs-Allsopp, *Lamentations*, 146.
182. Joyce and Lipton, *Lamentations*, 179.
183. Berlin, *Lamentations*, 121.
184. Middlemas, *Lamentations*, 61.
185. Brueggemann, *Deep Memory, Exuberant Hope*, 61.

are made out of deep conviction rather than out of a sense of distrust.[186] The voice of Lamentations is a complaint that God's power and faithfulness are not working, and the purpose of this complaint is not more narrowly to complain, but more expansively to move God to a decision and to activate the faithful God.[187]

Unlike most communal laments, which end with praise or the proclamation of hope/restoration, Lamentations 5 concludes with a sense of dejection. Nevertheless, it is also open-ended, as if the voices pass the microphone to God. Whereas God is silent in Lamentations, Zion is silent in Second Isaiah.[188] The cry of "no comfort" that flows through Lamentations is answered by the declaration of comfort that opens the very beginning of Second Isaiah (40:1). The voices in Lamentations cry out that God has forsaken and forgotten them (5:20), but Isaiah says that God will not forget (49:14–15). Isaiah 54:7–8 is the response to Lamentations 5:22. The voices in Lamentations say they have to buy water (5:3), but Isaiah proclaims that it is free now (55:1–2). Their land is conquered by foreigners and is desolate (5:2, 18), but in Isaiah, it will be restored (54:3). Isaiah creates a picture that contrasts with Lamentations and indicates reversal by using contrasting language. However, as Mandolfo argues, Second Isaiah does not fully answer the pain of Lamentations, such as giving the reason for destruction, and it uses and repeats the grammar of the existing prophetic books to some extent.[189] As many scholars agree, Lamentations and Second Isaiah are related and Second and Third Isaiah may have a relatively progressive view compared to Haggai, Zechariah, and Ezra-Nehemiah, in terms of dealing with Israel's suffering. However, Mandolfo's argument can be understood as meaning that the progressiveness may not completely respond to the pain of Israel in Lamentations and that a more radical response is necessary to emphasize Israel's great suffering appropriately. In this respect, Christ's passion, death, and resurrection can be portrayed as a divine lament, where God's response to human suffering is more tangible and concrete than that presented in Second Isaiah.

---

186. This is called a "genre of complaint." See below for the role and details of this genre. Westermann, *Praise and Lament*. However, there still is an irony here. Supplicants pray with hope because they believe God's love is faithful, but this love is actually completely untrustworthy. LeFever, *Understanding Prayers*, 31–34.

187. Brueggemann, *Theology of the Old Testament*, 321.

188. Tiemeyer, "Lamentations in Isaiah 40–55," 61.

189. Mandolfo, *Daughter Zion Talks Back*, 117.

Public Square: Lamenting Women

Biblical lament assigns significant value to the narratives of those who undergo suffering by incorporating and even foregrounding the voices of grief, anger, and dissent from those submersed in the distressing present.[190] Since the Bible is a story about relationships, the silence of God in Lamentations amplifies its pain. The voice of God in Isaiah, Jeremiah, and Ezekiel is dynamic and includes proclamations of both restoration and pain. In Lamentations, however, it is only the shameful and painful voices of the people that are voiced to God. The Bible allows these voices and those of everyone who is suffering to be expressed through the voice of Israel. The absence of the victims' names or specific causes of personal grief in Lamentations seems appropriate in this expression of general loss and grief.[191] Israel's pain represents the story of every painful voice beyond biblical times, those who have experienced wars, division, famine, despair, violence, and pain in life. Therefore, Lamentations functions as a repository of public lament, disclosure, resistance, and urgent calling, and helps us recognize the abyss, and draws on the power of newness for the whole world.

Also, the silence of God in Lamentations reflects the silence or denial of people. Daughter Zion is crying out to others who pass by: "Is it nothing to you, all you who pass by? Look and see" (Lam 1:12). Whether implicit or explicit, lament has political and social public implications.[192] Lament as a protest rejects the possibility of masculine concealment and the justification of violence along with the degradation of women.[193] Because Zion is depicted as a suffering, insulted, naked, and raped woman, many feminists have addressed issues of domestic violence, oppression, sexual abuse, patriarchy, and justice for the weak in their discussions of Lamentations. These reflections result in making room for a new way to meet God.[194] A wide spectrum of viewpoints in interpretation is presented, with viewpoints that range from arguments about the harm caused by Lamentations to the claim that the Bible promotes healing. Nonetheless, the public voice of the oppressed represented by a woman's voice can contribute to the multi-layered pursuit of justice and further healing.

---

190. Middlemas, *Lamentations*, 25.
191. Hillers, *Lamentations*, 5.
192. Thomas, "Feminist Interpretation(s)," 166.
193. Guest, "Hiding Behind the Naked Women," 413.
194. O'Connor, *Lamentations and the Tears*, 123.

Counter-Testimony

According to the core testimony of Israel, the text reminds us that God is the Almighty who creates the world, that God is a merciful God, and that the covenant between God and Israel represents the God of promise. This covenant contains both expectation and assurance that this promise will be fulfilled when Israel is in distress.[195] Lamentations as counter-testimony raises a question about core-testimonies of Israel, which say that God is always our refuge, strength, and help (Ps 46:1).[196] Brueggemann notes that such counter-testimony poses four questions: "How long? Why? Where? Is?"[197] The purpose of these questions is to ask God forcefully and urgently ask God to move positively toward them in faith. This call to accomplish this purpose is clearly revealed in Lam 5:1. The speaker uses three imperative verbs: זְכֹר, הַבִּיטָה, and וּרְאֵה. This powerful and direct call is repeatedly and collectively revealed through the voices of Lamentations (cf. 1:11, 20; 2:20; 3:19). The four questions have received strong support from verse 19. The doxology in verse 19 says that it is very difficult for God to be absent.[198] Therefore, verse 19 can be seen as reinforcing the tone of the "Why" in verse 20 and the tone of reproach by expressing the power of God rather than the purpose of praising God. In addition, Westermann does not understand verse 19 entirely as praise and considers the possibility that it represents a long distance between God and human suffering.[199] Dobbs-Allsopp also emphasizes the spatial separation between God and people. Though God sits in a heavenly dwelling place (v. 19), the earthly temple has collapsed, so human misery and God are far apart from one another, she suggests.[200] The idea that God reigns regardless of whether the temple stands can be a sign of hope for Judah. However, this hope is again shattered by the rejection of God in verse 20. The "why" question in 5:20 represents this frustratingly. Verse 20 is contrasted with God's ability to end the suffering mentioned in verse 19. Thus, the question in verse 20 can be "Nonetheless, why?" The faithful, merciful, and guiding God of core-testimony is now portrayed as a God who is unreliable, ruthless, and who has totally abandoned Israel in Lamentations 5. This sudden shift serves as the darkest counter-testimony in Israel's experience.

195. Brueggemann, *Theology of the Old Testament*, 169.
196. Brueggemann, *Reality, Grief, Hope*, 69.
197. Brueggemann, *Theology of the Old Testament*, 319.
198. Brueggemann, *Pathway of Interpretation*, 98.
199. Westermann, *Lamentations*, 216.
200. Dobbs-Allsopp, "R(az/ais)ing Zion in Lamentations 2," 47.

The speakers of Lamentations 5 get their own answer to "How long?" and "Where?" The answers are "forever" (v. 20) and "unless you have totally rejected us" (v. 22). This verse does not seem to refer to "where," but verse 22 is a cry that God is no longer with Israel. Rather than as a sign of distrust, the cry can be understood as a strong action to draw God's attention to their suffering. Besides, though Isaiah mentions that God has forsaken the Israelites "for a while," the abandonment of God "for a brief moment" (Isa 54:7) spelled death and disaster for that generation and an eternity-like long time.[201] God's silence places the entire book of Lamentations in the midst of silence and pain due to the desperate end of v. 22. The word, מָאֹס, which is interpreted as "utterly or totally," preceded by "reject," strengthens the resignation in contrast to the urgent appeal of v. 21.

Thus, Lamentations 5, especially verses 19 to 22, becomes one of the strongest and densest counter-testimonies. As a counter-testimony, Lamentations is an accusation against God's silence. It legitimates people's accusations by showing that accusations against God can be aspects of faith. However, the purpose of this complaint as another way to express faith is not to complain, but actually to move God and restore God's covenantal faithfulness.[202]

Rhetorical Plots

Since the five poems of Lamentations are not narratives and since they seem to lack an argumentative structure, dealing with plots may seem to be an inappropriate way to proceed. Nevertheless, I suggest it is still worth considering plots because Lamentations is a well-organized and planned piece of literature, communicated through rhetoric and image manipulation, and dramatized voices in five poems.[203] In addition, the experience of exile and war was a time when the paradigm shared with the community collapsed, and the paradigm reorganization or replacement was necessary.[204] Therefore, Lamentations may show how to communicate between traditional beliefs and the reality of suffering, ultimately proceeding to the theology of lament.

---

201. Berlin, *Lamentations*, 125.
202. Brueggemann, *Theology of the Old Testament*, 321.
203. Mintz, "Rhetoric of Lamentations," 4; Dobbs-Allsopp, *Lamentations*, 14.
204. Dobbs-Allsopp, "Tragedy," 34.

The Rhetoric and Plot of Lamentations

Lamentations 3 is often regarded as containing the most important message as the center of a chiasm, because chapters 1 and 5 are paired, 2 and 4 are paired, and chapter 3 is at the center.[205] Or, since the acrostic culminates in chapter 3, that text may be considered as representing the most important theological values and purposes. However, various rhetorical devices and styles gradually expand the language of suffering through compassion and amplification.[206] The contrast or contradiction compares Zion's former glory with its present despair. Contempt and insults stimulate empathy.[207] Though languages of sin are also found, the words lack specificity, and the confession of sin is contextually impaired (1:18; 3:42–43).[208] God's silence also amplifies Israel's suffering. Lamentations shifts from a basic desire to voice pain to a desire to explain, and this shift draws readers to the interests of the survivors through the power of persuasion.[209] Specifically, Lamentations as a liturgical poem is desperately trying to persuade God.[210] In this sense, the goal of Lamentations can be set as an expression of sorrow, a desperate desire for salvation, and a persuasion to rouse the compassion of God and of readers and to make them pay attention to the suffering.[211] According to this goal, the structure decreases due to the acrostic and qinah meter, but at the same time the voice of the isolated speaker is gradually heightened by the voices of the witnesses and the community.[212]

---

205. The technique of putting the most important words of the chapter in the middle verse following the parallel structure in the poem. For example, Amos 5 presents chiasm as follows.
    5:13: lamentation
       5:4–6: call for repentance
          5:7: charge of Israel's sin
             5:8a–e: hymn of God's majesty
                5:8f: Yahweh is his name
             5:9: hymn of God's majesty
          5:10–13: charge of Israel's sin
       5:14–15: call for repentance
    5:16–17: lamentation

206. Andrée, *Gilbertus Universalis*, 79.
207. Andrée, *Gilbertus Universalis*, 81.
208. Dobbs-Allsopp, "Tragedy," 45, 48.
209. Linafelt, *Surviving Lamentations*, 49.
210. Linafelt, *Surviving Lamentations*, 50.
211. Dobbs-Allsopp, *Lamentations*, 25.
212. Mintz, "Rhetoric of Lamentations," 12. The we-voice that was not in chapters 1 and 2, then appeared partially in chapters 3 and 4, and entirely in chapter 5.

Lamentations 1. The first-person speech invites readers to face, hear, and experience the hardships and pains of Zion's voice.[213] The rhetorical question is important because it makes hearers understand that there is no sorrow like Zion's sorrow (v. 12). "Passerby" is a term used in Hebrew poetry to refer to a witness of pain and this question serves as an urgent plea for empathy. The question is an important beginning to the process of the formation of empathy for the transmission of emotions that will unfold in the future through the language of pain.[214] The first chapter makes "a topography of pain."[215]

Lamentations 2. Zion realizes she cannot heal her wounds on her own and seeks a healer for those wounds (vv. 13–16), but realizes those efforts are not enough; thus, she tries to return to God, the author of destruction (vv. 17–19).[216] This rhetorical question-and-answer process proves that in the end God is the only Savior. This acknowledges that God is the healer, and at the same time it is a protest against the only savior God who has allowed Zion's excessive suffering, and it is an appeal to the covenant God who is silent yet holds the power of salvation. This reality is sharply contrasted with the unilateral wrath of God, bringing sufferers deeper into despair.[217] The narrator sees the overwhelming nature of Zion's pain. In addition, the narrator in chapter 2 accepts Zion's wounds as part of her/himself (vv. 11–13) and is moved to empathy for Zion's suffering as a person who is in solidarity with Zion's anger against God.[218] In the rhetorical questions of 2:20–22, cannibalism and children's suffering are named as horrors to reinforce the complaint to God because their enemies "have killed them, slaughtering without mercy" (v. 21). Also, the image of the ruined temple raises the issue of God's presence (vv. 1–8). If God allowed the destruction, then apparently God's ears are blocked to the voices of pain (v. 56).[219]

Lamentations 3. Expressing the pain intensifies physical and psychological suffering.[220] The transition, from the fragmentary hope of the I-voice waiting for the good Jehovah (vv. 25–26) to the we-voice, makes use

---

213. Dobbs-Allsopp, *Lamentations*, 50.

214. Provan, *Lamentations*, 48; Albrektson, *Lamentations*, 68; O'Connor, *Lamentations and the Tears*, 25; Parry, *Lamentations*, 57.

215. O'Connor, *Lamentations and the Tears*, 28–29.

216. Dobbs-Allsopp, *Lamentations*, 78.

217. Dobbs-Allsopp, *Lamentations*, 81.

218. Linafelt, *Surviving Lamentations*, 51; O'Connor, *Lamentations and the Tears*, 37.

219. Dobbs-Allsopp mentions that the poet consciously centers the human element in the rhetorical flow as a whole. Dobbs-Allsopp, *Lamentation*, 89.

220. Dobbs-Allsopp, *Lamentation*, 135.

of strong rhetoric. The voice in the third poem confesses faith in a God filled with anger, one who pursues sufferers, kills without pity, and remains indifferent to their prayers. However, the advocacy for God, hope in God, and the willingness to repent to overcome suffering (vv. 33–39) ultimately move back to despair (vv. 40–47). Instead of waiting in silence (vv. 51–66), the speaker decides to mourn without ceasing until God turns back (vv. 48–50). The rhetorical question of 3:37–39 can function to stiffen the next verses of complaint (vv. 42–47). Despite God's restorative and blessing power (vv. 37–38), enemies still open their mouths (v. 46), God is covered with wrath, is killing, and is not forgiving (vv. 42–44). This can lead the reader to understand that the voice experiences deeper suffering because the theological knowledge or wisdom that has previously been heard is broken and fails to offer hope.

Lamentations 4. Among the five poems, this poem reveals most poignantly the nature of suffering and death (vv. 4–5, 8–10, 18–19). As O'Connor said, the poem feels depleted and conveys a sense of being far away, so that not only structural shrinkage but emotional shrinkage is felt.[221] Chapter 4 expands "Lamentations' reach and perspective," in preparation for a longer sequence in chapter 5.[222] Chapter 4 functions as a "rhetorical gambit," focusing on various types of people, expanding the voices of chapters 1—3, and ultimately supporting the we-voices of chapter 5.[223]

Lamentations 5. Extended grievances, manifested as collective voices, progressively broaden to encompass various contexts, including wider geographical areas and diverse age ranges. As readers read more and more poetry, the psychological distance from the other's describe\d pain decreases, and they begin to internalize the experience: "What begins as contemplation of another's experiences ends with the interiorization of these same experiences and their accompanying grief, shame, revulsion, anger, and, yes, even protest."[224] Lamentations 5:19–22 bursts forth in the most intense emotions, emphasizing God's strength and mercy (vv. 19, 21) and reinforcing the image of abandonment (vv. 20, 22). The nuance of "nevertheless" is hidden between verses19/21 and verses 20/22.

In sum, based on the increasing sense of communal lament, Lamentations' rhetorical plot can be seen in general as a movement from expressions of pain, to persuasion, to an attempt at resolution, to deeper despair, and finally to sympathy for pain. The partial collective voice in chapters 3 and 4

---

221. O'Connor, "Lamentations," 1059; Dobbs-Allsopp, *Lamentations*, 129.
222. Dobbs-Allsopp, *Lamentations*, 129–30.
223. Dobbs-Allsopp, "Tragedy," 41.
224. Dobbs-Allsopp, "Tragedy," 41.

prevents the development of hope and emphasizes pain, thus inviting readers to testify to the pain and to the silent God expressed by the we-voice in chapter 5. Furthermore, the voices in Lamentations continue to plead with God to be a witness to their suffering (1:9c, 11c, 20a; 2:20a; 3:56–61; 5:1), Eventually, the silence of God is broken, and God bears witness to the suffering in Lamentations (cf. Isa 47, 54). This can be seen as suggesting a bigger plot for Lamentations in the relationship with other biblical books.

Abused Nation and Women

As preachers, we confront the challenge not only of how to interpret Lamentations but also of how to convey its messages to our congregations. The ethical concerns echoed in Lamentations should not be dismissed, and we need to resist the urge to unravel systematically and definitively the calamities it portrays, along with their significance and applicability to our present circumstances. In this sense, reading Lamentations solely as a descriptive view of suffering may undermine sufferers' agency and may depict them as dependent and passive victims.[225] However, "the vulnerability and yearning expressed in Lamentations does not necessarily equate [to] total powerlessness, nor does the post-conquest trauma inscribed in the book solely function on the level of description."[226] Lamentations, at the very least, bears witness to the sustained trauma of enduring imperial oppression, rather than a singular catastrophe that would have granted her the time and space to gather her grief.[227] The empire devastates the collective of subjects known as "we," encompassing women, virgins, princes, elders, young warriors, and boys.[228] The afflictions of the body, manifested through specific body parts, further underscores the holistic nature of colonial suffering: our necks (v. 5), with our soul (v. 9), our skin (v. 10), our heart (v. 15), our head (v. 16), our hearts (v. 17), and our eyes (v. 17).

The rhetoric of the acrostic, functioning as a mode of contextualization, expresses a yearning for an envisioned alternative world and can serve as a projection of counter-identity.[229] The fifth poem intentionally emulates the acrostic structure, albeit without employing an alphabetic sequence, to convey a sense of cumulative passion. The collector lays "hold of two interlocking hemistiches, creating a world of bounded singularity and sensational

225. Cuéllar, "Collecting Impulse," 280.
226. Cuéllar, "Collecting Impulse," 276.
227. Cuéllar, "Collecting Impulse," 276.
228. Cuéllar, "Collecting Impulse," 285.
229. Cuéllar, "Collecting Impulse," 277.

symmetry."[230] Susan Pearce recognizes this deliberate collection as having a political role, and as fulfilling a specific social and cognitive function.[231] The inclusive "we" in Lamentations 5 can also be understood as a response to the persistent distress arising from the erosion of social relationships and ties.[232] In this light, as a book read together by a community, Lamentations emerges as an embodiment of collective agency and may symbolize an enduring effort to challenge imperial dominance.[233]

Furthermore, the personification of cities in Lamentations provides readers with an opportunity to engage directly with the personified female figure.[234] The names assigned to these anthropomorphized cities serve as a reminder that a woman who recounts a tale of anguish and brutality is not an anonymous woman but rather a woman who possesses an identity as a cherished covenant heir of Yahweh.[235] This rhetoric of naming compels readers to confront the narrative without looking away. The act of exploitation in the first poem of Lamentations, for example, accompanied by evocations of sexual violence, can be read as extreme depictions of trading all possessions, including one's own body, for survival.[236] As readers, we are implicated in our own complicity; we too have witnessed the exposure of Daughter Zion's vulnerability, we too have witnessed the stain of blood on her garment, and we too find ourselves among those who have failed to offer her solace.[237]

As Mandolfo observes, for Christians the words of the Bible possess inherent power, demanding that preachers approach the text with a particular ethic.[238] When it appears that the voiceless are articulating their thoughts, a critical consideration arises as to whether they genuinely speak from a standpoint of disenfranchisement, or whether their expressions emerge within a framework crafted by those wielding greater authority within the realm of discourse.[239] Homi Bhabha argues for a "hybridization" of discourses that disallows "a stable unitary assumption of collectivity."[240]

230. Cuéllar, "Collecting Impulse," 284.
231. Pearce, *On Collecting*, 33.
232. Cuéllar "Collecting Impulse," 285.
233. Cuéllar "Collecting Impulse," 279.
234. Wendland, "Naming Jerusalem," 72.
235. Wendland, "Naming Jerusalem," 73.
236. Wendland, "Naming Jerusalem," 71.
237. Joyce and Lipton, *Lamentations*, 15.
238. Mandolfo, *Daughter Zion Talks Back*, 27.
239. Griffiths, "Myth of Authenticity," 75.
240. Bhabha, "Signs Taken for Wonders," 153.

By aligning ourselves in solidarity with the oppressed within our texts, we can actively oppose the structural afflictions afflicting the world.[241] Moreover, this epistemic interpretation extends not solely to the contemporary context but also reaches into the biblical past, enabling us to seek unity with those whom the biblical narrative silences and marginalizes.[242]

More on Rhetorical Plot of Suffering for Preaching: Wider Contexts

The rhetoric of Lamentations amplifies the voice of suffering and gaining sympathy, which can be helpful for lament-driven preaching. Lament preaching is based on the larger movements of the crucifixion-resurrection and suffering-hope frames. However, this movement is dynamic rather than straightforwardly linear. Therefore, there can be various ways to set a plot within a larger framework of movement, for example, within a circular structure or an unending plot.

The circular structure is different from some well-known narrative arcs. For example, in *Bongsan Talchum*, a Korean mask play, the *Mial* episode starts with the reunion scene of an elderly couple. The couple lost track of each other as they tried to survive in the panic of war (or uproar) in their town.[243] They looked for each other throughout the nation. In this sense, the reunion of the couple seems to be the end of the story. However, a new conflict arrives with the appearance of a concubine. The plot of such a narrative is not driven by a curiosity about what will happen in the future, but curiosity about how to resolve things that the audience already knows are the driving force of the story.[244] This structure creates repeated waves by causing the story to fluctuate through convergence and diffusion like Lamentations. Lamentations is likely to resolve the pain in chapter 3, but the pain gets deeper and the despair becomes denser, avoiding an easy conclusion.

Though Hebrew (Rabbinic) tradition rereads verse 21 once more after 22, preventing the fifth from ending with despair, Lamentations indeed exhibits an endless plot.[245] Lamentations' rhetoric makes the sufferers' pain most dramatic and does not let God's words overturn or assuage their expressions of suffering. The resolution is delayed though, as Brueggemann says, for "Second Isaiah should not be permitted to 'solve' the grief of the

---

241. Mandolfo, *Daughter Zion Talks Back*, 27.

242. Schüssler Fiorenza, *Rhetoric and Ethic*, 12.

243. Lee, *Korean Mask Paly*, 236. This script is organized based on oral tradition and does not explain the specific reason for the separation of the couple.

244. Son, "Study on the 'Yeonsan' Structure," 79.

245. Re'emi, "Theology of Hope," 132.

lament too soon or too completely."[246] "History happens in the midst of silence that is at the edge of absence. It happens first of all in tears that are long and salty, that yield only late, very late, to hope."[247] This is the "open-end." Harris and Mandolfo propose that verse 22 opens space to continue mourning.[248] The space after 5:22 is the point where God's sorrow and silence meet at the end of the torment of human suffering and the manifestation of anger. It is a moment of silence in which we have seen but have not spoken to each other. Thus, Lamentations leaves the end open instead of ending with God's voice, offering a place where the sufferers lament as much as they need to, complain to God, ask for others' sympathy, protest together, witness others' pain, and wait in faith for their restoration by God.

The Portion of Hope in Lamentations

In searching for hope in Lamentations, many scholars try to decipher hope from the third poem, from Second Isaiah, or from the resurrection of Christ. These are useful methods. The memory about our faithful God (Lam 3:21–26) can be a hope, whether or not it moves back to despair because the memory of God's faithfulness allows us to anticipate a reprise of such faithfulness. The hope of Christ's resurrection needs to appear because it is the only genuine power that can save sufferers from endless suffering. Nonetheless, preachers may not need to remove all hope from the poignant suffering voices in Lamentations itself because "honest talk about God and to God in the midst of suffering is the only way to realistic hope."[249] In Lamentations 5 the genre of complaint does not stem from "distrust," but comes from trust in God as core-testimony, God alone can put an end to this unbearable situation and restore it. "The evidence given in the text tells against the core testimony, but at the same time appeals to the core-testimony, asking that this particular circumstance should be drawn into the positive reality there attested."[250] The urgency of the situation and the intensity of the pain led them to truth-telling about their tremendous loss.

Lamentations reveals the human will for life, profoundly manifested, and serves as an expression of faith.[251] Lamentations has a deep suffering voice and tone, but within this, the recovery and vitality of life resist

246. Brueggemann, *Introduction to the Old Testament*, 342.
247. Brueggemann, *Introduction to the Old Testament*, 343.
248. Harris and Mandolfo, "Silent God in Lamentations," 142.
249. Davis, *Preaching the Luminous Word*, 221.
250. Brueggemann, *Theology of the Old Testament*, 321.
251. Dobbs-Allsopp, *Lamentations*, 2.

the dominance of suffering.[252] As Dobbs-Allsopp mentions, the rhetoric in Lamentations seeks "one object, God, and one desire, to see suffering relieved."[253] There is no place to go and no way to solve the pain without God. Those who lament pray with trust in God and show the will to continue lamenting about their suffering until God renews them and the land. Thus, the overall rhetoric aims to reactivate God's favor and love.[254] Their groaning is urgent, very powerful, and provocative. The unresolved ending in Lamentations 5 coexists with hope, reveals the mystery of faith, and exists until the full kin-dom of God comes, revealing its value. In relation to Christ's crucifixion and resurrection, Lamentations can work as a metaphor for the period from Holy Friday until Easter, a metaphor which embraces suffering and nurtures hope.[255]

CONCLUSION: LAMENT IN LAMENTATIONS

The reality of darkness exists until the eschaton. Human pain exists and will exist in any place and at any age; its victims are all full of the "honest cry of darkest despair."[256] Sadly, however, lament as a way of dealing with poignant suffering seems to be largely overlooked in today's church, even though lament continues to be an appropriate response to numerous painful situations in human life.[257] Luke A. Powery's sermon allows churches to see why they pay minimal attention to pain:

> I know we have problems in the church with the notion of lament. I know some love praise and worship (hey!). I know some embrace the top of the mountain and have a hard time dealing with the rough side of the mountain. I know we've been co-opted by the capitalistic principalities and pristine powers of prosperity-gospel preaching, naming it and claiming it, a bigger house and a bigger car and a bigger bank account. I know we love a Santa Claus God who we can call up on the mainline and tell him what we want and God will grant us like [a genie] our every wish just the way we like it. I know we've been under the hallucination of gospel music theologies like "let's get back to Eden and live on top of the world" when we've never been on

---

252. Dobbs-Allsopp, *Lamentations*, 47.
253. Dobbs-Allsopp, *Lamentations*, 48.
254. Lakkis, "Have You Any Right to be Angry?," 174.
255. Brueggemann, *Theology of the Old Testament*, 401.
256. Swenson, *Living Through Pain*, 140.
257. Lakkis, "Have You Any Right to be Angry?" 181.

top of the world. I know we, in the church, can be socialized liturgical zombies and get caught up in fancy phrases like "when the praises go up, the blessings come down."[258]

The declaration of premature victory over suffering often leads to imperfect ideas of resurrection and imperfect hope. The Bible does not say only happy things concerning the resurrection because we also live with the cross (Mark 10:38; 16:24; Rom 6:5). The Bible speaks not only about the good parts of life but about all its parts, including pain, scars, and weakness. Good Friday leads to the morning of the resurrection. However, the scars of Friday remain on the body of Christ. And these scars are a permanent warning against any premature proclamation of hope.[259] Lamentations as a communal lament in preaching can bring the language of grief into a liturgy as a central part of biblical faith and devotion, just as the Gospels describe Christ's suffering.[260]

The book of Lamentations seems to end with grumbling and sighing, but this does not mean it embodies a negative or passive attitude. It rather stands as an accusation against the reality of injustice, it offers comfort to the weak, and it seeks justice. Brueggemann says, "that our sense of loss and sadness is serious and honorable, and one need not prop up or engage in denial."[261] Mourning is a channel for calling on God and the community to hear from those with wounds and those in suffering. Lamentations is a place where the restoration of language takes place. It is a place to recall and restore the language of suffering. In Lamentations 5, the perfect agent of lament becomes the collective 'us.'[262] Singing Lamentations is not for the past, but rather for the present and future of the community. Besides, Lamentations may enable people in pain to discover new ways to communicate with God. Lament is an act of hope that believes that there is no situation beyond the power of God.[263] The last verse of Lamentations shows that even renewed faith and trust do not provide absolute certainty: only God can do that.[264] In this sense, this biblical lament is another means of faith approved by God that allows us to express suffering, to witness, and to yearn for recovery. As the language of grief, especially used in communal

---

258. Powery, "My God, My God, Why?"
259. Brueggemann, *Theology of the Old Testament*, 332.
260. Dobbs-Allsopp, *Lamentations*, 36.
261. Brueggemann, *Cadences of Home*, 12.
262. Dobbs-Allsopp, *Lamentations*, 33–34.
263. Brueggemann, *Old Testament Theology*, 29.
264. Renkema, *Lamentations*, 179.

liturgical situations, Lamentations shows the possibility and value of lament in preaching as a way to deal with suffering in faith.

Preaching lament does not conclude on Sunday; rather, it encourages the everyday practice of lament to deal with suffering beyond Christian discourse. As we have seen in this chapter, lament was neither confined to nor used only by faith communities. Practicing lament in ancient and biblical times was not only an appeal to God, but also an appeal to find people to lament as witnesses of suffering in the human community and as a resistance to injustice. In the next chapter, we will probe the idea that lament promotes resilience in the wider community beyond the boundaries of churches. Also, we will identify how such lament has become a medium for resolving personal and public grief in Korean culture, by examining Korean history and culture and discussing its universality and value within a modern context.

2

Lament as a Reflection of *Han* (한, 恨) and as a Way of *Hanpuri* (한풀이)

IN THE STUDY OF LAMENTATIONS, we discussed the various functions and interpretive issues of biblical lament. When humans face unbearable suffering, lament can be a way of calling upon God and a means by which to recall and restore the language of grief in communities. Communal lament in the Bible refers to a hopeful act, whose intention is to cultivate the resilience of the faith community and to reaffirm trust in God, express suffering, witness, resist injustice, and speak of longing for recovery.

However, lament constitutes a significant ritual for dealing with suffering, persistently observed across a diverse array of cultures. The discourse of lament extends beyond the confines of historical and cultural contexts linked with biblical traditions. This chapter will show how communal lament has been used and has influenced how people deal with suffering and hope in Korean culture. Through cultural and social studies, this chapter examines whether and how the dynamics of lament provide a transition from suffering to hope, promote communities' resilience, and express the suffering of broader communities beyond faith communities. This chapter especially probes the roles of communal lament in light of a historical, cultural, and homiletical understanding of Korea, applying the concepts of *han* and *hanpuri* as a movement from suffering to hope. It also considers the 2014 *Sewol* ferry tragedy as a watershed incident that has revitalized public lament in Korea, in public and religious spheres.

THE CONCEPTS OF *HAN* AND *HANPURI* IN KOREA

Han (恨) means "a state that keeps holding the wounds in the heart as an idiograph of 忄, which means heart and 艮, which means being still."[1] Comparing *han* as it is understood in China and Japan, the emotions commonly mentioned are 怨 (complaint, blame, resent) and 嘆 (lament, cry, groan).[2] From Korean literature, *han* is understood as a more complex and diverse emotion:[3] (1) as 情恨 (representation of longing for someone or something lost), (2) as 願恨 (infinite dreams held by finite humans), (3) as 怨恨 (having aggression toward the opponent), (4) as 痛恨 (various complex emotions accompanied by the concept of pain)[4], and (5) as 餘恨 (continued suffering inside).[5] The New Korean Reformed Version of the Bible translates *han* as "to loosen or solve *han*" in Gen 27:42, Prov 23:11, Lam 3:58–59, Dan 7:22, Luke 18:3–8, 2 Tim 3:3, and Ps 72:4. "Redress a grievance or exonerate" has a similar meaning when it is used to refer to an orphan (Isa 1:17, 23), the needy (Prov 31:9), and the poor (Prov 29:14). *Han* cannot be defined merely as a grudge, bitterness, or sadness.

Hanpuri is not a certain fixed state, but a fluid concept that includes the process of moving *han* to *puri*. The metaphors of *han* are widely understood as a very intricately entangled knot or a tightly formed blood clot or lump of rock in a human's soul and something deep in the heart.[6] Hence, *puri* means to untangle, release, resolve, liberate, or dissolve *han*. *Puri* means to comfort, consume, and sublimate the sorrow of *han*.[7] In addition, when the meaning of *han* and *puri* are presented together, and when combined with the term *Minjung*, *han* can be better understood.[8] As a more collective feeling, *han* is inscribed in the history of oppression, the tyranny of the ruling class, and religious ideology.[9] Like a gene that has shaped the identity of Korea, *han* has the archetypes and creation principles of Korean culture.[10] *Han* is also connected with the heart of caring for others.[11] *Han* refers to awaiting

1. Lee, *Essay on Koreanology*, 1:276.
2. Kim, "Study of Education," 303.
3. Kim, "Study of Education," 303–4.
4. Shin, *Pungryu*, 256–57.
5. Jung, "Poetics of Korean Traditional Emotion," 112–13.
6. Jung, "Approach of Pastoral Care," 246–51.
7. Choi, "Creating a Culture of Reconciliation," 234–36.
8. Park, *Korean Preaching*, 15.
9. Park, *Korean Preaching*, 18.
10. Jung, "Poetics of Korean Traditional Emotion," 108.
11. *Pansori* and other literary works including *Heungbuga* are often used in conjunction with *han* and *jung* (情). Cheon, "On the Structure of '*Han*: 恨'," 171–72.

reunion, healing, and reconciliation beyond revenge.[12] *Han* may exist both in the ruling class and in subjugated classes, but the minjung's *han* has its roots in survival, justice, and ideals, and believing in the hope of tomorrow.[13]

Korea has traditionally solved *han* with various cultural expressions, such as humor, sarcasm, song, and dance, as well as social forms, such as an uprising of the people, and religious services such as *gut* (a religious rite of shamanism). In these various ways, lament has acted as an important expression of *hanpuri* conducted in various social spaces. Hence, *hanpuri*, also called *hyehan*, goes beyond tolerating and alleviating pain and instead exposes pain, shares stories of pain, and demands justice.[14]

BACKGROUND UNDERSTANDINGS ABOUT *HAN* AND LAMENT IN KOREA

This section introduces several important historical, cultural, and theological contexts to show how *han* is formed and to illustrate the public practice of lament.

Historical Background of Suffering

The Japanese Colonial Period (1910–45)

In the early 1900s, the Japanese Empire disseizes sovereignty of Joseon (the last dynasty of Korea, 1392–1910). Following Japan's victory in the Russo-Japanese War (1904–5), the Protectorate Treaty between Korea and Japan concluded in 1905 and the Japan-Korea Unequal Treaty of 1907 was imposed by force. As a result, the Korean army and police were forcibly dissolved, and Korea's diplomatic and administrative rights were surrendered to Japan. In 1910, the Korea-Japan Annexation ended the Joseon Dynasty, launching Korea's thirty-six years of the Japanese Colonial Period. Since political and social leaders lost their roles as a result, the people turned to church leaders to assume those leadership roles.[15] The Korean church maintained some autonomy thanks to being organized into different denominations; it was the period when the institutional churches were formed.[16]

---

12. Suh, "Formation of *Han*," 88–89.
13. Cheon, "Study on the Principle of Reconciliation," 1549.
14. Park, *Wounded Heart*, 105.
15. Lee, *Lee Gi-Pung*, 35.
16. For more detail, see Park, *Korean Christian History* 2, 73–79.

Early missionaries in Korea were more focused on individual salvation than on the political situation of Korea.[17] In September 1901, the Presbyterian Council declared non-politicization, meaning that the Korean church pledged its loyalty to the emperors and rulers (of Japan), that the Church would not engage in politics, and that political issues would not be discussed in the church.[18] By almost twenty years later, Korean Christianity had become socially reformative, and secured a new position in society through its active participation in the 3.1 (national resistance) movement (1919). With all that came a public explosion of Korean people's *han*. Although early Christian missionaries had supported to make Korean Christianity nonpolitical, Korean Christianity suggested the ideological foundation of the national movement by sublimating the spirit of resistance and national consciousness to the dimension of faith.[19] In response to this, the Provisional Government of the Republic of Korea was established in Shanghai in April 1919 to unify the entire independence movement, and systematic armed independence struggles were continuously carried out. In 1930, the government began to push for shrine visits and worship. Since Shinto worship represented a religious rite dedicated to venerating the spirit of Shinto, Japan's indigenous religion, it inevitably clashed with Christian doctrine, expressly forbidding idolatry. A substantial number of Christians refused visiting shrines at the beginning. As a result, full-scale church persecution began, and a small minority paid a huge price for the anti-shrine worship movement in which they participated. From 1938, Japan established a policy to obliterate the Korean nation, including its language, and Koreans were forced into wars for Japan. Korean people suffered from severe famine and the constant threat of death.

After the failure of the March First (or 3.1) independence movement, Protestant leaders who had been actively involved in the movement began to distance themselves from the national problem. Church leaders focused on the stability of church organizations and expansion. Instead of weakening social reform and resistance, the commentary on the doctrine of religion was strengthened and the form of faith which emphasized individual cultivation and sanctification. Compared to the *Baekmokkanyeon*, a collection of sermons from the 1900s and 1920s, *Joseon Pulpit-35 People's Sermons*, published in the latter half of the 1920s, contains a more developed explanation

---

17. Kim, "Study on the Principle of Preaching," 116–17.

18. Noh, "Church and Policy." This resolution of the missionaries was distributed through *The Christian News*, October 3, 1901.

19. Park, "Christian Faith and National Consciousness," 259.

of religious doctrines and the supernatural quality of Christianity.[20] With daily problems being neglected by preachers, theology focused instead on the afterlife and mysticism, mainly through redemptive preaching. In addition, the pattern of sermons, as shown in the *Joseon Pulpit-35 People's Sermons*, emphasized the piety, repentance, and sanctification of individual believers. This was somewhat different from the repentance characteristic of the great revival movement in the Korean church in 1907, and was likely because the social and structural problems were also reduced to the level of individual spirituality, leading to the acceptance of the existing political and social order and the inculcation of guilt in individual believers. The church regarded the misery of the nation and the poverty of individuals as due to the lack of individual repentance.[21]

At the beginning of the 1930s, Christianity was perceived as one of the threats to Japan.[22] At this time, the largest issue facing the church was the matter of the shrine visits.[23] There were some preachers who resisted shrine worship, but most submitted to the threat of Japan and went along with it, ostensibly in the name of preserving the Korean church organization and authority.[24] In the 1930s, the sermons tended to blame life's problems on the individual, on selfishness, and to focus on personal, inner issues, detached from the national and historical scene.[25] The sermons in *Collected Sermons in Commemoration of the Jubilee* in 1940 describe the gospel and faith as affirming the existing order—in other words, Japanese colonial rule. In short, preaching socio-structural evil, civilization, and order as products of faith eventually "colonized" the oppressed, instilling in their own consciousness a sentiment of self-hatred.[26]

The Korean War (1950)

On August 15, 1945, Koreans celebrated the liberation of both Christianity and the nation.[27] Patriots who had been engaged in independence movements and agents of the Provisional Government of the Republic of Korea returned home, but internal politics was confused by the trusteeship of the

---

20. Park, "Christian Faith and National Consciousness," 262.
21. Kim, "Give Us Enthusiasm," 32–33.
22. Kim, *History of Preaching in Korea*, 210.
23. Kim, *History of Preaching in Korea*, 214.
24. Park, "Christian Faith and National Consciousness," 252.
25. Park, "Christian Faith and National Consciousness," 267–68.
26. Park, "Christian Faith and National Consciousness," 263.
27. Yu, *Vein of Korean Theology*, 145.

superpower countries. Korea became two countries: The Republic of Korea (South Korea) and the Democratic People's Republic of Korea (North Korea).[28] At this time, one of the biggest tasks of the Korean government and churches was to clear away the remnants of Japanese colonialism. In this period, incumbent clergy sought to secure their positions within the church, with some clergy venturing into politics. Released saints who had opposed shrine visits, prioritizing church reconstruction, advocated repentance, self-restraint, and church discipline for shrine worshippers were a guiding principle for Korean church reconstruction. A pronounced conflict arose between the released saints and the church authorities who had already in power and who endorsed shrine worship and resisted the request of repentance. This is tenuously connected with the idea that the reconstruction movement of the church clearly revealed the nature of the purification movement.[29]

Since the Korean War, preaching about repentance had increased because most preachers thought the Korean War was caused by the sins of Koreans.[30] Amid the chaos, the Korean War, which broke out in 1950, was like reopening a wound. Many churches were destroyed, church leaders were taken prisoner, and martyrs were sacrificed.[31] People in Korea were once again trapped in poverty and suffering. Because of this war, many South Koreans became anti-communist in orientation.

Sermons in the 1950s were therefore primarily about the historical rule and judgment of God. The preachers who supported a pre-millennialist vision placed strong emphasis on the spiritual world knowing only too well that the human world is filled with suffering. They wanted to establish how

---

28. In December 1945, at a tripartite conference in Moscow, the trusteeship was approved. The Soviet Union established the northern region of the Korean Peninsula as a satellite state, and the US governed the southern region. Provisional Government agents insisted on establishing a self-governing unification government, but Rhee Syngman hoped for the sole rule of the United States, and South Korea's sole election was held. The Institute of the History of Christianity in Korea, *History of Korean Christianity*, 3:196–97. Un-Yong Kim estimates that as the Syngman Rhee government was established, Christianity tended to be in close contact with "the pro-US anti-communist policy" and those who supported the unification policy of the Syngman Rhee regime, advocating the achievement of reunification even through the mobilization of force. Kim, *History of Preaching in Korea*, 457.

29. For more details see Oh, "Calvin's View on Schismatic Movement," 203–19.

30. Yum, "Theological Analysis," 245.

31. The total population of South and North Korea was about 30 million, and about one-sixth of the total population was killed or injured by the Korean War. Civilian victims also suffered a great deal of damage. Also, because the social and economic foundations of South and North Korea were thoroughly destroyed, Korea had to rely completely on US economic aid.

different the world of God is and presumably to attract those beaten down by the Korean War and other events.

Military Dictatorship (1960s–80s)

In light of the Korean War (1950), a majority of South Korean people thought that if they did not strengthen their anti-communist stance, Korea's national base would be shaken. This strong resistance to communism unfortunately led people to support the military dictatorship. Some Christian representatives and missionaries wanted to recover the stability of the country, and their desire was closely related to the pro-US/anti-communist policy of Korea's first president, Syngman Rhee.[32] However, when President Rhee revised the Constitution to allow himself to become a third-term president, and when his party consequently held an illegal election, a protest broke out in Masan on April 11, 1960. Joo-Yeol Kim vanished following his involvement in a protest against the fraudulent 3.15 elections. Kim Ju-yeol, a demonstrator, was teargassed, and subsequently, the police disposed of his body in the sea. This discovery incited public outrage, catalyzing the April 19 Revolution—a democratic uprising against the corruption of the Syngman Rhee government. More than forty students from Korea University were injured by armed political thugs after the student rebellion was launched on April 19.[33] The Rhee regime suppressed protests by force, resulting in more than 100 deaths and 450 injuries. The student protests prompted the older generations to join the protest; 1,566 students and citizens were subsequently killed when they were confronted by a heavily armed army that was equipped with tanks.[34] The Korean churches who were attached to the regime (for example, through their advisory roles) could no longer avoid their responsibility in the regime's corruption and violence. Movements arose, calling for repentance and self-examination.[35] The National Council

---

32. Hee-Kuk Lim presents several reasons for the close relationship between missionaries, Protestant leaders, and Rhee: (1) Some US missionaries arrived in Korea not solely as religious missionaries but as advisors to the US military government. The US Military Administration offered substantial support for churches and their members; (2) Rhee acknowledged and put into effect certain policy proposals advocated by Protestants; (3) Protestant pastors frequently intervened in political matters and personnel recommendations, leveraging their personal relationships with Rhee. Lim, "Political Participation," 19–20.

33. Park, *Korean Church History*, 3:74.

34. Kim, "Reminiscence and Prospects of 4.19," 19.

35. Elders and pastors, regardless of denominations such as Presbyterian, Methodists, and the Holiness Church, participated and held a national evangelism movement with the motto, "return to God." Park, *Korean Church History*, 3:87.

of Student Associations, which recognized that the revolution of ideology and life must take place together to overcome political and moral corruption and confusion, promoted the Enlightenment Movement that was based on the soul of Christianity.[36] Ik-hwan Moon (1918–94) preached, "From the president up to the common people, we should lament in sackcloth with ashes on our heads.... There is no democracy in the military world."[37] In the 1970s–80s, political confusion became more serious. Demonstrations by students against the military dictatorship continued. However, Korea's economy was developing rapidly amid this turmoil.

Tensions stemming from unstable economic growth, social and psychological disruptions due to industrialization and urbanization, along with bureaucratic controls to manage unrest, persisted.[38] Seeking stability amid this tension resulted in a significant influx of individuals into the church. During this phase of church expansion, themes such as evangelism, faith for blessings, and the infusion of the Holy Spirit emerged as prominent subjects in sermons.[39] Furthermore, the modernization movement of the 1960s and beyond, coupled with national and individual aspirations to overcome poverty, gave rise to sermons focusing on prosperity.[40] While some religious sects became more involved in social issues as a means of engaging with the challenges of the times, the Korean church as a whole did not share that conviction.

The Cultural Background of Suffering

The foundation of Korean thought is based on local beliefs that were held from the time of the society's foundation—over 1,500 years of Buddhist thought, and over five hundred years of Confucian thought, to which Christian and Western ideas were later added.[41] Thus, these traditions have greatly influenced Koreans' thoughts, lives, and ethics.

---

36. Park, *Korean Church History*, 3:89.
37. Moon, "Will Democracy Succeed in Korea?," loc. 268.
38. Kim, *History of Preaching in Korea*, 605.
39. Kim, *History of Preaching in Korea*, 607.
40. Kim, *History of Preaching in Korea*, 607.
41. Lee, "Syncretism Ideology," 233.

Ingwauengbo (인과응보, 因果應報, *Retributive Justice*)

Korea's interpretation of suffering has been influenced by this multi-religious culture. The oldest interpretation of suffering is *Ingwauengbo*, which teaches that a person suffers because of having done something wrong.[42] Shamanism, which had been the dominant belief and practice among Koreans in the past, held a worldview that the natural gods and ancestral gods determine how humans are blessed and cursed.[43] However, Buddhist belief states that suffering comes from past actions and that human actions can change the future.[44] The public was comforted by the idea that living well or righteously in the present life can lead to comfort in the next life.[45] Ingwauengbo served as moral justification of the ruling class, that enjoys blessings in the present life.[46] Confucianism interprets natural catastrophes or illnesses as warnings sent from heaven. Confucianism interprets suffering as fate when suffering cannot be explained by Ingwauengbo logic. This interpretation may well have been an obstacle to compassion for those who were suffering. Although this idea contributed widely to the formation and maintenance of individual and social order, it also contributed to the tight connection that Korean preachers made between pain and sin, where they combined Ingwauengbo ideas with theology.[47]

The Honor-Shame Culture

The Korean honor-shame culture is related to the patriarchal social system based on strict Confucian norms that were accepted after the middle of the Joseon Dynasty.[48] This culture has had a particularly negative impact on women. For in Confucian society, the sexual honor of a woman is related to

---

42. Kang, "Understanding of Suffering," 58.
43. Nam, "Medieval Korean Society and Buddhism," 96.
44. Kwak, "Confucian Philosophical Interpretation of Pain," 289–308.
45. Jeong, "Korean Philosophy," 246.
46. Jeong, "Korean Philosophy," 249–50.
47. Kim, "Fidelity Types and Buddhist Roles," 258. Although fidelity does not have to be reciprocated, it forms the idea of causal retribution that takes it for granted that the result of fidelity is derived as a desirable result, and has a positive function of establishing, maintaining, and developing social order based on that idea. Kim, "Fidelity Types and Buddhist Roles," 284.
48. If guilt is an emotion that accompanies human sinful behavior, then shame is an emotion associated with denial of human existence. Yim, "Study on the Korean Women's Shame," 266–67.

the family's honor.[49] More specifically, the chastity of a woman is essential to the social reputation of her husband. It is also related to her mother's chastity, and to her father's honor. A mother's chastity also affects her son's honor. Thus, married men's extramarital sexual relations are looked upon with relative tolerance, while any such relations women pursue are regarded as serious insults to their husbands and families. The stringent and discriminatory criteria imposed upon women have rendered it challenging for them to avail themselves of protective measures against violence within the prevailing social framework. From the early 1930s to 1945, while Japan was using a lot of forced labor for their war, they created military sex slavery.[50] Korean girls were forced to fulfill the sexual desires of the Japanese military in the war.[51] They had to give their bodies to twenty to thirty Japanese soldiers a day in places like a narrow warehouse.[52] That overwhelming mental and physical suffering caused severe damage to many sexual slaves. Many committed suicides because they could not return home on account of the shame associated with such (forced) labor.[53] They could not speak to their families or to others about their pain. They were afraid that the honor of their families would be destroyed because of them. At the same time, they were ashamed of themselves, even though they were not at fault.

> 13-year-old, to a naked and exhausted body
> when military boots attack like a bomb shell . . .
> without time to weep bitterly. . . .
> Because my womb became decayed
> I cannot be a mother or a wife

49. Kim, "Psychological-Social Understanding," 242.

50. Korea suffered two major events in the 1900s: the Japanese colonial period (1910–45) and the Korean War (1950). I grew up listening to my family's stories related to these events. My aunt carried my father's older brother on her back to run away from guns and swords. They suffered from hunger and fear of death. My mother-in-law's hometown is in North Korea and her family members were all refugees. All Koreans have these stories. They not only lost their loved ones, but also were forced to live scattered, far from one another. These events have become national traumas.

51. Jeong, "Formation of Depressed Women's Subjectivity," 79. The phrase "Comfort Women" is a term intended to conceal the (sexual) violence of war. Japan's sexual slavery system was defined as an example of military sexual slavery by the UN Commission on Human Rights. Japan used the words comfort women and comfort facilities as intentional euphemisms used to minimize its crime. These words should be corrected to "Japanese sexual slavery women" and "brothel."

52. Testimony of surviving "comfort women": "On Sunday, it is busy. Usually, we dealt with 30–40 soldiers a day. I did not know if it took ten minutes or twenty minutes. . . . I closed my eyes." Kim, "Incomplete Stories," 8.

53. The women who were afraid that their families would be pointed out by society because of what they been forced to do, patriarch banished to a silent existence.

> I cannot see my home and parents
> hide in day, breathe in night. . . .
> By whose rough conspiracy was my life pushed into an incineration plant of history?
> Someone please remembers my blood clot [*han*] in the sky.[54]

They were deprived of their right to speak the truth and their pain was not named. The survivors' trauma resulted in permanent and excruciating memories. The honor-shame culture has never allowed "comfort women" any relief from their unbearable *han*. The socially tacit agreement within this culture has contributed to the accumulation of *han* by making the victims unable to reveal the truth and unable to mourn the suffering of the violence committed against them as women—by government, the military, individual soldiers, and their families.

Patriarchy

Family and kindred in ancient society had a bilineal system in marriage, inheritance, and descent, which survived until the Goryeo Dynasty (936–1391).[55] However, the Joseon Dynasty (1392–1909), which took Confucianism as its ruling ideology, reformed the marriage, funeral, ritual, and inheritance systems. These were now focused on paternity in order to establish a new understanding of kingship and status in society. Thus, patriarchy had become firmly established by the middle of the seventh century, and this intensified women's suffering in the late Joseon Dynasty.[56] Despite the many positive aspects of Confucianism, it has also had negative effects, for example increasing women's suffering by creating vices such as 七去之惡 (seven conditions for expelling a wife) and 三從之道 (three principles that women should follow).[57] Because the rules did not allow women to go

---

54. Gwon, "Military Sexual Slavery's Secret History 3."
55. Lee, "Korean Patriarchy and Women," 161.
56. Lee, "Korean Patriarchy and Women," 161–62.
57. The scripture that systematizes Confucianism's view of women and ethics is Yegi (禮記). Yegi's view of women served as a norm restricting women's activities, and the gender-discriminatory view is dominant. Nam, "Confucian View of Women," 279–81; Kim, "Confucianism and Feminism," 399–428, 401. Samjongjido (三從之道) refers to the three principles that a woman must follow. They obey their parents when they are young, obey their husbands when they are married, and follow their sons when the husband dies. *Encyclopedia of Korean Culture*, s.v. "Samjongjido (三從之道)." Chilgeojiak (七去之惡) is (1) Not serving the parents-in-law well, (2) Not having a son, (3) Committing adultery, (4) Jealousy, (5) Hereditary diseases such as leprosy or epilepsy, (6) Talking too much, and (7) Stealing. *Encyclopedia of Korean Culture*, s.v. "Chilgeojiak (七去之惡)."

outside of the house gate after dark, if her house were ablaze women were required not to come out but to burn to death.[58] 男尊女卑 (the superiority of men over women) was also formed in the seventeenth century because of 朱子學, which is one principle of Confucian philosophy. As a result, as the regulations that controlled women became stricter, and men began to restrain them and made women increasingly subordinate.[59] Also, society regarded women as bringing bad luck and destruction, and wives as the private property of husbands, which connived to make domestic violence socially acceptable.[60] Women's married life manifested all these difficulties. When a woman married, she had to go to the house where the man lived, and the harsh married life she often endured at that house became *han*.[61] Married life required strict obedience and required her to produce a son, while society ignored her harsh repression.[62] In this sense, patriarchy has created a female *han* by contributing to various conditions of oppression of women, regardless of women's class or economic status.

The Bansang System (반상--, 班常--, A Status System)

The *bansang* system refers to the aristocratic bureaucracy of the Joseon dynasty (1392–1910).[63] *Ban* refers to *Yangban*, which is an occupational group that receives a stipend from the government, and *sang* refers to a merchant group. More particularly, the *Bansang* system consisted of the *yangban* with a ruling class, a middle class, peasants as a subjugated class, and slaves as the lowest class. By law, movement between statuses was not permitted. *Yangban* citizens enjoyed all the socioeconomic privileges and maintained their status through marriage to other members of the *Yangban* class.[64] In this hierarchical bureaucracy, except for the privileged few, all people suffered

---

58. Lee, *Korean Woman's Lessons*, 33.
59. Kim, "Confucianism and Feminism," 401n1.
60. Bang, "Korean Consciousness Structure," 67, 74.
61. Bang, "Korean Consciousness Structure," 76–77.
62. Bang, "Korean Consciousness Structure," 77–78.

63. Kye, "Birth and Diffusion," 105. Two theories about class in the Joseon Dynasty were proposed: *Yangcheonje* and *Bansangje*. Bansangje argued that there was an exclusive class based on blood ties, while *Yangcheonje* understood Joseon as an equal society composed entirely of free citizens except for the *nobi* (slaves), without acknowledging the aristocratic character of the *Yangban*. However, considering that slaves constituted 40 percent of the population from the fifteenth to the mid to late eighteenth century, the political structure of the Joseon Dynasty could be seen as an aristocratic bureaucracy. Refer to Palais, "Confucianism and the Aristocratic/Bureaucratic Balance," 428.

64. Park, *Korean Preaching*, 17.

from harsh living conditions, and often rebellion took place.⁶⁵ The middle class or peasants, who suffered from poverty, became slaves themselves, and this situation was often abused by the *yangban*.⁶⁶ Most of the ruled classes were exposed to the risk of hunger, infection, natural disasters, and the people suffered from the corruption, intimidation, and injustice inflicted by the ruling class, *yangban*.⁶⁷ The *han* of these subjugated classes has been projected into many literary works as well as recorded in documents.

> It's been three years since I have gone begging not to starve to death from this great famine. . . . I was left on the road and suffered from hunger and cold. I cried day and night and descended to the point of starvation. . . . I write this document with the intention of selling myself and my children forever, and I will receive 10 *Nyang* (375g) gold as needed to save my parents' lives from starvation.⁶⁸

Theological Background of Suffering

Drawing upon historical, cultural, and sociostructural experiences, the Korean church has formulated various theological interpretations and alternatives addressing the suffering encountered by believers. These theological pursuits exhibit variable emphasis, at times focusing on eschatological hope, at other times highlighting the pursuit of temporal well-being, and occasionally manifesting as forms of resistance against social and political oppression.

Historical Pre-Millennialism

For Korean preachers, the eschatological sermon was a very important topic for preaching believers about their immediate context. In other words, anticipating the imminent second coming of Jesus while living under the pressures of Japan and enduring the suffering of life provided

---

65. Park, *Korean Preaching*, 18.
66. Bak, "Girls Sold as Nobi," 186–87.
67. Bak, "Girls Sold as Nobi," 196–98.
68. In the twenty-third year of King Jeong-jo's reign (1799), Yongdan, an eight-year-old girl, prepared this document to sell herself to a noble family in order to prevent her family from starving. However, the style of the writing suggests that it was actually the family that initiated the sale of the young child. 古書: 古文書展示會 at Yeungnam University Central Library, 1997, in Bak, "Girls Sold as Nobi," 188–89.

believers with great support and hope.⁶⁹ Therefore, an important theme in the early Korean church sermon during the Japanese colonial period was eschatological faith related to repentance, regeneration, and salvation. Early missionaries brought with them belief in historical pre-millennialism, and missionaries who arrived in the 1920s introduced belief in dispensational pre-millennialism.⁷⁰

Pre-millennialism refers to the belief that the church would pass through the tribulation and, immediately, enter the millennial kingdom marked by the second coming of Jesus.⁷¹ Since historical pre-millennialism recognizes that the church is saved after passing through the final tribulation, those who looked for stability, while facing anxiety, easily accepted this apocalyptic faith as the gospel. The emphasis on this eschatological faith has created a variety of heresies, but it has played a positive role when society was in a period of uncertainty, for example by consoling the suffering congregations, and allowing the opponents of shrine worship to overcome jail and torture.⁷² This eschatology also had an escapist character.⁷³ These eschatological beliefs distracted people from their present suffering and made it more difficult for them to express their pain. Though pre-millennialism helped people to endure the suffering caused by their harsh conditions and to see hope in the future, it provided limited help in dealing with the present pain.

Religious Nationalism

The sermon as resistance to injustice was closely related to the national situation. Korean preachers equated the history of Israel with the history of Korea, calling for a repentant attitude because they understood the internal cause of the destruction of the nation to be the result of the sins of the Korean people. In particular, sermons preached before the March First Independent Movement were focused on stimulating the reality of colonial Joseon and raising the issue of ethnicity. Preachers used the language of the Bible, such as that of the Babylonian captivity or the Exodus, in a metaphoric way:⁷⁴

69. Kim, "Eschatology of the Korean Church," 263.
70. Min, *History of Christian Churches in Korea*, 134.
71. Min, *History of Christian Churches in Korea*, 270.
72. Kim, "Eschatology of the Korean Church," 269.
73. Kim, *History of Preaching in Korea*, 180–81.
74. Park, "Christian Faith and National Consciousness," 254.

> At this time, the Israelites have been taken to a country called Babylon and have been in a great struggle for fifty years.... When they were in their homeland, they lived a life of free people. Today they live a painful slave life. Today, Babylon is a flourishing country, its people are suffering from hunger and a serious illness, which pressure both the spiritual and physical sides.[75]

In the historical situation of the time, the congregation easily understood that Israel was Joseon and Babylon was Japan. People believed that the day would come when Joseon would be free from Japanese oppression and able to worship freely, just as the Hebrew people had settled in Babylon and had t returned to Jerusalem years later to re-build the temple.[76]

The suffering of Korea was also interpreted as the suffering servant mentioned in Second Isaiah. This interpretation is closely related to Korean nationalism because the suffering and oppression are interpreted through the lens of God's purpose for the world. In other words, Koreans thought they were God's "chosen people" or a "new Israel."[77] Therefore, "preaching suffering and nationalism certainly reflects the ethos of the Korean People."[78] This idea gave Koreans the power to fight injustice, but also placed too much emphasis on sin and repentance. In other words, people could cry and repent of their sins, but it was hard for them to cry about their own suffering.

Faith for Blessing

The social unrest of the 1950s was severe because of the fear of death, separation from family, and survival itself. Besides, year-long droughts and floods and infectious diseases intensified poverty and social unrest.[79] The condition of absolute poverty might have contributed to the substitution of materialism for humanism, which has traditionally been a fundamental value in Korea.[80] The public's strong desire to escape from their pain transformed Christian faith into a form suitable for the pursuit of temporal welfare, which was reinforced by the rapid industrialization and growth ideology of Korean society.[81] Kim mentions that the spread of *Kibok* faith

---

75. Han, "True Tears," 107–9.
76. Lee, "What I Have," 160.
77. Lee, *Korean Preaching*, 79.
78. Lee, *Korean Preaching*, 79.
79. Kim, "Kibok Faith," 10.
80. Kim, "Kibok Faith," 11.
81. Kim, "Kibok Faith," 13–14.

LAMENT AS A REFLECTION OF HAN (한, 恨)

(faith for blessing) came from the pulpit and the sermons of repentance and judgment were weakened after the war.[82] In other words, believers started to want concrete solutions in their lives. People gathered in prayer meetings and revival meetings in hopes of miracles to treat diseases, and to be granted spiritual gifts.[83] In the 1960s, churches emerged that emphasized not only health but also material blessings.[84] Churches felt that quantitative growth proved God's blessing.[85] As church growth began to be important, the place of lament in the church, including in its preaching, rapidly disappeared. Furthermore, since the mid-1970s, believers have continued to seek more wealth. Prosperity theology, which became popular in the United States in the 1980s, had a great influence on Korean churches. Many pastors considered the megachurch to be an alternative church to lead the twenty-first century and used prosperity theology as a tool for church growth.[86] The concept of threefold blessing—that Jesus transformed present life from curse to blessing, the human body from death and disease to life, and that he healed the human soul—is based on prosperity theology and was emphasized by David Yonggi Cho. The Pentecostal churches proclaimed that.[87] This approach weakened the sense of God's judgment, the power of evil, and the power of sin. Pursuing only blessing can result in the misinterpretation of the life of those who have gone through economic hardships, physical illnesses, or difficult lives, seeing these problems as a painful and heavy judgment of God.[88] Many sermons included stories of success and triumph, which carried the danger of excessive optimism.

---

82. Kim, "Kibok Faith," 15.

83. Kim, "Kibok Faith," 18.

84. Kim, "Kibok Faith," 19.

85. Yi, "Modern Man with Premodern Religiosity," 213–14. The 1970s was a period of growth for all Christian denominations. The Methodist Church and Holiness Church grew steadily, and the Pentecostal Church grew rapidly. All other denominations more than doubled in membership. Park, *Korean Church History*, 3:280–81. Rapid growth was based on gospel congregations in the 1980s. Christianity grew from 4.3 million in 1975 to 6.5 million in Korea.

86. Ryoo, "Theological Critique of the Prosperity Theology," 8.

87. Kim, "Kibok Faith," 25. Cho, a Pentecostal pastor and founder of the Yoido Full Gospel Church, a globally prominent and expansive congregation, aimed to address diverse challenges for belivers in his sermons. His messages depicted God as a bestower of both material and spiritual blessings, featuring elements such as miraculous healings, emphasis on the Holy Spirit's baptism, and personal testimonies.

88. Kim, "History Buried in the Triple-Time Salvation," 47.

Minjung Theology

In the 1970s a whole slew of events became topics of theological discourse, including the Cuban Revolution, the Cultural Revolution, the Vietnam War, the Second Vatican Council, the strengthening of the Cold War system, the development of technology, the structural poverty of the Third World, and racism.[89] This period also saw the introduction of the Theological Declaration of Barmen of the German Confessional churches and the theology of Dietrich Bonhoeffer; German theologian Juergen Moltmann visited Korea in 1975 to address the hope in the people's struggles; and theologians, G. Gutierrez, James Cone, and C. S. Song encouraged the theology of social participation in the progressive camp of the Korean church.[90] In addition, the political and social background of the 1970s became the theological and ideological foundation of *minjung* theology.[91] The concept of *minjung* (meaning the public, or the under-privileged) implies a class, but it goes beyond a simple understanding of the concept of the public.[92] *Minjung* theology is a task of theological identification of minjung events.[93] *Minjung* theology emphasizes the concept of "Jesus outside the camp" (Heb 13:13), which refers to the place of residence of the alienated people. This shows that minjung theology is not only concerned with political and economic alienation, but also with the criticism directed to the privilege of existing churches.[94] *Minjung* theology was born from the experience of people who suffer, who fight for human rights and democracy, and who share hope.[95] The accumulated *han* of people in the context of severe human rights oppression after the military revolution (May 16, 1960) considered and resisted

---

89. Chai, "Theological Foundations," 13.

90. Human Right Commission of The National Council of Churches in Korea, *Democratic Movement in the 1970s*, 1:40.

91. Park, *Korean Church History*, 3:152.

92. Park, *Korean Church History*, 3:29.

93. Ahn, *Ahn Byung-Mu Collection*, 2:7.

94. Ahn, *Ahn Byung-Mu Collection*, 2:43–44.

95. Chai, "Theological Foundations," 18. The most negative view of *han* is that it refers to one who indulges in lament, grief, or sorrow, one who seeks sentimental reconciliation out of a sense of resignation, nihilism, or defeatism. This perspective views *han* as the internalization of suffering, restraining emotional content within oneself. The second view of *han* is a psychological interpretation. This interpretation suggests that people who feel frustration, unconscious hatred, or resentment place the responsibility for their frustration on the other party. The third view is of *han* is based on the logic of dual opposition, which centers how *han* arises and how it is resolved. This refers to the inherent power that causes continuous sublimation. Hong, "Problem of *Han* in *Minjung* Theology," 140–45.

social, political, and economic issues collectively.⁹⁶ *Minjung* theology tried to draw a dynamic and subversive peculiarity *han* has. *Minjung* theology is considered *han* as an explosive and moving force to overcome the mass of suffering accumulated from the dark ages of Korea.⁹⁷ In this sense, the way minjung theologians do theology is to unite the two stories of minjung's *han* and the gospel.⁹⁸

THE MOVEMENT *HAN* TO *HANPURI* THROUGH LAMENT

A Korean American theologian, Andrew Park argues that *han* can be revealed in active ways, such as through revenge or revolt, that it can entail a sense of bitterness or resentment, but that it can also be revealed in passive ways such as through resignation or corporate despair and helplessness.⁹⁹ That *han* allows one both to externalize and internalize one's feelings, and to transcend one's suffering means that three forms of *han* are useful.¹⁰⁰ This chapter looks at how *han* becomes *hanpuri* and how lament functions in this movement, based on these three categories: externalization, internalization, and transcendence.

Externalization of Suffering through Social Movements

In what follows, we consider two aspects of *han*: "active *han*[, which] is closer to aggressive emotion, [and] inactive *han*[, which] is similar to an

---

96. Park, "Christian Social Ethics," 124.

97. *Minjung* theology has attracted attention as an independent theology of Korea, but it has not been integrated into mainstream theology in Korea because of the difference in values, the problem of Christology, the different contexts, and the challenge of existing authority and power. Park, "Critical Review of Christology and Hamartiology," 184. *Minjung* was perceived as the subject, not the object, of salvation. Jesus served as both the personification and symbol of *minjung*. Suh, *Study of Minjung Theology*, 65. *Minjung* theology regards the Lamb who takes away the sins of the world as *minjung*.

98. Park, *Korean Preaching*, 14.

99. Park, *Wounded Heart*, 31–41. Park put Lamentations in the category of passive unconscious communal *han*, but the act of lament is not always passive or unconscious. Lament can work as a strong active trigger to *hanpuri* and there are many cases in Korean tradition in which lament was used to respond to or treat *han* in an intentional way.

100. These categories follow Kwang-don Jeon's analysis in *In the Beginning, There Was Han*.

acquiescent spirit."[101] In Korea, active *han* was revealed by the public's anger. The independence movement in Korea and the democracy movement are clear examples of the externalization of such anger. The so-called "comfort women" whose *han* society ignored and neglected offer an example of inactive *han*. Externalization of *han* signals people's suffering publicly, and can shift public perceptions and social structures. Candlelight vigils to publicize the *han* of "comfort women" are an example of how previously inactive (or suppressed) *han* can be externalized and lamented by the public.

Social Movements

Han that spurs tenacity in the lives of the oppressed has often erupted into social revolutions.[102] Among them are the protests held by *Seongkyunkwan* (an educational institute) in the Joseon Dynasty. *Keundang* (捲堂, 권당) was a means of protesting the kingship, and its intensity varied depending on the times and circumstances.[103] *Keundang* represented a collective protest where students collectively boycotted classes and work, serving as a mechanism to scrutinize the monarch, akin to the contemporary role of the press.[104] Among the diverse instances of *Keundang*, *Hogok* (號哭) *Keundang* refers to the act of weeping while marching to the palace.[105] Sometimes marchers untied their hair and wailed out loud.[106] Such resistance was

---

101. Park, *Wounded Heart*, 15.
102. Suh, *Study of Minjung Theology*, 114.
103. Kim, "Study on *Keundang* and *Kongkwan*," 253.
104. Kim, "Study on *Keundang* and *Kongkwan*," 263. The Joseon Dynasty is grounded in "*Minbon* (民本) thought," which considers the people as the fundament of the nation, and "*Duckchi* (德治) thought," which means to rule the subjects with virtue. The Joseon Dynasty is a Confucian state with the political idea of governing the country according to public opinion. Kim, "Study on *Keundang* and *Kongkwan*," 254. Since the purpose of establishing *Sungkyunkwan* was to research and spread the study of Neo-Confucianism and to cultivate human resources that fit the theory of Neo-Confucianism as social guidance, *Sungkyunkwan* served as a vanguard to protect a particular way to study. It was relatively easy to speak up and voice one's opinion because the students were able to live in a group so that self-government activities were also possible. Their opinions were respected as public opinion and had a considerable influence on the politics and society of the time. Lee, "Study on *Keundang* and *Kongkwan*," 32–34.
105. In the fourteenth year of the reign of King Jungjong (1519), when Gwang-jo Jo was imprisoned, about 150 students from Sungkyunkwan petitioned for Jo's release. Records from the time reveal that the sound of their lamenting vibrated throughout the palace. Veritable Records, *King Jungjong*, vol. 37.
106. Veritable Records, *King Jungjong*, vol. 43. The traditional Korean burial process, rooted in the heritage of the Joseon Dynasty entailed a ceremonial observance where the living would ceremoniously uncoil their hair, don burlap garments, don

typically employed when bureaucrats wanted to reveal something that was wrong and make a request to right it.[107] There is also a record of the wailing of the marching people who filled the roads.[108] During the Joseon dynasty, the act of lamenting was one factor in successfully checking the power of the monarchy and of revealing and protesting social injustice, regardless of lamenters' status or gender. In the twentieth century, the act of public lament appeared as a more radical form of social movement. It appeared in the March First Independence Movement (1919) and the Democratic Movements (1960, 1987). The Japanese government brutally massacred some people who participated in the (nonviolent) March First movement, and arrested and tortured others.[109] The motivation for the March First Independent Movement was *han* embodied as a longing for Korean independence and as an expression of the accumulated feelings from daily life under military rule and being exploited by Japan.[110] Japan dominated Korean finances, collected extreme taxes, nationalized all Korean land, asserted the right to punish people without trial, banned the freedom of the press, sanctioned a religion that controlled ideology, and banned the Korean language.[111] In this way the Japanese implemented the national annihilation policy in all areas, and the doubtful circumstances of Emperor Gojong's death by poison in 1919 overlapped with the resentment of the loss of the country, and while the March First Movement sprang up simultaneously in multiple locations across the country.[112]

Recall also that it was at this time that Syngman Rhee's illegal election occurred, and that a protest broke out in Masan in 1960. Many innocent students and people were killed on the streets. In 1972, President Park initiated the Yushin Constitution, which was intended to remove the restriction of political reappointments and to limit the rights and freedoms of the people, and thus to make the power of Park's regime absolute and permanent.[113] Under Yushin, the public's fundamental rights were thoroughly

---

straw footwear, and observe a three-day fast, or forgo several meals. A representative of the bereaved who had lost a parent, so called Sangju, she is considered as a transgressor.

107. Veritable Records, *King Sejong*, series 1, chapter 1.

108. Veritable Records, *King Sejong*, vol. 34; *Diary of Gwanghaegun*.

109. According to contemporary Japanese statistics, 7,509 people were killed and 15,961 were injured during the protests in the three months after the 3.1 movement. In addition, 46,948 people were detained, and forty-seven churches, two schools, and 715 private houses were burned down.

110. Yoo, "3.1 Movement," 91.

111. Rhodes and Campbell, *History of the Korea Mission*, 501.

112. Kim, *Shortened History of 3.1 Movement*, 9, 20, 28.

113. Park, *Korean Church History*, 3:104.

ignored. It limited physical freedom, and condoned unlawful arrests, detentions, searches, interrogations, punishments, and forced labor.[114] On May 18, 1980, the tragic Gwangju Democratization Movement resulted in the indiscriminate killing of innocent citizens by the new military coup forces led by Doo-hwan Chun. They assaulted and killed ordinary citizens and children who had nothing to do with the protests, controlled the media, inflicted havoc through random shootings from helicopters, and raped women.[115] Those who sought to reveal the truth of what the government had done were simply imprisoned. And yet, even though everyone was panicked by the fear of death, social anger rose in the hearts of the people and exploded in the form of resistance. In 1987, the deaths of Chung-Cheol Parks, who was tortured unjustly, and of Han-yeol Lee, both patriotic martyrs for democracy, became a catalyst for the June Democracy Movement.[116] The public flocked to the streets to mourn, crying out for democracy because they had hope that a system that suppressed and killed them could be overthrown, and they spoke out to resist the despair of the evil and violence of the world. The Christian Youth cried out:

> Leader: Oh Yahweh, when will you listen to this cry?
> Together: When will you resolve unjust things?
> Leader: . . . Do you ignore our hard life?
> Together: Only plunder and oppression are seen here, only arguing and quarrel take place
> Leader: Law falls to the ground
> Together: Justice has been toppled.[117]

The Candlelight Protest for "Comfort Women"

The issue of military sexual slavery in Japan was not discussed officially until fifty years after the end of Japanese rule. The reality of "comfort women" was known to the public by Jeong-ok Yoon, one of the first to publicize

---

114. Lee, "Life of Korean *Minjung*."

115. Jung, "High School Student Became a Monk."

116. The media intentionally erroneously reported Jong Cheol Park's death as stemming from sudden shock; however, subsequent revelations disclosed that the fatality resulted from brutality and torment, eliciting a public outcry. His death spurred multiple simultaneous demonstrations on a national scale. Park, *Korean Church History*, 3:492–93.

117. Kim, *32nd Annual Mission Education Conference Source Book*, in Park, *Korean Church History*, 3:488–89.

the "comfort women" issue in 1988.[118] In 1991, after Hak-soon Kim gave the first testimony as a survivor, other survivors began to testify. In 1992, when it began to become public that children aged seven to twelve had been forced into sex slavery, the issue of "comfort women" finally also emerged as a social issue.[119] Over the years, the women survivors revisited and shared their nightmares with one another, nightmares they wanted to forget. By facing the pain rather than trying to forget it, they exposed their shame publicly as a real lament for themselves. When the community began to mourn the truth and pain of the military sex slaves, they began the process of resistance with truth-telling in response to the decades in which these crimes had either been deliberately glossed over by the government, or the government had blamed the women for what happened to them, or it had forced the women to conceal the pain caused by unjust power. This shift in response, this going public with the truth, meant that there were finally others raising their voices on their behalf with empathy, not just sympathy or repression or total silence.

Many people of all genders and ages lit candles and walked in procession to mourn with the "comfort women." Since January 8, 1992, every Wednesday a rally is held for the "comfort women," and on November 1, 2023, the 1,620th rally was held. Indeed, rallies for this cause had been spreading throughout the world.[120] Those who attended the Wednesday rallies had been demanding a sincere apology from Japan, a recognition of what had happened to these women as actual crimes, and a revelation of the whole truth about "comfort women." Korea demanded formal reparations including the inclusion of the truth about "comfort women" in Japanese history textbooks, the construction of a memorial tower and historical archives, and punishment of all those who had planned and carried out this war crime. However, to this day Japan has not agreed to these requirements, and the controversy persists.

Even though *han* will persist until the Japanese government admits its fault and makes reparations, and eventual reconciliation possibly occurs, the "comfort women" movement has meanwhile not stalled: it has continued to be engaged in the restoration of women's rights not only in Korea but throughout the world, and it will act as a communal voice to overcome *han* altogether, including the *han* passed down from generations past, to the

---

118. Chung, "Christian Women's Contribution," 296.

119. Women's Division of the Institute for National Democracy Movement, "Humiliated Diplomacy with Japan," 132.

120. Wednesday rallies were also held in thirty-seven cities in twelve countries. Kim, "Cry of Justice."

present, and into the future.¹²¹ Within the movement, laments have a role in connecting the memory (which is the memory of the generation who suffered) with the postmemory (which is the memory of the next generation who received it).¹²²

The external movements of *han* have had remarkable results that have changed social values and beliefs. However, these external movements are not a desire for resistance or mere revenge but are a passionate and persistent expression of people who are still waiting for healing and reconciliation. *Han*-driven movements have contributed to independence and democracy in Korea. In this context, *hanpuri* can mean clarification of truth, divergence, and liberation of *han*.¹²³ Communal laments have empowered people in bringing *han* to *hanpuri* of the future and present, in uniting the voices of mourners, and in creating a space where sadness is shared and resolved.

Internalization of Suffering through Narrative Expression

The internalization of *han* refers to trying to achieve *hanpuri* through indirect expression, and to dealing with *han* from the inside. At times when *han* could not be released explicitly and publicly, the public has expressed *han* through cultural discourse by releasing and sharing the sentiment of *han* through folk tales, novels, plays, masked dances, folk songs, *pansori*, poems, and paintings.¹²⁴ Such cultural expressions allows one to release in a psychological way the *han* that has accumulated, and in so doing to heal the wounds of *han*, at times even eradicate *han*, but in any case to share the experiences of *han*, remember the pain of *han*, convey the message of *han*, and create a new story to take the place of the story that involves *han*.¹²⁵ In Korean folk art, Korean sadness and joy and humor, as well as shade and brightness and other artistic means of expression, appear connected to each other. Likewise, lament is an important linguistic and cultural expression of ritual meaning.¹²⁶ Though there are many ways of expressing *han*, in this book I focus on expressing *han* through language, because language has long acted as a witness, messenger, ritual of *han*, and a medium by which to release *han*. Traditional *han* narratives in *Pansori*, *Talchum*, and *Gut*, literature, and public wailing acts of expressing suffering are notable examples.

121. Hong, "Saga of the Japanese Wartime Sexual Slavery," 218.
122. Hirsch, *Family Frames*, 23.
123. Suh, *Study of Minjung Theology*, 115.
124. Jeon, *In the Beginning*, 326.
125. Jeon, *In the Beginning*, 327.
126. Moon, "Crossing Relationship," 66, 87.

Pansori (판소리, Epic Chant)

Pansori is a performance in which sounds, words, and gestures are enacted to the beat of a drum, weaving together various elements of a long story.[127] *Pansori* has the breadth and flexibility to accommodate a wide range of audiences, but, fundamentally, the *han* of *pansori* can be seen as representing the *han* of the public.[128] In the openness and aesthetics of art, *han* is expressed publicly and accuses the social system of injustice and misuse of authority.

The plot of the *pansori* or epic chant has long been used as an important means to bring catharsis from *han*.[129] For example, the plot of *Chunhyangjeon*, one of the famous pansori narratives in Korea consists of (1) the occurrence of *han* due to the frustration of love and social injustice, (2) increasing anger and resentment against the persecution of *yangban*, (3) overcoming the painful situation, and (4) practicing reconciliation and tolerance by releasing *han*.[130] Lament expresses pain in the first and second phases, and empowers those involved to endure and overcome the reality of suffering in the third phase.[131] Most *pansori* follows the same narrative arc, with an introduction, development, turn, and conclusion, but it is circular rather than linear.[132] In the plot, *han* is released through the repetition of tension and relaxation, rather than all at once. The continuous feeling of sadness is overwhelming for a person; the repeated creation of tension and relaxation leads to release, *hanpuri*.

One of the important attributes of *han* is expressed as an earnest wish.[133] In *Shimcheongga*, one of the famous pansori narratives, a daughter sacrifices herself, hoping her father will open his eyes: "As soon as I [*Shimcheong*) was born, I lost my mother and had only a father who was blind. I would be able to open my father's eyes if I offered three hundred measures of rice. But I am poor, so I only have my body."[134]

Pansori was believed to be like a soothing sound that releases the painful knots hardened by *han*.[135] People expected that *pansori*—as a repetitive

---

127. *Encyclopedia of Korean Culture*, s.v. "Pansori (판소리)."
128. Cheon, "Study on the Principle of Reconciliation," 1548.
129. Park, *Korean Preaching*, 57.
130. Cheon, "Study on the Principle of Reconciliation," 1556.
131. Cheon, "Study on the Principle of Reconciliation," 1559.
132. Park, *Korean Preaching*, 57–59.
133. Kim, "Study of Education," 319–20.
134. Kang, *Jaehyo Shin Pansori*, 361.
135. Lee, "Namdo People 5," 174–75.

sound of *han*—would accumulate and permeate their lives and eventually overcome *han*, bringing about forgiveness and nurturing resilience.[136]

*Talchum (*탈춤*, Mask Dancing)*

Talchum is a public play or performance usually centered on play, humor, and satire; it typically ends with *gut*, a ritual of shamanism.[137] The reason why such humor and satire work as a driving force for catharsis or *hanpuri* is that the reality of *han* is reflected in ridiculous masks and exaggerated gestures that are shared in *talchum*. *Nuckduri* (complain, grumble, moan) as the act of *hanpuri* is lament in *talchum*.[138] It can be seen as a process of projection that reveals the difficulties of life. For instance, a grandma in *Hahoetal Nori* sings of her discontent during her life as a woman.[139] In *Yangju Byeolsandae Nori*, *Chwibali* uses the form of lamentation to express his suffering as a father.[140] Expressing one's *han* externally rather than simply keeping it in one's heart can help to express what one has long suppressed unconsciously in public. *Talchum* was also a desperate attempt to transform the absurd world by publicly naming the moral contradictions of the ruling class and criticizing the public themselves:[141] "Alas, Alas, what sorrow it is! . . . You take a field filled with water, you take a female servant like a swallow and a male servant like a flying hawk with their child, you give me only the sand field, and you even give me male mice, female mice. . . . How can I live with children?"[142] This *Nuckduri* represents women's *han* due to social discrimination in the Joseon Dynasty. More specifically, it criticizes the situation in which an unfaithful husband expels his wife from the home, without giving her anything at all to be able to make it in life. If *talchum* is a dramatization of the repressed unconscious, with *talchum* itself being part of the healing process, it is thereby able to contribute to healing in a community.[143]

---

136. Lee, "Namdo People 5," 31.

137. Korean mask dance has been used in a variety of contexts, including in funerals, shamanistic rituals, plays, etc. Lee, "Therapeutic Aspects of Korean Mask Dance," 29. Also, mask dance has a role in a ritual banquet in that the public enjoyed Gut at the end and a shamanistic ritual before the performance. Ju, "Study about the Theater," 178.

138. Kim, "Folk Imagination of Modern Korean Poetry," 130–31.

139. Ju, "Study about the Theater," 184.

140. Ju, "Study about the Theater," 185.

141. Choi, "Creating a Culture of Reconciliation," 235.

142. Lee, *Korean Mask*, 230.

143. Ju, "Study about the Theater," 176. Ju says that the techniques of projection and metaphors in mask dance enable an examination of treatment, such as through theater therapy and group therapy.

The plot of talchum places importance on each episode, rather than merely on its causation.[144] For example, the *Miyal Halmi* episode manifests in diverse Korean *talchum*; in *Bongsan Talchum*, originating from the Hwanghae province, it is positioned at the conclusion, while in Gyeongnam province's *talchum*, *Deulnoreum* or *Ogwangdae*, the *Miyal* episode is placed in the middle of the performance.[145] This may not seem logical, but rather than showing that only conclusions are important, this type of plot which emphasizes each episode, shows that all the episodes are important. The *talchum* plot reveals the circularity and continuously shifting nature of life, and no single episode assuming a predominant role throughout. As death and life fluctuate, the play holds both at the same time. This is for the purpose of discovering and enjoying the complete reality of life, not just to focus on life's suffering.[146] Also, this structure does not use curiosity about what will happen in the future as the driving of the story, but it instigates curiosity regarding the diverse ways in which what people already know is coming will be fulfilled.[147] As mentioned in the first chapter, this may allow a new perspective compared with the plot of Lamentations. If the third chapter of Lamentations had been the last chapter, the voices of suffering might not have been noticed as much as they are now. The plot of the sermon that considers lament can also express lament itself as a part of life rather than only as the process of going to hope, and by doing so, it can create a place of respect and understanding of the reality of pain itself.

*Daesungtonggok (*대성통곡, 大聲痛哭, *Wailing Aloud Together)*

The literal meaning of *daesongtonggok* or *gok* (哭) is to cry out loud according to certain formalities and procedures to express sadness (cf. Judg 21:2; Zech 3:12).[148] The culture of *daesongtonggok* is unique to Korean funerals; the ritual is hard to find even in Japan or China.[149] It is an act of expressing sadness through a loud cry of *han* related to the dead, but it also holds the hope of reunion with the deceased.[150] At the end of the invocation of the dead—the first ceremony in a funeral process in which ones calls the name of the dead person three times from the roof in order to hold the soul at the

---

144. Chae, "How Would the Alienated Class," 212.
145. Chae, "How Would the Alienated Class," 212.
146. Son, "Study on the 'Yunsan' Structure," 79.
147. Son, "Study on the 'Yunsan' Structure," 79.
148. *Encyclopedia of Korean Culture*, s.v. "Gok (哭)."
149. Jung, *Entertainment Economics*, 89–90.
150. Jung, *Entertainment Economics*, 91.

house during the funeral—men loosen their hair and begin to cry out loud, or daesongtonggok.[151] The funeral includes a *gut* or complaint intended to meet the dead and the living in one space and to relieve their *han*.[152]

The great sacramental wailing does not occur only at the funeral but emerges amid a social crisis or through the actions of gathering together to cry out recalling particular instances of injustice and pain. At a rally calling for the apology of Doo-Hwan Chun, who slaughtered those who participated in the May 18 Democratization Movement in Gwangju, a mother confessed, "I had lived with *han* that formed a huge blood clot for 39 years after losing my son at the time of May 18," and sat on the floor and cried out loud and then people cried together.[153] At a meeting held in front of the *Sewol* ferry memorial altar and during the long battle for clarification of the truth of the *Sewol* ferry, the great wailing was also an element.[154] Through *daesongtonggok*, people felt close to *hanpuri* by being heard, by testifying, by remembering, and by empathizing with their *han*.

Gut (굿, A Ritual of Shamanism)

In the context of folk beliefs, *han* refers to the complexity of the consciously or unconsciously intertwining of the frustration of desires and wills, the resulting catastrophes of life, and the paranoid and compulsive attitude and injury of the mind.[155] Through a folk rite known as *gut*, people have resolved *han* both at the individual and communal level. A shaman was a priest *of han*.[156] Narrative was and is a key element used by shamans to resolve *han*.[157] For example, the story of Princess *Bari*, who was abandoned because she failed to meet the expectations of her father for a male heir, is used in rituals for the dead. The shaman recites the story of *Bari* and entrusts the deceased person's soul to her, as she is the one who leads the dead to heaven.[158] At such gatherings with a shaman, living people respond to their pain or guilt

---

151. Kim and Moon, "Study on Funeral Culture," 81–82. Early Christian missionaries decried the tradition of Daesongtonggok, hoping to eliminate the customs of loosening one's hair and crying loudly. Yi, *Korean Christianity and National Consciousness*, 428.

152. Kim and Moon, "Study on Funeral Culture," 83–84. For details, refer to the next section on the *gut*.

153. Lee, "Punish Doo-Hwan Chun."

154. Yoo, "I Wish You Shared Sadness."

155. *Encyclopedia of Korean Culture*, s.v. "Han (恨)."

156. Park, *Korean Preaching*, 19.

157. Park, *Korean Preaching*, 23.

158. Park, *Korean Preaching*, 24.

by wailing and lamenting, all while listening to the shaman re-tell the *han*-ridden narrative of *Bari*. Through this process of listening and lamenting, the *han* of both the dead and the living is resolved.[159] In *Younggaewoolim*, a *gut* in Jeju province, as one of the ways to resolve *han* through the *gut* rite, the shaman tells a *han*-ridden story of the dead, wailing loudly.[160] The shaman recounts the soul's *han* about life and the sadness of death, intercedes on behalf of close relatives who are crying, and then the gathered people burst into tears together.[161] Through *Nuckduri* (complaint, grumble), which is a lament in the *gut*, people can experience purifying their emotions through the empathy that results when god and humans, and humans and humans exchange *han*-stories with each other and become united.[162] *Gut* reminds mourners that there are people who witness and participate in others' suffering and *gut* assembles *han* of a multitude of participants and observers to enact the ritual of *hanpuri* and facilitate the process of healing.[163]

Literature

As a language of lament and as the voice of *han*, literature has indirectly exposed people to *han* and shared *han* with others to comfort people in pain and to unravel the *han* they are experiencing internally. Literature has not only expressed *han* but has also revealed the reasons for *han*, such as injustice and other evils of society.

The Invocation of the Dead (招魂), by the Korean poet Kim Sowol (1902–34), who lived a short life during the Japanese colonial period, is superficially a poem poignant lamenting the loss of a loved one and the yearning for the one. However, the in-depth meaning of the poem can be interpreted as *han*, signifying the poet's loss of his homeland, Joseon, and the invocation of the dead articulates a profound longing to restore sovereignty to the nation that has been lost, embodying the sentiment of *hanpuri*. In essence, the lament in this poem serves a protest against Japanese imperialism.

> O shattered name!
> O name parted from me in mid-air!
> O name without owner!

---

159. Ahn, "Pastoral Care for Korean Souls," 144.
160. Moon, "Crossing Relationship," 97.
161. Moon, "Crossing Relationship," 97.
162. Kim, "Folk Imagination of Modern Korean Poetry," 145.
163. Jang, "Study of the Historical Trauma," 263.

O name I'll call until I die!
...

I call your name till I can't bear the grief of it.
I call your name till I can't bear the grief of it.
The sound of my call sweeps forward but
sky and earth are too far apart.

Though I turn to stone standing here
O name I'll call until I die!
O you whom I loved!
O you whom I loved!¹⁶⁴

Comfort Woman, a novel by Nora Okja Keller,¹⁶⁵ is written in a cross-narrative style and unfolds through the perspectives of Beccah, the daughter, and her mother, Soon-hyo (also known as Akiko), who was forced into becoming a "comfort woman."¹⁶⁶ Born in the United States, Beccah hesitated be part of her mother's life, but upon the death of her mother, she finally began to find out about her mother's life and opened her eyes to her mother's pain.¹⁶⁷ Soon-hyo connects with the spirit of Indeok (originally referred to as Akiko by Japanese soldiers. Following Indeok's demise, Japanese soldiers referred to Soon-hyo as Akiko, using the same Japanese name as that given to Indeok) who ravaged and killed as a sex slave, and has taken over Indeok's *han* in her life and narratives. The manifestation of the ghost of Indeok is based on the local Korean belief about *han* that if the deceased person is insufficiently mourned, it appears as a ghost. In the novel, the soul of Indeok opposes Japanese imperialism and male sexual violence. The ghost is a dual device that links past scars and present life. Soon-hyo (Akiko)'s reinterpretation of the death of Indeok shows the possibility of resistance and the will to reveal her own scars.¹⁶⁸ This narrative of sorrow testifies to the history of women's *han* that occurred under Japanese colonial rule.¹⁶⁹ The novel

164. 招魂 means to invoke the soul of a dead. It is an act of *gobok* ritual (皐復儀式), which is one of the common ritual procedures of invoking the name of the dead three times from the roof or yard toward the north while fluttering the garment of the dead. Kim, "Invocation of the Dead."

165. As a Korean American writer, she first recognizes the tragic colonial history of military sexual slavery by opening herself to what newspapers are saying, as well as to people's testimonies, and direct or indirect testimony. These give her a great shock, and at the same time, a sense of guilt and sense of duty. Lee, "Traveling or Troubling Memories," 279–80.

166. Kwon, "Mode of Remembering," 218.
167. Keller, *Comfort Woman*, 173–83.
168. Kwon, "Mode of Remembering," 224.
169. Gil, "Possibility of Ghost Life," 210.

names and unravels a disenfranchised *han* by lamenting the dead and by voicing the truth that resists enforced silence.

Literature plays a crucial role in aiding individuals in deriving the internalized and accumulated grief that precipitated the formation of *han*. By encapsulating this grief in embodied imagery, literature facilitates the emotional sublimation of the internalized *han*.[170] Literature enables catharsis by dealing with the suffering of the times and the experiences of despair and loss in individual suffering through a particular style of mourning.[171] Literature as lament may seem extremely personal, but it has been effective in appealing to the universality of suffering and by encouraging people to mourn, like the voices heard in Lamentations.

Transcendence

Han has established close affiliations with various religions. Attempts to resolve *han* spiritually help transcend the reality of *han*. Such efforts do not simply pass *han* on to a transmundane world. Instead, it heals *han* and encourages people to be resilient while still holding and wrestling with *han* in the power of God.[172]

Tongseong Prayer (통성기도, 通聲祈禱, Praying Aloud Together)

Tongseong prayer, a practice which began during the early revival movement in Korea, literally means *a prayer with a loud voice together*.[173] It can be regarded as a liturgical sublimation of the collective *han* come from anger and grief experienced due to the loss of the country to the Japanese. *Tongseong* prayer as "a prayer of lament, especially, a communal lamenting prayer" includes fervent appeals for the restoration and salvation of the nation to God

---

170. Jung, "Poetics of Korean Traditional Emotion," 121.

171. O, "Korean War and a Matter of Mourning," 227.

172. Jeon argues that this struggle with *han* is called "crawling." In this praxis of *han* one does not pass through of pain all at once: it entails a struggle that is gradually achieved through unending screams, shouts, and gestures. Jeon, *In the Beginning*, 329–30.

173. The missionaries struggled to find the correct word to translate *tongseong* prayer in English. North Presbyterian missionary G. Lee called it "audible prayer," the United Methodist missionary G. H. Jones called it "united audible prayer," and Canadian Presbyterian missionary W. Scott translated it as "prayer of unison." Rhie, "Early Korean Indigenous Church Formation," 54. Tongseong prayer was introduced as a unique form of prayer in Korea in the Worship Book of the American Methodist Church published in 1993.

expressed in a loud voice.[174] *Tongseong* prayer has contributed to the growth of the Korean church by cultivating a remarkable history of prayer.[175]

In addition, during the 1907 Great Revival Movement in Pyongyang, *tongseong* prayer led an individual and collective movement of repentance. The public confession of sin, which began with an elder, Seon-ju Gil, spread to the whole congregation, and their prayers continued from 8 pm to 5 pm. It was repeated for many days:[176] "the whole audience began to pray out loud, all together. The effect was indescribable. Not confusion, but a vast harmony of sound and spirit, a mingling together of souls moved by an irresistible impulse of prayer. The prayer sounded to me like the falling of many waters, an ocean of prayer beating against God's throne."[177] Noting that the people lived with ethical, economic, religious, and political *han*, *tongseong* prayer can simultaneously mean a *tong* (通, communication) *seong* prayer, which means to be connected with God and neighbors and *tong* (痛, pain, lament) *seong* prayer as a prayer of those who have pain.[178] *Tongseong* prayer functions as a Christian way to resolve the pain and resentment of *han* through the Holy Spirit.[179]

Thus, the intention of *tongseong* prayer is to bring the reality of one's suffering to God. It is also a communal prayer of lament prayer, that intercedes on behalf of the community's pain, reveals the power of evil and sin in the world, and expresses an earnest hope to get out of the situation of crisis.[180] In this respect, the voice in Lamentations closely resembles *tongseong* prayer.

Language of Grief in the Korean Pulpit

In the era of Japanese occupation (1910–45), there was a great burden on many preachers to preach about the sadness of the times, a sadness caused by the political and ideological interference of Japan. Though many Korean preachers preached that the nation's suffering was entirely the result of sin, other preachers lamented and embraced the suffering of the time and the people. Sung-Bong Lee preached: "It is the empathic attitude of crying with those who cry and being happy with those who are happy. How precious

174. Kim, "*Tongsunggido*," 301.
175. Kim, "*Tongsunggido*," 299.
176. Baird, "Spirit among Pyeng Yang Students," 65.
177. Blair and Hunt, *Korean Pentecost*, 71.
178. Rhie, "Early Korean Indigenous Church Formation," 58.
179. Kim, "*Tongsunggido*," 300, 308.
180. Kim, "*Tongsunggido*," 300, 314.

it is! ... Shoulder the responsibility of their family, their church, and their country and pray with tears."[181] Chi-Seon Kim (1899–1968) also preached that tears for the nation will move God and that God will save Korea: "We have a mission to appeal to God with tears for thirty million people. For the evangelization of the nations. ... We must spread the tears of nationality and testify of Christ."[182] Yong-Do Lee (1901–33) began to sing a hymn and then started to cry: the entire congregation cried when they saw their preacher crying. As Lee's crying became severe, the hall became a sea of crying.[183] Lamentations was his sermon.

Since the military coup of May 16, 1961, Korea has become a controlled society.[184] Chung-Choon Kim (1914–81) preached that he could not think only about his own salvation and turn away from others' pain, injustice, and poor and miserable reality: "If God's people tolerate or connive that the history of this country depends on one human's desire for power, then human rights are violated and freedom is imprisoned. We cannot keep silent about social evil, political evil, and materialist evil because we have a desire that our nation in which we live can be a kingdom of God."[185] Kyung Chik Han (1902–2000) could not hide his bitterness when he preached: "In 1950, because of the Korean War, the lives of millions of dear young people fell on this land. ... But this year, more than 100 young students like flowers fell here. ... Whenever I think of young men's blood drenching our land, I can't tell you enough how bitter and terrible it is."[186] Cardinal Stephen Suhwan Kim's Christmas message (1922–2009) likewise shows his interest in social justice and asks the powers that be:

> I would like to sit down on this Christmas night with all those suffering, those who mourn, and those who are in distress. I want to share your pain, your encounters, your sorrows. ... If there is no practice of justice in us, we are hypocrites and betray the incarnate Christ. ... We know that the roots of our endemic corruption and social unrest are in the present system of absurd power and financial power ... if we seek to solve problems only by coercive means that ignore fundamental human rights, then our nation may have no place to go.[187]

181. Lee, "God's Beloved Son," 109, 111.

182. Kim, "Tears of Loving National People," 23, 28.

183. Hymn 149 was "Nearer, My God, to Thee." Byeon ed., *Rev. Lee Yong-Do Collection 6*, 28–29.

184. Yum, "Theological Analysis," 248.

185. Kim, "People of God," 583.

186. Han, "For Our Nation," 342.

187. During the sermon at the midnight mass at Myeong-dong Cathedral on

Gyu Tae Son (1940–) preached lament for others as the sincerest attitude:

> It is difficult to participate in the suffering of others, but there is no more noble human act than it. There are innumerable people in this world suffering from physical conditions and social circumstances. The love for these people will be the attitude of those who mourn. Though many socially underprivileged are suffering in today's fiercely competitive capitalist society, few are lamenting for them. . . . We have been taking no measures for those who have suffered. . . . Grief is the human's most honest state of mind. In the penitence of sin, in sharing, or in suffering, in our way, lamenting is the sincerest attitude toward ourselves and others.[188]

Although the sermons excerpted above may have the potential to be estranged from the meaning of the Bible due to excessive social references to human rights and democratization and may be criticized as being "like stories in newspaper editorials," they embody the incarnated spirit of Jesus, who entered into the suffering of people.[189] Through lament, the voices of *han* in preaching have made congregations aware of the urgent need for God's redemptive action in the suffering, and they contributed to speaking of the close connection with Christ's cross and resurrection. Lament as transcendence in Christian view has been the energy to sustain Koreans' life full of suffering and the explosion of *han* as resistance to social injustice and evil.

In summary, social, cultural, and religious dimensions are brought together in people's lives. Attempts to share, name, remember, resist, and dream of a better future admit the reality of their suffering has appeared through the circular process of *han* and *hanpuri*. Lament, not only as a language of grief but as a dynamic space and medium, is what keeps *han* moving on to *hanpuri*. In this way, lament has variously permeated social, cultural, and religious movements in Korean culture, and has shown itself to be a valuable way of dealing with universal human suffering beyond Christian values.

December 24, 1971, live broadcasts were stopped when Cardinal Kim strongly criticized President Park's extension of power. Lee, "Comfort from the Christmas Message of 1971."

188. Son, "Blessed Are Those Who Mourn."
189. Um, "Morphology of Contemporary Korean Church Sermons II," 126.

REVITALIZING LAMENT AFTER THE *SEWOL* FERRY TRAGEDY

As the economy and democracy have stabilized, Korean churches and society have gradually lost their traditional expression of lament, and instead have pursued an ideology of secular blessing and growth. The Korean church has used lament mainly as a means of repentance for sin and it has rarely engaged in lament for suffering itself. After the *Sewol* ferry tragedy, lament is as it were enjoying a revival and reappreciation as a way to deal with pain and find hope.

Sewol, the Name of Suffering

The *Sewol* ferry incident, which occurred on April 16, 2014, is one of the most important events in Korean modern history, and is often recalled in the same breath as events like the Korean War (1950) and democratization movements against the military dictatorship.[190] In the *Sewol* tragedy, 304 people lost their lives, including 261 high school students. The incident was a shocking event that came to symbolize many of the weaknesses of Korea, including political and economic corruption, systemic avoidance of responsibility, and inexperience in resolving cases. This incident was traumatic for most Koreans who watched the children sink into the sea and drown. Immediately after this incident, the people who watched the tragic deaths said they would fight for justice and never forget the victims. But over time, politicians and some citizens have turned their attention away from the victims and some have even ridiculed the bereaved families.[191]

The many Korean churches which did not address the tragedy or lament the pain it caused experienced a backlash due to the powerful trauma of the *Sewol* ferry incident. The Korean Church did not know how to address the grief, how to speak about sorrow, or how to comfort the people who were in pain. Some influential preachers ignored their pain with a theology of vested rights. They explained pain as a result of a lack of faith and concluded that all of these things were due to sin. As one preacher says, "It is time to keep silence."[192] This denied the voices of sufferers. The Korean churches failed to cope with the issue of suffering when they faced the social

---

190. Lee, *Sewol Ferry and Korean Feminist Theology*, 19.
191. Lee, *Sewol Ferry and Korean Feminist Theology*, 20–21.
192. He promptly clarified his contentious sermon. However, it is regrettable that he did not pay more attention to their wounded hearts. No matter what his intention was, people were feeling hurt by the words of the preacher. Lee, "Pastor Lee."

issues they had ignored and the sufferings from which they looked away or which they regarded as evidence of a weak faith.[193] Kwang Jak Cho, the vice-president of The Christian Council of Korea, said: "The poor house children can go to *Bulguksa* on a school trip, but I do not know why they made this disaster by the ferry to Jeju Island."[194] Sam Hwan Kim preached that God made the *Sewol* ferry sink and insisted that the youth were scapegoats whose tragic deaths would save the nation.[195] Jung Hyun Oh was criticized for advocating for a person who said the victims and the bereaved families and friends of those who died on the *Sewol* ferry were "uncivilized."[196] The bereaved family sued Pastor Kwang Jak Cho and Jung Hyun Oh, and Korean society lambasted the entire Korean church.[197]

The incompetent government and corrupt politics and economy made the hearts of the public turn cold. For them, it was clear that politics had priority over people's lives. Members of an extreme right group mocked the deaths of the victims. Even the survivors of the incident could not speak their truths to the world because they were afraid of being publicly condemned. No one accepted responsibility for the incident, and indeed the investigation into the incident was abandoned, and the people's pain was ignored. After September 30, 2016, the regime forcibly terminated the Special Investigative Committee of *Sewol*. However, thirty-one investigators continued their investigations on behalf of the general public, held a meeting, and decided to publish a book, *Turned Away and Avoided*.[198] They protested the unjust termination of their investigation with a hunger strike, and for three months conducted their own investigation and hearings. However, the regime shut them down and they were forced to end their activities without fulfilling the one-and-a-half-year investigation required by law. This tragedy triggered traumatic and powerful *han* among Koreans.

---

193. Hwang and Han, "Bereaved of Sewol Ferry." N. T. Wright presents three consequences as characterizing the problem of evil. The first is that if evil does not attack us directly, we ignore it. Second, we are surprised when we face evil. Third, as a result, we react to evil in immature and dangerous ways. The Korean churches responded in this third way to the Sewol tragedy. Wright, *Evil and the Justice of God*, 23–24.

194. *Bulguksa* is a relatively cheap place for a school trip in Korea. The intention of the speaker was to blame the victims for not going to a cheap place although they were poor. Song, "Fourth Anniversary of Sewol Disaster."

195. Song, "Fourth Anniversary of Sewol Disaster."

196. Choi, "Controversial Advocacy."

197. Hwang and Han, "Bereaved of Sewol Ferry."

198. Sewol Special Investigative Committee Investigators Association, *Turned Away and Avoided*.

Theological Reflection about the *Sewol* Tragedy and *Han*: Public Lament as Memory, Resistance, and Resilience

Many Korean theologians agree that theologies after the Sewol incident should be different. Kyung Il Chung pointed out that a theology that is insensitive or indifferent to social suffering is no longer acceptable, and that there is an urgent need for a theology that responds to suffering and responsibly participates in others' pain.[199] He also criticized the refusal of the Korean church to lament: "Compared with the church's inability to lament, the mourning of the bereaved family and citizens was more religious than were the churches. Beyond lamenting for others, they felt others' pain as their pain."[200] Chang Hyon Park emphasizes that theology after the *Sewol* tragedy should be a theology of memory.[201] He further argues that Korean Christianity needs to nurture the socially positive function of religion to provide a model of the future, comforting and supporting those who are in pain.[202] Kyo-Seong Ahn posits that the *Sewol* incident exposes the absence and deficiency in public faith, highlighting the question of theodicy connects to the inquiry into human existance. This implies that grappling with theodicy in suffering entails a task linked to humanity within Christian faith.[203] The query, "On that day, where was God?" reverberates back to the question that God poses to us, "[when] I was hungry . . . I was thirsty . . . I was a stranger . . . naked . . . sick and in prison (Matt 25:42–43), [where were you?]."[204] Certain theological discourses, emphasizing the significance of 'being together' and 'staying,' have also emerged, highlighting the imperative for churches to lament the loss of empathy. Additionally, these discourses stress the need for churches to articulate their theology and descern their role in the context of public suffering.[205] Dong Chun Lee observes the tendency of selfishness in perceiving disasters as personal incidents and critiques the lack of responsibility in attributing the issue of suffering to theodicy. Lee emphasizes the need for nurturing collective memory and cultivating a public spirituality.[206] Ji Sung Lee argues that the Korean church needs to face the uncomfortable truths, to look at what they have

---

199. Jung, "Lament, Remember, Resistance," 172–73.
200. Jung, "Lament, Remember, Resistance," 178.
201. Park, "Theology of the Post-Sewolho (*Sewol* ship) Calamity," 346–47.
202. Park, "Theology of the Post-Sewolho (*Sewol* ship) Calamity," 347.
203. Ahn, "Study of the Construction of the Post-*Sewolho Sinhak*," 71.
204. Ahn, "Study of the Construction of the Post-*Sewolho Sinhak*," 71.
205. NCCK Sewol Disaster Preparedness Committee, *To Be With.*
206. Lee, "Christian Ethics Reflection on an Attitude," 250–55.

been missing or deliberately overlooking, not to forget those painful things, and to learn to participate in them rather than turn away from them.[207] In this respect, theology after the *Sewol* tragedy has claimed that its task needs to include lament as an act of resistance against injustice, participation in the pain in the world, and offering hope for the resurrection which restores justice.

Practicing Lament in Pulpits after *Sewol*

Unfortunately, despite such calls for change, the language of mourning has been almost entirely absent in Korean churches even after the Sewol tragedy. Nor have theological responses to injustice and suffering around us generally been reflected from Korean pulpits. Nevertheless, some few preachers have included the language of grief in their sermons and have attempted to offer hope in suffering.

Ji-cheol Kim preaches that our pain is healed through Jesus' suffering and that we need to put our pain in God's hands: "When we enter into Jesus' pain, our pain begins to heal. When we enter into Jesus' discouragement and despair, healing occurs in us. Because no one has experienced such great despair, pain, and loneliness as Jesus did. There are all my sins, all my despair, sickness, lament, and all human problems in Jesus' cross."[208]

Ji-cheol Kim and Yoon Jae Jang preach that we can overcome suffering through lament. They also mention the power of lament in the wickedness of the world.

> A man with a heart of lament is a man who got the calling from God. The place of lamenting in our hearts is our workplace. It is a blessing to mourn. . . . A community that does not feel pain is a group of dead people. A culture and civilization without mourning will be dismantled on this earth. When there is a mourner, a country can survive. Seeing injustice and evil and mourning create justice in the land. . . . Lamenting is possible when you love. When you risk your life with concern, sincere lament arises. . . . Only those who mourn can win in the reality of suffering.[209]
>
> What we have to mourn and lament today is sorrow for the wickedness of this world. Today, the weak and the innocent

---

207. Lee, "Study on Suffering Narrative for Sympathy," 91–94.
208. Kim, "Eloi, Eloi Lama?"
209. Kim, "Blessing of Lamenter."

suffer. However, each one person is trapped in their own sorrow and is not concerned about having compassion for others' sorrow even though humans can understand each other only through pain and sorrow.... Therefore, blessed are those who mourn. Blessed are those who mourn because of the suffering of their neighbors and the world. These are those who weep together in a union with the lament of the Holy Spirit.... Weep for the pain of the world.... Set aside theological controversy and political ideology in the presence of the sick, hungry, naked, cold, and lonely. Cry together, just as Jesus did.[210]

Soo-Il Chai considers the church of Jesus Christ as a community of remembrance and testimony. In his sermons, lament works as a form of remembering and testimony. He says that anyone who participate in another's sufferings is in God and that love is manifested in actions, not ideas.

> Love is a response to the love of Jesus, who gave up his life, made himself a peace offering, and loved us first, and this love inevitably and specifically toward neighbors and the whole world: How can God's love stay in one if the one does not have righteousness although the one sees one's brothers and sisters in need?... In April, the month commemorating the Lord's crucifixion and resurrection, we remember April 3, 1948 (Jeju massacre), April 8, 1970 (*Wow* apartment collapse), April 9, 1965 (*Inhukdang* case executions)... April 15, 2019 (*Jeamri* massacre), April 16, 2014 (the *Sewol* tragedy), April 19, 1960 (4.19 Democratic Revolution), April 28, 1995 (Daegu Metro gas explosion), and April 29, 1932 (Bong-gil Yun's bombing of Shanghai). We cannot and should not forget these events; we must persist in bearing witness to them across the ages. This is because, even if we are not all eyewitnesses, the Church of Jesus Christ is a community of remembrance and testimony.[211]

Jae Hyuk Jin emphasizes the significance of a lamenting community, urging us to mourn our weaknesses and lament the pain of others:

> If we sincerely stand before the Lord with a poor heart, our souls should groan.... Can we say that the community is alive if there is no lamenting that the pain and suffering of the nation accept as our pain and weep for it?... When we lament, we can see our calling. We cannot cry together without the heart that loves others and laments for them. The lamenting is another important

---

210. Jang, "Power of Lament," para. 12, 14, 20.
211. Chai, "One Who is in God," para. 32.

work, a mission that we must bear and serve in our lives. The moment when we mourn with the lament of God, God gives it to us as our mission.[212]

On Easter Sunday, Jong Hwha Park's sermon begins with lament, devoid of theological judgment or premature resurrection proclamations. The only hope he expresses is that the pain of the victims and the bereaved will reach the cross of Christ:

> Today is Easter. But it is too sad and dark. . . . I feel so heartbroken when I think of them. . . . Lord, who died for us, our young men are still in the waters of the sea. Take your cross there. Bear their small crosses unto your grand cross. Allow your cross to swallow their cross of suffering and death. In your resurrection, encompass their resurrection together.[213]

After the *Sewol* ferry capsize, lament theology and preaching as communal lament have appeared as a space waiting for *hanpuri* and community resilience beyond isolation due to pain, as a space waiting for the expression of *han*, and for resistance against social injustice. In the cyclical movements of *han* and *hanpuri* that are repeated in life until the kin-dom of God comes, lament is s a dynamic movement that seek true hope, not escape, and a space in which to respect *han* and then let it be taken up.

CONCLUSION: THE UNIVERSALITY AND POSSIBILITY OF LAMENT IN *HAN* AND *HANPURI*

Han is everywhere there is oppression. Ji-hye Hwang translates "124 was spiteful" in *Beloved* by Toni Morrison as "The address 124 is laden with *han*."[214] This is the place where Sethe, a fugitive slave, tragically ends the life of her two-year-old daughter. Her rationale stems from the fear that, upon recapture, her slave status could be inherited by her daughter. As Baby Suggs says, "Not a house in the country ain't packed to its rafters with some dead Negro's grief."[215] With such images in mind, it is not surprising to translate grief as *han*. At the end of *Beloved*, the women of the village hear the story of Sethe, whom they turned away and cut off, and go to 124 to confront her pain and the pain in them all. Then, they resonate with each other's suffering

---

212. Jin, "Lamenting Community."
213. Park, "Resurrected!," para. 1.
214. Morrison, *Beloved*, 3; Hwang, "'Han' Ethos," 295.
215. Morrison, *Beloved*, 6.

and mourn through songs.²¹⁶ We might understand this to be their own *hanpuri* ritual. For indeed, *han* is the universal emotion of the oppressed, the afflicted, the weak, and those who have painful memories.

Although the method of untangling *han* may be different in each culture, lament can be a way to deal with suffering and nurture community resilience in many cultures through crying together, expressing sadness, resisting injustice, and participating in grief based on *hanpuri*'s trajectories, which are external, internal, and transcendent.

Through these first and second chapters, we have seen that communal lament has been used to deal with individual and communal suffering not only in the Bible but also in various aspects of culture and society. For Christian communities in particular, the practice of lament has resonated in the close relationship between the crucifixion and the resurrection. Thus, in the next chapter, we will examine the theological rationale for the value of lament-driven preaching based on Christ's crucifixion and the resurrection, as the center of God's act of salvation. Also, by bringing divine lament into the interpretation of human suffering, we will also look at how preachers can enlarge their interpretations and name the complex interpretive issues.

---

216. Hwang, "'*Han*' Ethos," 308.

3

The Theology of Lamentation(s) in Paschal Triduum Narratives[1]

PREVIOUS CHAPTERS HAVE SUGGESTED lament as an appropriate way to deal with suffering in society as a whole as well as in Christian communities, recognizing that to lament does not liberate a person from suffering or cure them. This chapter identifies particular principles that are important for a theology of lament. It does so by looking at how divine lament presents the crucifixion and resurrection as God's definitive intervention in the suffering of the world. Christ's cross and resurrection are for Christians the most complete and definitive "place" where God is revealed, where all wrongs are rectified, and where all pain is embraced and resolved.[2]

Many interpreters and preachers we will encounter in this chapter have emphasized a close theological connection between human suffering and the crucifixion and resurrection. Lament preserves and promotes

---

1. The Paschal Triduum is a series of rituals of the early church, rituals centered on the passion and resurrection that were elaborated in the fourth century and developed into the Holy Triduum service, which is celebrated on three consecutive days, Thursday through Saturday of Easter. Talley, *Origins of the Liturgical Year*, 37–38. Protestants, influenced by the Roman Catholic Church's earlier reforms, celebrated the Paschal Three Days in their own tradition. Despite the diverse denominational, historical, and regional understanding and practicing of the Paschal Triduum, the intrinsically unitive nature of Easter constitutes a commemoration of the passion, death, and resurrection. Bradshaw and Hoffman, *Passover and Easter*, 177. Thus, this book comprehends the Paschal Triduum narratives as encompassing the events of the passion, death, and resurrection. Also, I am greatly indebted to Fleming Rutledge's analysis on Jesus' crucifixion and resurrection throughout this chapter.

2. Rutledge, *Crucifixion*, 11.

a transitional space between suffering and hope where God meets us and shows faithfulness regarding human suffering.

This chapter explores lament in the Triduum narrative as an expression of divine participation and solidarity in the reality of suffering, rather than as an expression of divine-human distance and divine judgment of human sin. The theology of lament in the narratives of the Paschal Triduum resonates beautifully with that expressed in the book of Lamentations, enabling readers to hear the suffering of humans and God articulated. The Paschal Triduum narratives extend the scene of lament as an eschatological response to the suffering of the entire creation. The redemptive nature of divine lament allows us to envision the changed reality of lament through redemptive nature of divine lament and to look at the dynamics of lament from the perspective of cross and resurrection without ignoring the reality of human tragic loss and unbearable suffering.

The chapter begins by naming the chief causes of people's lament, focusing on the human experience of suffering. It then examines the human need for lament by looking at the relationship between God's absence and the impossibility of humans solving suffering. The second half of the chapter explores the divine response to sufferers' laments, including the Paschal Triduum narrative. I approach the Paschal Triduum narrative from the perspective of lament rather than as an argument about doctrine convinced that the story of divine and human suffering requires a new hearing, one that goes beyond the formal and authoritative definitions of doctrine. Since this hearing based on our understanding of lament drives our epistemic and creative action in relation to God and life, this chapter shows that this understanding that appears so clearly in the Triduum narrative also works vividly in our hearts and lives in various ways.

HUMAN LAMENT

What causes human lament? Lament arises from the vast web of suffering, which derives from intersectional oppressions, from a responsible and valid guilt for wrong one has done or wrong that has been done to one, from social evil, and from alien powers which cannot be explained or overcome in the human sphere.[3] All of these call for divine redemptive action. Here I am not trying to articulate separate, distinct categories of lament. For they are all intertwined, being simultaneously individual and corporate, spiritual and physical. Recognizing the powers of sin and death helps to reveal a spiritual realm and the part this plays in regard to systemic or collective

---

3. Rutledge, *Crucifixion*, 209.

evil. Since human suffering comes not merely from humans' wrongdoing or from social structures and systems, to consider evil in its entire variety of forms reminds of the holistic, eschatological, and cosmic nature of fallen creation.

Naming the Causes of Human Lament

The Power of Sin and Death

Lament involves individual and communal confession of sin and a plea for God's mercy for delivery from the gravity of sin. And yet, paradoxically, lament emanates from God's grace. This is because people can realize their sin by presenting "the news of God's prevenient purpose through the cross of Christ."[4] That means the decision to repent is not enough to overcome individual wrongdoing or guilt and the realization of sin itself is God's grace.[5] When human beings realize their responsible guilt, they can start a sincere lament for forgiveness and redemption.[6]

People tend to deal with sin as a problem of individuals, not as a problem of society, let alone of the world. Examples of society's sins are wars, poverty, the abysmal conditions of laborers, immigrants, prisoners, our pollution of land, racism, and so on. Indeed, "such a chasm, and the suffering it causes, is the result of sin in which our whole society participates."[7] This tendency to individualize sin comes from the bondage of sin and its ubiquity.[8] People are often numb to the power of sin or numb to how much the world is infected by sin.[9] For this reason, the unusual act of a communal lament may actually be more effective in awakening people to recognize their enslavement to the power of sin.[10]

The lament caused by sin is deeply related to the alien powers of sin and death. The existence of evil is not abstract; it cannot be equated with human sin, nor is it separate from sin.[11] The enslaving power of sin cannot

---

4. Rutledge, *Crucifixion*, 169.
5. Rutledge, *Crucifixion*, 171.
6. See chapter 2, "Tongseong Prayer."
7. Rutledge, *Crucifixion*, 176–77.
8. Rutledge, *Crucifixion*, 181. Rutledge has a twofold understanding of sin: as responsible guilt and as an alien power.
9. Rutledge, *Crucifixion*, 193–94.
10. Rutledge emphasizes "Sin's power to enslave," mentioning that the power of sin is "not something we commit; . . . [but something we] are in." Rutledge, *Crucifixion*, 195.
11. Barth argues that alien power is a complex mystery, a "God's own affair," something beyond the comprehension of human reason. Barth, *CD* III/3:360.

be conquered through human willpower or human abilities.[12] "Wrong is not mysterious but evil suggests a mysterious force that may be in business for itself and may exploit human agency as part of a larger cosmic conflict between good and evil, between God and Satan."[13] Repentance is not sufficient to correct the situation: something must happen on the side of God, and an invasion from the outside must occur in the realm of the power of sin and death.[14] Only through δικαιοσύνη, the rectifying power of God, can people be delivered from the power of death because it is God in Christ who overcomes death's power, invading the realm of death.[15] In lament, people call upon God's faithfulness to defeat the power of sin and death. Thus, lament is not merely about confessing wrongdoings or a sign to restore what is lost: it is an expression of humans' desperate desire to survive suffering derived from the powers of sin and death.[16]

Social Injustice

Discourse on injustice is found in many places in the Bible, and is related particularly to prophets' laments: "How long will the land mourn?" (Isa 24:4; Jer 12:4), or "why do you look on the treacherous, and are silent when the wicked swallow those more righteous than they?" (Hab 1:13).[17] This lament from injustice is related to the structural evilness of domination. While the crucifixion of Jesus may be seen as the work of Jewish leaders, of Jews who were hostile to Jesus, and of Roman rulers, blame cannot be apportioned to one particular group. For these individuals were deeply embedded in a 'system of domination' that was larger than them, a system that enslaves and prevents them from considering alternatives to the ways of domination and violence.[18] Thus, Christ's fight was not with people but with the powers of the world that hold people captive and make them accomplices to

---

12. Barth, *CD* III/3:202.
13. Morrow, *Evil*, 51.
14. Rutledge, *Crucifixion*, 192.
15. Rutledge, *Crucifixion*, 368–69.
16. Rutledge, *Crucifixion*, 204. Rutledge argues that confession is not the cause, but the sign. In this sense, confession is a response to the recognition of sin, so it is not limited to the form of lament.
17. Brueggemann notes that counter-testimony poses four questions about the core-testimony: "How long? Why? Where? Is?" Brueggemann, *Theology of the Old Testament*, 319. The purpose of these questions is forcefully and urgently to ask God to move positively toward them.
18. Campbell, *Word before the Powers*, 59.

domination (Eph 6:12).[19] Today, the results of this system of domination are wars, nuclear threats, illness, pain, terrors, the tainted natural ecosystem, socioeconomical brokenness, political exploitation, and so on.[20] Thus a lament from injustice is closely linked to the suffering of the poor, the oppressed, the voiceless, and the abandoned.[21]

The issue of injustice which calls forth lament is also usually based on the sins of denial or on the apathy of the public. Denial resists seeing the reality of suffering.[22] The optimism which allows humans to forget the evils they commit may also contribute.[23] Though Jerusalem says peace, there is virtually no peace but instead suffering from injustice (Jer 6:13–15; 8:10–12). However, when God helps people face pervasive injustice in the world, they can lament it (Lam 1–2; Jer 7:29; 8:18–22). The nonviolent resistance to injustice as lament such as fights of Martin Luther King's nonviolent marches and the democracy movement in South Korea, among others, exposed this power and opened the way for its dismantling to begin.[24] Though Rutledge says we can only "share the sufferer's pain in silence and . . . hate these things with a perfect hatred," lament can be a form of resistance to the injustice of structural evil.[25] This is because this lament does not ignore suffering; instead, it enters into it, it shares the pain, and it does not stay silent, but rather reveals the pain.[26]

---

19. Campbell, *Word before the Powers*, 61.

20. Rutledge makes a distinction between moral evil and impersonal or random evils. Moral evil has victims and perpetrators, whereas catastrophes like floods and earthquakes result only in victims. Rutledge, *Crucifixion*, 450.

21. Rutledge mentions that the Christian life involves suffering like the suffering of Jesus. She argues that it is not the ordinary suffering that comes to everyone, but the particular affliction that must come to those who bear witness to the Lord's death. Rutledge, *Crucifixion*, 566–67. I partially agree, as I discussed above. Kazoh Kitamori claims that if any want to participate in the cross, they can serve God through sharing others' pain. Kitamori, *Theology of the Pain of God*, 50–52.

22. Brueggemann, *Disruptive Grace*, 137.

23. Rutledge, *Crucifixion*, 199.

24. Campbell, *Word before the Powers*, 63.

25. Rutledge, *Crucifixion*, 447–48.

26. Denial is one of the most powerful factors that prevent people from acknowledging pervasive suffering from evil today. Amnesia, indifference, and ignorance cannot avoid the blame for creation's pain. See Ku, "Resisting Apathy and Amnesia."

The Power of Evil: Fallen Creation

Lament also comes from the power of evil throughout the whole of creation.[27] Beyond the problem of social injustice, we may recognize the power of sheer evil that is utterly separated from pure goodness. Evil may be said to be the power that takes over and manipulates principalities and powers in the world, the power that is the focus of eschatological wrath.[28]

All over the world, there are crying children, exploding bombs, screaming people, and bodies piled high. There are natural disasters and unexpected losses caused by floods, earthquakes, illnesses, and plagues. Paul says that the power of evil wields its strong influence over all creatures (cf. Rom 8:18–27) and that creation longs for the Savior. That means "nothing is excluded from the fated suffering, and no period of time has been free of lament and pain."[29] The problem of ubiquitous evil has led to questions about whether God or God's purpose is good, whether "suffering can be justified by a greater good," and whether everything happens for a reason.[30] The existential challenge of pain and evil neutralizes most attempts to separate the discussion of evil from God; "human justice cannot make right what was wrong," and only God can take something wrong and make it right.[31] There is "no explanation and there can be no morally sufficient reason," for evil.[32] Instead, we can resist it and be angry at it by calling for God's restorative power.[33] We lament as some kind of response to the pain that comes from "the absence of God, the power of evil, and the unjust suffering in the world."[34]

---

27. The origin of evil is endlessly controversial and cannot be explained. For example, Rutledge refers to the first story of the fall in Genesis, pointing out the paradoxical and enigmatic points: God has created the serpent, which lures Adam and Eve to do evil unto death, but the Bible focuses on the revolt of humans against God, not on the serpent, Rutledge, *Crucifixion*, 418.

28. Rutledge, *Crucifixion*, 377, 382.

29. Öhler, "To Mourn," 163.

30. Rutledge, *Crucifixion*, 432–33.

31. Rutledge, *Crucifixion*, 133, 143.

32. Rutledge, *Crucifixion*, 429, 444.

33. "My eyes are spent with weeping; my stomach churns; my bile is poured out on the ground because of the destruction of my people. Our Lord, don't forget how we have suffered" (Lam 2:11; cf. 5:1).

34. Rutledge, *Crucifixion*, 444–45.

Lament as an Expression of the Need for Action

The person who suffers may face a collapse of language, an inability to articulate sorrow. Lament can break the silence of sufferers and enable "opening the way to a deeper struggle with God."[35] Patrick Miller writes of lament that is directed to God in the hope of getting divine answers: "When the victims of oppression and suffering cry out to the Lord, God hears their cries of pain and sees their trouble and comes to deliver them."[36] Based on the causes of lament in the previous part, this section looks at how lament can be formed.

A Plea for Mercy

Sin is basically the brokenness of the relationship between God and human beings. The promise which God will answer if Israel confesses their sin (Neh 9:28; 2 Chr 6:39) is in danger because of the experiences of a silent God (Pss 89:46, 90:13; Lam 3:49–50), God's rejection (Jer 5:7; Lam 3:42; Hos 1:6, Amos 7:8), or the punishment/retribution of God (2 Chr 6:23; Ps 1:5; Isa 1:28; Ezek 7:27). The plea for God's mercy may not take the form of a simple expression of suffering, but instead a strong commitment to turning back to God, forsaking the way of evil (Isa 55:7; Jer 36:3; Ezek 18:30). Thus, lament for divine mercy is a confession that "all for sin would not atone but only God can supply the remedy for sin."[37] The power of sin must be solved by God's power of righteousness. God's grace precedes the recognition of sin, confession of sin, and abandonment of sin.[38] Like the eyes of Christ that looked at Peter, who denied him three times, in Christ our masks are taken off when God looks at us, and our desires and secrets are exposed (Luke 22:61).[39]

---

35. Pleins, *Psalms*, 27.

36. Miller, *Deuteronomy*, 182.

37. Rutledge, *Crucifixion*, 181. The voice of Lamentations implores: "Restore us to yourself, O Lord, that we may be restored (Lam 5:20)." It expresses that God has the agency to restore them from pain.

38. Rutledge, *Crucifixion*, 168–69. Rutledge points out, "The relation of justice to mercy is not always clear in particular cases of barbarism." Marshall mentions that mercy is about helping to achieve justice. He sees justice in terms of the restoration of relations. Discourse on justice, centering on the restoration of relationships, provides a new lens for looking at biblical justice. For more concerns about restorative justice, see Zehr, *Changing Lenses*. As the repetition of the Exodus and the events of the Cross reveal, the justice of God is not destroyed by mercy but rather is constantly changing. God goes through anger toward recovery.

39. Rutledge, *Undoing of Death*, 95.

Also, a lament for communal sin can have strong participatory aspects beyond the personal or symbolic. Rutledge considers the communality of pain and lament (1 Cor 12:26) and the longing and belief in God's deliverance that is inherent in lament.[40] She makes no clear distinction between individual sin and community sin, because she understands suffering and salvation to be a communal event. Rutledge focuses on realizing and acting on the wickedness of social sins in which humans unconsciously or consciously engage. Rutledge's point of view is in line with that of Dietrich Bonhoeffer, who points out that the church is a "collective-I" through which it confesses and acknowledges its guilt.[41] Nonetheless, lament resists "the temptation to absorb the problem of suffering into guilt and sin."[42]

A Plea for Justice

Lament as a plea for justice includes both vertical and horizontal aspects. The vertical aspect is a plea to God for justice, a plea to move and intervene in the reality of present suffering. God's justice will assuredly be realized on Earth (Isa 1:16–17; cf. Exod 23:6; Deut 24:17; Ezek 45:9; Mic 2:1–3; 3:9–12; Luke 4:16–21).[43] This is because justice is not merely the desire of God, but the very existence of God and the core of God's ministry.[44] God is the source and center of all justice; God permits Scripture writers to put the blame for unrighteousness even upon Godself.[45] God is said to hear the cries of the fatherless and widows and to work for the oppressed and the afflicted in society (Exod 22:22–23). Anger rather than denial is needed for those

---

40. Rutledge, *Undoing of Death*, 331.

41. Bonhoeffer, *Life Together*, 137–41. Bonhoeffer laments: "The church confesses that it has not professed openly and clearly enough its message of the one God, revealed for all times in Jesus Christ and tolerating no other gods besides. . . . [I]t has misused the name of Christ by being ashamed of it before the world and by not resisting strongly enough the misuse of that name for evil ends. . . . [I]t is guilty of the breakdown of parental authority. . . . [I]t has looked on silently as the poor were exploited and robbed. . . . [It] confesses its guilt toward the countless people whose lives have been destroyed by slander, denunciation, and defamation. . . . By falling silent, the church became guilty of the loss of responsible action in society, courageous intervention, and the readiness to suffer for what is acknowledged as right."

42. Farley, *Tragic Vision and Divine Compassion*, 52.

43. Rutledge, *Crucifixion*, 109–11.

44. Marshall, *Little Book of Biblical Justice*, 22. To verify it, Marshall mentions Gen 18:25; 2 Chr 12:6; Neh 9:8; Pss 7:9; 89:14; 97:2; 103:17; Isa 24:16; 30:18; 45:21; Jer 9:24; Dan 9:14; Zeph 3:5; Zech 8:8; Rom 3:26, 9:14; 1 Pet 2:23; Rev 15:3.

45. Marshall, *Little Book of Biblical Justice*, 23.

who are abused and oppressed by the system.[46] However, humans cannot enforce human justice proportionate to the crime.[47] In this respect, justice is God's intervention for those who cannot help themselves.[48] That anger is God's wrath against all things against redemptive purposes, and it was first in God's heart.[49] Thus, lament makes a plea for God to break God's silence and inactivity. We may lament to be assured of God's attention to the pain of injustice and to call for God to act.

The horizontal dimension of lament is linked to the public place and time. Sufferers need someone to acknowledge their pain sincerely and name it.[50] Rather than only be an accusation against the reality of injustice, lament can also be a voice that comforts the weak and seeks justice, and a practice of justice that calls for God's redemptive action.[51] Such anger is not merely an emotion.[52] The outrage of a witness can function as the beginning of the recovery of justice in sufferers' lives. This is because "to be outraged and to take an action on behalf of the voiceless and oppressed is to do the work of God."[53] As a plea for justice, it includes not only socioeconomic or political justice in the present but also the righteousness of God as a power of intervention for apocalyptic hope. A "forgive and forget" syndrome, rooted in our boundless optimism, might have contributed to the absence of communal lament.[54] However, Lament resists triumphalism, the silence of God, and people's denial of structural injustice.

---

46. Rutledge, *Crucifixion*, 129.

47. Rutledge, *Crucifixion*, 121. There is a possibility of turning the oppressed into oppressors.

48. Rutledge, *Crucifixion*, 132, 134.

49. Rutledge, *Crucifixion*, 129, 131. Rutledge considers God's anger not as a burning emotion, but as a way to correct all wrongs.

50. Rutledge notes the story of Jim Wang, and his wife. He was innocent, but his family has experienced severe suffering because of the failure of justice. For more details, see Rutledge, *Crucifixion*, 127–28.

51. For the relationship between the Bible and triumphalism, see Brueggemann, *Theology of the Old Testament*, 329.

52. Rutledge, *Crucifixion*, 30. Rutledge compares such outrages to "blood boiling," asking: "if our blood does not boil at injustice, how can we be serving God?" See 131–32.

53. Rutledge, *Crucifixion*, 143.

54. Rutledge, *Crucifixion*, 116, 123. Rutledge considers forgiveness too easy to say—even if it is because of the cross—in the face of injustice. She criticizes some Christians who believe that forgiveness is the essence of Christianity. See Rutledge, *Crucifixion*, 142.

A Plea for Release from the Abyss

The abysmal realm is a place of shadow like *Sheol*, a realm of death like Hades, a place of painful punishment like Gehenna.[55] There is no comfort, no hope, no thanksgiving, and no God in this place. Indeed, the abyss is not a place but "a domain where evil has become the reigning reality."[56] The abyss, in the sense we are using it, is related to a status of bondage caused by human's "sinful passions" (cf. Rom 7:5) that creates separation from God.[57] Lament that arises from the abyss involves a strong longing for eternal liberation from the power of evil (cf. John 8:36; Rom 6:16) and a rejection of eternal separation from God. Because evil is a cosmic force that destroys the creation and holds some authority over the world, fallen creatures cannot escape from under evil's reign or God's wrath of their own accord (cf. Ps 49:15; Dan 8:24). The plea for deliverance from the abyss means an earnest request to be reckoned, not as cursed, but as a righteous person under God's reign. The plea is to restore the wrong and broken world through God's eternal and apocalyptic victory.

Evil cannot be explained and cannot be destroyed by humans. We cry out with Job as a response to suffering: "Let the Almighty answer me!" (Job 31:35) The language of grief will not stop until their prayers reach God, will not remain silent, and will continue to lament until the sole Redeemer moves (cf. 1 Kgs 8:30–39); "blessed are those who mourn, for they will be comforted" (Matt 5:4a).

The Silence of God

Here is a cry of an embattled person: "Why does the way of the guilty prosper? Why do all who are treacherous thrive?" (Jer 12:1b). "O Lord, how long shall I cry for help, and you will not listen? . . . Justice never prevails" (Hab 1:2, 4). When God is seemingly absent in silence, when God seems not to be moving, and when the promises of the Bible are no longer kept, the sufferers can feel that they are abandoned, accursed, and excluded from God.[58] There is no human dignity and in its place are shame, disgrace, rejection,

---

55. Rutledge, *Crucifixion*, 406.

56. Rutledge, *Crucifixion*, 417.

57. The abyss is the eschatological place into which all evil powers will be cast (Rev 20:3) and is often used in the Bible to curse the enemy (Ps 140:10; Jer 48:28).

58. Rutledge, *Crucifixion*, 77.

powerlessness, and weakness.[59] Furthermore, "God's deliverance is deemed neither likely nor inevitable" (cf. Dan 3:16–18).[60]

Scholars have long considered God's silence from different angles. I-Gon Kim argues that the lament about God's absence is speaking of a place of God's presence.[61] Samuel Terrien calls it "presence in absence."[62] As Israel experiences it, the silence of God can be felt as if God has turned away God's eyes, but not "completely" (Lam 5:20, 22). Rutledge finds in Abraham's narrative a fickle, arbitrary, and cruel God who "commands that Abraham slaughter his own son."[63] There was silence instead of lament "at the outermost limit of human experience."[64] Rutledge argues that "perhaps, this event may be understood as encompassing all the incomprehensible silence of God from that day forward."[65] This is because, in the midst of silence, Rutledge finds Christ who is the Lamb on the cross as a substitute for Isaac.[66] Jesus' earnest prayer in Gethsemane is also unanswered with God's silence. Jesus remains alone and afraid. This continues in Jesus' lament on the cross, "my God, my God, why hast thou forsaken me?" God's silence encompasses Christ and the voices of those who suffer.

At the same time as Christ breathes his last, the Temple veil is torn in two (Matt 27:50–51; Mark 15:37–38; Luke 23:45–46). Lament flows from the torn veil.[67] God's silence was in the fullness of pain and sorrow. Christ enters the abyss with the ultimate pain that Abraham felt and the weight of sin and death that humans have borne. The strictness and limitations of the Holy of Holies were at once solved and confirmed by Christ's death.[68] This can be thought of as the openness of God to sufferers who can pour out their grief before God in the name of Jesus Christ. Though God's silence is broken by the word of God who is Jesus Christ, the silence of God strongly

---

59. Rutledge, *Crucifixion*, 79–80.
60. Levenson, *Creation and the Persistence of Evil*, xix.
61. Kim, "Theology of Lament of the Abandoned," 319.
62. Terrien, *Elusive Presence*, 320–37, 323.
63. Rutledge, *Crucifixion*, 259.
64. Rutledge, *Crucifixion*, 265–66.
65. Rutledge, *Crucifixion*, 265.
66. Rutledge, *Crucifixion*, 266.
67. Unbearable grief, shame, and rage in response to Jesus' death compel God to step out from behind the curtain in all God's desperate glory. In Jesus' death, we, at last, get a full-frontal glimpse of God. God's lament removes the dividing line between the holy and the profane. As the curtain is rent in two, so too the old division between sacred and profane is forever torn apart. Dykstra, "Rending the Curtain," 56.
68. Rutledge, *Crucifixion*, 267–70.

resists an easy remedy.[69] Kathleen O'Connor argues that "God's silence gives reverence to voices of anger and resistance, of hope and despair."[70] Thus, the silence of God can be understood as God's will in listening to the sufferers, and God's rejection of the oppression of the disenfranchised, providing it with space.[71] God not only listens to sufferers but responds and acts. Jesus' death, burial, and resurrection have verified it.

DIVINE LAMENT IN PASCHAL TRIDUUM NARRATIVES

Human lament is not required to get God's response.[72] The works of grace on the cross and in the empty tomb are inherent to the nature of God from the beginning. Some may think that, if it were, humans would not have to account for their sins or sufferings, nor would they have to cry out to God earnestly because God is going to figure out the wrong things without cooperation from human will. However, the Paschal Triduum narratives that encompass Christ cross, death, and resurrection are the divine response to human suffering and need to be understood in the context of the divine-human relationship. God heard the cry of suffering in Egypt, heard the torment of Zion crying in the ruins of the temple in Jerusalem, and finally died under the power of evil before the judgment seat. It is an urgent, decisive, and complete response, accompanied by Jehovah's tears, anger, sincerity, and fierce compassion to hear the pain of fallen creatures.[73] The divine redemptive action in the Paschal Triduum narratives is an expression of empathy with human suffering, and complete participation in human suffering.

The promise of recovery in Second Isaiah after the voice of Lamentations resonates with, extends, and in fulfilled in the death, descent, and resurrection of Jesus.[74] The Bible shows readers how the suffering in Lamentations 5 resonates with the suffering servant in Isaiah 53 and the crucified Jesus (Mark 15), in terms of silence (Isa 53:7; Lam 5:20, 22), rejection by others Isa (53:3; Lam 5:8–9), being stricken (Isa 53:4; Lam 5:7, 16), being afflicted (Isa 53:4–5; Lam 5:11–16), experiencing injustice (Isa 53:8; Lam 5:2–5), being severed from God (Isa 53:8; Lam 5:20–22), and finally buried

---

69. Rutledge, *And God Spoke to Abraham*, 309.

70. O'Connor, "Voices Arguing about Meaning," 29.

71. Harris and Mandolfo, "Silent God in Lamentations," 152.

72. Rutledge, *Crucifixion*, 247.

73. Wright says that God has heard the cry of the people through the suffering of the Israeli representative and works to free them. Wight, *Evil and the Justice of God*, 93.

74. Parry, *Lamentations*, 167.

(Isa 53:9; Lam 5:5, 10, 17, 22; cf. 3:55).[75] The phrase "the blood of the righteous" (Lam 4:13) connects the destruction of the temple with the shedding of blood (Matt 23:35, 37–39).[76] When all the passersby clapped their hands, whistled, and shook their heads to insult daughter Jerusalem (Lam 2:15), Christ on the cross was also insulted (Mark 15:29–30).

The scene of Lamentations leads us to see Jesus, weeping over Jerusalem (Luke 19:41–44). In the Midrash, the rabbinic imagination depicts the God of Lamentations as a human king mourning the loss of his dead son, similar to what Daughter Zion does: wears sackcloth (2:10), sits on the ground (1:1–2), is naked (1:7), is silent (2:10), weeps (1:2), and sits alone (1:1).[77] The similarities between these lamenting practices and suffering bring God closer to the experience of Zion's loss and death, bringing it from heaven to earth, from silence to mourning in a way that is immanent and participates in the suffering, and moves from punishment to comfort.[78] Christ's body and soul contain both divine and human suffering.

At the birth of Jesus, there was lament from Ramah (Matt 2:18; cf. Jer 31:15).[79] Jesus was born and raised amidst loud lamentation from all mothers who had lost their sons. Lament opens the discussion of Jesus' birth and anticipates his ministry for sufferers, the oppressed, and the weak. Christ gave himself to save us from all aspects of individual failure and systemic evil.[80] Finally, we meet Jesus' own lament on the cross when he is being delivered for the sake of all people who believe in the name of Jesus. The lament of the triune God is now incarnated: "Jesus entered the deepest darkness and took upon his lips the faithful lament of the God-bereft soul (Ps 22:1). It is for us that Jesus did so, making our lamentation—all lamentation—and the cause of lamentation his own."[81] Thus, the divine lament in the Paschal Triduum narrative is possibly considered "as a story of powerful resurrection—this is, after all, the most vulnerable of stories, a story of suffering and absence, of negation and of death."[82] This is a narrative of "a God of tears and compassion, who suffered in his suffering people, who was

---

75. Willey, *Remember the Former Things*, 227; Parry, *Lamentations*, 167.
76. Parry, "Jesus and Jerusalem." 253.
77. Thomas, "Rabbis Talk Back," 271–72.
78. Thomas, "Rabbis Talk Back," 272.
79. Duff, "Recovering Lamentation," 11.
80. Rutledge, *Crucifixion*, 193.
81. Bartow, "Till God Speaks Light," 162.
82. McCarroll, *Waiting at the Foot of the Cross*, 89.

moved by their sighs and lamentations, who was angered by their meanness of mind."[83]

Crucifixion

Crucifixion is: (1) an expression of God's love; (2) includes fear, hatred, shame; (3) is a declaration that Jesus died for sin; and (4) is the result of the state of the world and the suffering of humankind.[84] The cross reveals both the pain, brokenness, dependence, and frailty of the human condition, and the power and possibility of God's love revealed in and through the very real limits of creation.[85]

Mirroring the Reality of Human Sin

Descriptions of the cruel reality of the crucifixion show that the death of Christ is not abstract, but represents vicious and the most extreme form of punishment of the day, including public lashing, ridicule, and contempt.[86] The meaning of the cross should not be weakened as a mere religious symbol if we acknowledge the cross to be an appropriate form of execution to address humanity's darkness-bound bondage and God's wrath.[87] This is because the reality of the cross shows an awful means of death typically used for "the dregs of humanity": it is public, deliberate, shameful, inhuman, and cursed (Deut 21:23; Gal 3:13).[88]

The Messiah's cruel death is a display of human evil.[89] The horror of the crucifixion confronts the hideous side of human nature.[90] On the cross, Christ mourns and prays for God's forgiveness for the ignorance, sadism, and sins of man that men do not realize themselves.[91] In this regard, the cruelty of the crucifixion shows that Christ embraces all aspects of human

---

83. Caputo, *Prayers and Tears*, 336.
84. Rutledge, *Crucifixion*, 46.
85. McCarroll, *Waiting at the Foot of the Cross*, 89.
86. Rutledge, *Crucifixion*, 93–94. Rutledge devotes the second chapter of *The Crucifixion* to arguing that not only the fact of the Messiah's death but also the way of death was God's purpose. Rutledge, *Crucifixion*, 104.
87. Rutledge, *Seven Last Words from the Cross*, 44.
88. Rutledge, *Crucifixion*, 74.
89. Rutledge, *Undoing of Death*, 145.
90. Rutledge, *Crucifixion*, 197.
91. Rutledge, *Seven Last Words from the Cross*, 11.

suffering, shows God's faithful and decisive response to the extreme fallen state of men, and shows God's deep sorrow for human suffering.

Christ's way of death was apparently unnecessary, and Christ suffered an unnecessary increase in suffering, like those who suffer through excessive malice.[92] This event emphasizes the state of humanity and the powerful solidarity of Christ that God wants to show even at the cost of unnecessary and unwarranted pain. The meaning of Jesus' lament in Gethsemane may be not so much in anticipation of his death, but because he knew he was bearing "the burden of the sin of the world" on the cross.[93] Outside the city of Jerusalem, where the road to the cross begins in earnest, Jesus wept not for himself, but for the city. "All these tears and every tear that has ever been shed by anyone anywhere are rolled up into the tears of Jesus. Jesus weeps for us. The Son of God weeps" for us.[94] On every path of human tears, wherever human pain flows, it merges with the tears of Christ.

Atonement for Sin

To discuss atonement for sin, we need to consider a basic assumption: human beings are under the bondage of evil powers. According to the Passover and exodus (Isa 53; 1 Pet 2:23–24) narratives, Jesus as a paschal lamb has delivered people from the suffering of earthly death, the power of slavery, and the eternal death at the final judgment.[95] This blood sacrifice conveys that sin must have atonement in terms of justice, and it demands the cost of atonement. That is, this sacrifice concept places emphasis on death of "self"-giving for the "ungodly" (Rom 5:6).[96] It connects with the ransom and redemption motif in The First Epistle of Peter that talks about how only the death of Jesus can address the fall of man and the gravity of sin: "Christ also suffered for sins once for all" (3:18).[97]

However, conceptualizing Jesus solely through the "pay for" sin can foster a perception of God as capricious and transactional.[98] This is because the parable of the lost son depicts a father who forgives and rejoices over his lost son, regardless of ransom with blood, and God forgives because

---

92. Rutledge, *Crucifixion*, 563.
93. Rutledge, *Undoing of Death*, 134.
94. Rutledge, *Undoing of Death*, 8.
95. Rutledge, *Crucifixion*, 219–20.
96. Rutledge, *Crucifixion*, 253, 276.
97. Rutledge, *Crucifixion*, 294.
98. Park, *From Hurt to Healing*, 128.

God wants to transform a world of injustice and violence with God's love.[99] The ransom is not what God requires in return for salvation for sin: that self-sacrificing love existed before creation, and it is not dependent on any external factors. Payment was made by Christ-self in the triune God in order to correct what was wrong.[100] Christ is not sacrificed to satisfy the Father's wrath but is with the Father.[101] Thus, the crucifixion of Christ can be understood as a metaphor for the love of a suffering God. As George Hunsinger writes,

> There is no sorrow God has not known, no grief he has not borne, no price he was unwilling to pay. . . . [I]t is a love that has endured the bitterest realities of suffering and death. . . . Christ's blood signifies . . . the divine commitment to rescue, protect, and sustain those who otherwise be lost. . . . Christ commits himself to others and offers them his life.[102]

Furthermore, the discourse on the atonement of sin eventually reaches the final judgment, addressing the ontological dimension of individual and collective sin within the social and global context of a systemic structure.[103] To be specific, the themes of the Day of Yahweh in the Old Testament and the last judgment in the New Testament concern the "justification of the ungodly" based on apocalyptic victory and resurrection.[104] This judgment motif includes the theological theme that there is no righteous one (Ps 14:3; Rom 3:10) and divine-human reconciliation in the category of *dikaiosis* (rectification/justification).[105]

Even though the declaration of being "righteous" by God on the final day is already a reality in the present, it is essential to acknowledge the challenge posed by the current provisional triumph.[106] It is expressing the essence of the Christian life, which necessitates existence within tension, struggle, and suffering. However, the validation of this struggle by the resurrection energizes the community of believers, turning the tension between present realities and the anticipated future aspects of reconciliation into a source of motivation rather than a cause for paralysis.[107]

99. Park, *From Hurt to Healing*, 128.
100. Rutledge, *Crucifixion*, 296, 298.
101. Rutledge, *Crucifixion*, 279.
102. Hunsinger, *Disruptive Grace*, 362.
103. Rutledge, *Crucifixion*, 304.
104. Rutledge, *Crucifixion*, 303.
105. Rutledge, *Crucifixion*, 346.
106. Rutledge, *Crucifixion*, 333, 341.
107. Rutledge, *Crucifixion*, 343.

Deliverance from the Power of Sin and Death

Another narrative of what happened on the cross paints a cosmic and eschatological picture. Biblical narratives depict the *Christus Victor* motif as a narrative of God's continuous struggle against and eventual triumph over cosmic and human forces that resist God and pose a threat to God's creation.[108] Jesus on the cross is not passively suffering, but actively participates in the apocalyptic war against the rule and power under the control of sin.[109] However, the victory of God may be originated from the lamentation of Jesus.

The scene of Gethsemane is a space for getting ready for the pivotal confrontation with the forces of darkness.[110] The atmosphere of Gethsemane is laden with the fear of death, rejection, pain, hurt, forsakenness, and loneliness.[111] This shows God knows human suffering and is struggling in the midst of it. In this sense, the victory on the cross strongly expresses the apocalyptic view by gathering all suffering and violence to Godself and opening up a new vision (Rev 21:4), without losing the sense of human reality in suffering.[112] Christ not only understood human suffering and experienced it, but Christ also assumed its place. In this substitution, Christ on the cross is stoned, slaughtered, enslaved, defiled, and replaces traitors, apostates, murderers, and everyone else.[113]

---

108. Boyd, "Christus Victor View," 25. The First Testament depicted God's battle with sea monsters, which were believed to threaten the creation. Boyd, "Christus Victor View," 25. The examples of God's war with sea monsters are in Pss 29:3–4; 74:10–14; 77:16, 19; 89:9–10; Prov 8:27–29; Job 7:12; 9:8, 17; 26:12–13; 38:6–11; 40:15–34; Ezek 29:3; 32:2; Jer 51:34; Hab 3:15; Nah 1:4. The Bible witnesses God's wars with Satan in the Second Testament. "The various kingdoms of the world can be described as a single kingdom under Satan's rule (Rev 11:15)"; John mentions "the whole world lies under the power of the evil one (1 John 5:19)," and Paul also recognized "the god of this world has blinded the minds of the unbelievers (2 Cor 4:4)." Jesus' war is against the powers of the world, including not only "rulers, principalities, powers, and authorities (Rom 8:38; 13:1; 1 Cor 2:6; 15:24; Eph 1:21; 2:2; 3:10; 6:12; Col 1:16; 2:10, 15)" but also "dominions (Eph 1:21; Col 1:16), cosmic powers (Eph 6:12), thrones (Col 1:16), spiritual forces (Eph 6:12), elemental spirits (Col 2:8; Gal 4:3) and other spirit entities." Boyd, "Christus Victor View," 28–29. Early Christians and Paul expected God's intervention to destroy the power of sin and make people free from the bondage of sin. Boyd, "Christus Victor View," 29.

109. Rutledge, *Crucifixion*, 379–81.

110. Rutledge, *Crucifixion*, 371, 373–74.

111. Rutledge, *Crucifixion*, 373.

112. Rutledge, *Crucifixion*, 382.

113. Rutledge, *Crucifixion*, 473.

In addition, the contrast between Adam and Christ shows that God's action is infinitely greater than all calamities (Rom 5:12–21).[114] In the crucifixion, Christ is not just an agent or advocator because Christ is united with men in the adversary's realm and transfers man to new sovereignty.[115] This means not only that all the misery and suffering of history will disappear in the end times, but that even now the power that Christ has accomplished for all creation is working for it. This is connected to considering how individuals or communities that have embraced the "mind of Christ" (1 Cor 2:16) can live in the present.

The Lens of Lament for Rethinking Crucifixion

In relation to the discourses on crucifixion discussed above, a lament lens sheds light on several points that require consideration in addressing human suffering.

(a) God's wrath has always been an aspect of love and an aspect of God's powerful work in achieving righteousness.[116] God's wrath is aimed at refining impurities.[117] Here, if "δοκιμήν (character)" is emphasized too much, it can produce a passive attitude toward suffering, or people might think suffering is used as a tool to test the faith of believers (cf. Rom 5:4–5). Though the wrath is correcting the wrong, not evil, this view could have a sufficient effect on reducing lament to the voice of those who do believe or cannot endure. This brings two challenges: whether the sufferer should be silent about pain in endurance (Lam 3:26–28), and how to distinguish the pain of good purpose from God's wrath.[118]

(b) God's absolute agency resolves human suffering and humans are called to participate in God's fulfillment.[119] The shape of the participation is manifested in the ministry and everyday life, emphasizing the hope of an unrealized future, and expressing the essence of a Christian's life in tension, struggle, and suffering.[120] Although the act of righteousness is both passive

---

114. Rutledge, *Crucifixion*, 540.
115. Rutledge, *Crucifixion*, 552, 557–58.
116. Rutledge, *Crucifixion*, 323, 325.
117. Rutledge, *Crucifixion*, 324.
118. See Ku, "Lament as Resistance and Rage," 7–12. My article posits that God's wrath can be viewed as a divine lament against injustice.
119. Rutledge, *Crucifixion*, 325. Rutledge uses civil rights movements as examples of both where righteous and honest behavior occur and of participation. Rutledge, *Crucifixion*, 343.
120. Rutledge, *Crucifixion*, 343.

and active, dealing carefully with this point is important because the lament as witness, resistance, and participation is sometimes very active and can be overly moral so that human agency invades divine agency or makes a list of to-dos.

(c) Sometimes, emphasizing Christ who knows suffering can empower sufferers to go to the throne of Christ and claim a space that allows them to speak their suffering out loud. The very blood of Christ leads sinners and sufferers into a space where they can pour out their poignant sorrow and mourn before God in faith (Heb 10:19). Lain American and Asian theologians take seriously this concept in the context of their life situations. In Latin America's mestizo Christianity, the allure of Latino perspective lies in its portrayal of Jesus of Nazareth as a man of sorrow.[121] Having suffered at the hands of Spanish and American colonialism and military dictatorship for over three hundred years, and having fought to regain their survival and human dignity, Filipino women find Christ's suffering, death, and resurrection mirrored in their own suffering, death, and resurrection.[122] Asian women's theology is intricately intertwined with the narrative of women's suffering, as numerous Asian women have endured millennia of prejudice, discrimination, widespread socio-political exploitation, and structural vulnerability within male-dominated Eastern cultures.[123] These manifold oppressions have eroded women's autonomy and relegated them to insignificance. The laments arising from the deepest corners of this existence resonate with the agony of the God who cried out from the cross—the God who endured suffering under diverse oppression, the suffering God who was subjected to death, stripped bare, insulted, and spat upon by military and political forces. Christ is the one who knows sorrow and the one who becomes insignificance. Rather than serving as a model for emulation, in this sense, Jesus Christ is a God who shares in suffering and weeps alongside them. The crucifixion with its extreme suffering of that human Jesus, is where his divinity is best revealed and where he offers a realistic memory and presence for salvation.[124]

(d) On many occasions, interpretations that seek meaning or purpose in inexplicable suffering and provide simplistic explanations can be rejected. As we explore in the book of Lamentations, the communal complaints and

---

121. Elizondo, *God of Incredible Surprises*, 13.

122. Chung, *Struggle to Be the Sun Again*, 63.

123. Kwok, "God Weeps with Our Pain," 92.

124. Elizondo, *God of Incredible Surprises*, 13, 100. On Good Fridays, the trial, crucifixion, and funeral of Jesus are reenacted at the San Fernando Cathedral in San Antonio and elsewhere in Latin America. The narrative of Good Friday across time and space meets our narrative here and now. Elizondo, *God of Incredible Surprises*, 103.

questions in the fifth poem remind us that no one can truly comfort the sufferers, and no one can clearly offer the reason for their pain. Neither the events of the cross nor Christ's lamentations in response to human suffering provide justification for enduring all suffering nor can they be used as a panacea.

For Black people, the motif of Good Friday refers to "a form of existential crucifixion" of enslaved Africans who experienced the transatlantic slave trade.[125] The existential crucifixion continued as slaves were not only forced to give up their names, culture, and ultimately their identity, but were also subjected to disease, unfair treatment, horrendously crowded and unsanitary conditions, malnutrition, and, if they became ill, abandonment at sea.[126] Violence was a means of capture, and slavery was a means of maintaining control. Slaveholders considered slaves to be socially dead or made them so.[127]

The lament of crucified Jesus, "Why" represents a perpetual, global objection to human suffering and the inherent injustice in a world where the innocent suffers and malevolence prevails. However, "the silence that greeted his question is exactly the same as the sad silence in cancer wards and concentration camps."[128] This may suggest that God, in his profound grief, is mourning alongside them in their existential pain rather than furnishing answers.

(e) The understanding of atonement also needs to be considered in a variety of contexts. The statement that Christ died for our sins is not entirely consistent with the confession that Christ died, because the latter encompasses more meanings and contexts.[129] Andrew Park compares the *han* of Tae-il Chon, a Korean laborer who sought to draw attention to the injustice of his labor conditions through suicide by fire, with the *han* of Christ, suggesting that the full meaning of the cross cannot be derived from the doctrine of sin alone. Based on Mark 10:45, ransom is understood as redeeming an inheritance, a slave buying freedom, and the ransom of Jesus here is not

---

125. Hall, "Middle Passage," 46.
126. Hall, "Middle Passage," 47.
127. Lauber, *Barth on the Descent into Hell*, 154.
128. Lewis, *Between Cross and Resurrection*, 56.

129. Schüssler Fiorenza, *Jesus*, 123. Atonement rituals had the power to remove sinful behavior that violated the covenant relationship. Schüssler Fiorenza argues that this covenant renewal was linked to the "Day of Atonement" (Lev 23:27–32), when the sins of the people were symbolically blotted out by being ascribed by proxy to a "scapegoat" that was then driven into the wilderness. In this cultural context of Judaism, the formula "Christ died for our sins" is bound to take on cultural color. Schüssler Fiorenza, *Jesus*, 124. The covenant-based concept of atonement must be carefully distinguished from the concepts of reconciliation and justification.

an image of atonement but rather an image of ransoming enslaved people or prisoners of war being set free by the death of Christ. This is the freedom from ruling powers (Rom 5:14, 17) that is referred to in Revelation and in Paul's letters.

(f) One should not forgive and forget without justice but needs to strive to "behold and remember" as an act of lament for suffering (cf. Lam 5:1). Meanwhile, if a preacher or a community aims to convey the concept of forgiveness within the pursuit of justice, it is essential to ground it in the lament of God as an inbreaking force in suffering, who has the capacity to bring about "perfect justice come out in the world."[130] Of course, we conscientiously reject the dichotomy between the guilty and the innocent in relation to the redemptive action of God. We also avoid adopting a biased perspective favoring either side.[131] Nevertheless, we acknowledge that throughout history, numerous individuals have suffered as a result of colonialism. Jesus also the Galilean was one of the colonized peoples of the empire and wrestled fiercely with colonial realities.[132] Charles E. Farhadian evokes memories of Papua, Indonesia, emphasizing the parallel between the suffering of Jesus and that of the Papuan people. Jesus endured suffering in a colonial context, and Papuans affirm their own experiences of suffering from state violence in the context of Christ.[133] This collective memory serves as a source of hope for the future. This is because Jesus' fellowship with the outcasts and those experiencing oppression demonstrates God's engagement in suffering within an oppressive environment. This participation can be regarded as a manifestation of God's love, as Jesus perceives the pain of the sufferers and, by remembering and entering into their pain, leads them to hope.

(g) Dealing with suffering in relation to the crucifixion of Jesus is satisfied not only with a theological-interpretive approach. Although it is essential to ensure theological validity and diversity in the analysis of cross motifs, a focus on the suffering itself is also crucial through the lens of divine lament in the crucifixion. Understanding Jesus' lament on the cross in light of Psalm 22, Gustavo Gutiérrez argues that Jesus appropriated this psalm, which originated from the suffering of a psalmist on behalf of one's people, and made it his own.[134] This act demonstrates a radical communion with human suffering. Gutiérrez calls this communion the message of the

---

130. Rutledge, *Crucifixion*, 124.
131. Wright, *Evil and the Justice of God*, 27–29.
132. Horsley, *Jesus and Empire*, 15–17.
133. Farhadian, "Emerging Theology," 200.
134. Gutiérrez, *On Job*, 99–100.

cross: "Communion in suffering and in hope, in the abandonment of loneliness and in trusting self-surrender in death as in life."[135] The cry of Jesus on the cross makes the cry of every person of sorrow in human history, both individual and collective, more audible and more penetrating.[136]

Contemplating the diverse dimensions of the cross through the lens of lament is to encounter an expression of God's mysterious and abundant love. This love hears human suffering, intentionally bears that suffering, experiences death in God's absence, enters under the power of death, and ultimately brings about a future that humans cannot imagine or envision.[137] This divine lament, which is inherent in God's purpose of confronting suffering and the force of evil in the world, becomes even more pronounced through the descent of Christ.

Burial

On the day of burial, death is given the time and space to exist in its own right, in all its coldness and powerlessness.[138]

> The apostles wait in the emptiness. Or at least in the non-comprehension that there is a Resurrection and what it can be (John 20, 9; Luke 24, 21). The Magdalen can only seek the One she loves—naturally, as a dead man—at the hollow tomb, weeping from vacant eyes, groping after him with empty hands (John 20, 11, and 15). Filmed over with an infinite weariness unto death, no stirring of a living, hoping faith is to be found.[139]

This existence is only possible if *"unus ex Trinitate passus es"* both in Jesus' human nature and in Jesus' divine person, for it is only by virtue of his divine person that he can enter into the desperate situation of a free human being vis-à-vis God, in order to transform it from a dead-end to a situation full of hope."[140] The Saturday tomb preserves a radical separation in death and hell, while simultaneously upholding unity and wholeness for the

---

135. Gutiérrez, *On Job*, 100.
136. Gutiérrez, *On Job*, 101.
137. Lauber, *Barth on the Descent into Hell*, 151–52.
138. Lewis, *Between Cross and Resurrection*, 37.
139. Balthasar, *Mysterium Paschale*, 43.
140. Balthasar, *Dramatis Personae*, 239.

triumph of the resurrection.[141] It is directed towards all of humanity, including sinners, enemies of God, and those who deliberately reject this love.[142]

Descent into Hell

The descent into hell provides a way to consider the existence of radical evil and adversity in order to register the worst aspects of human nature, to explore how God solves adversity and expands the solution cosmically, and to help believers resist horrors, "in memory of the victims and in solidarity with those who mourn inconsolably."[143] To do so is essential because it allows humans the opportunity to look with theological imagination and canonical grounding at the open-ended space after the desperate cry of Lamentations 5:22, and to contemplate how God enters into the space of complete human hopelessness in response to their lament. The descent into hell narrative will also play an important role in understanding Christ's death and resurrection as a response to human suffering.[144] Though the gospel writers remain silent about the time after death and before the resurrection, by considering the hidden time of Christ's descent into hell we can construct a theology that breaks theological silence and resists the smooth progression from death to life.[145]

Various Christian traditions have confessed this through the Apostle's Creed, with the phrase "descended into hell" first found in the second century and universally adopted in the eighth century.[146] Some Roman Catholic and Lutheran traditions understand the phrase as a figurative description of the torments of hell, while the Reformed tradition interprets it as "the soul's most profound torment of abandonment by God."[147] The traditional interpretation of Christ's descent into hell is that Christ actively goes to hell to bind evil and save the saints.[148] Some traditions reduce Christ's descent to a period of waiting for the resurrection, as one way of explaining what happened on Good Friday.[149] Such multiple and varied interpretations have arisen because the Bible itself does not provide a comprehensive explanation

---

141. Lewis, *Between Cross and Resurrection*, 224.
142. Lauber, *Barth on the Descent into Hell*, 153.
143. Rutledge, *Crucifixion*, xix, 397–98.
144. Rutledge, *Crucifixion*, 398.
145. Rambo, *Spirit and Trauma*, 46.
146. Cahill, "Descent into Solidarity," 237.
147. Cahill, "Descent into Solidarity," 237–38; Rohls, *Reformed Confessions*, 96.
148. Cahill, "Descent into Solidarity," 238.
149. Cahill, "Descent into Solidarity," 241.

of the time between Christ's crucifixion and his resurrection. We only find fragmentary hints of it in passages like Psalm 16:10 and 1 Peter 3:19. However, this mysterious gap prevents us from understanding the events of the cross solely as anything other than a symbolic or metaphorical event.

John Calvin wrote that Christ "bore the weight of the divine anger, that, smitten and afflicted, he experienced all the signs of an angry and avenging God."[150] This reading makes Christ an active agent in the descent event.[151] However, according to Balthasar, Christ's descent is a "contemplative and objective (passive) moment" as distinguished from the subjective and active suffering of the passion.[152] Balthasar argues that death itself is a state of pure sin and pure condemnation, pointing out that it is absolutely impossible to come back to life after the absolute emptying of life.[153] We may consider these two together: Jesus' descent into hell involves both the passivity of being dragged as a dead man into the realm of the dead, as well as the active element of Jesus' will.[154] It reveals the mystery of God's own divinity, who united Godself with man's sinfulness and bore God's own judgment.[155] It also reveals the mystery of God's own love, which is realized in the freedom of God's perfect love, not as a descent necessitated by the perfection of God's own purpose, but as pure grace without price. This love of God is not capricious but flows from the very character of God's being.[156] That Jesus, as God and as man, knows, suffers, and overcomes the suffering of creation is an expression, not a denial, of His omnipotence and shows him as a creative and free participant, not a passive victim, in the dynamic of divinity and history.[157] While the doctrine of the two united natures of Jesus Christ in relation to the Trinity is diverse and still controversial, the understandings of the doctrine does not exclude a God who participates in suffering.[158] "Only as triune can God be identified with humanness and suffering, while remaining Lord and God."[159]

---

150. Calvin, *Institutes of the Christian Religion*, 2.16.11.
151. Cahill, "Descent into Solidarity," 239.
152. Balthasar, *Mysterium Paschale*, 131.
153. Balthasar, *Mysterium Paschale*, 132.
154. Lauber, *Barth on the Descent into Hell*, 149.
155. Lauber, *Barth on the Descent into Hell*, 150.
156. Lauber, *Barth on the Descent into Hell*, 150.
157. Lauber, *Barth on the Descent into Hell*, 159.
158. Lauber, *Barth on the Descent into Hell*, 162.
159. Lauber, *Barth on the Descent into Hell*, 197.

The narrative of Christ's descent may start with the scene of death on the cross that has been allowed to remain in ruin, darkness, and silence.[160] There is nothing but God who can break this silence. Lam 5:22 also shares this silence. The silence that follows the earnest cry is left behind in the time before God's word is heard. When "[Jesus] breathed his last . . . the rocks were split. The tombs also were opened, and many bodies of the saints . . . were raised" (Matt 27:50–52), then Christ descended to the gates of death and Hades.[161]

Rutledge uses several words to describe the space into which Christ descended after his death: Sheol is a space, "a shadowy subexistent state" that God does not remember (Ps 6:5), a space that is disconnected from God, a space without praise (Ps 115:17), full of silence, darkness, and hopelessness (Ps 94:17), and a space that has lost all strength and vitality (Isa 14:10).[162] Hades is "a realm of death, . . . a place of punishment for the ungodly."[163] And Gehenna is the eschatological "hell of fire" at the last judgment.[164] Hell is a place from which humans cannot escape without God's active rescue.[165] In this sense, Jesus who descended into hell, is separated from God: "in the symbolic space between cross and resurrection, Christ was utterly cut off from his powers, from his Father, from any hope of redemption or victory, and that precisely in this kenosis his solidarity with us and with our lot was complete."[166] In the "devil's kingdom," the darkest place, Christ bound himself with Satan and became imprisoned in order to bring about the complete victory by plundering the devil's hideout.[167] Descent into hell is the final and definitive action of God against the powers of evil that humans cannot resist. Ultimately, this confirms "there is no realm anywhere in the universe, including the domain of Death and the devil, where anyone can be cut off from the saving power of God."[168] Psalm 139:7–10 beautifully witnesses to this when its ways, "if I make my bed in Sheol, you are there" (v. 8b).

---

160. Rutledge, *Undoing of Death*, 137.
161. Rutledge, *Undoing of Death*, 190.
162. Rutledge, *Crucifixion*, 399; Balthasar, *Mysterium Paschale*, 161.
163. Rutledge, *Crucifixion*, 400.
164. Rutledge, *Crucifixion*, 401.
165. Rutledge, *Crucifixion*, 406.
166. Rutledge, *Crucifixion*, 407. Balthasar also supports it: "he is in solidarity with the dead." Balthasar, *Mysterium Paschale*, 149, 160.
167. Rutledge, *Crucifixion*, 413.
168. Rutledge, *Crucifixion*, 461.

The concept of hell can be necessary to recognize the reality of the power of radical evil.[169] The classical definition of evil, *privatio boni* (privation of the good) allows us to consider that hell is not a place, but the rule of evil and death.[170] In this sense, being a Christian with a sense of present war may involve adopting a language of resistance to evil.[171] Nonetheless, the descent narrative manifests God's presence, without loosing the gospel should constitute good news not only for victims but also for perpetrators, including passive bystanders.[172] This is because under certain circumstances ordinary people can do evil and terrible things, and Christ died for the sins of all, including the unrighteous.[173] Through Christ's descent into hell, salvation has come even to those who have lost the way and are hopeless.[174]

Holy Saturday

The narrative of Christ' descent into hell is closely related to the theology of Holy Saturday in terms of Christ being in solidarity with all human suffering. The theology of Holy Saturday emphasizes the place of suffering of both Jesus and humankind. Adam Tietje regards Holy Saturday as "the most fitting place to theologically ground the spiritual care of war-wounded souls."[175] The in-between day shows God's solidarity with "our God-abandonment" (Rom 8:39).[176] The day represents "the dark night of the soul," and "full descent" without a hope of recovery. From this understanding, Tietje shows the connection between Holy Saturday and lament, arguing that lamenting is what believers need in order to experience life at the edge: "The survivor

169. Rutledge, *Crucifixion*, 458.

170. Rutledge, *Crucifixion*, 425, 459–60. Rutledge presents one of several consensuses of tradition, "God permits the evil to operate within appointed bounds," pointing out that we should discern between God's intentional will and God's permissive will. See Rutledge, *Crucifixion*, 427. Rutledge thinks the discussion of evil should be more than a philosophical issue but should be engaged in faith and life, saying: that "the horrendous evil can actually destroy a person's self, whether the body is destroyed or not, presents a particularly acute challenge to belief in a God of mercy." See Rutledge, *Crucifixion*, 430. Balthasar says that hell should be understood as an inner spiritual state, not as a place. Balthasar, *Mysterium Paschale*, 163.

171. Rutledge, *Crucifixion*, 450.

172. Rutledge, *Crucifixion*, 453.

173. Rutledge, *Crucifixion*, 454–55.

174. Balthasar, *Mysterium Paschale*, 160.

175. Tietje, *Toward a Pastoral Theology*, 2. Tietje emphasizes the relationship between Holy Saturday and sin, rather than identifying it as a cosmic conflict or giving it apocalyptic meaning.

176. Tietje, *Toward a Pastoral Theology*, 47.

must reckon with the fact that neither revenge, nor forgiveness, nor compensation will erase the trauma. The only way forward is through the pain of mourning."[177] Tietje says that lament is putting an expression of courageous faith, resistance, anger, sorrow, and disappointment before God.[178] Tietje argues that sufferers need to be invited to see their suffering in the light of Christ's cross and descent into hell because God was with those who suffered in the grave, and Christ came down to the deepest level of our sorrow in the abyss of sin and death.[179] Shelly Rambo says Holy Saturday is a place of witnesses, where death and life are connected in a unique relationship.[180] Rambo notes that what persists between death and resurrection is another extended form of pain beyond physical pain and death, such as extreme loneliness, abandonment, and disconnection.[181] But she sees a new beginning in the wound. In this sense, "descent into hell," may suggest a place to bridge the movement from suffering to hope. In the discontinuous and continuous space of the abyss, Christ's agency emerges as an existential mode of love.[182] Christ's suffering is a love that embraces and affirms the world.[183]

The space between the cross and the resurrection can be considered as a place of testimony rather than as a description of evil or theodicy.[184] It is also a space where divine lament and human lament converge in robust solidarity through God's intervention into a state of eternal condemnation. In this regard, Christ's descent into hell can be understood as a response to the unanswered question of Lamentations 5:22. In God's silence, lamenters see God who comes to the depths and is really dead and buried.[185] This space witnesses God's and people's suffering and connects death with life.

Rutledge and Miroslav Volf see Holy Saturday as the perfect triumph of Christ's cosmic conflict, whereas Balthasar sees it both as a space of inner or spiritual wounds such as of absence, emptiness, loneliness, and also as the pinnacle of divine love.[186] Rambo and Tietje understand Holy Saturday

---

177. Tietje, *Toward a Pastoral Theology*, 44, 78.
178. Tietje, *Toward a Pastoral Theology*, 86.
179. Tietje, *Toward a Pastoral Theology*, 96.
180. Rambo, *Spirit and Trauma*, 46.
181. Rambo, *Spirit and Trauma*, 49.
182. Bartlett, *Cross-Purposes*, 260.
183. Lee, *Marginality*, 99.
184. Rutledge, *Crucifixion*, 434.
185. Rutledge, *Crucifixion*, 409.
186. Volf, *End of Memory*, 180, 298. Balthasar says that Christ's love in the abyss on Holy Saturday is far from the image of triumph. Rambo says that Christ's love in Balthasar's Holy Saturday theology is "weary love," but not a tragic death. Rambo, *Spirit and Trauma*, 71.

through the lens of the wounded. Despite the difference in emphasis due to the difference in theological lens, the unknown realm is a space of amazing solidarity with Christ and a space where dramatic pain is expressed in the perfect Trinity that bears all human suffering. Ultimately, this space unfolds into the final drama of salvation, providing eternal liberation and deliverance from all forms of suffering—guilt, the dominion of Sin, Death, and Evil—resisting the hasty move towards Easter.[187]

Thus, Holy Saturday is the time to face Jesus' death and God's silence. At the deepest point of sorrow and suffering, Jesus is shaping the strongest solidarity with us. Jesus responds to sufferers with his soul and life, actively and passionately staying with man at the end of suffering.

To summarize, Christ participates in people's suffering through his own suffering. His suffering is the incarnated lament of God. The lament from Jesus' suffering does more than give a foretaste of the apocalyptic struggle. This characteristic is an important aspect of the Christian life which is waiting for God's kin-dom in an apocalyptic sense, resisting, witnessing, and participating in pain in the world. Christ trespasses into "the system of terror" to break the vicious "cycle of violence."[188] A sense of Christ's lament shows that lament as resistance does not accept injustice passively but acts on it to overcome, breaking into the denial-filled world to reveal injustice, to build justice, and to embody the kin-dom of God with nonviolent actions, in the self-sacrificing manner of the Holy Spirit. Divine lament embraces physical, mental, and spiritual suffering. Jesus still laments for all pains with and in us through the Holy Spirit.

The realm of anonymity, strangeness, and emptiness between Jesus' death and resurrection sometimes disconnect the two events. As a disconnect, this realm prevents both the finality of Calvary and the unexpected surprise of Easter from being undermined when Christ's resurrection is explained in terms of the predictable cycles of life that naturally follow death—death and birth, sleep and wakefulness, night and morning, etc. In other words, because Jesus died in death, and because no natural rhythm of creation, no cyclical experience, can raise Christ from the grave, the resurrection does not merely embody the permanence of human life, but is the ground of hope for humanity and the universe.[189]

187. Some scholars criticize Balthasar, arguing he has placed too much emphasis on suffering when describing the cross and descent into hell. They tend to separate Holy Saturday from the death of the cross. Such people may look away from the suffering of the cross, may separate the triune God, and may ignore the suffering of the sinless one turning to be sin. Refer to Webb, "Why von Balthasar Was Wrong."

188. Volf, *Exclusion and Embrace*, 291.

189. Volf, *Exclusion and Embrace*, 60.

Resurrection

There are therefore two repeating categories of evil power: sin/guilt and slavery/bondage/oppression.[190] Atonement is generally needed for the former category and deliverance for the latter.[191] That means all suffering needs to be comforted and healed by God's redemptive power. In this sense, the Easter narrative is God's powerful conquest over the forces of evil that threaten God's creation and the wrongdoing that leads humanity to self-destruction.[192] However, the resurrection of Christ cannot nullify the narrative of crucifixion. This is because the life of resurrection in this world, although liberated and assured in the confident hope of eternal life, must "always be marked by the signs of the cross" until the day God wipes every tear from our eyes.[193]

The understanding of the resurrection narrative can shift from salvation through sacrificial suffering to the transformative potential of relational and participatory lament. Engaging in lament within the context of resurrection constitutes a form of resistance against the assumption that all individuals share identical losses or aspire to equivalent restoration. Lament serves as a protest against oversimplifying the notion that all suffering can be interpreted solely through the narratives of the crucifixion and resurrection. Furthermore, it challenges a passive interpretation of these narratives as mere exercises in patience and waiting. The lament in resurrection does not prompt us to avert our gaze from devastation and suffering in pursuit of their resolution, but rather urges us to confront this severity, chaos, and shattered state.[194] It does not advocate for blind optimism, but rather signifies an earnest quest for rejuvenation and hope within the embrace of God's providence.[195] It is a hope that no one will be subjected to the enduring and life-altering consequences of prolonged imprisonment within an utterly flawed system.[196] Thus, this section will explore how resurrection operates in both the future and the present, without losing or lessening significance of Christ's crucifixion and while preserving the empowering force that enables humans to embrace hope for resurrection amid their suffering.

---

190. Rutledge, *Crucifixion*, 216.
191. Rutledge, *Crucifixion*, 216.
192. Lewis, *Between Cross and Resurrection*, 65.
193. Lewis, *Between Cross and Resurrection*, 45.
194. Kaveny, "Anger, Lamentation, and Common Ground," 682.
195. Kaveny, "Anger, Lamentation, and Common Ground," 683.
196. Kaveny, "Anger, Lamentation, and Common Ground," 677.

Comfort in Tension

The response to human suffering is not merely divine compassion, but also divine redemptive and definitive action in Christ's death and resurrection. The resurrection shows how the powers that are against God can be overcome and exterminated.[197] Jesus' resurrection is "the first act of the One who has conquered the power of death."[198] In the resurrection, "Death has been swallowed up in victory" (1 Cor 15:54).[199] Jesus' resurrection is God's response, not only to the lament of God's people but to Jesus' lament on the cross.[200] This is because "the cross reveals God's own acceptance of lament, and the resurrection bears witness to the transformation of lament in eschatological reality which is brought about by the Spirit 'already.'"[201] Thus, the crucifixion and resurrection of Christ are God's offer of comfort and God's response to the repetitive disappointments in history and to the groaning of the whole of creation.[202]

For human life, God's capacity to rectify what is wrong is shown through faith in the resurrection of Jesus Christ.[203] In the story of two ordinary, unknown disciples encountering Jesus on their way to Emmaus, it may seem that nothing is happening. Yet it is a tremendous thing to recognize the risen Christ and to know Christ who is a companion on our path, whose presence is burning in our hearts, and who is awakening hope.[204] When believers associate themselves with Christ's "godforsaken death" in baptism, they simultaneously partake in Jesus' resurrection and become part of a new community.[205] The new community "includes not only the promise of eternal life but also a radically transformed life now, with the power given through the Holy Spirit right this minute."[206] The Bible testifies not only to their anticipation of the future but also to their earnest endeavor in entrusting God's message of reconciliation to the world in the present, as they serve as "ambassadors for Christ" (2 Cor 5:20).

---

197. Rutledge, *Crucifixion*, 505.
198. Rutledge, *Crucifixion*, 418.
199. Rutledge, *Undoing of Death*, 248.
200. Novello, "Jesus' Cry of Lament," 39–40.
201. Harasta, "Crucified Praise and Resurrected Lament," 205.
202. Rutledge, *Crucifixion*, 356.
203. Rutledge, *Crucifixion*, 610.
204. Rutledge, *Undoing of Death*, 271.
205. Rutledge, *Crucifixion*, 143. Cf. Rom 6:5.
206. Rutledge, *Bible and the New York Times*, 158.

In this regard, the comfort of Christ's resurrection is not a self-satisfying consolation. The relationship between resurrection and lament can be understood as a call to live as an ethical response of those who are convinced of the reality of the resurrection. John Wesley recognizes the tension of life after the resurrection, noting that sin continues even after the resurrection and its relationship to personal spiritual growth:

> How naturally do those who experience such a change imagine that all sin is gone; that it is utterly rooted out of their heart, and has no more any place therein! . . . Temptations return, and sin revives; showing it was but stunned before, not dead. . . . They find one or more of these frequently stirring in their heart, though not conquering; yea, perhaps, "thrusting sore at them that they may fall."[207]

Nonetheless, just as we witness the ongoing crucifixion within eschatological tension, God persistently embodies the transformative power of resurrection against the numerous situations and powers that condemn people to diverse forms of death.[208] In this regard, the power of justifying the unjust world makes people press on towards until God's words, justification, and promise are fully accomplished at the end. For this reason, it is necessary to discuss *dikaiosyne theou* as the divine power empowering this transformed life.

Dikaiosyne Theou

The lexical meaning of *dikaiosyne* encompasses justice and righteousness. When coupled with the word, God, it can signify the covenantal faithfulness of God and the rectifying power in an eschatological sense.[209] Thus, *dikaiosyne theou* is the power of reckoning us as righteous and rectifying all wrongs. By invading the enemy's territory, *dikaiosyne* is a final rejection of violence and injustice.[210] The continuity of God's covenant faithfulness throughout history paves the way for all to become part of God's family through the faithfulness of Christ. Also, the faithfulness of the Holy Spirit in eschatological approach, aligns with God's salvation ministry, progressing towards the final restoration of all creation, by ongoing facilitating faith communities to recall and actively engage in the restoration of the self as

---

207. Wesley, "Sermon 43," 25.
208. Elizondo, *God of Incredible Surprises*, 128.
209. Wright, *What Saint Paul Really Said*, 104–10.
210. Rutledge, *Crucifixion*, 505.

the beloved, the restoration of knowledge, and the restoration of the grand narrative—symbolized by the cross and resurrection.[211] *Dikaiosyne*, thus, offers the very reason for our claim on God (Lam 5:1, 20, 22) and our faith in a God who laments, heals, restores, and creates.

This power not only encompasses eschatological implications but is also intricately linked to the exigencies of current existence. It represents God's visible and active engagement in human history rather than a passive endurance of present suffering and injustice with a view towards a future culmination. For faith communities and individuals, *dikaiosyne theou* empowers everyday life not only to long for God's righteousness but also to participate in God's righteousness in everyday life. As articulated in 2 Corinthians 5:20, "we entreat you on behalf of Christ," implying that God appeals to the world "through us." This underscores an active collaboration wherein God works within us, enabling the embodiment of covenant faithfulness, positioning us as God's fellow-workers.[212] Christian communuties can serve as the reminding language of God, *dikaiosyne theou*.

In this regard, for seeming to be sole interested in personal forgiveness than in social justice, Christianity may need to be criticized. This because being angry and speaking out on behalf of those who are speechless and oppressed is participation in God's work: "God is overcoming evil, delivering the oppressed, raising the poor from the dust, vindicating the voiceless victims who have had no one to defend them."[213] Christian communities can participate in resistance to injustice every day, because God's war is with "the weapons of self-giving love and identification with those who suffer."[214] This means a sacrificial life that can be realized as a "mutual self-offering."[215]

Drawing from Romans 1, situations where injustice and incomprehensible evil seemingly prevail over good have persisted throughout history. Nevertheless, the belief in God's faithful promise operating in every circumstance, even in unrighteous conditions, persists. Despite challenges such as conflict, famine, poverty, and disease, *dikaiosyne theou* remains the reason for the conviction that God is actively working among us, providing evidence of God's ongoing work. The vocation of the Christian community is to stand on the side of righteousness and proclaim divine intervention in earthly suffering.[216] This life can be enacted in the Spirit of God who leads

---

211. Wright, *Paul in New Perspective*, 173–74.
212. Wright, *Justification*, 166.
213. Rutledge, *Crucifixion*, 328.
214. Rutledge, *Crucifixion*, 275.
215. Rutledge, *Crucifixion*, 275.
216. Rutledge, *Crucifixion*, 144.

us to lament for the sufferers. In lament, we can call on God in "hope against hope" (Rom 4:18): "God is continually pushing into the occupied territories with dynamic force."[217]

Lament as a Way of Being: A Cruciform Life

The gospel is not about human potential but about God's power.[218] On the cross, believers died with Christ and were raised again by the resurrection of Christ. Believers live by changing the direction of life with a new identity due to the very Spirit who "intercedes with sighs too deep for words" (Rom 8:26).[219] Humans cannot always distinguish evil, cannot punish evil with complete justice, cannot entirely resolve contradictions, and cannot completely change the world by pure subversion. Nonetheless, Humans' participation is not passive because the realm often referred to as the "now and not-yet," does not position us within an exclusive spiritual sanctuary that is isolated at the boundary where the anticipated kingdom of God exerts its utmost influence.[220] In the temporal domain situated between the present moment and the envisaged future, and within discernible indicators of suffering and struggle, humans, as collaborators with God, may actively confront, accompany, and bear witness to suffering. This engagement involves participating in God's decisive role in addressing and understanding the complexities of human affliction.

Joining the death and resurrection of Christ does not mean escape from the cosmic war, but rather means entering a life of suffering for the gospel and living between the first and second coming of Jesus.[221] According to Mark Taylor, resurrection signifies "a mode of remembering and living" rather than a supernatural belief that Jesus' body was reconstructed into a celestial form.[222] Taylor views these memories and ways of living as the social spaces where these practices release their power of liberating for change.[223] In the coexistence of the powers of evil and the new creation between the already and the not-yet, Christians are called to enact "social reversal" as eschatological transformation.[224]

---

217. Rutledge, *Crucifixion*, 357.
218. Rutledge, *Crucifixion*, 553.
219. Rutledge, *Crucifixion*, 553–54.
220. Rutledge, *Crucifixion*, 45.
221. Rutledge, *Crucifixion*, 389.
222. Taylor, *Executed God*, 19.
223. Taylor, *Executed God*, 19.
224. Myers, *Who Will Roll Away the Stone?*, 401.

This transformed identity also brings about a major change in the reality of lament. The changed reality of lament still works for expressing tragic loss, resisting injustice, naming evil, and calling on God. But in the light of the resurrection, it also insists that the victory of Christ is both now and final: death or despair is not the last word, Christ is with us in the midst of suffering, the Holy Spirit as a source of *dikaiosyne* powers us, and God is ultimately sovereign. The identity of a new lament expands the realm of lament into resurrection.

The lament coming from "ontological transformation" is a dynamic reality that connects to the issue of ethics.[225] Rutledge argues that Christians are called to live in a "cruciform" way that resembles the only one who can cry out in the seemingly endless reality of suffering, who gives himself up for betrayal and allows himself to be exposed, naked, crucified, pouring out blood, sweat, and tears, and who can keep his promise to bring a new life.[226] Rambo asserts that living a cruciform life, embracing solitude akin to Christ on behalf of others, serves as a significant model for imparting the *mysterium* of Holy Saturday as a testimony.[227] Tietje argues that just as Christ's prayer of mourning was in solidarity with us, so too we should participate in the prayers of those who weep.[228] Wright lends strength to the present ethical mandate, emphasizing the significance of "The continuity between the present body and the future resurrection body" (cf. Rom 12–14).[229] This continuity emphasizes that Christians' actions with their bodies is important now and in eschatological terms.[230] This ethical vision empowers us to transcend the ways in which social divisions can keep us apart.[231] In this sense, the changed reality of lament is closely attached to the suffering of others and it has communal aspects that include a sense of nowness.

Picking up and carrying one's cross means "total reorientation of the self toward the way of Christ." This transformed identity also calls people to participate in God's justice.[232] God's justice is intended for all especially for the marginalized; as As the Bible says, "What to me is the multitude of your sacrifices. . . . I have had enough of burnt-offerings. . . . [M]ake yourselves clean, . . . seek justice, rescue the oppressed, defend the orphan, plead for

---

225. Rutledge, *Crucifixion*, 564–65.
226. Rutledge, *Undoing of Death*, 17.
227. Rambo, *Spirit and Trauma*, 69.
228. Tietje, *Toward a Pastoral Theology of Holy Saturday*, 86.
229. Taylor, *Executed God*, 19.
230. Wright, *Surprised by Hope*, 290.
231. Myers, *Who Will Roll Away the Stone?*, 402.
232. Rutledge, *Crucifixion*, 44.

the widow" (Isa 1:11, 16–17).[233] Following Christ as a communal action poses a counterculturaI challenge to the ethics of individualism and competitive materialism.[234] According to Mary Gray, the endeavor of gathering the fractured fragments of creation commences with attentive listening to the voices of the marginalized, subsequently giving rise to the formation of a language for the soul—a labor that interlinks the spiritual dimension with the pursuit of justice.[235] Christ gathers the shattered fragments of creation, and through a process of mending and healing, brings them to wholeness, ultimately leading to redemption. This is the work of God. Yet it is also the endeavor of all communities dedicated to bearing hope.

In terms of the necessity of lament, people may question why we need to lament if God is active in the world anyway, with or without our laments. However, lament itself is a gift of God's grace given for human resilience, not as a necessary condition for God's salvation. In other words, lamentation is not only for calling on God's redemptive action, but can be a confession of trust in God and a channel of dialogue with God. As Hunsinger claims, "We thus facilitate healing when we help the afflicted cry out their sorrow, rage, and tears to God. Prayers of lament—crying out to God for deliverance—seem to be faith's only alternative to despair."[236]

In this respect, people living in the tension and pain of the already-not-yet need to maintain a sense of lament while acknowledging God's powerful agency for salvation and life. As "a whole book of the Bible is entitled Lamentations," we are allowed—and indeed encouraged—to blame, question, and challenge God, and to throw our misfortunes in the face of God.[237] Also we need to maintain our ability to be "shocked, grieved, even enraged."[238] We shall articulate our sorrows, acknowledging that God's love will ultimately prevail as the final word. We will continue to fight, kick, and scream in this wicked, dark valley of tears until the Lord comes again.[239]

---

233. Rutledge, *Crucifixion*, 109. Justice is clearly revealed in the Bible. Rutledge mentions that the biblical references to justice show that "God is attentive to the material details of human need," presenting Exod 23:6; Deut 24:17; Ezek 45:9 as textual evidence. She argues that justice is central to God's nature and that God is against every form of injustice. Isaiah also notes that God rejects worship which is not linked to justice. See Rutledge, *Crucifixion*, 110–11.

234. Grey, *Beyond the Dark Night*, 40.

235. Grey, *Beyond the Dark Night*, 14–15.

236. Hunsinger, *Bearing the Unbearable*, 17.

237. Rutledge, *Undoing of Death*, 330–31.

238. Rutledge, *Crucifixion*, 589.

239. Wright, *Evil and the Justice of God*, 105–6.

LAMENT AS IN-BETWEEN-EPISTEMOLOGY WITH PASCHAL TRIDUUM NARRATIVES

The existence of the Paschal Triduum narratives that embraces mortality and overcomes it through an abundance of love forms the foundation for the divine hope for those who are unwell and sinful, those approaching death, and those who have already died.[240] Inevitably this prompts us to wonder how to embody the Paschal Triduum narratives within a world facing the specter of death and shackled by the persistence of malevolence and unfairness; and what is the genuine significance of the church, which not only shoulders the burden of the crucified God's cross, but which also embodies (within a world in decline) Christ's body, where the demise of God transpired.[241]

In-Between as Lament Space

The life, death, and resurrection of Jesus all aimed to liberate the oppressed from suffering and bondage.[242] Scholars such as Jung Young Lee, Sang Hyun Lee, and Virgilio Elizondo have written suggested that the incarnation of Christ represents God's self-marginalization.[243] This God not only associates Godself with those on the margins but also beckons us into these marginal spaces, where creativity, resistance, solidarity, and openness to the new thrive.[244] Jesus here is identified as a man of sorrow, grief, and love. Jesus embodies the creative essence of God's love, and we become part of this essence through our own experiences of marginalization.[245] The Triduum narrative of the triune God, as manifested through Christ, profoundly exemplifies this marginal mode of thinking. The inseparability of death and resurrection is a crucial aspect of this narrative.[246] Even when the world

---

240. Lewis, *Between Cross and Resurrection*, 256.
241. Lewis, *Between Cross and Resurrection*, 257.
242. Park, *From Hurt to Healing*, 20.
243. Lee, *Marginality*; Lee, *From a Liminal Place*; Elizondo, *God of Incredible Surprises*.
244. Yang, "Towards a Chinese Theology of Displacement," 201.
245. Lee, *Marginality*, 99. The resurrection of Jesus signifies the dawn of a new era. When Jesus reveals himself to his marginalized and scattered disciples, they acknowledge him as Lord. The Holy Spirit bestowed upon them enables people from all nations to establish a shared understanding without resorting to confusing language. This event gives rise to a fresh community, uniting them to coexist harmoniously. Lee, *Marginality*, 96.
246. Lee, *Marginality*, 72.

hesitates to accept him as the Son of God, His affirmation and heavenly confirmation do not pull Christ away from the periphery. Instead, through the narrative of Jesus' death and resurrection, he reconciles two distinct worlds, integrating and harmonizing them within himself, and transcending potential dichotomy.[247]

Xiaoli Yang identifies the liminal spaces within the Bible as paradoxical realms situated between the wilderness and the promised land, homelessness and home, and Good Friday and Easter Sunday.[248] The act of incarnational lamentation in the face of suffering, coupled with hope in God, fosters active engagement and collaboration with God's ongoing creative process in the world.[249] Yang articulates, "This [incarnational act—lament over suffering and hope in God] is the path of embracing brokenness as children of God. They join creation in a collective 'groaning in one great act of giving birth' (Rom 8:22), resonating with the essence of birthing pains and the joy of receiving new life."[250] Lee Sang Hyun perceives the life, death, and resurrection of Jesus as a "liminal space." For instance, Jesus' public ministry bridges the liminal gap between the cross and the space he opens through his compassionate healing of marginalized individuals.[251] Within this realm, he establishes a sense of community through mutual acceptance and respect, empowering them to embark on a new journey. This liminal space embodies total comprehension and embraces the entirety of the fallen creation, with God also participating in the suffering of this realm.[252] While social marginalization and peripherality endure, the apprehension of that marginalization is no longer accompanied by fear.[253] Through Jesus' resurrection, his disciples lead lives dedicated to realizing God's love and justice in the world.[254]

Scholars employing the concept of the 'liminal not only acknowledge the presence of two opposing camps but also emphasize the significance of its 'inter' element, reflecting their inherent dynamism and ever-evolving

247. Lee, *Marginality*, 85.
248. Yang, "Towards a Chinese Theology of Displacement," 207.
249. Yang, "Towards a Chinese Theology of Displacement," 211.
250. Yang, "Towards a Chinese Theology of Displacement," 211–12.
251. Lee, *From a Liminal Place*, 82. Lee's conceptual grasp of *communitas* is similar to the interpretation of Christ's solidarity with humanity as discussed by other scholars. Lee says that "Communitas with others is a way of relating to others with respect for all their differences, in other words, respect for others in all their otherness." Lee, *From a Liminal Place*, 151–52.
252. Lee, *From a Liminal Place*, 81.
253. Lee, *From a Liminal Place*, 86.
254. Lee, *From a Liminal Place*, 85.

nature. This intricate interplay draws those situated in the in-between space into a realm of "multi-and-inter" awareness and practice.[255] Individuals who keenly perceive the coexistence of Good Friday and Easter, inhabiting the space in between, cultivate an ability to view Good Friday through the lens of Easter and vice versa. This dual perspective enables a clear recognition of both the experience of suffering on Good Friday and the experience of hope on Easter, while existing within this intermediate realm. The domain of Holy Saturday serves as a catalyst for embracing the dynamic and creative essence of the in-between, rather than settling for a singular viewpoint. This understanding of in-between space enables us to perceive that God's action is not linear and quantitative, but rather qualitative and three-dimensional. Thus, lamenting in-between is to embrace hope from resurrection and to reveal life and reprieve amidst the cross, without diminishing a sense of suffering in the marginal space.

Embodying the Paschal Triduum Narratives In-Between

Through the incarnation and death of Jesus Christ, God does not merely align with human suffering or assume human suffering; rather, God suffers.[256] Divine love is not refined through suffering, nor does it immerse itself in the realms of suffering, death, and hell for self-fulfillment. Instead, it does so for the sake of the world's life.[257] This perspective on trinitarian life and divine suffering embodies both mystical and practical dimensions. It straddles the border between excluding from God all inner human experiences and suffering, while simultaneously affirming that the potential for those experiences and suffering resides within God.[258]

Miguel A. De La Torre characterizes *han* as a companion to the disenfranchised—the individuals enduring injustice, the powerless, the voiceless, and the marginalized.[259] He contends that it is within this han-laden periphery that the dominant culture discovers its path to redemption. This capacity to perceive and acknowledge this *han* sparks a healing process, enabling the wounded individual to mend the wounds of others. A man fell into the hands of robbers (Luke 10:25–37). That man was a member of the oppressive dominant culture that marginalized the Samaritan—the very man who, along with the inn keeper, cared for him. Yet, through his own inner

---

255. Phan, "Experience of Migration," 189.
256. Lauber, *Barth on the Descent into Hell*, 138.
257. Lauber, *Barth on the Descent into Hell*, 148.
258. Balthasar, *Dramatis Personae*, 324.
259. De La Torre, *Reading the Bible from the Margins*, 26.

han, this man from Samaria managed to develop empathy for the wounded person, and in so doing the *han*-bearing community became a catalyst of healing in a *han*-bearing world.[260] Christopher Munzihirwa, who became an outspoken protector of the Hutu refugees after the genocide began in Rwanda in 1994, says, "There are things that can be seen only with eyes that have cried."[261] Munzihirwa frequently employs this phrase—a critique of violent politics and a prophetic rationale for a novel nonviolent social reality he terms "the way of Christ"; this prophetic lament holds profound social and political implications.[262]

Thus, as a community of lament, our objective is to contemplate the implications of demonstrating communal sensitivity towards the suffering endured by both ourselves and by individuals or communities grappling with a wide range of afflictions and to take decisive action. Lament helps shape how the situation itself can be perceived in various ways, how theology is practiced in different contexts, and how multi-faceted themes can emerge from the same situation.[263] This is not an attempt to manipulate theology to suit our needs, but rather to ask whether the reality in which we find ourselves allows us to form and practice our own theology in a creative way.[264]

Lamenting with the Marginalized

The suffering of crucifixion includes not only of spiritual and mental suffering but most definitely and primarily also physical suffering. Amid unequal power structures and intrinsic social injustices, the human body becomes a conspicuous manifestation of oppressive authority, bearing witness to various concealed and blatant forms of suffering: torture, beatings, gas chambers, imprisonment, and more.[265] Therefore, the evocation of the resurrected body of Christ, which endured similar mistreatment yet triumphed, can serve as lament to defy earthly power. Such invocation of lament also provides solace and support to individuals enduring affliction under oppressive regimes.[266]

---

260. De La Torre, *Reading the Bible from the Margins*, 27.
261. Allen, *Global War on Christians*, 49.
262. Katongole, *Born from Lament*, 163.
263. Fernandez, *Toward a Theology of Struggle*, 26.
264. Elizondo, *God of Incredible Surprises*, 105.
265. Punt, *Postcolonial Biblical Interpretation*, 190.
266. Punt, *Postcolonial Biblical Interpretation*, 190.

The life, death, and resurrection of Jesus Christ have taught us that God is a liberator not only from the confinements of individual sin, but also from the collective sins that devastate the existence of those residing on the fringes of society.[267] This representation of Christ challenges a powerful and privileged Christ. Much as Gemma Cruz does in the context of migration is this representation of Christ, and thus Christian spirituality epitomizes a descent into the valley of injustice, "from belonging to non-belonging, from relational connectedness to family separation, from being to non-being."[268] As marginalized minorities, migrants often suffer economic deprivation, political disenfranchisement, and cultural displacement, and are almost always exposed to the worst human rights violations, racism, and xenophobia.[269] The lament of the poor and oppressed pierce the superficiality of outward culture to reveal the naked truths of human existence. Through such laments we catch hints of God's presence with them on the margins of society.[270] In their extraordinary stories of hunger, thirst, marginalization, nakedness, disease, and imprisonment, we can see the face of Christ crucified, a lamenting God.[271]

Lamenting with Women

One of Christ's images on the cross can convey the idea that God's suffering for the sake of others saves the salvation of the world. While this represents one among several motifs behind Christ's crucifixion, it may, at times, be interpreted in a negative way as an expression of unconditional obedience and sacrifice to the will of power. In such an interpretation, self-sacrifice and obedience are likely linked to the primary Christian virtues and defining characteristics of a person of faith.[272] Especially for women within the patriarchal framework, rather than promoting ideas and values that emphasize blind obedience to authority figures and view forgiveness as the virtue, the actions and image of Christ need to be re-told and re-imagined for women as *das Symbol von Ganzheit und Leben* (the symbol of wholeness and life).[273] This is because an understanding of the cross, derived from women's experiences of various sufferings, should be grounded in their existential and

---

267. De La Torre, *Reading the Bible from the Margins*, 135.
268. Cruz, *Toward a Theology of Migration*, 141.
269. Min, "Migration and Christian Hope," 197.
270. Groody, *Border of Death*, 32–33.
271. Groody, *Border of Death*, 32–33.
272. Schüssler Fiorenza, *Jesus*, 107.
273. Moltmann-Wendel, "Zur Kreuzestheologie Heute," 557.

relational perspectives, rather than relying solely on the principle of forgiveness of sins.[274] In this context, lamentation serves to bring forth existential and relational perspectives of women who have experienced suffering. For example, lamenting with the sense of women's suffering in the surrogacy experiences of black women encourages people to question whether their status as surrogates for Christ, who went to the cross to redeem sinful humanity, holds redemptive power for black women or whether it reinforces the exploitation and surrogacy that accompanies the surrogacy experience.[275] In this respect, lament allows us to recognize the many nameless individuals crucified. An act of lament with women's suffering experiences refutes justifying the suffering of those victimized by patriarchal oppression, including domestic and sexual violence. Communities attuned to suffering lament the homogeneity and single interpretation within Paschal Triduum narratives that have been shaped by powerful or dominant forces. They endeavor to draw forth concealed and overlooked experiences, narratives, and memories, with the intention of comprehending Jesus and, in turn, gaining insight into ourselves.

Such perspectives find meaning of the theology of the cross within the context of historical facts of unjust oppression, experiences of the struggle for a different world, and the unjust suffering of the dehumanized leading to sacrifice and death.[276] In doing so, those who lament suffering discover themselves as a historical agency capable of naming and transforming dehumanizing circumstances that lead to the death of oppressed and disenfranchised people.[277] Thus, lamentation within the Paschal Triduum narratives speaks not only of future hope in eschatological language but also of a present hope accompanied by vision and action.[278]

Lamenting with Political Discourses

If we set aside the exploration of the divine "will to die" for the purpose of atonement, which encompasses divine images of merciful death, deification, and glorification, we can perceive that the cross is an act of (political) execution.[279] Crucifixion was an act of humiliation, torture, and execution designed to deal with those deemed most threatening to the Roman Empire

274. Moltmann-Wendel, "Zur Kreuzestheologie Heute," 554.
275. Williams, "Black Women's Surrogate Experience," 9.
276. Schüssler Fiorenza, *Jesus*, 130.
277. Schüssler Fiorenza, *Jesus*, 130.
278. Schüssler Fiorenza, *Jesus*, 120.
279. Taylor, *Executed God*, 6.

and its interests.²⁸⁰ To understand the cross as an execution—and to give it theological meaning—is to trace functions in solidifying political and cultural discourses of supremacy and domination beyond Roman domination of Palestine and white supremacist rule.²⁸¹ The cross is the punishment for those who challenge and work to dismantle "hegemonic and imperial codes," just as we look for the suffering of Christ in the pain-ravaged faces of the oppressed.²⁸² Fernandez says we need to move beyond crying for deliverance to political struggle, which is not a future refuge but a way of dwelling on earth where heaven is earned through struggle.²⁸³

Within the associations of crucifixion and execution, the tragic Atlanta spa shooter who targeted Asian women (March 16, 2021) is an invitation for us to consider the crucifixion of Jesus not only as a spiritual and abstract event but also as a political event—of terrorism.²⁸⁴ Terrorism aligns with the notion of a pervasive "mass death sentence" imposed by systems of slavery, white supremacy, hegemonic masculinism, genocide, and holocaust.²⁸⁵ This clearly affirms the necessity of lament in addressing veiled and muted suffering imposed by the terrorism system, explicitly exposing social injustice. The structural violence of this time and history is hung next to the cross. From a political perspective, Jesus' lament is related to the way of the cross in the existential, political, and historical reality of Jesus' own life; Mark Taylor calls this the "politics of remembrance model."²⁸⁶ Taylor's model involves remembering the ways in which the cross in Jesus' day targeted "the racial/ethnic other, those deemed inferior by gender and sexuality, and also the poor."²⁸⁷ This reflection allows us to see violence against various 'others' in the modern day. In so doing, we reconstruct the historical past in the present.²⁸⁸ It does not reduce the events of Jesus to historical material but makes them an organism of history that expresses our time.²⁸⁹

Since we encounter the same crucible of suffering, akin to that of crucifixion, even after the resurrection—the daily ordeals, torments, terrorism, etc. inflicted by structural oppression—an appreciation of Jesus' voluntary

---

280. Sugirtharajah, *Postcolonial Criticism and Biblical Interpretation*, 95.
281. Taylor, *Executed God*, 7.
282. Sugirtharajah, *Postcolonial Criticism and Biblical Interpretation*, 95.
283. Fernandez, *Toward a Theology of Struggle*, 55.
284. Taylor, *Executed God*, 8.
285. Taylor, *Executed God*, 9.
286. Taylor, *Executed God*, 16.
287. Taylor, *Executed God*, 17.
288. Benjamin, "Literary History and the Study of Literature," 464.
289. Benjamin, "Literary History and the Study of Literature," 464.

suffering can sometimes dilute our sense of unity with those who endure oppression.[290] The gospel that truly fosters such unity is intricate and challenging, centered around a notion of 'life in opposition' capable of withstanding and challenging the dominion of ruling powers. Relinquishing the deity of political dominion signifies not disengaging from political discourse and strife, while evading the adoption of hierarchical and violent structures that brand individuals and groups as threats or inferior—an ordeal that various forms of immigrants have continually borne.[291] In this regard, lament can be a way of being. It signifies a novel approach to perceiving and understanding God's triumph, materializing as an imaginative victory by the marginalized, surpassing the might of the oppressors.[292] When we the radical acceptance of life as it is, even during the most agonizing moments, the inception of a resurrection experience has already begun.[293]

Lamenting with Dedicated and Determined Action

Jon Sobrino uses the concept of "crucified people" to make a connection between suffering people and Yahweh as a suffering servant. Sobrino argues that "in these crucified people, Christ acquires a body in history, and that the crucified people embody Christ in history as crucified."[294] The crucified people, due to their very existence, are the greatest witnesses and protesters against injustice, even when they are not actively fighting for justice, and even when they are silenced through violence.[295] Those who endure injustice bear the sins of their oppressors on their shoulders and contribute to eradicating sin and exposing the problem, serving as carriers of historical soteriology. Although, compared to the death of Jesus the deaths of the oppressed masses do not fully account for the active nature of the anti-kingdom struggle or the freedom with which this struggle was undertaken, these crucified people nonetheless create solidarity between the people and the Church in a mutual, open, and committed way.[296] They are "in my flesh I am completing what is lacking in Christ's afflictions" (Col 1:24).

---

290. Taylor, *Executed God*, 31.
291. Taylor, *Executed God*, 36.
292. Taylor, *Executed God*, 48.
293. Elizondo, *God of Incredible Surprises*, 101.
294. Sobrino, *Jesus the Liberator*, 255.
295. Sobrino, *Jesus the Liberator*, 258.

296. Sobrino, *Jesus the Liberator*, 261, 271. Biblical scholar John P. Meier criticizes Sobrino's reference to the historical Jesus. For Meier, the historical Jesus is the Jesus whom we can locate through the methods of historical criticism. Meier, "Bible as a

This perspective aligns with Korean Minjung theology, which considers Christ as one of the people. Similarly, Filipino Christianity also theologizes their participation in the struggles of the people.[297] For them, to follow Jesus is to know where Jesus is: standing with the victimized, the rejected, the oppressed, and the marginalized, as the cross of Jesus represents the highest expression of solidarity.[298] In this regard, Eleazar Fernandez goes on to say that eschatology needs to be interpreted "in light of suffering (theodicy) and struggle (politics)" rather than the quest for immortality.[299] In a theology of struggle, the crucified Christ is not a passive and meek one, but one who struggles with those who suffer, and Jesus' suffering is a struggle that encourages others to do the same.[300] Although Fernandez does not see crying as a form of active resistance, as we see above, lament (beyond crying) as an expression of grief or suffering is a strong action against injustice. Lament works beyond the groans of a suffering generation. Its prophetic laments and cries serve as a call to action for resistance to evil and for a world in which no one is forced to carry a cross. Divine lament is an act for the "renewal" that has already been granted to us and to the world. It is prayer for the peace and reconciliation that have already been achieved, and is a striving for the freedoms that are guaranteed.[301] This is because resurrection is a force that transcends the survival of the soul and beckons for the transformation of the world we inhabit.

CONCLUSION: HOPE AGAINST HOPE

The theology of lament is intentionally situational because it prioritizes particularity as the primary locus of reflection on the truth of things. It is

---

Source for Theology," 6. Latinx scholars, however, have a more expansive understanding of the word "historical." According to Ignacio Ellacuría's understanding, demonstrating the influence of a particular concept in a specific context is also considered as historicizing; that is, historical reality is understood as the totality of reality given in a more open and qualitative form. Ellacuría, *Filosofía de la realidad histórica*, 43–44, cited in Lasalle-Klein, "Postcolonial Christ," 146. Sobrino sees the quest for the historical Jesus in Latin America as a benchmark for discipleship: discovering the living sign that God historicizes its affirmation by raising Jesus from the dead. The historical Jesus is understood as the life, practices, words, actions, attitudes, and spirit of Jesus of Nazareth, and thus the reality of Jesus of Nazareth is comprehended as history, including his crucifixion and resurrection. Sobrino, *Christ the Liberator*, 50, 225, 228, 264.

297. Fernandez, *Toward a Theology of Struggle*, 22.
298. Fernandez, *Toward a Theology of Struggle*, 125.
299. Fernandez, *Toward a Theology of Struggle*, 31.
300. Fernandez, *Toward a Theology of Struggle*, 103.
301. Lewis, *Between Cross and Resurrection*, 66.

through lamentation that emerges from the specificity of historical reality and experience that we perceive the intimations of God's presence in it.[302]

On the basis of the previous chapters, we can now define lament as an impassioned expression of, witness to, and personal and/or social protest of those who suffer in the face of evil and injustice, a longing for God's saving presence. For God, lament is used as a way to respond to and to express solidarity with human suffering, to show humans another aspect of God's image, and to reveal a strong sense of divine compassion. Also, because of divine lament, humans can embrace hope and express lament that is transformed in the reality of suffering.

An essential concept within lament theology resides in the notion of "hope against hope" (Rom 4:18). Hope against hope appears in the narrative of the morning when Abraham had to travel to sacrifice his only son Isaac (Gen 22:3–4), in the narrative of God's wrath (Mal 3:2), and in radical evil like the Holocaust and the Cambodian genocide.[303] Hope against hope is holding on to hope even in the darkest night of suffering. It is a confession that God is the Only Hope, but it does not lose sight of evil and suffering. Thus, it contrasts with boundless optimism and positive thought.[304] Those who hope against hope are full of the passion of despair and blame like the voice in Lamentations, contrasting hope with hopeless sadness.[305] Nonetheless, hope against hope verifies the faith of the community in *dikaiosyne* which is "a continual going-out in power to effect what it requires."[306]

Believers then and now have assumed that the Messiah would not only bring about the political liberation of the people and a transformation in historical circumstances, but also that he would alter history itself, bringing an end to suffering, marginalization, and exile.[307] Perhaps this is why the concept of a crucified messiah, a vulnerable messiah, a weeping messiah, a rebel, a murderer, a robber, a humble man, a slave, and a member of a subjugated people was and is so challenging to embrace. However, God's cosmic engagement with suffering, as unveiled in the Paschal Triduum narratives, invites us to respond by participating in divine hope and becoming "entangled" in that narrative.[308] In every facet of life, Christ is risen and extends an

---

302. McCarroll, *Waiting at the Foot of the Cross*, 90.
303. Rutledge, *Crucifixion*, 263, 325, 434.
304. Rutledge, *Crucifixion*, 434.
305. O'Connor, *Lamentations and the Tears*, 97.
306. Rutledge, *Crucifixion*, 144.
307. Copeland, "Cross of Christ and Discipleship," 183.
308. Jüngel, *God as the Mystery of the World*, borrowed from Schapp, *In Geschichten verstrickt*.

invitation to those who grieve with him, encouraging participation in God's movement to establish order, peace, and justice in communities that mirror the anticipated kin-dom of God.[309] This is not a hope grounded in fantasy but in the reality of Christ crucified and resurrected, a hope that simultaneously shapes the lives of believers.[310] Practices of nonviolent solidarity, pursuing justice with love, and caring for the impoverished and oppressed all indicate that we are walking the "way of Jesus."[311]

To possess hope is to acknowledge our limitations—our inability to liberate ourselves, cure our ailments, soothe our fears, resolve our predicaments, and dictate our fate.[312] This conscious surrender of self is the essence of engaging with Paschal Triduum narratives, and it is the merging of our lamentation with the lamentation of God's Spirit that opens up possibilities. Thus, lament in hope against hope may work a way of being between the first and the second coming of Jesus with the strange image of God, who laments. This God makes all those who suffer and lament have hope against hope by verifying God's love through God's lament.

---

309. Lewis, *Between Cross and Resurrection*, 319.
310. Moltmann, *Ethics of Hope*, 85.
311. Copeland, "Cross of Christ and Discipleship," 191.
312. Lewis, *Between Cross and Resurrection*, 307.

4

The Role of Lament in Preaching

THE PREVIOUS CHAPTERS LOOKED at the meaning and roles of communal lament in the Bible and in society and discussed a theological understanding of lament. The meaning of divine lament, as a response to human lament based on the cross and resurrection, is the foundation of the practice of lament, which generates hope without losing sight of the reality of pain. To combine the previous discussion about lament with preaching, this chapter investigates lament as a homiletical practice.

This entails an exploration of how sermons have addressed experiences of suffering, the role that lament has played in preaching about such suffering, and the dynamics involved in the interplay between suffering and hope within the context of preaching.[1] Lament in recent homiletics is encountered in diverse themes, encompassing listeners, public crises and justice, intercultural and feminist issues, lectionary sources, and theology. Lament preaching invites listeners to disclose their pain, aiming to bring diverse experiences of suffering closer to them. This approach often necessitates

---

1. Paul Scott Wilson classifies the Post-New Homiletics trend as the Radical Postmodern school separated from New Homiletics. See chapter 9 in *Preaching and Homiletical Theory*, 135–58. He introduces John McClure, Joseph M. Webb, Christine M. Smith, L. Susan Bond, and Lucy Rose as members of this radical school. Wilson's criticism of the radical school is that their preaching as an ethic puts more weight on human behavior than on God's action. Wilson, *Preaching and Homiletical Theory*, 137. Also, not all homiletics since the 1950s is called New Homiletics. For example, James Cox's book *Preaching* was published in 1985 and was used as a preaching text, but his work is positioned rather more in line with traditional propositional sermons. In other words, truth is presented largely as clear propositions in terms of content; it is logical and rational, with little room for the imaginative and mysterious. Language is functional rather than poetic, and Cox's approach generally presents propositions that have a deductive and non-narrative form. Rose, *Sharing the Word*, 16–18.

the presentation of a rich and interpretive description that employs vivid, concrete, and heuristic language tailored to the hearers' context. Lament has been strategically incorporated into various rhetorical aspects of preaching, including narrative and plot, metaphor, imagination, and tension, to effectively navigate the theme of hope amidst suffering. Some preachers have developed theological and homiletical frameworks that articulate the dynamic interplay between suffering and hope. Notably, the Trouble and Grace school of preaching provides a foundational framework for understanding the transitional role of lament.

SUFFERING DISCOURSES IN RECENT HOMILETICS

The New Homiletic is a movement in preaching which started in the 1950s and has greatly influenced today's preaching. Instead of the logical, rational, propositional, deductive, and expository approaches of previous types of preaching, the New Homiletics has combined an understanding of imagination, language, metaphor, narrative, images, performance, words as events, inductive learning, horizontal authority, social context, and justice.[2] Some of these characteristics have effectively offered a place to deal with suffering in hope.

Focus on Listeners and Experience

A predominant trend within the homiletics movement since the 1950s reflects a shift towards more direct engagement with listeners and human experiences, in contrast to earlier sermons that primarily aimed to 'deliver' the gospel.[3] This transition has established a close link between preaching language and lived reality. For instance, articulating aspects of the divine inherently involves addressing human experiences, as the encounter with God significantly impacts the tangible aspects of human existence.[4]

Charles Rice points out that in the overall process of writing a sermon, the language fundamentally reflects the experience of listeners. Both application and exegesis/exposition are "filtered through the preacher's own subjective awareness of himself and his congregation."[5] Criticizing a

---

2. Wilson, *Four Pages*, 6. For seeing a brief development of New Homiletics, see Allen, *Renewed Homiletic*, 7–10.
3. Rose, *Sharing the Word*, 71.
4. Neal, *Overshadowed Preacher*, 206.
5. Rice, *Interpretation and Imagination*, 95.

"heteronomous view of the world," and "positivism as a non-experiential reductionism" that may make humans try to disconnect themselves from realms of experience that they cannot manipulate or control, Rice also emphasizes preaching the integrated view that is able to see the reality of the world as both tragic and comic.[6] Fred Craddock proposed inductive preaching in which the listeners travel toward the conclusion together in communion with a preacher, rather than passively accepting the conclusions delivered by the preacher. Craddock stressed the use of a concrete experience as a source of a sermon and a sermonic movement through creative usages of an analogy and the identification with the listener to integrate the experience into learning.[7]

David Buttrick argues that listeners have a variety of stories that relate to their perception of the world around them, and the stories are rearranged as "our story" through sharing, that ultimately gives them a shared identity.[8] Buttrick referred to the sermon as "a double hermeneutic" that interprets the biblical text and the listener's situation.[9] He criticized the preaching that speaks of God as someone who acted in the past, and which loses connection with the God who works in today's society.[10] In other words, Buttrick believed that sermons need to reflect today's experiences of the listeners. In this sense, Buttrick argued that it is necessary for preachers to concern themselves with those who suffer and to have a clear and deep sense of the social system that imposes suffering and that oppresses.[11]

A more radical understanding of the listeners can be seen in the work of Lucy Rose and John McClure, who use the image of a roundtable to exemplify what happens during a sermon.[12] That image indicates an open conversation including "disvalued, muffled, or extinguished" voices in a community.[13] Rose reduces the gap between the preacher and the congrega-

---

6. Rice, *Interpretation and Imagination*, 49–50.

7. Craddock, *As One without Authority*, 59, 61–62. Through the former, he intended to help the audience to make decisions themselves by identification with what the audience listens to, and through the latter, he intended for the listeners to reach their own conclusions rather than passively accepting the conclusions presented by a preacher.

8. Buttrick, *Homiletic*, 8, 10. Buttrick noted that we will eventually be able to possess a transformed story due to the encounter of our story with the story of God. Buttrick, *Homiletic*, 11. If there is no story that will change, no story has changed: "By locating our storied lives within a framework of beginning and end, Christian preaching poses the possibility of faith" Buttrick, *Homiletic*, 13.

9. Buttrick, *Homiletic*, 258–61.

10. Buttrick, *Captive Voice*, 10.

11. Buttrick, *Preaching the New and Now*, 21.

12. Rose, *Sharing the Word*, ch. 5; McClure, *Roundtable Pulpit*, 51.

13. Rose, *Sharing the Word*, 125.

tion yet further by emphasizing "co-dependency."[14] Rose also claims that sharing openly in a sermon the autobiographical experiences of members of a congregation as a form of public discourse allows believers within the community to re-kindle and manage their own experiences and personal memories of suffering and abuse that have been repressed.[15] McClure calls the form of communication that relies on the unauthoritative and empathic imagination "interchangeable experience."[16]

Some preachers highlight the need to consider social location. Jacquelyn Grant suggests that the experiences related by White Women's Christ and Black Women's Jesus may not be the same.[17] This means that the social location indicates different experiences in the wider and diverse world. Such concerns for social location have continued to shape postcolonial discourse. Postcolonial discourses are related to the voices that have been oppressed and forced into silence by colonial powers. In terms of the agency of voices, it is essential to recognize the social locations of the congregation when preachers project their own theology and values onto a biblical text.[18] Doing so can be a way to respect the congregation's multi-faceted voices and de-centered experiences free from "the limited perspectives of male Eurocentric biblical and theological interpretation."[19] Postcolonial preaching is an endeavor to "find a 'voice' to speak against such an oppressive system" which has created a false identity for the people whose access to power has been denied.[20]

The importance of human experience and the roles of listeners in a sermon have both been criticized for giving precedence to human experience and for ignoring the specificity of the preacher's role.[21] However, the preachers who recognize the importance of listeners and experience have played and continue to play a role in guiding the congregation to participate in preaching in a way that respects their experiences, rather than giving a one-sided answer or compelling a focus on the preacher's own experience.[22] The emphasis on the audience and their experiences has created an

---

14. Rose, *Sharing the Word*, 90. Rose considers a congregation as a community of self-directed interpreters. Rose, *Sharing the Word*, 117.

15. Rose, *Sharing the Word*, 125.

16. McClure, *Other-Wise Preaching*, 51.

17. Grant, *White Women's Christ and Black Women's Jesus*.

18. Allen, *Preaching and the Other*, 75–94.

19. Allen, *Preaching and the Other*, 78.

20. Jimenez, "Toward a Postcolonial Homiletic," 167.

21. Campbell, *Preaching Jesus*, 132; Neal, *Overshadowed Preacher*, 43.

22. Rose, *Sharing the Word*, 92.

opportunity to listen to and lament sufferings and has provided a place for disenfranchised and muted voices, thus expanding the possibility of facing social evil and the reality of suffering in the world. Through bringing into their sermons the voices of multiple experiences, including of suffering, preachers have shown that to develop a sensitivity to humans, to read the Bible through the lens of human experience, and to engage it in that light can be the basis for the proclamation of hope in the realm of death.[23] Such emphasis on listeners and experience is also linked to ethical discourses that are closely related to public crisis and social injustice.

Public Crisis and Social Injustice in Ethical Discourse

Recent homileticians have used ethical views to address social injustices and public crises. This interest has been focused by what has been called the Radical Postmodern school, but is not limited to it. This school pays attention to the ethics of the social suffering that is inflicted on specific groups of society, but it gives relatively little emphasis to God's agency.[24] Ethics-driven preaching is a much broader category and has two outstanding characteristics: a strong sense of social evil, and a communal purpose. These characteristics are found not only in sermons, but in prophetic, pastoral, feminist, liberation, cross-cultural discourses, and in concerns for the crisis of creation. They predominantly establish a dynamic interplay between suffering and hope in preaching, while encouraging the utilization of the inherent potential in both poles.

Prophetic Consciousness

Ethics-centered preaching lays claim to a form of prophetic consciousness. The word, "prophetic" is often used in relation to God's judgment on sins and injustice in the biblical tradition.[25] However, it also encompasses hope (liberation, restoration, salvation, etc.) based on the covenant of God. Abraham Heschel focuses on both doom and hope, arguing that most prophets in the Bible demand not only justice but also "consolation, promise, and the hope of reconciliation."[26] The prophets in the Bible make proclamations

---

23. Powery, *Dem Dry Bones*, 114.
24. Wilson, *Preaching and Homiletical Theory*, 139, 145.
25. Wogaman, *Speaking the Truth in Love*, 3.
26. Heschel, *Prophets*, 12.

about a wider world as well as the life of faith communities.[27] Thus, we may find that prophetic consciousness is based on a communal setting and a sense of polar thought. Prophetic preaching with prophetic consciousness may be related to social and political transformation or judgment and be understood as a message about the kind of worthy and reasonable life required of a people before God will accept their worship (Isa 1:11–17).[28] Though the meaning of prophetic preaching can vary, prophetic preaching may have formed a huge umbrella under which can be included pastoral and social consciousness related to the life/identity/mission/ethic of God's people and their moral concerns with oppression and social evil.[29]

Brueggemann is one of the most insightful voices calling preachers to prophetic witness. Brueggemann's approach to preaching has a dual focus: lament and amazement. For Brueggemann, the prophetic voice is called to build an alternative community and to resist "religion of static triumphalism" and "politics of oppression and exploitation."[30] Brueggemann presents lament as expressing pathos on suffering brought about by the power of death and judgment.[31] Lament, he says, is a cry that penetrates into the apathy and denial of imperialism.[32] Brueggemann considers mourning as an essential community practice (cf. Amos 5:16): "First the prophet states his own grieving. Then he 'goes public' and includes the 'professionals.'"[33] Importantly, Brueggemann not only pays attention to the mourning of the prophet and the people, he also hears the voice of God's mourning overlaid with the voice of the prophet.[34] Then, Brueggemann brings in "the language

27. Wogaman, *Speaking the Truth in Love*, 5.

28. Kim, "Prophetic Preaching," 197. Turner defines prophetic preaching as "a form of proclamation that critically questions the status quo, offers theological insight into the current situation, and challenges people to repent by performing God's justice and extending God's compassion." Turner, "Prophetic Preaching," 101.

29. Brueggemann, *Prophetic Imagination*, xxv. Many preachers, including Wilson, Wogaman, and Allen, have considered prophetic and pastoral preaching as being not in conflict but interrelated. Wilson, *Preaching and Homiletical Theory*, 119; Wogaman, *Speaking the Truth in Love*; Allen, "Relationship Between," 173–90. Stanley Hauerwas argues that prophetic tasks need to be theological and pastoral based on Christology and a community. Hauerwas, "Pastor as Prophet," 158–59.

30. Brueggemann, *Prophetic Imagination*, 3, 7.

31. Brueggemann, *Prophetic Imagination*, 46. Imperial consciousness refers to the system that dominates the world and represses people on the fringes, the system that pursues abundance. It prompts persons to give up their power to move toward a new life. For more details, see chapter 2.

32. Brueggemann, *Prophetic Imagination*, 49.

33. Brueggemann, *Prophetic Imagination*, 53.

34. Brueggemann, *Prophetic Imagination*, 54.

of Amazement" as a language of true novelty that redefines the situation of suffering.[35] This is a subversive language in which God, who seemed helpless, reclaims God's kingship.[36] However, this assertion of God's strength may weaken the idea of a lamenting God, and speaks negatively about God's absence in reference to the times when the powerful God is not experienced. Nevertheless, lament and amazement have given preachers insights into the power and hope of God invading and overcoming the world's power and social injustice.

Walter Burghardt argues that God shows justice in a way that defends the people, punishes covenant violations, and does not forget the forgotten.[37] Burghardt says that God's presence, in which he cares for and responds to suffering, can be proclaimed by reinstating the rights of those who suffer.[38] From his understanding, a preacher betrays the prophetic call if the preached message does not reach all human life, especially the marginalized edges of human life.[39] While he does not specifically identify which people suffer injustice, Burghardt gives witness to various examples of real sufferings and tries to bring them into a sermon as a matter of justice. By contrast, Barbara Lundblad argues that fear should be named and addressed, and that emphasis on grace subsequently becomes the most effective antidote to fear, for it is the assurance of grace that becomes the foundation for change.[40]

Leonora Tubbs Tisdale identifies twelve prophetic preaching forms, including "problem-resolution-new possibility," "question-answers," and "moving from ease to dis-ease."[41] Lament is the eleventh form. Tisdale mentions that the "sermon's appropriate role is to invite the congregation into a place of mourning and weeping in solidarity with those who are suffering."[42] Tisdale presents two sermonic examples that speak of staying in the place of suffering. These sermons can sometimes take place at the time of large national disasters or in sermons on Holy Saturday. Still, inviting people to stay in pain can be difficult and can seem to diminish God's action of redeeming, empowering, and sending healing into the world.

Tisdale speaks of the injustice and suffering caused by this world with a powerful emphasis on "no" in her sermons. By doing so, she reveals what

35. Brueggemann, *Prophetic Imagination*, 67–74.
36. Brueggemann, *Prophetic Imagination*, 70.
37. Burghardt, *Preaching the Just Word*, 3.
38. Burghardt, *Preaching the Just Word*, 56.
39. Burghardt, *Preaching the Just Word*, 58.
40. Lundblad, *Transforming the Stone*, 18, 29.
41. Tisdale, *Prophetic Preaching*, 63–88.
42. Tisdale, *Prophetic Preaching*, 82.

occurs in the violence promoted in the name of silence and obedience.[43] She concludes by encouraging us to find the courage to claim the freedom God has won for us in Christ Jesus, saying "no" to any attempts to hurt or subjugate us.[44] For Phil Snider, preaching as resistance is an attempt to change the world, not simply to portray the pain of the world, and is a collective act of liberation that is rooted in deep solidarity by fostering an experiential place that celebrates the wonders and beauty of God's justice and love.[45] Snider proposes three sermonic elements to deal with social justice: seeing the broken world, experiencing the God who changes, and responding to God's justice and love as a responsibility to the gospel.[46]

Prophetic preaching played an essential role in bringing homiletic attention to those who have been suffered from social injustice. Considering that "suffering is central to the prophetic consciousness," preaching on social justice or crisis issues with prophetic consciousness calls for lament as a form of resistance aimed at dealing with structural suffering.[47] Lament entails expressing and bearing witness to the suffering caused by social injustice before actively resisting it. In this context, lament is inseparable from the individual or community's situation and position in life, connecting lament with pastoral consciousness.

Pastoral Consciousness

In homiletics, sermons focused on pastoral issues have been sometimes been called therapeutic preaching, life-situation preaching, pastoral preaching, and counseling preaching.[48] Pastoral consciousness in preaching places an emphasis on the congregation's needs, especially the concrete problems of suffering, or the challenges of human life.[49] The context of the congregation becomes an important part of a sermon, and the preaching is understood as the dialogue that takes place between the preacher and the congregation.[50]

---

43. Tisdale, "God's No and Ours," 202–3.

44. Tisdale, "God's No and Ours," 204–5.

45. Snider, "Introduction," 3.

46. Snider, "Introduction," 5.

47. Brueggemann, *Prophetic Imagination*, xxix.

48. Such pastoral consciousness in preaching has developed since the 1920s. Coffin, *What To Preach*, 119; Luccock, *In the Minister's Workshop*, 50; Oates, *Christian Pastor*, 110; Kim, "Homiletical Evaluation and Suggestion," 301.

49. Wimberly, *Moving from Shame to Self-Worth*, 16; McKenzie, "Popular Psychology and Preaching," 405.

50. Fosdick, *Living of These Days*, 96.

Donald Capps suggested that pastoral consciousness in preaching shows respect for polar thought in the movement from suffering/trouble to heal/resolve, or from starting with human problems and providing resolutions in the word of God.[51] Pastoral preaching carries the risk of diminishing communal aspects of the preaching. It may seem to suggest that there is a solution for or an answer to all human problems, and sometimes it is possible in such preaching to downplay the power of sin and evil.[52] Yet, highlighting the reality of human suffering and human needs of restoration/healing has also created room for lament in preaching.

Susan Bond maintains that the therapeutic pastoral counseling movement of the mid-1950s introduced human needs as a pastoral concern.[53] Harry Emerson Fosdick developed such an approach to preaching, criticizing a tendency to obsess over textual interpretation, regardless of the context of a congregation.[54] Fosdick recommended that a sermon address the "vital concern" that a congregation faces.[55] Fosdick stressed the importance of understanding the life situation and troubles of a congregation and insisted that sermons address a wide range of social issues beyond personal issues.[56] Wilson assesses Fosdick's sermons as moving "from problem to solution, from quandary to hope, and from primarily intellectual appeal to primarily emotional."[57]

When preaching with pastoral awareness is too focused on how to "treat" the suffering of the congregation, this can diminish the recognition of the complexity of suffering and the power of sin, especially in terms of communal sectors. To be specific, forgiveness is related to a sense of guilt so that many preachers are more focused on guilt than on shame when they preach the crucifixion of Christ or Bible stories. However, when preachers search the biblical text, they find that many scriptures contain a sense of guilt-shame together, as does the book of Lamentations. For example, in

---

51. Fosdick, *Living of These Days*, 97. Capps suggested four stages: identification of the problem; reconstruction of the problem; diagnostic interpretation; and treatment and intervention. Capps, *Pastoral Counseling and Preaching*, ch. 2. Capps brought into and applied the four elements of his counseling session to preaching. Capps, *Pastoral Counseling and Preaching*, 37.

52. Buttrick, *Homiletic*, 277.

53. Bond, *Trouble with Jesus*, 23.

54. Fosdick, *Living of These Days*, 92.

55. Fosdick, "What Is the Matter with Preaching?," 134.

56. Fosdick, "What Is the Matter with Preaching?," 134; Kim, "Homiletical Evaluation and Suggestion," 307.

57. Wilson, *Concise History of Preaching*, 158; see also Macvaugh, "Structural Analysis," 533–34.

addressing the pain associated with the prodigal son, which is entangled with guilt and shame, Neil Pembroke preaches hope not solely through the discourse of forgiveness but also through the discourse of acceptance.[58] Pembroke argues that the prodigal son's shame is appropriately based on his moral failures that resulted in dishonor to himself and his family. The prodigal son considered his father as one who was dead. The son had lost everything and was so hungry he wanted to eat the slops fed to the pigs (Luke 15:13–16).[59] As for the shame, Pembroke shows hope through the act of "acceptance" by bringing the son back into the family and community.[60]

G. Lee Ramsey emphasizes the language of preaching, language that can proclaim salvation from sin, liberation from social injustice and for the healing of wounds, and he does so without overlooking the brokenness of humans who fail to build a caring community.[61] A church as a caring community exists for the "care of each other and the world."[62] Ramsey uses "a Christological motif of suffering-resurrection" as a lens through which a congregation sees the world.[63] The view through this lens helps the congregation to understand the presence of God through the Holy Spirit in social injustice and the gravity of human suffering for those who long for resurrection and redemption.[64] He also argues that it is possible for faith communities to discern that God is on the move in the world through efforts such as the civil rights movement that struggles against social structures that perpetuate injustice.[65]

Kathy Black's *A Healing Homiletic: Preaching and Disability* is distinctive in its prophetic and pastoral approach. She resists traditional interpretations of the disabled, such as understanding disability as punishment for the parents' sin, as a way of glorifying God, or as a "bad example of [what] we should not do," connecting a deaf person and a person who ignores God's call.[66] She challenges biblical literary and metaphorical application on disability in biblical interpretation.[67] Black argues that dealing with suffering

---

58. Pembroke, "Theocentric Therapeutic Preaching," 253.
59. Pembroke, "Theocentric Therapeutic Preaching," 253.
60. Pembroke, "Theocentric Therapeutic Preaching," 254.
61. Ramsey, *Care-Full Preaching*, 81–95.
62. Ramsey, *Care-Full Preaching*, 60. Ramsey argues that a preacher is "the one who spots the problem." Ramsey, *Care-Full Preaching*, 95.
63. Ramsey, *Care-Full Preaching*, 116.
64. Ramsey, *Care-Full Preaching*, 116.
65. Ramsey, *Care-Full Preaching*, 116–17.
66. Black, *Healing Homiletic*, 62.
67. Black, *Healing Homiletic*, 17–22.

requires patience, courage, and inner strength. She sees sufferers as people who are blessed with admirable qualities instead of looking at them as cursed by disabilities.[68] Black broadens the discourse about the disabled to include the poor and the oppressed. She argues that the doctrine of pain redemption becomes "judgment on the powerless and a rationale for injustice" and she instead focuses on "blessed are you."[69] Kathy Black uses a lament lens in her sermon, which addresses pain in people who live with birth and acquired disabilities.[70] Her mourning moves to healing by reminding us of God's nature. Black proclaims that God is not the one who chooses and creates disabilities, and that God is there to give us opportunities to heal and change in every moment of our lives.[71]

A deeper understanding of psychology enables us to have a broader view of the Bible and allows us to understand how to think of the relationship between human suffering and the Bible and how God responds to such human wounds. Also, telling a story of sufferers may support the meaning-making process as a hermeneutical approach, and this creates a link between preaching and pastoral care.[72] Nonetheless, if preachers focus only on personal emotional suffering, they may ignore the power of structural evil and illness and lose sight of a communal sense of pain. Furthermore, if preachers write a sermon by determining a specific issue to address in it, there is a risk that their interpretation of the Bible will be biased or too purpose-oriented.

Feminist/Womanist, Liberation, and Cross-Cultural Discourses

Preaching in regard to social justice issues and public crises can be considered from feminist/womanist, liberation, and cross-cultural perspectives based on the theme of respect for diverse voices and the wholeness of the larger community. Feminist scholars have focused on the issue of oppression experienced within established social structures. These include gender discrimination and violence against women, issues frequently found in the Bible. Basically, women preachers had to fight to reach ordination under an "onslaught of forced resignations, firings, and systematic purges."[73]

---

68. Black, *Healing Homiletic*, 19.
69. Black, *Healing Homiletic*, 21–22.
70. Black, "Why Me?," 192–93.
71. Black, "Why Me?," 197–98.
72. Wimberly, *Moving from Shame to Self-Worth*, 16.
73. Flowers, *Into the Pulpit*, 24.

THE ROLE OF LAMENT IN PREACHING 137

Female preachers insist that sermons respect the voices and experiences of women.[74] They also argue that biblical interpretations need to consider the view of the powerless, especially women who are often overlooked and are treated with silence and oppression.[75] In light of the violence and suffering that real women continue to suffer, feminist theologians have sought alternative metaphors that reject the metaphors of abuse, tolerance of violence, and gender-stereotypes evident in the Bible.[76] Although the feminist approach has resulted in a wide range of biblical interpretations, the basic feminist approach is to employ a hermeneutic of suspicion because, as Elizabeth Schüssler Fiorenza points out, standard biblical interpretations present "a religious justification and ideological legitimization of patriarchy."[77]

Christine Smith starts her preaching with deep lament for violence against women.[78]

> I want to mourn, to remember, to bring to memory, to give voice. I want to graft to my human heart the senseless pain, the violent deaths, the cruel invisibility of all these girls and women throughout time; and I want to do this in some desperate hope that in lamenting the suffering, remembering the forgotten, and speaking the unspeakable, something redemptive, something saving might happen among us.

The sermon laments the interpretation of Jephthah's daughter's loss merely as a tale of Jephthah's faithful obedience (Judg 11:29–40). It also underscores the enduring pain of women, who are still marginalized and disregarded today under male dominance and power. To participate in this suffering, Smith calls on collective lament, drawing a parallel to the solidarity exhibited by the daughters of Israel for Jephthah's daughter. At the end of the sermon, Smith recounts her experience observing the dedication of two nurses at a Nigerian clinic in the sorrowful reality of women and children succumbing due to limited healthcare. Smith posits that the perpetual struggle of not allowing women to perish and of participating in the suffering of the muted is both a form of lamentation and a sacred act. Smith suggests that the ongoing struggle to prevent women from perishing and to

---

74. Smith, *Weaving the Sermon*, 99; Rose, *Sharing the Word*, 97.

75. Claassens, *Mourner*, 98–99.

76. Claassens, *Mourner*, 22.

77. Norén, *Woman in the Pulpit*, 89–90. (1) Biblical feminists use the Bible as a primary source of theology, (2) liberation feminists use liberation theology focused on women liberation, and (3) radical feminists reject both Scripture and tradition because they understand both are too oppressive. In Schüssler Fiorenza, *Bread Not Stone*, xi.

78. Smith, "Unspeakable Loss," 164–69.

engage in the suffering of the silenced is both a form of lamentation and a sacred act: "These Nigerian and German nurses have heard the wailing of the daughters of Israel for Jephthah's daughter and they have joined in the faithful movements, actions, and wordless rituals of their lamenting."[79] Her preaching moves from suffering in the world and in the Bible to hope in human ethical action.

Womanists have raised the discourse of racism and classism beyond sexism.[80] These are Black feminists and feminists of color who are aware of latent racial biases even in feminist circles. Susan Bond, a white scholar, engages in the discourse on Western imperial culture, recognizing the similar experiences of oppression that are common among Asian and African women.[81] Bond also expands the womanist discourse to include cultural specificity through expressing women's suffering in the Third World.[82] Womanists encourage women not to accept passively forced obedience or suffering as beneficial.[83] In the relationship between women and suffering, Asian Womanists project an image of a mother weeping for her children's suffering in the suffering of Jesus.[84] Jesus and mothers are portrayed as people who are accustomed to suffering. A woman is considered to be the one who is able to recognize the violence of oppressors or the suffering of oppressed people and who can understand the suffering of Jesus.[85] In this sense, womanists recast the image of women which has been twisted by social and cultural oppression while placing value on the testimony of women's lives and experiences.[86] Also, this discourse ultimately brings into preaching the kind of womanist rhetoric that truly fights for the integrity and liberation of all

---

79. Smith, "Unspeakable Loss," 169.

80. Walker, *In Search of Our Mothers' Gardens*, xi; Grant, *White Women's Christ and Black Women's Jesus*, 198. Johnson notes that it is imperative for the scope of feminism to include social conditions, namely, a story of similar racism, classism, and sexism. Johnson, *Womanist Preacher*, 108.

81. Bond, *Trouble with Jesus*, 98–106.

82. Bond, *Trouble with Jesus*, 99.

83. St. Clair, "Womanist Criticism," 171.

84. Lee, "One Woman's Confession of Faith," 215. Hong Kong theologian Kwok Pui-lan also points out the similarities between the image of a suffering God and Asian mothers, bringing a mother weeping for her children into theological discourse. Kwok "God Weeps with Our Pain."

85. Lee notes that the action of Maria who poured perfume on Jesus' head was come from the understanding of the reality of Jesus' suffering among women who have suffered and shared more of the suffering of history. Lee, "One Woman's Confession of Faith," 216.

86. Johnson, *Womanist Preacher*, 110.

oppressed people.[87] Womanists use communal "emancipatory praxis" to overcome oppression and to maintain a sense of wholeness.[88] Feminist/womanist and liberation preaching share their key concerns related to the equality of all humans and to liberation from abusive social structures.[89]

Liberation preaching is rooted in liberation theology with "the perspective of the traditionally powerless" as they experience the gospel.[90] Liberation theology emphasizes "praxis" as its "particular struggle and action" against oppressive structures.[91] Analyzing, participating in, and resolving suffering today are their main concerns.[92] Liberation hermeneutics also looks at the Bible through the eyes of the oppressed and emphasizes the message of solidarity, freedom, and liberation.[93] Correspondingly, liberation preaching has a strong ideological sense; Justo and Catherine González argue that biblical interpretation and preaching must have a real intervention in the process of liberation: "The word of the gospel . . . comes to us clearly in the painful groans of the oppressed."[94] They suggest five strategies of preaching and they argue that liberation preachers need to delineate clearly and sharply the relationship between power and the powerless, to identify what is unjust in the Bible within the current historical and political context, and to consider the fact that the Bible may have different perspectives depending on its varied contexts and settings.[95] Thus, "ideological suspicion" and the contemporary situation of suffering and oppression become the center of hermeneutics.[96] In liberation preaching, God is identified as the one who frees us from both oppression and sin.[97] From this perspective, the overly

87. Johnson, *Womanist Preacher*, 124.
88. Allen, *Toward a Womanist Homiletic*, 81.
89. Farris, "Hermeneutics," 34.

90. González and González, *Liberation Preaching*, 13. The liberation concept arose in Latin America, whose people experienced oppression from ideological forces in the 1960s. Jimenez, "Liberation Criticism," 45.

91. González and González, *Liberation Preaching*, 22. Latin American liberation theology prefers the term praxis rather than practice because praxis claims "a commitment with a community of oppressed people, a commitment to struggle for social, economic, and political change." Jimenez, "Liberation Criticism," 46.

92. González and González, *Liberation Preaching*, 106. Jimenez suggests the See-Think-Act strategy. Jimenez, "Liberation Criticism," 46.

93. Jimenez, "Liberation Criticism," 45.

94. González and González, *Liberation Preaching*, 68, 108.

95. González and González, *Liberation Preaching*, 69–93. (1) Ask a political question; (2) Reassign the cast of characters; (3) Imagine a different setting; (4) Consider the direction of the action; (5) Avoid avoidance.

96. González and González, *Liberation Preaching*, 93.

97. Harris, *Preaching Liberation*, 21–22.

simple dichotomy by which the oppressor is evil and the oppressed good, can distort preaching.[98] Nonetheless, when identifying the existing oppression it is also critical to name the social movement that is based on God's intention to make the world a community of justice and love.[99] Carolyn Ann Knight accuses the current era of suffering and oppression presents God's parallel vision of the broken world:[100]

> I submit that what we are experiencing right now—ethnic-cleansing in Bosnia and Mississippi and Arkansas, bombings in New York and Oklahoma, Birmingham and Atlanta; high unemployment, no health care, poor child care, insecure social security, babies dangling from bridges, babies with bullets, children with guns, run-away teenage pregnancy, children with no hope, mothers who can't cope, fathers on dope; more black men in jail than in college; women forgotten too soon; men gone too soon; children dying too soon; sisters waiting to exhale; brothers trying to get paid; heroes becoming zeroes; many of us kept out, kicked out, knocked out, locked out, pushed out, put out, pulled out, phased out; the hopelessness and despair that pervade sour communities—what we are experiencing right now is an aberration. We are wandering in a wilderness called the United States. This is not who we really are.[101]

Knight's liberation preaching names, ponders, and liberates the oppressed identity.[102] And then, liberating preaching encourages a congregation to take on a new identity and to participate in deep devotion empowered by God.

> But you have to travel farther than the slave ship, segregation, and second-class citizenship to know who we are. . . . We need to remember the great ancient cities that we built; the many contributions that we made to science and medicine, literature, the arts, religion, business. . . . We must never forget that God has always done great things through Africans. Weare formed out of adversity. From it we have fashioned our unique perspective on humanity and divinity. . . . You are a great people. You have an internal mechanism to help re store our families, save our babies, empower our women, and reclaim our men. More than

---

98. Allen, *Patterns of Preaching*, 224.
99. Allen, *Patterns of Preaching*, 223–24.
100. Knight, "If Thou Be a Great People," 226.
101. Knight, "If Thou Be a Great People," 227.
102. Knight, "If Thou Be a Great People," 227.

that, we have an Eternal Motivator who is with us. . . . God never sends us where God has not already been. . . . Jesus has already met the challenge. "On a hill far away stood and and old rugged cross, the emblem of suffering and shame." Jesus went into the hill country and made it a highway to heaven.[103]

In the realm of the suffering experienced by individuals/communities facing oppression and marginalization, the immigrant context grapples with intersectional oppressions akin to the context of feminist, womanist, and liberation preaching. Lamentation readily surfaces in certain cross-cultural preaching, as the backdrop of suffering stemming from various power dynamics frequently intertwines with the struggle to survive within distinct social locations and diverse socio-cultural structures. These must take into account differences in gender, age, race, and theology.[104] Nieman and Rogers suggest a form of lament and praise as cross-cultural strategies to "validate that every portion of our lives can be honestly brought before God and will be met by divine mercy."[105] Matthew Kim suggests that people are looking for opportunities to lament because of the pain of society, insisting that preaching should have 'contextual compassion' by revealing silent pain and creating a place for the voice.[106] Kim argues that preachers need to respect others' suffering, not to judge, and not mitigate quickly or disregard congregations' suffering.[107] Kenneth Davis argues that preachers should listen to the lament of people as preparation for preaching because the Hispanic tradition values the connection between faith and life.[108] In a sermon about violence and suffering arising from being "different," John McClure encourages the congregation to abandon using its strength to dominate each other and instead to empty themselves in imitation of Christ's self-giving way.[109]

> We are different. This is the human condition. It is both beautiful and tragic. It is beautiful because it opens spaces for endless varieties of creative relationships. It is tragic because the simple, beautiful differences between us can become a door through which evil can enter—an evil that turns benign difference into malignant alienation. How does this happen? It happens as we

---

103. Knight, "If Thou Be a Great People," 227–28, 230.
104. Nieman and Rogers, *Preaching to Every Pew*, 146.
105. Nieman and Rogers, *Preaching to Every Pew*, 151.
106. Kim, *Preaching with Cultural Intelligence*, 144–45, 175.
107. Kim, *Preaching with Cultural Intelligence*, 59.
108. Davis, "Cross-Cultural Preaching," 40.
109. McClure, "Alienation > Emptying > Compassion," 250.

lose sight of the face of the other. We lose sight of the other person as vulnerable and fragile—as we are.[110]

In feminist/womanist and liberation preaching, lament is a form of naming and resisting the absurdity of injustice as a way to deal with suffering. Since cross-cultural preaching deals with the pain arising from the perception of cultural differences and vulnerabilities that come from those differences, lament in cross-cultural preaching is a means of expressing suffering and calling out for solidarity and respect for that beautiful diversity.

The three streams of preaching related to public suffering and crisis are closely linked to the praxis and Christian ethics or calling. These ethical approaches typically are biased in favor of the oppressed and are based on a procedural approach requiring fairness.[111] Such sermons, when focused only on human action, may seem to ignore the God who laments, moves, and redeems the sufferers, the oppressed, and the muted. However, these approaches do let us see how the various theological-homiletical concerns about the oppressed and social injustice have addresses suffering. Here, lament not only works as a resistance to injustice but also leads the congregation to hope as well as to participate in suffering by revealing, naming, and remembering the suffering, and showing God's willingness to rectify the world. In this way it enables us to see the image of God who laments with and for sufferers.

Suffering and Nature

A few scholars speak of suffering and nature in terms of lament. For example, Elizabeth Achtemeier deals with the antagonism between nature and the human species, and she presents the pain of creation as an ethical realm. Achtemeier finds that some relationships cause suffering: humans can and do damage nature (cf. 1 Sam 17:37; 1 Kgs 20:36; 21:19; 22:38), and nature can hurt humans (Ps 91:13). Some passages in biblical scripture give witness to how God protects humans against the threats of nature (Ps 91:12–13), whereas God also at times uses nature as a tool for judgment (Jer 5:5–6; 15:3; Ezek 5:17).[112] Achtemeier rejects the interpretation of natural disasters as punishment for sin, but she urges us to repentance and to turn our lives to God because she understands that humans and the world have fallen

---

110. McClure, "Alienation > Emptying > Compassion," 251.
111. Campbell, "Ethics," 116.
112. Achtemeier, *Nature, God, and Pulpit*, 107–8.

captive to the power of sin.[113] This shadow side of our captivity has made all creation lament for salvation (Rom 8:22).

John C. Holbert says that non-human creation mourns the same way as human beings do: "the groaning world might find release from its pain, giving birth to a new world of hope for all of God's cosmos, loved and redeemed by Jesus Christ."[114] This reminds us that salvation is intended for the entire cosmos. If preachers regard the destruction of nature as God's action, they can overlook the fact that much of nature's suffering has been caused by humans. In this context, a more inclusive approach is needed—to preach lament by crying, repenting, and renewing.

Preaching that stresses ethics or praxis has a relatively connection with lament.[115] This is because the sermons mostly move to hope or liberation by telling about the power of death and expressing anger before injustice "with the tears of grief and lament."[116] Specifically, communal laments have built a vital channel to overcome grief when a community falls into grief by understanding the painful situation and by expressing another way of faith.[117] This is because communal lament includes "invocation of the divine presence, explanation of the community's complaint, confession of trust in God, supplication for help" as well as being a voice for social action in the public square.[118] However, sermons that emphasize mainly moral behavior may weaken the aspect of revelation and may regard preaching as a social function or regard the gospel as righteousness based on praxis, leaving God out.[119] Also, the dichotomy between the oppressor and the oppressed can make people feel hostile to "people" rather than to the power of the world or evil. Besides, ethics or praxis is not a definitive solution or liberation for the oppressed. Thus, including lament in preaching for social justice and public crisis needs to draw out the pain of the world, to converse with God about pain of every possible kind, from anger and mourning, to tears and doubt, in our effort to reveal what God does in it, and to be invited to engage in God's work to rectify all wrongs with the guidance and aid of the Holy Spirit.

---

113. Achtemeier, *Nature, God, and Pulpit*, 109, 144.
114. Holbert, *Preaching Creation*, 64.
115. Brown and Miller, "Introduction," in *Lament*, xv.
116. Campbell, *Word before the Powers*, 119, 187.
117. Allen and Bartholomew, *Preaching Verse by Verse*, 128.
118. Allen and Bartholomew, *Preaching Verse by Verse*, 128.
119. Wilson, *Preaching and Homiletical Theory*, 140, 145; Campbell, "Ethics," 115.

The Holy Spirit and Creation's Suffering

The Epistle to the Romans witnesses to the Holy Spirit as God who laments for the suffering of all creation with inexpressible groans (8:26). Here, lament can be expressed as God's pathos and solidarity with those who are in pain and the Holy Spirit connects human lament and divine lament as a power to encourage people to lament. In this sense, understanding the Holy Spirit as the God who weeps with sufferers gives us a way to deal with the communal experience of suffering in our preaching.

Preachers in the African American tradition have put special emphasis on the importance of the Holy Spirit in preaching.[120] The Holy Spirit has been considered "not the Spirit as a principle of divine activity in human history, but as a very present help in the time of weakness . . . blending his sighs and groans with the persisting will of God."[121] The historical and cultural enslavement experienced by the African American community is a painful example of the experience of suffering.[122] The story of God is a liberation story which gives the African American community a sense of freedom and promises delivery from oppression. The unique and communal suffering experience of African American communities has influenced the way their communities understand the Bible and apply it to their lives.[123] Preaching has made an important contribution to the way in which the African American community deals with suffering thanks to their understanding of the working of the Holy Spirit.

For Henry Mitchell, the Holy Spirit is the one who brings "the supreme celebrative experience" and "an experiential encounter with the Word."[124] Mitchell urges preachers to be sensitive to "the primacy of need" for those who are trapped in human predicaments, regarding the weekly celebration as a word and gospel experience.[125] His sermons move from life situations/hardship to celebration. Frank Thomas's sermon form is similar in composition to Wilson's four pages of the sermon in its structural contexts because he finds "bad news" and "good news" in the text and in our time.[126] Thomas also has a behavioral purpose statement and celebration that goes beyond

---

120. Thomas understands preaching as "a spiritual gift." Thomas, *They Like to Never Quit Praisin' God*, 30.

121. Forbes, *Holy Spirit and Preaching*, 73.

122. Holmes, *Joy Unspeakable*, 55–56; Wilson, *Setting Words on Fire*, 135.

123. LaRue, *Heart of Black Preaching*, 1.

124. Mitchell, *Recovery of Preaching*, 67; Mitchell, *Celebration and Experience*, 11.

125. Mitchell, *Recovery of Preaching*, 142.

126. Thomas, *They Like to Never Quit Praisin' God*, 122–23.

this four-page structure.[127] In this movement, the Holy Spirit enables a congregation to experience the transformation of grief and loss through the assurance of grace.[128]

For James H. Harris, the Holy Spirit is a spirit of liberation, which he understands as a God who is present in our real lives and actions, helping us out of our suffering.[129] Though lament is not expressed as a work of the Spirit, Harris refers to lament and trust as characteristics of a relationship with God.[130] Harris claims that every situation in pain should be recognized as torment and those who suffer should cry out for God's help: "when the preacher speaks of God, people cry and shout, weep and mourn, believing that God is able to do all things."[131] Harris argues that it is necessary to worship and to proclaim Christ as the truth in order to move from torment to tranquility.[132] The understanding of the Holy Spirit's work in preaching was explored as lament by black preachers, especially Luke Powery.

Otis Moss III, Barbara Holmes, Luke Powery, and Cleophus LaRue discover that the celebration has a need to recover an understanding of lament, to prevent the disappearance of the lament tradition.[133] Powery argues that lament is essential in effectively preaching the gospel because it is an expression of the Holy Spirit.[134] The Holy Spirit animates hope, embraces death, and is a source of freedom to support those who suffer, who are associated with the suffering, and who support the oppressed.[135] Also, the Holy Spirit is a source of strong hope that represents God's intervention and work, and is a being who shows divine agency in hope.[136] To Powery, the Holy Spirit possesses the power of language that creates new reality.[137] Preaching is an expression of the Spirit as movement from lament (crucifixion) to celebration (resurrection).[138] This is what LaRue calls the "emotive

---

127. Thomas, *They Like to Never Quit Praisin' God*, 123.

128. Thomas, *They Like to Never Quit Praisin' God*, 86.

129. Thomas, *They Like to Never Quit Praisin' God*, 33, 38.

130. Harris, *Preaching Liberation*, 23.

131. Harris, *Preaching Liberation*, 22, 108.

132. Harris, *Preaching Liberation*, 109–10.

133. Moss, *Blue Note Preaching*, 4; Holmes, *Joy Unspeakable*, 95; Powery, *Spirit Speech*, 35; LaRue, *Rethinking Celebration*, 25–26.

134. Powery, *Spirit Speech*, 35.

135. Powery, *Spirit Speech*, 51, 78.

136. Powery, *Dem Dry Bones*, 100.

137. Neal, *Overshadowed Preacher*, 39.

138. Powery, "Holy Spirit/Passion," 310.

movement."¹³⁹ Holmes moves lament to ritual empowerment: "crisis contemplation emerges in two situations that require ritual lament and one instance of ritual empowerment."¹⁴⁰ The African American traditions tend to blend lament and celebration in one song, and Crawford calls this trend the bitter-sweet flavor or trouble-glory fusion.¹⁴¹ As Harris states, "black preaching is indeed exciting and jubilant, but it is also sad and reflective. It represents the ebb and flow of the Holy Spirit that correlates with the ups and downs of life."¹⁴²

In preaching, lament that appears as the action of the Holy Spirit can be argued to enable listeners to express pain without being silent and allows them to understand the God who laments with us, beyond a mere emotional thing.¹⁴³ Ultimately, lament has functioned as a transitional stage in a movement toward celebration, resolution, and healing.

Theodicy and Suffering

Looking through a theological lens, we see that Christian lament is deeply connected to repentance for sin and the power of evil in the world, though the specifics have changed with the advance of scientific knowledge.¹⁴⁴ Medieval society believed God to be the cause of all suffering.¹⁴⁵ Due to the "irrationality and inexplicability of innocent suffering," the deadly Lisbon earthquake disaster in 1755 not only challenged faith in a loving and powerful God but also raised questions about God's reign.¹⁴⁶

Thomas Long argues that God does not cause the suffering maliciously and that evil is a mysterious power that human beings cannot explain and control. Long rejects the idea that all suffering is the result of the misuse of human free will. He denies that sin or evil is necessary for "soul-making" in order to accomplish a higher good.¹⁴⁷ Long presents lament, or the cry unto God, as natural for preachers. It is a Christian's deep reaction to sin and evil and is a turn to God in pain and protest.¹⁴⁸ Long argues that preachers

---

139. LaRue, *Rethinking Celebration*, 14–15.
140. Holmes, *Joy Unspeakable*, 65.
141. Crawford, *Hum*, 67–68.
142. Harris, *Preaching Liberation*, 52.
143. Mitchell, *Celebration and Experience in Preaching*, 19–20.
144. Steimle, "Preaching and the Biblical Story," 211.
145. Long, *What Shall We Say?*, 6.
146. Long, *What Shall We Say?*, 17, 21.
147. Long, *What Shall We Say?*, 69, 75, 77.
148. Long, *What Shall We Say?*, 125–26.

should abandon efforts to justify innocent suffering or come to a theological resolution about suffering, but instead should consider God's suffering in Christ.[149] "God's power has ultimately to articulate itself in divine solidarity with the sufferer; that is, in the weakness of suffering love," he says.[150]

Jürgen Moltmann says, "in the wider sense of salvation as the overcoming of death and the raising to eternal life, people are healed not through Jesus' miracles, but through Jesus' wounds; that is, they are gathered into the indestructible love of God."[151] In this respect, lament has provided a response to theodicy. Lament is another form of theology and is a form of language available to those who harbor unanswerable questions about pain and envision a silent God whom they see as the ultimate light of hope.

Lectionaries and Suffering

Holmes insists that Black tradition seems to have forgotten how to lament and repent, noting that it is hard to find lament in Black worship, even during Holy Week.[152] Given Lamentations and lament psalms in lectionaries, the lectionary volume titled "Year C" has the most lament scripts (about 37 percent of the total psalms recited for that year). It is not a negligible percentage; however, lament in the pulpit can be challenging to find, often overlooked either due to the difficulty in properly interpreting suffering or the tendency to quickly pass over it. Allen argues that some texts with suffering can be "ethically or theologically problematic."[153] Lectionaries appear to steer clear of many controversial texts, often excluding the most challenging parts, such as the ending of Psalm 137, which implores God to dash their babies against rocks.[154] Similarly, for the book of Lamentations, Chapter 3 is predominantly included because it contains elements of hope and praise, diverging from the tone found in the book's other chapters.

Although lament is a custom in the Christian Bible, lament may not have held an important place in pulpits, leaving the impression that preaching suffering was only loosely associated with lament. However, a part of the tradition and practices as verified by recent homiletic scholarship confirms that lament in sermons has been shaped not only by dealing with personal

149. Long, *What Shall We Say?*, 45, 56, 64.
150. Hall, *God and Human Suffering*, 156.
151. Moltmann, *Way of Jesus Christ*, 110.
152. Holmes, *Joy Unspeakable*, 70.
153. Allen, *Sermon Tracks*, 54–55.
154. Allen, *Sermon Tracks*, 55. In terms of communal lament as anger related to Psalm 137, see Ku, "Lament as Resistance and Rage," 7–12.

suffering or repentance but by dealing with the power of evil and suffering in the world. In many respects, lament has been used as a meaningful medium to deal with pain.

FEATURES OF THE NEW HOMILETIC THAT SUPPORT LAMENT

The New Homiletic has a variety of features—narrative, imagination, and metaphor—that together have contributed to developing and supporting lament. Lament has been understood as a language of the gospel in the dynamics of suffering and hope through stories, images, metaphors, symbols, saga, sermons, songs, letters, and poems.[155]

Narrative and Suffering

Alasdair MacIntyre points out that narrative is a basic and essential genre for the characterization of human behavior.[156] Because we all live the narratives that make up our lives, we understand our own life from the perspective of the narrative we live in, and the narrative is suitable for understanding others.[157] It is not surprising, therefore, that religious experience takes a narrative form.[158] Also, narrative has a strong communal character: "Narrative of any one life is part of an interlocking set of narratives."[159] It expands into history. In fact, a significant portion of our cognitive processes can be narrative-dependent.[160] Specifically, since evil is inexplicable, it has to demand a form other than a causal explanation. Here, narrative may be the only form capable of showing behavior without explanation.[161] Thus, narrative works as a large umbrella that gathers under it several different and interrelated forms.[162] This feature is also applicable to the homiletic field.

---

155. Rutledge, *Crucifixion*, 9.
156. MacIntyre, "Virtues," 94.
157. MacIntyre, "Virtues," 97.
158. Metz, "Short Apology of Narrative," 255.
159. MacIntyre, "Virtues," 103.
160. Hauerwas and Burrell, "From System to Story," 168.
161. Hauerwas and Burrell, "From System to Story," 181.
162. Campbell, *Preaching Jesus*, 120.

Plot in Narrative

In the context of preaching, narrative as a plot has been actively developed by New Homiletic scholars because it allows a sermon to have a sense of movement, like a journey, and it generates an experience. Narrative plots have "continuity and movement."[163] As Wilson argues, the gospel is a movement, not an abstraction or a static thing, and through its movement it seeks to answer theological questions.[164] In Eugene Lowry's understanding of plot, based on Aristotle, many narratives begin with contradiction or conflict, proceed to struggle, and finally end with resolution after a reversal.[165] Lowry's plot structure intensely engages congregations to the extent "when it gets worse to some point of no return."[166] This complication stage takes listeners to the point of getting lost before being found.[167] Lowry's plot structure may allocate a place for lament within the narrative, positioning it as a role in confronting the inherent loss and evil in the world. This goes beyond regarding lament merely as a tool for explaining or justifying suffering on the path to hope. This is because the complication that occurs in the second stage "deepens the grasp of the symptom of human malady," rather than focusing on a solution to theological or biblical conflict.[168] Eslinger determines that the diagnosis in the second (complication) stage is essential because through it human problems and the answers of the gospel can be correlated.[169] Lowry also suggests a "strategic delay," which refutes a sudden jump to a conclusion.[170] In this regard, the plot seems to reserve lament as the place where the suffering can be considered in depth.

David Buttrick says that to preach God's work preachers need opposition from human experience or the scriptures, such as the absence of God, suffering, confusion, and misunderstanding.[171] Fred Craddock argues that once a sermon awakens fear or desire in the inner flow of human beings, preachers can speak reliably and graciously about it.[172] And Wilson says that "moving from trouble to grace helps ensure that grace is strong and

---

163. Lowry, *Homiletic Plot*, 16.
164. Wilson, *Four Pages*, 149–50, 189.
165. Lowry, *Sermon*, 23.
166. Lowry, *Sermon*, 68–69.
167. Lowry, *Sermon*, 70.
168. Lowry, *Sermon*, 68–69.
169. Eslinger, *Web of Preaching*, 37.
170. Lowry, "Narrative Renewed," 62–63.
171. Buttrick, *Homiletic*, 30, 44–46.
172. Craddock, *Preaching*, 87.

reinforces the overall movement of the faith," because the movement can be shaped into a form that reveals a strong need for grace when dealing with suffering.[173] Wilson recommends that lament be employed in the first half of a sermon.[174] As something with a critical role in the movement from "suffering to hope," lament has not always been noticeable in pulpits. Yet the movement—such as from trouble to grace, from conflict to unfolding, from oppression to liberation, or from wounds to healing—does make room for lament.

Storytelling to Communicate the Experience of Others

Many scholars testify to the benefit of storytelling as a way to deal with suffering and to make sense of hope in suffering. As Joni Sancken notes, a story allows listeners to resonate with others and with God's actions in their lives.[175] Charles Rice says that liturgies and stage plays have something in common in that they have a "combination of tragedy and the comic." Thus in sermons stories can serve as a suitable container for lament and hope through the mutual resonance of the story's participants.[176] Wilson says the story is the first direct record of pain and injustice, that it enables reflection on the experience, and that it breaks down barriers to others.[177] Metz argues that a story is not an artificial and private composition, but is aimed at social criticism, and that the narrative memory of salvation in history allows both the history of pain and salvation to be expressed without being diminished.[178]

Biblical narratives are no exception. Eslinger observes that the Bible's authors use the narrative form to resolve problems of theology and suffering, such as the righteous cry (Job 21:7).[179] This is because, rather than debating right and wrong, narrative includes a variety of ideas.[180] Eslinger notes that apocalyptic literature with images of suffering and calamity also

---

173. Wilson, *Preaching and Homiletical Theory*, 98.
174. Wilson, *Setting Words on Fire*, 135.
175. Sancken, *Stumbling over the Cross*, 196.
176. Rice, "Theater and Preaching," 19.
177. Wilson, *Imagination of the Heart*, 205–6.
178. Metz, "Short Apology of Narrative," 256, 258.
179. Eslinger, *Web of Preaching*, 72.

180. Hauerwas and Burrell, "From System to Story," 169. The discourse of abortion is much more complicated than the question of right and wrong with the basic moral principle that all life is sacred. Its narrative contains such complexity. Wilson argues that stories are often the way to hear difficult problems without hostility, while the language of persuasion can approach pain abstractly or ignore the suffering. Wilson, *Imagination of the Heart*, 203–4.

gives hope and courage to the faithful in times of tribulation and reveals its meaning through a solid connection with the narrative.[181] Theissen also argues that the hidden God and the revealed God work more appropriately within the narrative "than any abstract theodicy."[182] Storytelling in preaching, thus, contributes to making emotional, spatial, and temporal sense of lament, leading listeners to wait for the hope that comes from God.

Although narrative preaching may not guarantee lament and can be vague in terms of expressing the theological or doctrinal causes of lament and the source of hope, a narrative can function effectively in sermons as a tool by which to testify. It does not explain or judge suffering and can communicate hope in the midst of suffering. As a result, preachers invite the participation of listeners with truthfulness through the universality of painful stories.[183] In addition, the narrative draws human suffering into God's salvation story.[184] Narrative in the pulpit has included various stories of suffering in order to bring hope to the places where there is sorrow.

Metaphor, Analogy, and Suffering

The dictionary definition of metaphor is "an expression that describes a person or object by referring to something that is considered to possess similar characteristics."[185] Metaphor connects by conveying meaning from a word, image, idea, or situation to another word, image, idea, or situation. Metaphor is basically movement between these two poles. George Lakoff notes that metaphors are not merely verbal expressions, but the spiritual experience of linkages that, because they are based on our familiar world, enable us to access difficult situations or hidden meanings.[186] Moreover, when such expansion of self-experience deals indirectly with inner problems, then symbols and metaphors offer some healing effects.[187]

Various metaphors are also found frequently in the Bible and have been used in sermons for effective gospel communication since the New Homiletic stream began (and of course long before!). As figurative language

---

181. Eslinger, *Web of Preaching*, 72–73.
182. Theissen, *Sign Language of Faith*, 76.
183. Hauerwas and Burrell, "From System to Story," 168, 173.
184. Hauerwas and Burrell, "From System to Story," 183; Metz, "Short Apology of Narrative," 258.
185. Cambridge Dictionary, s.v. "Metaphor," https://dictionary.cambridge.org/dictionary/english/metaphor.
186. Lakoff and Johnson, *Metaphors We Live By*, 7.
187. Jung, "Metaphor," 217.

tools, analogy functions in a sermon in a manner similar to simile and metaphor: it draws a comparison between two things. An analogy involving stories functions like an extended metaphor. Thus, in a sermon, metaphor and analogy are closely related.

Lamentations, for instance, is full of metaphors of grief, and a preacher can take a motherless metaphor from among them and develop a sermon. Susan Bond forms her entire sermon by comparing people who have become "emotionally homeless" in postmodern reality to a state where everything is captured in a period of exile. "In Isaiah's world, everybody is on hold and hopeless. There's no safe place anymore. They're convinced that the world is in trouble, but they feel helpless to change things. They want a place where they can lock the doors and make the world go away"[188] The postmodern era is compared to the biblical exile era and this metaphor explains the characteristics of the period. According to Buttrick, all approaches to the mystery of God are metaphorical.[189] Buttrick says specific images are used symbolically for the poem of liberation and hope, but they imply the language of reality that we can see and understand.[190] An analogy can also be used in a creative way to understand inductive movements.[191] Craddock noted the possibility that analogies derived from others' lives can be applied to the lives of the congregations as a way of learning that expands or reveals experiences, although analogies may not provide conclusive evidence for the resolution of a sermon.[192]

Wilson pairs metaphor in sermons with metonymy.[193] Metaphor and metonymy are two important kinds of non-propositional thought processes in which different meanings are related.[194] Roman Jakobson says that one of these two relationships will emerge at every language level.[195] Metonymy generates chains of thought through repeating words or images. It helps the multiple episodes to unify, connect, and develop into a single idea.[196] Metonymy in sermons establishes history, tradition, lasting revelation, and hope for the future.[197] It is used to reinforce theological expression, con-

---

188. Bond, "Coming Home," 66–67.
189. Buttrick, *Preaching the New and Now*, 121.
190. Buttrick, *Preaching the New and Now*, 124.
191. Craddock, *As One without Authority*, 59.
192. Craddock, *As One without Authority*, 60.
193. Wilson, *Practice of Preaching*, 221.
194. Taylor, "Category Extension by Metonymy and Metaphor," 324.
195. Jakobson, "Metaphoric and Metonymic Poles," 43.
196. Wilson, *Practice of Preaching*, 227.
197. Wilson, *Practice of Preaching*, 231.

necting the sign of God with the greater truth, connecting an idea or image with a larger Christian story, and transcending space and time.[198]

By contrast, metaphor unites two things that may not normally be related to evoke new and fresh ideas through forming a third identity, the product of the tension between them.[199] To be specific, the stories of those who have experienced God's forgiveness can act as a metaphor for God's forgiveness and a story of finding social justice can become a metaphor for "demonstrations of God overturning the world, making the impossible possible."[200]

In this regard, metaphor and analogy have made our "conceptual boundaries" elastic and permeable.[201] They have enabled preachers to use appropriate words to express their thoughts, attitudes, and feelings, to dismantle the existing frame, and to express tension.[202] Metaphor and analogy have functioned not only to express and reveal pain but also to dismantle the dichotomous border between pain and hope, or between the future and present, fostering dynamics between the polarities.

Imagination/Image and Suffering

A preacher tries to bring biblical scenes alive, to capture people's needs today, and to demonstrate faith. Imagination is needed for this—the ability to see the familiar in new ways. Imagination is sometimes used in a negative way to picture something that is not true.[203] However, imagination also allows us "to see this world as it is, with Christ in the midst of our brokenness," and it gives us the ability to imagine "a world already transfigured by Christ's love, already penetrated by the new order."[204] Barbara Brown Taylor suggests that the main function of the church is to imagine, and that this act of imagination enables us to form a mental picture of the self, of neighbors, of the world, and of the future, and to picture a new reality.[205] The power of imagination can similarly work the power of reality, and it can bring a physical change to the person who imagines it. Just as a vivid depiction of a ship in a storm can evoke a sense of nausea in the reader, as if they were

198. Wilson, *Practice of Preaching*, 231–34.
199. Wilson, *Four Pages*, 68–69.
200. Wilson, *Four Pages*, 196.
201. Black, "More about Metaphor," 33.
202. Black, "More about Metaphor," 22–23.
203. Craddock, *As One without Authority*, 77.
204. Wilson, *Imagination of the Heart*, 16.
205. Taylor, *Preaching Life*, 39.

standing on the deck of that ship. Therefore, Taylor notes that imagination can bring about changes in our lives beyond affecting just ourselves.[206] "To believe that is an act of faith, which is an imaginative act."[207]

Craddock noted that preaching requires evocative images that play a role in recreating experiences and insights.[208] Craddock argued that imagination and hope are related to each other, but that imagination needs to reflect reality and not fantasy.[209] For example, rather than abolishing the image of pain and replacing it with hope, preachers have a new perspective and image of pain. Thus, Warren Wiersbe claims that presenting biblical pictures of death can comfort people while maintaining their connection to the new day.[210] According to Brueggemann, the imaginative task of the preacher is to grasp the promise of the newness of God that is still working in our history and to draw it into the hearts of the audience.[211] To do so, he says that preachers should create symbols that can reveal the future through their imaginations, publicly express hope and aspirations, and use language that is specific.[212] The following sermon excerpt by Martin Luther King, Jr. shows a notable example of imagination in preaching:

> [Lament] But one hundred years later, the Negro still is not free. One hundred years later, the life of the Negro is still sadly crippled by the manacles of segregation and the chains of discrimination. One hundred years later, the Negro lives on a lonely island of poverty in the midst of a vast ocean of material prosperity. One hundred years later, the Negro is still languished in the corners of American society and finds himself an exile in his own land. . . . [Hope with imagination] And so let freedom ring from the prodigious hilltops of New Hampshire. Let freedom ring from the mighty mountains of New York. Let freedom ring from the heightening Alleghenies of Pennsylvania. Let freedom ring from the snow-capped Rockies of Colorado. Let freedom ring from the curvaceous slopes of California. But not only that: Let freedom ring from Stone Mountain of Georgia. Let freedom ring from Lookout Mountain of Tennessee. Let freedom ring from every hill and molehill of Mississippi. From

---

206. Taylor, *Preaching Life*, 44.

207. Taylor, *Preaching Life*, 46.

208. Craddock borrows Heidegger's expression. Macquarrie, *Martin Heidegger*, 48, quoted by Craddock, *As One without Authority*, 77.

209. Craddock, *As One without Authority*, 79–80.

210. Wiersbe, *Preaching and Teaching with Imagination*, 252.

211. Brueggemann, *Prophetic Imagination*, 62.

212. Brueggemann, *Prophetic Imagination*, 63–67.

every mountainside, let freedom ring.... Free at last! Free at last! Thank God Almighty, we are free at last!²¹³

Images are also important in preaching. Indeed, Buttrick claims that "Homiletic thinking is always a thinking of theology toward images."²¹⁴ Image is the ability to bring objects in the world to the mind and through them to mediate perception and recognition by opening the self (one's own or another person's) to the world.²¹⁵ Images are like work that gives meaning through imagination.²¹⁶ Imagination comes from hope; imagination and hope are closely related.²¹⁷ Brueggemann points to the images used in the Gospel of Matthew of a Father God who is a creator and has arranged the world in abundance, and to Isaiah's images of a Mother God who is feeding the child.²¹⁸ And using this, he brings the image of orphan into the situation of the audience. "We begin to worry about having enough stuff as if we were fatherless, about being forgotten as if we were motherless. And we begin to think only of ourselves, and we readily become scavengers.... [W]e take what belongs to others, doing damage to the body politic because we think only of ourselves and our survival and well-being."²¹⁹ Brueggemann then shows the audience the image of our world against the image of God's world. "It occurs to me that our society now is a place of anxiety and threat and selfishness and narcissism and self-indulgence, as though we were fatherless without resources and motherless and forgotten."²²⁰ Brueggemann overthrows the image of orphan: "This is the news. We are not orphans."²²¹

This declaration means that though we have lived as orphans according to the world's values, now we can imagine and live a new life because of God's values. The proclamation becomes a new language that is in complete contrast to the previous language and digs into people's imagination "This is an extraordinary mandate given to the sons and daughters of the mother-father God, to break the vicious cycles of orphanhood in the world.... It occurs to me that those who have mother and father, those who have been honored, beloved ... are able to ... care about the whole family and the

---

213. King, "I Have a Dream," xi–xvii.
214. Buttrick, *Homiletic*, 29.
215. Warnock, *Imagination*, 10.
216. Eslinger, *Web of Preaching*, 251.
217. Craddock, *As One without Authority*, 79–80.
218. Brueggemann, "Orphans Come Home," 60–63.
219. Brueggemann, "Orphans Come Home," 61.
220. Brueggemann, "Orphans Come Home," 61.
221. Brueggemann, "Orphans Come Home," 62.

whole neighborhood and the whole sweep of the community."²²² Through Isaiah's message proclaimed, people can imagine a new life not as an orphan, and through that imagination they gain the power to live an entirely different life in the face of particular realities of the world. Brueggemann might expect listeners to confess with him: "I have this image of a child who lies down at night safe, beloved, at rest, remembered by mother, protected by father, unanxious."²²³

Imagination and image have contributed to preaching. The images of mourning have been used in various sermons to deal with the reality of suffering and have played a role in reinforcing the call for new images to overthrow suffering and leading them to imagine a new world. However, there are also challenges in using images and imagination to deal with pain. For example, in Brueggemann's sermon above, image and imagination might hurt those hearers who are actually orphans and those whose homes are not safe due to domestic violence or child abuse, because the sermon pictures a home as a safe place. Kathy Black likewise cautions us about using certain physical images of some people to describe the sinful behavior of others, in so doing perhaps unwittingly ascribing sin to persons with disabilities.²²⁴ Therefore, using imagination and images for preaching hope in suffering needs to be done circumspectly and thoughtfully.

Dramatic Tension and Suffering

Lament functions as a transitional space facilitating the movement from "lament to hope," offering a way of being between suffering and hope. Sally Brown articulates a rhetoric of lament as a "cry of anguish, cry of resistance, or theological interrogation," ultimately evolving into a whisper of hope.²²⁵ The gospel holds both suffering and hope without nullifying either one. By generating a sermonic tension between the two poles, as in metaphor, tension mirrors and creates the reality of suffering and can draw it into a sermonic plot or movement toward hope. In inductive preaching, tension is established at the beginning of a sermon by raising a question or describing an event that needs to be resolved.²²⁶ A narrative plot in preaching starts with a conflict or a discrepancy and then goes deeply into a complication.²²⁷

222. Brueggemann, "Orphans Come Home," 62.
223. Brueggemann, "Orphans Come Home," 63.
224. Black, *Healing Homiletic*, 62.
225. Brown, "When Lament Shapes the Sermon," 33–35.
226. Gibson, "Point Form," 403.
227. Lowry, *Sermon*, 23, 66.

Some sermons that use polar thought also involve tension. Wilson's four-page sermon pursues the tension between trouble and grace, instead of washing away the trouble (which is dealt with on pages one and two) with grace (on pages three and four).[228] Because for Wilson the gospel includes both trouble and grace. Wilson argues "when [trouble and grace] are harnessed and held in tension, the gospel can be expressed and experienced."[229]

In preaching, lament works in this transitional and dynamic space or tension. This is because lament holds trouble (crucifixion) and grace (resurrection), maintaining the balance between the two poles and not negating one or the other. This characteristic of tension in preaching is essential for preaching hope within the reality of suffering, and for creating a tension between eschatological hope and present hope. Tension ultimately generates transformative or new meaning in faith. The awareness of this tension can contribute to revealing the reality of suffering in the resurrection, verifying the need for a movement from lament to hope.

In the example that follows, Charles Rice proclaims the sorrow of the world and the need for God's comfort in sermons during Holy Week.[230] He shows the idea of the changed reality of lament.[231]

> For to wait on the Lord as if the world were of no account is to miss the Kingdom which is in our midst.... We endure time as those who know that all our times are in his hands, past, present, and future. But while we wait in work and rest, we mourn for the world.... But all is not well, no more than in the old Jerusalem over which Jesus mourned. And we are never so much in his company, nor so near to the pathos of Gabriel's searching eye, as when we weep over the daily newspaper, over the life of the world.... But our weeping is not that of sentimentality or of despair, for that is not the mourning which is in itself blessedness. It is the comforted grief of those who have seen and who wait to see the salvation of God. For while we mourn over the world, we know the meaning of the promise, "Blessed are they that mourn."[232]

Rice concludes the sermon by mentioning that we can mourn and wait because we know the decisive story of Christ's salvation as both Alpha and Omega. Rice presents the Christian life in the dynamic of pain and hope

228. Wilson, *Four Pages*, 120.
229. Wilson, *Four Pages*, 120.
230. Rice, *Interpretation and Imagination*, 136–44.
231. Rice, *Interpretation and Imagination*, 141.
232. Rice, *Interpretation and Imagination*, 142.

and the lament as a way of life in which pain and hope coexist. Thus, tension pursues a balanced dynamic by accepting ambiguity that does not result in a single theological interpretation logically and propositionally, as in the traditional view. This trend may contribute to bringing the language of suffering into the language of worship and preaching.

In Rice's sermon, tension also shows that human life is still in the twofold reality of suffering and hope in the present.[233] Rice says that lamenters are waiting for God's comfort, and we must weep for the world while waiting for the kingdom of God to be completed.[234] He notes that lament belongs to those who know God's salvation.[235] Just as the cross and the resurrection exist simultaneously in the Christian gospel, so there is tension in life between the reality of suffering and hope from the ultimate victory confirmed by Christ's resurrection. This tension, like pulling on a rubber band, can seem to hinder the path to ultimate hope. However, preachers need to escape from the pressure to choose one or the other.[236] These two can coexist in a sermon, and in fact are truer to life when they do.

In summary, some features of recent homiletic discourses—such as narrative, metaphor, imagination, and tension—may assist the purpose of lament and deal with suffering.[237] Despite their limitations, these features have contributed to the development of a variety of linguistic and rhetorical strategies to make listeners aware of God's saving actions, including Christ's crucifixion and resurrection, without losing a sense of the suffering world. However, these features alone might not be enough. Preachers need to look at what theological perspectives can be used to form effective sermons to address suffering. The Trouble and Grace school may offer some theological emphases to preach suffering and hope effectively.

HOMILETIC THEORY TO DEAL WITH SUFFERING: TROUBLE AND GRACE

In this section, I examine the theological basis and preaching structure of Trouble and Grace school and how these studies have contributed to dealing with suffering. In addition, I look at the role of lament in this school. The aim is to show how the movement from suffering to hope via lament is theologically verifiable based on the theological concept of trouble-grace.

233. Bouer, "Enquiring into the Absence of Lament," 26.
234. Rice, "First and the Last," 137, 140.
235. Rice, "First and the Last," 141.
236. Eslinger, *Web of Preaching*, 70–71; Powery, *Dem Dry Bones*, 93.
237. Wilson, *Preaching and Homiletical Theory*, 136.

Law and Gospel

The pair, law and gospel, is one of the theological structures embedded in the very biblical text, particularly the New Testament and has developed throughout the history of Christianity. In the Reformed Church, the polarity between law and gospel became a center of Martin Luther's doctrinal teaching.[238] He himself noted that "Suffering and death are not excluded from the midst of life. . . . They are part and parcel of one's daily bread." Though Luther certainly does not neglect the experience of suffering in his writings, neither did he ascribe ultimate meaning to the experience of suffering.[239] Law and gospel seem to be separate ideas for Luther rather than one integrated and dynamic idea, and though he viewed law as a gift from God, he considered it to be inadequate for salvation.[240] The law seems to make people conscious of the possibility of salvation that is closed forever if we rely on our own abilities.[241] Luther's distinction between law and gospel has the tendency to foster a dualism between the worldly state and the Christ-based church, potentially disrupting the lives of believers who exist in both realms.[242]

John Calvin identified three functions of the law: the first use is to convict, the second is to keep people from falling into unrighteousness, and the third is to incite them to obedience through the promise of new life.[243] Using the metaphor of a mirror, Calvin says that law reveals a person's sinfulness and weakness, so that people see their existential reality through the mirror of law, making them aware of their need for the gospel.[244]

The theological frame of the law-gospel has evolved homiletically.[245] Richard R. Caemmerer instead uses the terms God's Judgment and God's Rescue.[246] He suggests that a preacher should hold on to three things: God's plan, God's judgment, and God's grace.[247] Caemmerer explains the meaning of death as a condition under the wrath of God caused by humans who

238. Joo, "Homiletic Geared towards Ethical Living," 14.
239. Bayer, *Martin Luther's Theology*, 11–12.
240. Cary, *Luther*, 10.
241. Pesch, "Law and Gospel," 95.
242. Couenhoven, "Law and Gospel," 184.
243. Calvin, *Institutes*, 2.7.12.
244. Calvin, *Institutes*, 2.7. 7.
245. For more details about the Law/Gospel and Trouble/Grace structures in preaching, see Wilson, *Preaching and Homiletical Theory*, 73–115. Wilson presents a holistic map of how this theological grammar has usefully served the pulpit as a homiletical structure, even beyond Luther's tradition.
246. Caemmerer, *Preaching for the Church*, chs. 4 and 5.
247. Caemmerer, *Preaching for the Church*, 15, 20.

have failed covenant relationships.[248] The cross and resurrection serve as the means of mercy by which human sin is atoned.[249] Caemmerer approaches the need for salvation by focusing on sin and judgment rather than pain.[250] Wilson criticizes Caemmerer's understanding and use of the law, saying it is merely "a finger of rebuke."[251] Such sermons, says Wilson, run the risk of treating people who protest against suffering or who fail to endure suffering as lacking faith or not coming under the grace of God. Also, by focusing only on the relationship between humans and God, people can lose their sense of the power of evil and reduce the problem of suffering to an overly personal and simplified relationship.[252]

Milton Crum and Herman G. Stuempfle Jr. further emphasize the movement from the law to gospel in Caemmerer's approach. Including the vertical perception of Caemmerer's law, Stuempfle imagines a "mirror of existence" as a horizontal level that reflects the fallen state of humanity and the world, such as anxiety, finitude, alienation, doubt, and despair.[253] As Wilson notes, Stuempfle has contributed to the description of corrupt or broken situations in the world and society, expanding the focus from individualism to society.[254]

Milton Crum itemizes "the five dynamic factors" in human change: symptom, root, result, gospel content, and new results.[255] Crum regards the experience of human fallenness as a symptom and tries to explain the root of the symptom by showing its result, and claims that the symptom should be changed by the gospel.[256] And "a new result as the transformed behavior" emerges through the affirmation of the gospel.[257] The way preachers deal with suffering is linked to the perception of sin and suffering as a result.[258] But for Crum, what human fallenness means as a symptom is sin, which

---

248. Caemmerer, *Preaching for the Church*, 24. For Caemmerer, gospel and law cannot be separated from each other.
249. Caemmerer, *Preaching for the Church*, 31.
250. Caemmerer, *Preaching for the Church*, 16.
251. Wilson, *Preaching and Homiletical Theory*, 82–83.
252. Refer to Caemmerer, *Preaching for the Church*, 18, 23.
253. Stuempfle, *Preaching Law and Gospel*, 23–25.
254. Wilson, *Preaching and Homiletical Theory*, 84.
255. Crum, *Manual on Preaching*, 112.
256. Crum, *Manual on Preaching*, 76.
257. Crum, *Manual on Preaching*, 116.
258. Crum, *Manual on Preaching*, 111, 115. Crum thinks that it is not enough for a sermon to end with moral advice or godly aspiration. Crum, *Manual on Preaching*, 114.

calls for conversion, and he does not discern the power of evil as a factor of fallenness.[259]

Frederick Buechner uses the language of moving from tragedy to comedy to fairy tale in a sermon.[260] The fairy tale consists of the amazing things that happen with God and gospel. Good and evil fight in a fairy tale and God wins.[261] Buechner refers to the existence of hope as a fairy tale in the best sense, beyond the walls of what some people perceive as the real worlds, recognizing the reality of suffering that persists even after the final victory of the good.[262]

Eugene Lowry's homiletical plot can be considered as law and gospel. Wilson compares Crum's and Lowry's plots and finds similarities.[263] For both, human suffering is covered in the first half of a sermon. Human fallenness, as Crum refers to it, focuses on the situation of sin, and Lowry deals with contradictions and questions in the Bible, not just sin.[264] Both present the root cause of the pain (Crum) or the analysis of the inconsistency (Lowry) in the next step, Lowry aims to recognize the depth of the problem, but does not explain or comment.[265]

For Richard Lischer, preaching the gospel includes the realization of the brokenness of humans as a situation in which God's presence is desperately needed, and God's redemptive action through the cross and resurrection of Christ as a gift of God's grace.[266] For him, the concern in preaching lies mainly in hearing the "two tones of God's word in relation to one another."[267] Lischer offers seven tips for using the law and gospel in preaching.[268] The tips are about the balanced use of the two poles, law and gospel. Lischer argues that being too obsessed with problem analysis

259. Crum, *Manual on Preaching*, 113–14.
260. Buechner, *Truth*.
261. Buechner, *Truth*, 82.
262. Buechner, *Truth*, 89.
263. Wilson, *Preaching and Homiletical Theory*, 88–89.
264. Lowry, *Homiletical Plot*, 28–52.
265. Lowry notes that the second is the most important step in his plot. This is because the second process determines the rest of the sermon, including the form of the good news. Lowry reflects on preachers' own involvement in the situation when attempting to diagnose a specific problem beyond preachers' experience, respects listeners' position, and suggests ways to ask. Lowry, *Homiletical Plot*, 41, 44, 47.
266. Lischer, *Theology of Preaching*, 32.
267. Lischer, *Theology of Preaching*, 34.
268. Lischer, *Theology of Preaching*, 43–46. His seven tips are: (1) The mechanical application of law and gospel; (2) Grace without Judgement; (3) Judgment without Grace; (4) Preoccupation with Analysis; (5) Moralism; (6) Preaching *about* the gospel; (7) Preaching the gospel in a law-tone.

may result in the reduction of the gospel, and that proclaiming the gospel without law may minimize the gravity of sin, death, and the power of evil. Lischer's tips include having a sense of eschatological importance and being wary of creating a list of moralistic virtues.

In relation to suffering, law and gospel have the potential to address not only with the notion of sin, but also the power of the world's structural evil.[269] Charles Campbell's exposing-envisioning frame moves by exposing the suffering of those oppressed by systemic illness and envisioning for people the evidence of resurrection as an alternative vision.[270] The exposing-envisioning form urges communal practice, by allowing the baptismal community to enter into grace through a new kind of life practice.[271] Though Campbell presents Christ's life, death, and resurrection as the way to envision redemption, Campbell's homiletic suggestion can undermine the direct movement of God, as people's experiences are used as evidence of the resurrection, not Jesus' actions to overthrow the system, and ultimately invite people into communal action. Wilson criticizes Campbell for tending to mute the voice of God.[272] Nevertheless, Campbell's exposing-envisioning frame contributes to the recognition and exposure of worldly power as an aspect of understanding suffering that has not been found in the previous discourses of law and gospel.

The law and gospel discourses posit that the necessity for grace arises from acknowledging human fallenness. These dialogues have influenced the perception of fallenness and the approach to addressing suffering. Consequently, the law and gospel's understanding of suffering has broadened from the personal to the communal, from sin to an awareness of the intricate power of sin and evil.

Paul Scott Wilson: Trouble and Grace

Wilson is a scholar who drew upon the theological and homiletical discourse of law and gospel to refine and operationalize the grammar of trouble and grace, making it accessible for preachers to compose straightforward yet impactful sermons. Wilson employs polar thought—trouble and gospel—to create tension between the two realms without separating them. Wilson's

---

269. Wilson, *Preaching and Homiletical Theory*, 96.
270. Campbell, *Word before the Powers*, 105–56.
271. Campbell, *Word before the Powers*, 133, 148, 154.
272. Wilson, *Preaching and Homiletical Theory*, 114.

endeavor aims to theologically fuse the two poles in a manner that mutually influences and depends on each other.[273]

Wilson's basic theological understanding is that the entire human species is under the influence of sin, which distorts human behavior and requires God's grace. Thus, trouble can be identified both in the biblical texts and in today's life, no matter how positively the Bible speaks.[274] Trouble coexists in tension with grace; indeed, preachers cannot talk about grace without reference to human sin and wounds.[275] Wilson draws on the image of vertical and horizontal trouble to deal with the suffering in today's world. The former is from individual sin, which can be solved by God's forgiveness. For Wilson, trouble is not a vertical judgment, but a faithful proclamation.[276] This is because when a person meets one's limitations and realizes that there is no savior but Christ, the one in faith cries out to God. The latter is a communal sense of "fall, the brokenness of systems, and the suffering of the vulnerable," which requires the subversive power of God in Christ.[277] In this regard, as Wilson argues, lament can be suitable for the discourse of trouble in any sermon, that is, as the first half of a sermon.[278] Wilson's concept of "trouble" provides a critical basis for the research of lament in preaching.[279]

For the other half, Wilson emphasizes God's action, which "has acknowledged the injustice, is empowering human work, and stretches from Easter to eternity."[280] Wilson contributes to the formation of a useful grammar for sermons based on the theological understanding of trouble and grace, showing how theology forms preaching: trouble in the Bible and the world, and grace in the Bible and the world.

Luke A. Powery: Lament and Celebration

Luke Powery proposes lament as a hermeneutical lens through which to view suffering.[281] He recognizes the power of death that causes suffering, including physical illness, disability, failure, violence, and a system of corruption and negativity. He calls these human experiences a "slow death"

273. Wilson, *Preaching and Homiletical Theory*, 92.
274. Wilson, *Four Pages*, 80.
275. Wilson, *Four Pages*, 111–12.
276. Wilson, *Four Pages*, 101, 111–12.
277. Wilson, *Four Pages*, 114–17.
278. Wilson, *Four Pages*, 139.
279. Powery, *Spirit Speech*, 93.
280. Wilson, *Four Pages*, 141.
281. Powery, *Spirit Speech*, 91.

or "little deaths."[282] Preaching lament, which is connected to the reality of human suffering, suggests that God is responsible for restoring what has become a tainted order and for re-establishing justice.[283] Lament as a gift of the Holy Spirit keeps the focus on God, without losing sight of human suffering.[284] Powery introduces several strategies for practicing lament in preaching:[285] (1) naming the human reality of pain correctly, (2) using imperative and direct language, (3) using self-inclusion, (4) explicitly noting faith in God/Christ, (5) moving toward celebration and praise of God, and (6) employing heightened, passionate rhetoric. Powery sets up celebration in response to grace, and lament in response to trouble, and also confirms that lament is the work of the divine and the human, united in the Holy Spirit.[286]

Powery says: "What one laments in preaching turns to celebration because of God's imminent intervention." Thus the dynamics of lament seem somewhat reduced, in that they are not connected to grace.[287] In terms of preaching continuity, lament seems to end in the sermon by reaching celebration, although Powery claims that lament contains hope for a change in life.[288] Powery insists that Christ's suffering needs to be preached, but that suffering does not seem to be identified as God's lament.[289] Nonetheless, for Powery, lament is a language of faith and he recognizes that preaching has a bi-focal nature like "sad joyfulness."[290]

Joni S. Sancken: Trauma and Healing

Joni S. Sancken speaks of trauma as the awareness of a "wounded soul" in dealing with suffering in the world.[291] She argues that trauma-aware preaching can educate people about trauma, reach out to sufferers, provide ears that are open to conversation, speak in a powerful way to those who need to hear God's promises, and offer theological tools for people to understand

---

282. Powery borrows the expression from Lathrop, *Pastor*, 125; Powery, *Dem Dry Bones*, 2–3.
283. Powery, *Spirit Speech*, 92–93.
284. Powery, *Spirit Speech*, 92.
285. Powery, *Spirit Speech*, 120–21.
286. Powery, *Spirit Speech*, 117.
287. Powery, *Spirit Speech*, 98–99.
288. Powery, *Spirit Speech*, 104.
289. Powery, *Dem Dry Bones*, 8.
290. Powery, *Spirit Speech*, 96; Raboteau, *Sorrowful Joy*, 37.
291. Sancken, *Words That Heal*, 2.

their experiences in faith.²⁹² Sancken's approach to suffering is a communal experience, in that she looks for a place where the community resonates with wounded people.²⁹³ To do this, churches need to be safe places that resist silence and amnesia, and instead speak of wounds, and lead the remembering and lamenting with compassionate witnesses.²⁹⁴ In dealing with suffering, Sancken makes the point that Christ's act of salvation reaches even *Sheol*. Lament can happen in the place of despair and hopelessness because Christ reaches into hell to break through all resentment and broken relationships, and the descent leads to a transition to resurrection. For a theological understanding of trauma, Sancken brings the Korean concept of *han*, an unhealed wound endured by traumatized people. The intention of Sancken's important work to understand *han* is to find a place for victims, criticizing a church and a criminal justice system that has focused more on criminals than on victims.²⁹⁵

Sancken says healing can be a sign of resurrection, but this may not be a good approach for those who are not healed physically, as Black argues.²⁹⁶ Sancken's main contribution is promoting the theology of Holy Saturday as a space for the wounded. This is presented as a place of healing and connects the salvific act of Jesus with the traumatized.²⁹⁷ Though an individual therapeutic approach may acknowledge the gravity of sin, the power of evil, and the responsibility of collective sin to weaken, Sancken extends the scope of God's care to all of society, because God's redemptive vision encompasses creation and all spheres of life.²⁹⁸ Also, Sancken's attempts to highlight both Jesus' vulnerability and ability is essential, because a Superman Christ can become distant from suffering people and aggravate a sense of the absence of God.

The Importance of God's Action in Hope

The experience of the gospel in the theological frame of trouble and grace primarily comes from God's redemptive action. Some polar frames might fit the trouble-grace dynamics, but preachers need to recognize that

292. Sancken, *Words That Heal*, 3.
293. Sancken, *Words That Heal*, 40.
294. Sancken, *Words That Heal*, 52, 54–55, 91.
295. Sancken, *Words That Heal*, 21.
296. Black, *Healing Homiletic*, 23–24.
297. Sancken, *Words That Heal*, 22–24; Rambo, "Spirit and Trauma," 14.
298. Sancken, *Stumbling over the Cross*, 13.

the possibility of resolution or hope in the trouble and grace structure is grounded in the action of God.

Christine M. Smith notes the crucial nature of weeping, compassion, and resistance in dealing with pain.[299] Smith also seems to use a trouble-grace frame. From a feminist perspective she examines the social and cultural oppression and pain that come from political and structural evil. The act of crying is needed to connect the congregation effectively to those who suffer from injustice and violence.[300] Smith argues "when preachers body forth passionate justice, it is life in the midst of death. When congregations respond by bodying forth dimensions of justice, it is hope amid despair."[301] Yet Smith neither investigates the agency of righteousness nor the distinctiveness of human misdeeds and the power of evil. This can lead to overlooking God's definitive action in the world and to avoiding the discernment of the oppressor from the oppressed and the innocent from the guilty within the power dynamics of society. Nevertheless, Smith emphasizes communal confession beyond individual repentance, in contrast to the temptation to portray the world a preacher wants, or simply to seek to relieve the pain without taking account of the complexity and truth of life.[302]

Grace as Smith understands it is based on the resurrection, and involves exploring a new language, image, and understanding to proclaim the life of resurrection faithfully.[303] To do so, Smith focuses on the power of resurrection in today's world and in the life of faith communities which "live in ways that create and embody hope."[304] Smith considers that the action and language of hope can come from resistance to suffering and oppression.[305] Smith argues that "from comfortable distance to weeping, from denial to confession, from complicity to resistance" one can find some sign of hope.[306] Smith emphasizes Christo-praxis as the very definition of being Christian, which means "identifying, naming, and participating in those activities in life that are truly redemptive," and imagining oppressed and condemned people as motivated to become "the locus of God's resurrection power."[307] Smith's view of resurrection seems human-centric.

299. Smith, *Preaching as Weeping*.
300. Smith, *Risking the Terror*, 14.
301. Smith, *Risking the Terror*, 4.
302. Smith, *Risking the Terror*, 4–5.
303. Smith, *Risking the Terror*, 1.
304. Smith, *Risking the Terror*, 2.
305. Smith, *Risking the Terror*, 14–15.
306. Smith, *Risking the Terror*, 7.
307. Smith, *Risking the Terror*, 36–37, 92, 99.

Though it may be necessary to testify how to make the resurrection accessible and available to communities, God needs to be revealed not merely as one who empowers humans and then steps back, but as a primary performer of redemption in the fallen world. Highlighting the power of the resurrection in today's life may diminish the eschatological and transcendental understanding of salvation/resurrection. It may overlook the fact that the fundamental understanding of the gospel lies in grace—before its political and social functions. Thus, in trouble-grace dynamics, it is important to proclaim how "God" is acting and inviting those broken and fragmented sounds back into the harmony of eschatological redemptive vision.

Based on the dynamics of the two poles, the Trouble and Grace school of preaching confirms that there is a place of lament between the two poles, and that neither pain nor despair is the last word in a sermon. Powery contributes to the discussion by establishing lament as a divine work of participating in the outcry of the world. Sancken's pastoral and practical approach also serves the school by creating a safe place for uncovering pain in preaching.[308] As Wilson emphasizes, God's action is important in order to prevent lament from being misused as part of a to-do list for suffering. Smith dedicated herself to disclosing disenfranchised grief and violence that stems from injustice, thereby breaking the silence of people's denial. However, Smith does not specify why the cross has the power to overthrow and tear open the darkness, or how God's salvation act is working amid suffering. Also, Smith's preaching against social injustice does not seem to distinguish clearly between participation in the cross and social ethics. These discourses have shown that preachers need to contemplate the agency of hope, the intricacies of hope, the complexity of suffering, and the diverse ways of responding to suffering, rather than move mechanically toward hope based on the theological notion of trouble and grace.

CONCLUSION: LAMENT AS UNSETTLING SPACE

Recent homiletics has dealt with suffering through various styles of sermonic rhetoric and their multiple features. In recent sermons, lament has by and large not been evident as a tool for suffering, but the discourses of this chapter show that there has been a place for lament to express and witness suffering, to resist injustice, and to call for hope, liberation, and healing. Also, the discourses on suffering in homiletics have expanded to encompass a universal and communal narrative.

---

308. Sancken, *Words That Heal*, 80–81.

In terms of the trouble-grace form as a theological framework on the basis of which to preach suffering and hope, I have shown that the dynamics between trouble and grace generate tension and are not separate from each other. Also, the tension in one supports and intensifies the other. However, I was not able to discern how tension operates as a spatial and temporal realm for the coexistence of suffering and hope, nor was I able to discern how tension provokes the detailed dynamics. Now we face the need to discuss in more detail how the tension communicates the gospel. The next chapter will do through an analysis of the dynamics between suffering and hope in a sermon.

In the previous chapters I have already examined the meaning and value of lament in dealing with suffering. Lament will not fade before the end of the sermon. Rather, lament in the sermon may imply the possibility of a shift to grace, like the scar of the cross on the resurrection body. Lament holds both suffering and hope. Thus, the next chapter will consider lament as a space of connectivity in preaching, and it will explore lament's possibility as the unsettling and transitional space of tension. Also, I will investigate several interpretive strategies in response to the previous chapters and examine some characteristics of lament-driven preaching as a way of preaching hope in suffering.

5

Lament-in-Hope

Lament-Driven Preaching as a New Approach to Proclaiming Hope

CHANGES IN HOMILETICS SINCE the 1950s have resulted in a meaningful discourse about how to speak and think about human suffering, whether it is presented linguistically, thematically, or theologically. The movement from trouble to grace in particular has shown that lament can be employed as an effective way for preaching to address suffering. As mentioned in the previous chapters, the dual identity of lament as holding both suffering and hope makes for an unsettling space. But precisely this also can also be the driving force that creates and promotes the dynamic energy found in the movement between suffering and hope. This chapter presents and evaluates the value of lament in preaching as a communal language by considering the various features of lament-driven preaching.

LAMENT FOR PREACHING

Human lament is an impassioned expression of, witness to, and personal and/or social protest of those who suffer in the face of evil and injustice, as well as a longing for God's saving presence. Divine lament responds to and expresses solidarity with human suffering for God is full of divine compassion. God's compassion is the foundation on which humans can build hope. In horrific situations, confidence in God enables human lament to be filled with hope. The theological task of preachers is to engage with suffering in the Bible and in the world in a way that proclaims hope by acknowledging and naming suffering. This section considers interpretive strategies through a pastoral lens to determine how best to use lament in preaching.

Interpretative Strategies for Preachers Addressing Suffering

Identifying Complex Causes of Suffering in Response to Christ's Crucifixion and Other Biblical Examples

In the study of Lamentations, I pondered the ambiguity and multi-layered meaning of the biblical voices of suffering. In the theological reflections on the crucifixion and resurrection, I considered the possible causes of lament and God's responses to lament. Knowing that the complexity of suffering stems from a sense of individual and communal sin as well as from the alien power of evil and death, how might preachers apply this understanding to their preaching?

I begin by considering individual and communal brokenness, for as Richard Eslinger says, preachers cannot properly speak of God's grace without understanding human sin and brokenness.[1] Humans are children of God and have a double self-image, one of which is stained with sin and rebellion.[2] Preachers address this stain, this human complicity with evil.[3] However, preaching that merely threatens or condemns sinners can be dangerous or inadequate.[4] For lament may act only as a way to expose human indifference to individual and collective sin, while avoiding appropriate blame.[5] By contrast, we can preach the cross of Christ in a way that energizes people to active resistance to social injustice and oppression that brings with it a sense of solidarity and compassion.[6] Here, Paul Wilson's understanding of Christ's ongoing crucifixion embraces the human condition of suffering after the fall, and is helpful for preaching: "God uniquely defeats the power of death and through the Holy Spirit continues to battle suffering and injustice. Sin and evil continue, but the final outcome is clear."[7] Christ's suffering shows sufferers they are not alone in their suffering, and confirms that there is hope on the cross where forgiveness and righteousness have

---

1. Eslinger, *Web of Preaching*, 211.
2. Craddock, *Preaching*, 88.
3. Brown, "When Lament Shapes the Sermon," 30–31.
4. Buttrick, *Preaching the New and Now*, 61.
5. Steimle, "Preaching and the Biblical Story," 198–211.
6. Brown, *Cross Talk*, 82.
7. Wilson, *Practice of Preaching*, 161; Wilson, *Four Pages*, 194.

been fulfilled.[8] Thus, preachers need a good theological understanding of both brokenness and God's work in order to preach about the complexity of suffering that contributes to individual and communal brokenness.

Second, naming evil powers is critical in the effort to deal with suffering. Evil is a power that transcends human understanding. It is an invasion into the goodness of creation. Evil is able to take a human captive and leave a person broken by the burden of the suffering it causes.[9] For that reason, we need to recognize the power of death and sin as the evil of the final enemy.[10] To try to understand evil within a system of reason can be to swallow up the voice of victims. We must understand that evil has been granted by God the right to exist.[11] Thus, the communal voice in Lamentations cries out to God to deliver them from the abyss. Sufferers experience "a comprehensive system breakdown" of which they are never in control.[12] This shows us that no one is able to tame or resolve the power of sin and death and that only God can master it. Preachers do not need to explain or interpret evil, but they should and can build a community that can absorb, resist, and transform suffering caused by the power of evil and sin.[13] Also, preachers can assure us of a God who resists evil and overcomes evil. As Darby Ray says, "Redemption from evil must mean more than suffering through it together. . . . [I]t must include resistance to evil, struggle against its causes, concrete efforts to undo it."[14] Preachers need not be afraid to face and preach the power of evil, trouble, and death because God ultimately will defeat the power of evil.[15]

Third, preachers may consider human anxiety, anger, or fear about the situation of suffering as a topic for a conversation with God. Such emotions are a very natural reaction in the reality of pain, and even the negative emotions expressed to God can, in themselves, sustain and revitalize the relationship with God.[16] Preachers have often used the example of Christ's cross to encourage Christians to be patient and to sacrifice in suffering. However, preachers need to remind that Christ's patience and obedience were not expressed in silence but in crying out to God in complete solidarity with human beings in pain. Expressing anxiety to God, encompassing even

8. Sancken, *Words That Heal*, 91.
9. Sancken, *Words That Heal*, 136–37.
10. Long, "Funeral," 389.
11. Johnson, *Quest for the Living God*, 50.
12. Lakkis, "Have You Any Right to Be Angry?" 170.
13. Swinton, *Raging with Compassion*, 35.
14. Ray, *Deceiving the Devil*, 89.
15. Sancken, *Stumbling over the Cross*, 21.
16. Sancken, *Wounds That Heal*, 76.

complaining to God, is not a sign of lack of faith but a sign of believing that God is big enough to deal with our painful cry.[17] In this sense, it can be unjust to preach that Christ's patience and obedience in suffering requires one to remain silent in one's pain or to accept one's pain passively, lest it cut off sincere dialogue with God. Preachers take precaution mistakenly and unjustly referring to "the mysticism of the cross" to justify pain to a sufferer.[18] No wonder that Jürgen Moltmann criticized the mysticism that forced peasants, Indians, and black slaves to accept their suffering as their crosses and told them it was appropriate and indeed God-ordained that they obey their unjust masters.[19] The mystery of the cross is not opium to sustain the afflicted in their suffering, nor does it justify suffering in a world of domination and oppression.[20] Rather, questions about the unbearable pain, the anxiety of death, or the nonsensicality of being are reasons to claim resilience and God's faithfulness. For God is not an oppressor but a listener, and by extension "The true power of the kingdom of God was not political but relational."[21] In all these ways preachers can use the language in the Bible to externalize the pain of the wounding experience and can use the voice of pain as a language of faith.[22]

Fourth, when talking about undeserved grief, preachers can remember "the pain of forgotten, unwanted, and unneeded people and should engage those who suffer the most in society."[23] Preaching can work as resistance by bringing to the fore memories of sin and violence.[24] Indeed, proclaiming forgiveness too hastily can aggravate the suffering of victims.[25] So one is wise to tread carefully and slowly if trying to get a perpetrator and victim to forgive and reconcile, lest one cause the victim even more suffering.

Fifth, to preach about parallel suffering experiences between the Bible and present-day situations can be a way to show God's continued involvement with people and reveal God's saving power and faithfulness.[26] Preachers can use biblical narratives as powerful tools to convey to the wounded the awareness and healing they need or want. For many of the Bible's stories

17. Sancken, *Wounds That Heal*, 29.
18. Moltmann, *Crucified God*, 48.
19. Moltmann, *Crucified God*, 49.
20. Moltmann, *Crucified God*, 49.
21. Charles and Rah, *Unsettling Truth*, 44.
22. Sancken, *Words That Heal*, 26.
23. Powery, *Dem Dry Bones*, 46.
24. Smith, *Preaching as Weeping*, 130.
25. Smith, *Preaching as Weeping*, 64–65.
26. Wilson, *Four Pages*, 139–40.

deal with traumatized individuals and communities and survivors of traumatic experiences.[27] The Bible through preaching can convey God's way of bringing life from death, which can, in turn, deepen the experience of the gospel.[28] However, preachers do well to interpret difficult Scripture texts circumspectly, taking care not to connect disability with an individual's sin, for example.

Sixth and last, when preachers employ Christocentric interpretation, they can (with caution) bring the cross into conversation with the Old Testament, either by taking the cross and the resurrection as a hermeneutical lens for a text, or by finding the resonance between the text and Jesus.[29] The image of Christ as a suffering servant who does not despise or hate the suffering of people is also a good theological way to interpret suffering.[30] However, preachers do well not to reduce Jesus Christ to being the answer to personal worries by universalizing and maximizing human experiences.[31] It is important to be open to what the cross can teach us in our preaching, rather than choose our metaphors simply to suit our preferences.[32] By the same token, we do well not to interpret people's suffering as a means of salvation, nor to say that God is glorified when the suffering of Christ is preached in connection with human suffering.[33] However, despite carefully resisting some traditional sacrificial theologies, preachers know the benefit of sharing the struggle of sufferers in their preaching.[34] And knowing that, preachers distinguish between the pain to resist and the pain that brings integrity.[35] For preaching about Christ's suffering can empower people to overcome suffering.[36] And it shows the life-giving power of God overcoming the power of suffering that destroys life and hope.[37]

---

27. Sancken, *Words That Heal*, 25.
28. Sancken, *Stumbling over the Cross*, 33.
29. Sancken, *Stumbling over the Cross*, 11, 159.
30. Wilson, *Four Pages*, 121–22, 201.
31. Campbell, *Preaching Jesus*, 141–45.
32. Brown, *Cross Talk*, 63.
33. Brown, *Cross Talk*, 90.
34. Smith, *Preaching as Weeping*, 161–62.
35. Brown, *Cross Talk*, 66.
36. Powery, *Dem Dry Bones*, 44.
37. Brown, *Cross Talk*, 79.

Virtually all suffering is complex; thus, generalizing pain can make it difficult to identify an effective response.[38] It takes effort to name, understand, and see the multitude of ways to respond to suffering experiences.[39]

Using Lament as Counter-Narratives for Collective Suffering

Common social master-narratives give people ways to identify what are generally considered to be normative experiences. We create counter-narratives when our own experiences don't match the master-narrative, or when we begin to question the basis of that dominant story.[40] That occurs, for example, when the narrative uses subversive rhetoric against the rhetoric of empire and violence.[41] However, a counter-narrative does not exist in a harmonious relationship with a master-narrative, but is in tension with it.[42] Recognizing and using an appropriate Christian counter-narrative—interrupting the master narrative—allows us to see who is not included in the dominant narrative and how it can affect society and people in marginalized groups.

Charles Campbell and John Cilliers describe the preacher as an "agent of interruption."[43] By using a counter-narrative, preachers bring the voices of those on the periphery to the seat of the privileged. Such counter-narratives can disrupt the powerful and the hold of the so-called wise and the powerful. One such counter-narrative is the narrative of the cross. Another is that of the new creation.[44] Counter-narratives may be seen as an attempt to disturb the taboos and boundaries of the pulpit itself.[45] Just as "lament is a way of protesting against the common theology" in faith, so too lament can function as an imaginative way to present a counter-narrative against the unjust world.[46]

---

38. Smith, *Risking the Terror*, 32. Smith argues that preachers refer to suffering most often in terms of individual human sinfulness rather than systemic and historical repression.
39. Smith, *Risking the Terror*, 34.
40. Andrews, "Counter-Narratives and the Power to Oppose," 1.
41. Claassens, *Mourner*, 9.
42. Andrews, "Counter-Narratives and the Power to Oppose," 2.
43. Campbell and Cilliers, *Preaching Fools*, 154.
44. Campbell and Cilliers, *Preaching Fools*, 154.
45. Campbell and Cilliers, *Preaching Fools*, 157.
46. Brueggemann, *Old Testament Theology*, 27.

Using Lament as a Form of Homiletical Rhetoric

Sally Brown argues that the rhetoric of lament, as "a cry of anguish, cry of resistance, or theological interrogation," is rhetoric that eventually leads to a whisper of hope.[47] The rhetoric of lament maintains a dynamic tension or space in which the movement of the Spirit occurs. It may set the direction and method of movement from death to life or from suffering to hope. The theology of Lamentations—from which neither is eliminated—shows the role of the lament rhetoric. There can be no real proclamation of the resurrection until human beings acknowledge the power of death and sin.[48] By doing so, the lament rhetoric aims "to move people so that the lament becomes their own and they seek the assistance of God."[49] Lament rhetoric can resist easy hope or solution through a strategic delay. For it can hold a space for pain, recognizing human limits against the power of sin and evil. And it can appeal to God, it can resist what is wrong in the world, and it can raise a collective voice of sympathy and testimony about pain as a way both of participating in suffering and of ultimately possessing the words of hope.

Taking Special Care with Bible Passages That Imply God's Violence

When preachers find God's violence in the Bible rather than God's love, mercy, and self-giving, they face interpretive difficulties. Old Testament prophets portray God's violence as a punishment for disobedience as part of the practice of God's sovereignty.[50] In addition, many biblical scripts about wars of conquest make God appear not to be good to all, raising questions about God's justice.[51] The marriage metaphor often portrays God as a husband of patriarchal authority and Israel as a weak, immoral wife.[52] Lamentations describes God as an enemy who tears Israel apart with a fierce anger.

R. N. Whybray noted that scholars are almost completely silent about God's violence.[53] Few deconstructionists have paid attention to it, he said, and even they have typically tried to *explain* God's abusiveness.[54] There have been several approaches to God's abusiveness: the

---

47. Brown, "When Lament Shapes the Sermon," 33–35.
48. Rutledge, *Undoing of Death*, 276.
49. Wilson, *Setting Words on Fire*, 137.
50. Brueggemann, *Theology of the Old Testament*, 381–82.
51. Brueggemann, *Theology of the Old Testament*, 382–83.
52. Brueggemann, *Theology of the Old Testament*, 383–85.
53. Whybray, "'Shall Not the Judge,'" 2.
54. Whybray, "'Shall Not the Judge,'" 2.

ignore-divine-violence approach, the justify-divine-violence approach, the reject-texts-about-the-abusing-God approach, and the God-is-both-abusive-and-loving approach.[55] Eric Seibert presents seven ways violence can be mishandled: (1) by justifying violence, (2) by interpreting certain kinds of violence as being for the greater good, (3) by categorizing violence as progressive revelation, (4) by interpreting violence as figurative or by otherwise mitigating our understanding of violence as truly violent, (5) by emphasizing Israel's law and moral superiority, (6) by recognizing and trusting unanswered questions, and (7) by defending divine violence.

Any attempt to find a balance between God's violent actions and other actions might be dangerous. The attempts to neutralize violence with a positive image can also be a risk.[56] Rather than attempting to explain why God's bad behavior in the Bible is somehow good, it might be better to be honest and show some integrity about the truly problematic nature of these texts. Instead, preachers can say that the Bible reflects the worldview, assumptions, and prejudices of individuals or communities living in ancient times.[57] They can also distinguish between human claims about God and the true nature of God by making a "distinction between God's direct actions and chaotic events that occur in the world."[58] The editors of the Bible made various attempts to alleviate the harshness of God's violence but did not change their perception that there was a dark side of God. They were aware of the complexities and apparent contradictions experienced by the Israelites in their relationship with God.[59] Indeed, Raymund Schwager finds that "the theme of God's bloody vengeance occurs in the Old Testament even more frequently than the problem of human violence. Approximately one thousand passages speak of Yahweh's blazing anger, of his punishments by death and destruction."[60]

This theological dilemma is not easily resolved. For historically, violent biblical texts have done enormous harm by justifying violence perpetrated against millions of people.[61] So we can welcome ideas of how to read texts in such a way that they do not perpetuate injustice, oppression, and murder.[62] Indeed, I suggest that preachers have the right and duty to investigate,

---

55. O'Connor, *Lamentations and the Tears*, 116–19.
56. Seibert, "Recent Research on Divine Violence," 14–19.
57. Seibert, "Recent Research on Divine Violence," 14–19.
58. O'Connor, *Lamentations and the Tears*, 120.
59. O'Connor, *Lamentations and the Tears*, 120.
60. Schwager, *Must There Be Scapegoats?*, 55.
61. Seibert, "Recent Research on Divine Violence," 10.
62. Seibert, "Recent Research on Divine Violence," 10.

question, and object to the texts, such as violence against women, genocide, and child abuse, that seem morally unacceptable to Bible readers.[63] Renita Weems is correct in emphasizing the importance of employing a double hermeneutic. For indeed, preachers need to research the violent and patriarchal God and still are open to learning something from the text while at the same time resisting the corrupt side of the text.[64] Rather than passively accept the idea of God's abuse, preachers can resist unsatisfactory interpretations of theological tradition, can reevaluate the situation of themselves and the congregation with the authority of experience, and in so doing can free up space for new ways of encountering and knowing God.[65] To be specific, if preachers want to deal responsibly with passages that contain violence, such as those on the conquest of Canaan, they should start telling the whole story without eradicating the violence.[66] By doing this, preachers will likely help develop compassion for the dead, not believing that some people in this world are worth killing, but resisting the justification of colonialism and war, murder and theft.[67] Preachers are well placed to propose a variety of views for consideration when discussing or preaching about today's issues of violence.[68]

Taking Special Care with the Apparent Absence of God

In Lamentations 5:19–22, there is a sense of *Deus absconditus*, which is strongly suggested by divine silence, and which contrasts with God's covenant faithfulness. If God's voice has sound, activity, embodiment, volition, and life, then God's voice means the essence of the covenant and God's existence.[69] The idea that God is absent can cause people great anxiety, anxiety that the word of God is removed from them. Yet, this can also lead people to discover that salvation or presence is not only manifested by the speaking God. God's presence is dynamically manifested in God's voice and God's silence (listening): "The only assurance the prophet has is that the faithful

---

63. Davies, *Immoral Bible*, 145–46. This ethical criticism can help criticize, challenge, and struggle rather than passively reading the text, but such an approach also risks readers accepting only the image of a God they like.
64. Weems, *Battered Love*, 100.
65. O'Connor, *Lamentations and the Tears*, 123.
66. Seibert, "Preaching from Violent Biblical Texts," 250.
67. Seibert, "Preaching from Violent Biblical Texts," 250–51.
68. Seibert, "Preaching from Violent Biblical Texts," 252.
69. Hudson and Turner, *Saved from Silence*, 25.

God, even in divine silence, hears and is moved by our human cry."[70] In addition, silence can be a strong manner of "speaking" even though the silence is not expressed or heard as sound. As one student has stated: "I was totally present with him. I was silent, . . . but in my silence, I have never been more voiced."[71] God who listens may encourage us to listen to sufferers as a way of mirroring the actions of God who sometimes chooses silence in staying alongside sufferers.

Samuel Terrien understands God's seeming absence as "presence deferred."[72] Luther's *Deus absconditus* indicates God hiding in an indirect and invisible way: "Yahweh is present in and attentive to the life of Israel in hidden ways."[73] Luther said that the truth is mystical and the footsteps of Christ are unknown in the cross and its suffering, because God is working not in dignity and almighty power, but in hidden power.[74] These perceptions offer a clue as to how a preacher can speak of God's presence in suffering. The preacher can see the paradox that God's revelation is hidden in pain, but that God's hiding becomes a revelation.[75] I-Gon Kim argues that the lament for God's absence is a place of God's presence, and that people meet the presence of God in the hidden God.[76]

On the other hand, God's silence per se is critical because it allows us to bring up the memories of many sufferings that have been paralyzed or left latent in us, and so allow the place of mourning. The silence may work as a reminder of human finiteness.[77] Also, lament in God's silence can evoke a sense of sinfulness and the memory of God's redemptive power. Though the silence of God in suffering firstly means the unanswered pleas, it unfolds people's indifference, denial, and individualism, reminding us of the necessity of divine response.[78] Lament is itself a strong desire to receive God's response; "Where is God? Why is He so very absent in a time of trouble?"[79] It is the "cry of dereliction."[80]

---

70. Hudson and Turner, *Saved from Silence*, 33.
71. Hudson and Turner, *Saved from Silence*, 11.
72. Terrien, *Elusive Presence*, 323.
73. Bruggemann, *Theology of the Old Testament*, 333.
74. Luther, *Lectures on Psalms II*, loc. 667–89.
75. Campbell and Cilliers, *Preaching Fools*, 176.
76. Kim, "Theology of Lament of the Abandoned," 319.
77. Dobbs-Allsopp, *Lamentations*, 152.
78. Thomas, "Holy Scripture and Hermeneutics," 15.
79. Lewis, *Grief Observed*, 9.
80. Rutledge, *Crucifixion*, 97.

Preachers and faith communities can follow the example of the voices in Lamentations and "confront God's silence straight on and navigate that silence as best [they] humanly can."[81] Furthermore, preachers can detect God's presence in a way that an audience would not expect by providing several (rather than only one) images of God. First, the image of God's struggle may show that God hides behind the mask of pain and reveals himself through the mask of pain.[82] When God protests against the injustice and violence inflicted on Jesus and creation, God's silence resonates, and the face of God's sorrow is encountered.[83] Furthermore, preachers can connect the image of a womb with God's silence. C. S. Song suggests that the silence of God is the womb that surrounds Jesus on the cross, that empowers Christ at the last moments, and that raises Christ into the resurrection of new life.[84] The metaphor makes it possible to express the space of silence as a space of waiting, embracing death, pain, and life. In addition, bringing the image of a weak God may work. Melissa Raphael attempts to revise an intrinsic image of God that traces the redeeming presence of God in Auschwitz in a way that does not collude with evil: "God is nonetheless an accompanying God whose face or presence, as *Shekhinah*, "She-Who-Dwells-Among-Us," goes with Israel, in mourning, into her deepest exile, even if Israel cannot see her in the terrible crush."[85] Raphael proposes motherhood as an alternative image for dealing with suffering and insists that the faces or other sides of God need to be seen.[86]

In this regard, it may be helpful to preach sermons that put God in the brokenness and despair of our fragile lives, rejecting quick resolutions and magical treatments, and recognizing that there is no guarantee of a happy ending in life.[87] Preachers may work to understand God's seemingly foolish wisdom and proclaim the fragile God from the broken body of Christ—as the fragility of God's power.[88] The eternal God is hidden behind the broken body of Christ. God seems to be absent but is, in fact, present: "There is no sense of absence where there has been no sense of presence."[89]

---

81. Dobbs-Allsopp, *Lamentations*, 154.
82. Campbell and Cilliers, *Preaching Fools*, 180.
83. Song, *Jesus*, 112.
84. Song, *Jesus*, 119.
85. Raphael, *Female Face of God in Auschwitz*, 5–6.
86. Raphael, *Female Face of God in Auschwitz*, 52.
87. Claassens, *Mourner*, 87.
88. Campbell and Cilliers, *Preaching Fools*, 176.
89. Taylor, *Gospel Medicine*, 83.

Featuring Lament as Part of a Polar Dynamics

In the previous chapter, I related the work of the scholars in the Trouble and Grace school to the two poles to preach the gospel effectively. They consider both trouble (or a problem) and grace to be important and they called for a unified relationship of the two poles because "sermons that only lament the world and provide social critique do not provide the necessary hope grounded in the Spirit of the Resurrection; and sermons that only celebrate do not present a realistic picture of human life grounded in the Spirit of the Crucifixion."[90] The relationship of the two poles needs to be understood as a dynamic tension between suffering and hope.

Preachers can conceive of the sermon as providing a space for this tension to be enacted. This dynamic creates an unsettling space that is full of new possibilities and is full of ambivalence and paradox.[91] The unsettling in-between space means the status of openness is not a stationary condition. In this regard, preachers can work as "boundary-crossers" who do not stay or belong to one side, who cross closed structural boundaries in society, and who move between future definitive hope and present painful reality and life and death through the Holy Spirit.[92]

In Korean culture, the performers of *talchum* worked in this way. Just as those performers gave comfort to and sustained the suffering public by breaking down the wall of status, by speaking of the sorrow of the common people, by criticizing the repressive and unjust system, by offering space for conciliation by speaking for those who have *han*, and by satirizing the nobles in their narratives, so too preachers can be border-crossers who preach hope in the time of suffering. Preachers as the border-crossers are identified by their tears and lament, and are those who look deep into the sufferings of life to fulfill their job, which is to sustain and explore the dynamic between suffering and hope.[93] They can proclaim God's salvation as an affirmation of the future, as affecting the present and driving the present when God's kairos time enters the unsettles space.

---

90. Powery, *Spirit Speech*, 100. Buttrick also argues that "only by preaching the future of God can a sense of God's presence once more fill the land," although "too much heaven can cause a careless neglect of earthly affairs." Buttrick, *Preaching the New and Now*, 22, 66.

91. Campbell and Cilliers, *Preaching Fools*, 42, 70.

92. Hyde, *Trickster Makes This World*, 6–7.

93. Campbell and Cilliers, *Preaching Fools*, 90.

Using Lament to Help People to Deal with Suffering

Lament has been the vocation of weeping women who, since ancient times, have played a central role in helping the community accept grief and nurture resilience.[94] In the Bible, weeping women were invited to remember the tragedy of Zion's destruction and to express their sorrow (Jer 9:17–20). This passage reveals the professionalism and wisdom of the lamenting women.[95] They mourned appropriately in light of the circumstances, rather than reciting the same words of mourning every time.[96] They led their community to mourn with them, as the Bible says: "teach to your daughters a dirge, and each to her neighbor a lament" (v. 20). In this space, women express emotions, name grief, testify to the horrific memories of death, challenge social complacency that ignores injustice, and lead communities in the first steps of their journey toward healing and recovery.[97] Calvin acknowledges that the prayers in Lamentations over the language of complaints and indignity can draw God's attention to salvation, and that Lamentations teaches a form of prayer that can arise to God in urgent and dangerous times.[98] Preaching lament can be a way of learning to accept suffering and to nurture resilience in troubled times at both the individual and communal levels.

Psychological Perspectives on Suffering

In psychology, the language of lament is considered a tool not only to express pain but also to satisfy adequately the needs of those experiencing the pain of everyday grief.[99] In psychology, the causes of lament have largely been understood as loss or "the deprivation of what we have become attached to."[100] The states of lament can be recognized by the frequency of the expression of some equivalent of a desire not to live; the feeling of being helpless, hopeless, forsaken, of having no desires. Religiously, this state is linked to the feeling of being abandoned by God and is often accompanied by a strong sense of guilt.[101] Kübler-Ross discerns five features of grief: (1) Denial, when the sufferer unconsciously brings into themselves only as

---

94. Lutz, *Crying*, 223.
95. Brenner, *Israelite Woman*, 38.
96. Dijk-Hemmes, "Traces of Women's Text," 84.
97. Claassens, *Mourner*, 27–30.
98. Calvin, *Jeremiah and Lamentations*, 595, 623.
99. Switzer, *Dynamics of Grief*, 16.
100. Bain, *Emotions and the Will*, 146.
101. Borgquist, "Crying," 163; Deutsch and Jackson, "Absence of Grief," 13.

much pain as they can handle;[102] (2) Anger, expressed in a variety of ways and directions, including against God.[103] Interestingly, here Kübler-Ross recognizes the need to provide a safe place in the church to express anger.[104] (3) Bargaining, in our case with God, which is typically attached to statements that begin with "What if?" and "If only." Bargaining can be a way of trying to control events. It can lead a sufferer to believe that they themselves can restore emotional order amidst the chaos.[105] (4) Depression, which can also be a way of exploring loss. During depression, it can be helpful and even necessary for someone else to stay with the depressed grieving person.[106] (5) Acceptance, which does not imply a state of complete recovery, but does mean that the awareness of the reality of the loss is complete and that a person has begun to learn to live with the loss.[107]

To heal the experience of suffering, Kübler-Ross and Kessler each in their own ways recognize both lament as "an expression of sorrow" and the importance of remembering and retelling the story of loss.[108] They argue that "if you do not take the time to grieve, you cannot find a future in which loss is remembered and honored without pain."[109] Thomas Eliot underscores the necessity for the externalization of the energy of sadness.[110] Harold Orlansky also emphasizes the role of iteratively discussing grief within the framework of mutual conversation as a means to disrupt the silence induced by the fear and anxiety of loss, a phenomenon that isolates the individual from society, resulting in profound loneliness.[111]

In this regard, scholars often note the importance of community lament. Jackson argues that comfort alone is not enough and that new relationships formed by discovering the universality of sadness within the community and by sharing pain can help those who have suffered a loss

---

102. Kübler-Ross and Kessler, *On Grief and Grieving*, 10. As denial gradually disappears, it is slowly replaced by the reality of loss.

103. Kübler-Ross and Kessler, *On Grief and Grieving*, 11.

104. Kübler-Ross and Kessler, *On Grief and Grieving*, 15. They say that a sufferer can feel that God is strong enough to bear the anger and strong enough to feel compassion and love for the suffering. Kübler-Ross and Kessler suggest not looking negatively at anger and not trying to find meaning and judging anger but feeling anger with respect. Kübler-Ross and Kessler, *On Grief and Grieving*, 16.

105. Kübler-Ross and Kessler, *On Grief and Grieving*, 19–20.

106. Kübler-Ross and Kessler, *On Grief and Grieving*, 24.

107. Kübler-Ross and Kessler, *On Grief and Grieving*, 25.

108. Kübler-Ross and Kessler, *On Grief and Grieving*, 229.

109. Kübler-Ross and Kessler, *On Grief and Grieving*, 207.

110. Eliot, "Bereavement," 663–64.

111. Orlansky, "Reactions to the Death of President Roosevelt," 253–54.

to develop resilience.¹¹² The grief in a community allows the opportunity to find the meaning of life, to contribute to the emotional care for the mourners, and to offer a language of grief and love.¹¹³ Deborah van Deusen Hunsinger recommends prayers of communal lament.¹¹⁴ Hunsinger pays attention to non-violent and compassionate language, rejecting languages of diagnosis, demand, and guilt.¹¹⁵ Such communal lament needs a safe and trustful relationship and a slow approach.¹¹⁶

In a psychological approach, lament is useful in dealing with personal grief and the suffering of loss: "mourning traumatic loss is an indispensable part of the healing process."¹¹⁷ Additionally, communal lament plays an important role in reintegrating sufferers into society and treating them—regardless of the physical and psychological causes or behavioral conditions. This pastoral sensitivity to the intertwined and complex relational aspects of hermeneutical and psychological concerns will enable a delicate yet comprehensive view of the application of lament to preaching, and is an important tool for addressing both community and individual suffering.

LAMENT-DRIVEN PREACHING

The interpretive and psychological strategies for dealing with grief explored above provide practical help for preachers trying to employ lament in their sermons. Note that in preaching, "lament is expressed on behalf of a community in such a way that a preacher enters the pain and is no mere detached observer."¹¹⁸

The Features of Suffering in Lament-Driven Preaching

People in pain have a variety of experiences, both mentally and physically. Among these, lament functions as a deep hope that goes beyond a reaction to pain or a simple wish. Lament can last a long time and be expressed over and over again, and by putting our stories before God, if necessary,

---

112. Jackson, *Understanding Grief*, 149, 160.
113. Switzer, *Dynamics of Grief*, 213.
114. Hunsinger, *Bearing the Unbearable*, 83–148.
115. Hunsinger, *Bearing the Unbearable*, 109.
116. Herman, *Trauma and Recovery*, 176.
117. Tietje, *Toward a Pastoral Theology of Holy Saturday*, 78.
118. Wilson, *Setting Words on Fire*, 126.

repeatedly, we can ultimately find hope, encompassing healing, forgiveness, and reconciliation.[119]

Naming and Witnessing to Sin, Evil, and Suffering

At the beginning of this chapter, I explored some complex causes of suffering. Naming and witnessing sin, evil, and suffering includes both discerning the causes of lament and God's response. The practices of naming and witnessing can be related to those who have lost their voice of suffering. Lament is a language of grief that gives voice to, names, and witnesses to disenfranchised grief.[120] Lament can thwart the denials and silence of pain. Preaching as a public place to lament invites people to move to 'our' pain from 'my' pain—to share in the pain and to help one another move towards hope. Preachers and the community become a common witness to the suffering that draws tears to the surface.[121] For all these kinds of "Lamentations create room within the individual and the community not only for grief and loss but also for seeing and naming injustice."[122] Thus, lament as a witness to and a naming of pain has a power that bursts forth from shared grief, as does *han*.

Sometimes, it is true, facing the pain encompasses one's shame publicly as well. But doing so is the starting point to naming festering pain. As Walter Brueggemann says, "our sense of loss and sadness is serious and honorable, and one need not prop up or engage in denial."[123] More than perhaps any other public figure, preachers are in a position to foster a safe place in which people's suffering can be heard with a mutual vulnerability. This practice of naming and witnessing to suffering rejects beautifying pain, or passive surrender, or suggesting that God creates suffering.[124] For the presence of the power of evil beyond the human sphere needs to be revealed and identified, it needs to be disentangled from human wrongdoing or avarice; The power of evil can only be defeated by God. Since lamentation calls out such a just action of God and invites that people participate in that action,

---

119. Tietje, *Toward a Pastoral Theology of Holy Saturday*, 91.

120. Doka, *Disenfranchised Grief*. This tells of sadness that is not possessed but is unrecognized, unshared, or not understood.

121. Brueggemann, *Disruptive Grace*, 130.

122. O'Connor, *Lamentation and the Tears*, 128.

123. Brueggemann, *Cadences of Home*, 12.

124. Long, *What Shall We Say?*, 133–34.

lament may "untangle complex knots of grief, despair, and violent anger that pervade society."[125]

Will Willimon presents religious rage as one of the methods for the "public processing of pain" through Psalm 137.[126]

> Every time the church tries to cover it up with our pretty vestments, and smiling preachers, and well-dressed congregation, Psalm 137 has said to all the broken hearted, "Come on in here. Bring your mourning to church. Let God have your rage. Weep with us!" . . . God can rage. Besides, Psalm 137 is in the Bible and the Bible is God's word and you and I, even in our modern arrogance, ought to be a bit reticent to expurgate or silence God's word. . . . Here, in Psalm 137, is the public processing of pain. Here, in church, before the altar of God, is strong, unrelieved anger, rage . . . When we edit out this Psalm, we also edit out all the alienated women, and abused persons, and lost, homeless, angry people in exile. Where will they go to express their rage? . . . Come, you hurting daughters of Zion, don't just grieve, rage with me. Did it ever occur to you that God may be as angry as you are? . . . I will not sing. I will not sit quietly and wail. . . . I will not keep quiet, not submit, not bow down, cave in, give up. Rage. I don't say that it's pleasant. I say that rage is real, honest, biblical, and faithful.[127]

Willimon preaches that hidden and disenfranchised pain needs to be named, witnessed, and expressed, even if it includes anger. In this case, preaching is an invitation the church to be angry for suffering, to testify, and to stay with the sufferers, resisting the dysfunctional understating of suffering which says "don't clench their fists and scream, don't rage. It is a rejection of practicing quiet acquiescence, patient acceptance, distortion the sufferers' voices into a whine, and resignation."[128] As Willimon reveals, utilizing the image of God's anger on behalf of sufferers against injustice can serve as a compelling metaphor and motivation for people to actively engage in vitalizing social justice.

---

125. O'Connor, *Lamentation and the Tears*, 131.
126. Willimon, "Religious Rage," in *Collected Sermons*, 106.
127. Willimon, "Religious Rage," 106.
128. Willimon, "Religious Rage," 105–6.

A Call for God's Action

Lament is a strong voice with petition as its primary task. It is a call for God's action. In the lament Psalms, there are repetitions of strong imperatives such as "look, remember, behold, awake, arise or deliver" (Pss 9:13; 22:21; 31:15, 16; 44:24, 26; 119:153; cf. Lam 1:20; 5:1). Israel complains that God does not protect Israel's legitimate rights. The voices of the book of Lamentations complain that God's power and faithfulness are not working. The purpose is not merely to complain, but actually to move God to faithfulness again.[129] The voices in Lamentations also persist in trying to engage God in God's silence (cf. Ps 109:1). "They make claims on God, demand attention, and beg for a future."[130] A plea to ask God to look directly at their suffering (Lam 2:20; 3:59, 63; 5:1) is not casual because they are in unbearable pain: their groaning is urgent, powerful, and provocative.

God's ultimate plan of salvation does not change according to human mourning. However, in terms of human-divine conversation, preaching lament can open another side of dialogue. As Brueggemann suggests, "The conversation also impinges upon the silent, absent sovereign and draws God back into the pain and hope of the world. The conversation transforms both parties, permitting communion."[131] When people accept their limitations, it is natural to call for God; as Luther notes, "the whole of human nature, seeing its wretchedness and filled with remorse, cries to the Lord for deliverance."[132] In the case of the *Sewol* ferry sinking, the bereaved paradoxically hope to enter the kin-dom of heaven with their children despite their resentment and fear of God.[133] Also, they confess that paradoxically they felt that only God can be trusted, even in the midst of dire suffering and silence from God. "Suffering of past and present must drive us toward God protesting, complaining, lamenting, grieving, crying out of the depths, insistently questioning 'How long, O Lord?' Rather than settling for a rational explanation, lamenting unto God, unto God in spite of everything, keeps hope alive."[134]

Similarly, in response to the despair of Ezekiel's Valley of Bones (Ezek 37:1–14), Teresa Fry Brown preaches, "How could so much promise be

---

129. Brueggemann, *Theology of the Old Testament*, 321.
130. O'Connor, *Lamentation and the Tears*, 127.
131. Brueggemann, *Finally Comes the Poet*, 76.
132. Luther, *Lectures on Psalms II*, loc. 714.
133. Kim and Kim, "Study on Experience of Bereaved," 103.
134. Johnson, *Quest for the Living God*, 67.

LAMENT-IN-HOPE

replaced, lost, stolen, strayed?"[135] Her sermon moves from the list of despair to the single revitalization possibility that can save the bones: the proclamation of God's word. The sermon may lead listeners to anticipate the words 'you shall live,' as they desperately call on God from their own despair.

> No vision, no wisdom, no ingenuity, imprisoned in societal graves of despair. They slipped into a form of spiritual and physical death right there in the valley.... Is it possible to restore life when Broken dreams, Broken relationships, Broken promises, Broken aspirations, Broken ministries, Broken spirits, Broken people have been pronounced dead?... Could God restore Hope? Overworked, underpaid, Ecclesiastical apartheid, no time to work out her own grief in disappointment, distrust, financial difficulty, Name-calling, Jokes to keep her in her place. Construction of barriers of race, age, gender, class, ability was used to strangle her articulation of possibility.... Like Israel, down in the valley with Ezekiel, Hope was part of the chosen ones of God, yet could not see God in the midst of the storm. Hope forgot the essence of her being.... Ezekiel responded, "Bones, hear the Word of the Lord."... What was dead was reconciled, restored by the power of God doing a miraculous work in the valley of seeming death.... It is not over until God says it is over. Hopelessness became hope in Ezekiel's vision. Death became life. God's promise was affirmed. Reconciliation was actualized.... God has the last word. Only by the grace of God is hope kept alive and well. When we reconnect to our understanding that God will do exceedingly abundantly above anything we ask, God will save us even from ourselves. God will not leave us without a comforter.[136]

Resisting Injustice: Truth-Telling

Letty Russell says "The true preaching... at least would have to be a word that speaks from the perspective of those who have been crushed and marginalized in our society. It would need to be a word of solidarity, healing, and love in situations of brokenness and despair and a disturbing and troubling word of justice to those who wish to protect their privilege by exclusion."[137] Such true preaching would indicate that forgiveness is neither

---

135. Fry Brown, *Weary Throats and New Songs*, 146.
136. Fry Brown, *Weary Throats and New Songs*, 145–52.
137. Russell, *Church in the Round*, 139.

"a substitute for justice, mere discharge of a victim's anger, mere assuaging of a perpetrator's remorseful anguish, one that demands no change of the perpetrator, nor righting of wrongs."[138]

The wrongs against "Comfort Women" were not righted for a long, long time. Their voices were ignored at first. And indeed, the issue of sex slavery in Japan has not been discussed officially in the last fifty years. When the Korean community began to mourn the women's pain, they began truth-telling as the beginning of resistance to the atmosphere of prettying up and concealing the pain caused by unjust power. It was the community's laments that showed that the pain the women suffered was not something shameful but the result of unjust women's forcible suffering. Lifting up the sufferers' own voices in lament was an act of resistance, a way of retrieving their own identities, a way of resisting what society had long defined as being acceptable.[139] The bereaved of the *Sewol* ferry disaster likewise explained that finding out the truth about the accident was what gave them real comfort and relief, and the way to reveal God's righteousness.[140] As O'Connor says, "Without the practice of public lament, justice is blocked, paralyzed, and unable to begin."[141]

Adorno suggests that resistance to social power means showing reality as it is. It means refusing false reconciliation with painful reality and showing the impossibility of reproducibility in a negative way.[142] This challenge is not an attempt to reject the things set in society, but to present a perspective different from what has already been established through criticism of the repressive violent tendencies of society by participating in suffering with solidarity.[143] This means that there is a possibility of justice in speaking the truth. Although complete justice comes from God, the civil rights movement and just practices such as telling the truth about history have been empowered by God's *dikaiosyne*, a rectifying power. This dynamic of the collective self has mirrored God's inbreaking with us in solidarity. Such truth-telling is not an ethic but a calling, as Jae Hyuk Jin preaches: "Can we

138. Volf, *Exclusion and Embrace*, 123.
139. Hudson and Turner, *Saved from Silence*, 13.
140. Kim and Kim, "Study on Experience of Bereaved," 102, 113.
141. O'Connor, *Lamentation and the Tears*, 128.

142. Adorno claims that limited subjective experience can take away the dignity of the most obvious. Adorno, *Negative Dialectics*, 213, 359.

143. What Adorno wants to criticize is not reason itself, but an instrumental reason that embodies the dominant logic by establishing a reason that is completely independent of the outside world. He does not intend to dismantle reason, but criticizes the notion of a good consciously or unconsciously forced by society. Lee, "Adorno's Negative Dialectic," 94.

say that the community is alive if there is no lamenting that for the pain and suffering of the nation except as our pain and weep for it? ... The moment when we mourn with the lament of God, God gives it to us as our mission."[144] Thus, lament-driven preaching is an act of invasion into the suffering from evil including injustice. Lament stirs and exposes unseen impurities at the root of society or in the hearts of individuals, and it bluntly accuses people of ignoring evil, making people long for eternal righteousness, *dikaiodyne theou*.

Lisa Rhodes' preaching breaks the silence, just as Esther did in speaking for her nation. In the following sermon excerpt, Rhodes laments the unbearable suffering caused by the social oppression that Black women have experienced, confesses the reality of their fear of truth-telling, and invites people to break the silence as an expression of their faith.

> Esther hesitated to give way to her secret. For breaking secrets can mean personal exposure, ridicule, and rejection. Young girls who are molested by family members, altar boys who are molested by priests, or women who are abused by spouses have extreme difficulty giving voice to their silent pain and suffering. Family members who have lost loved ones or experienced delays in their ability to give voice to their grief struggle. ... Homosexual and gay men and women and AIDS victims struggle with breaking the silence for fear of losing their jobs, their public offices, or their credibility. ... Sisters and brothers, we have been silent for too long. We have closed the doors to our emotional pain and suffering, and we will not say a word. ... Therefore, we say nothing about the interpersonal injustices, infidelity, and abuse. We continue to endure the escalating devastation in our communities, the alarming rates of divorce, teenage pregnancy, poor test scores, and low achievement. ... It's time to break the silence. Do not let fear of losing privilege, becoming vulnerable or exposed, hinder you from breaking the silence.[145]

Continuing Unfinished Stories

Lament becomes an important thread that enables the narrative of grief to persist across time, as Brueggemann argues that "Israel may despair; but it refuses amnesia."[146] The reappearance of voice allows listeners to remember

---

144. Jin, "Lamenting Community."
145. Rhodes, "It's Time to Break the Silence," 13–14.
146. Brueggemann, *God*, 17.

the stories, to accept responsibility for the history of forgotten incidents, and to mourn properly. This reappearance of voice is connected to an emotional posture that does not stay in oneself but looks at the suffering of the other and acts to address their pain. In preaching, this psychological and emotional intimacy prompts the congregation to remember one another's pain and accept it into their lives as a new way of life. This act can break the learned indifference and oblivion. It connects seemingly distant concepts including the church and the world, the past and the present, the individual and the other, and also the Christian and the non-Christian.[147] However, this unfinished story also encompasses God's faithfulness, accompanied by human stories in suffering. The crying, "gone is my glory!" (Lam 3:18) is a faithful remembrance of God that has now come to be in the particular narrative of Israel (Lam 3:21–26). The memory of the faithfulness of God enables anticipation of God's impending faithfulness.

Some people speak of this process of providing new healing memories to put alongside painful ones as a process of "postmemory"—it is the beginning of recovery.[148] A preacher can work as a narrator of postmemory by encouraging the congregation to resist those who would erase the pain or turn away from it.[149] Scars are not removed from one's wounded memory, but new narratives can help the wounded "to return fully to the self as socially defined, to establish a relationship again with the world."[150] In this process, remembering the voice of the wounded is essential for restoring their shattered heart and life. In order to keep their courageous truth-telling, a lament for their painful narratives must be heard so that the community does not forget them too easily.

The *Sewol* ferry incident occurred on April 16, 2014. Even seven years after the accident, one mother (and probably many more) was still

---

147. See Brydon's idea of psychological decolonization. Brydon, "Cross-Talk," 76.

148. As Hirsch mentions, writers have a role in connecting the memory (which is the memory of the generation who suffered and the next generation who received it) and postmemory (which is the person who suffered and the other person who received it) in terms of a close and lasting relationship with life. Hirsch, *Family Frames*, 23. This is akin to the role of the preacher, who acts as the bridge between the Bible and the modern world.

149. Postmemory is distinguished from memories in terms of the distance between generations and is also distinguished from history in terms of deep personal relevance. The characteristics of postmemory are related to the experiences of people who have grown up with their pre-birth stories, and Hirsh has developed this concept in relation to the children of Holocaust survivors. Hirsch, *Family Frames*, 22. However, I include into this term all people's painful experiences that have just happened and have been forgotten by people and society.

150. Culbertson, "Embodied Memory," 169–95.

experiencing the same pain as the day her lovely daughter drowned and was buried at sea. For such poignant suffering, preachers can continue to lament as a continuation of memory, as did this one:

> The state is attempting to bury the truth of the *Sewol* ferry incident in the past by leveraging its power. With power, the people are trying to erase the memories of the *Seowol*; and the church, in the name of faith, is trying to turn the truth of *Seowol* to heaven. What is different? Right now, they want to cry, they are in pain, and they are suffering. Now they want to know why their children died. Why bury the truth in the past? Why turn to heaven and turn to the future? Why do you not say, "I'm here to cry and mourn here and stay with them until the end"? Who says stop this lamenting? Our job is to be with them! We need to change our faith, our eyes to see the world. . . . This is the existence of believers' lives. So, alongside these mothers . . . to the end . . . by their side. . . . We should be at their side until they can be separated from their children in peace.[151]

Keeping the memory of suffering alive in preaching requires pastoral sensitivity. Preachers should think deeply about the historical burdens that victims of violence or those who suffer can bear. They need to feel a sense of solidarity and responsibility with individuals who encounter this pain rather than with particular ideology and politics (cf. Lam 5:7, 16).[152]

Also, memories are reconstructed starting from the present, not the past. The survivor's memory becomes a common memory in being alive in the midst of various ways of thinking and norms of society surrounding the survivor.[153] Perspectives, however, can be changed as the individual's position changes, and as the relationship with other environments changes.[154] Therefore, it is precarious for a preacher to deliver a sermon as if they comprehend and know all there is to know about any particular suffering, even if that suffering is identical or similar to the preacher's own experience.

---

151. Lee preached for "*Sewol* Tragedy Second Anniversary Memorial Prayer Meeting" on April 12, 2016 in Ku, "Theologians in the Era of *Sewol* Ferry."

152. Dealing with the problem of sexual slavery in the Japanese military is not limited to this problem but will play an important role in looking at the wounds of the colonies. It can be expanded to postcolonial discourse by not confining itself to Korea but also offering the possibility to consider the past history of East Asia. Yu, "Ethics of Representation," 77–95.

153. Halbwachs, *Collective Memory*, 44–49. For example, the testimony of "Comfort Women" is an eye-witness account by other "Comfort Women" and also an experience story of a Korean woman who survived the colonial era.

154. Halbwachs, *Collective Memory*, 48.

If unfamiliarity with an event far exceeds the preacher's experience, it is dangerous to testify to the truth.[155] For such testimony can be an appropriation of the other's truth in my own way.[156] In this case, the meaning of participation or empathy in order to correctly reproduce the painful voice of the other can instead start by acknowledging differences rather than by identifying with the other.

In terms of communal memory, a preacher can be a witness as can anyone in the community. The preacher's testimony can represent the other voice, which is absent.[157] In this case, however, some memories are unnamed and there is a risk of forming universal and special stereotypes when minority subjects are included in the majority discourse.[158] For example, in a situation of oppression, if the Black experience is perceived as analogous to the Asian experience or the experience of any other ethnic group, then Asian or other group experiences and interventions may face marginalization.[159]

Using story, preachers can enter a witness's own mind and memory, without judging the testimonies by some theoretical framework.[160] Such use of narrative testimony can be criticized by scholars who do not value individual experiences in preaching, but reproducing pain needs to be based on survivors' experiences. O'Connor's interpretation of Lamentations also supports this context as a theology of witness. Such a valuing of survivors' stories does not weaken God's authority or God's agency. Rather, a theology of testimony reinforces the necessity of God's prompt and urgent intervention. It does not remove the sufferers from listeners' lives as "other," but instead it can play an important role in getting people involved in sufferers' lives within the memory structure. The language of memory and regeneration can be a common language. It can allow us to realize who we are by revealing the dynamics that already exist and by making the voice and language heard.[161] Thus, lament-driven preaching is continuously uncovering narratives of those who suffer so that makes their pain and their truth are not easily forgotten.

155. Chun, "Beyond Politics of Memory," 476.
156. Chun, "Beyond Politics of Memory," 477–78.
157. Beverley, "Margins at the Center," 16.
158. Julien and Mercer, "De Margin and De Centre," 455.
159. Julien and Mercer, "De Margin and De Centre," 457.
160. Yang, "Testimony and Writing History," 60–98.
161. Yang, "Testimony and Writing History," 92.

Preaching and Holy Saturday

Lamen-driven preaching offers a place for the wounded to be included in the discourse between the suffering of people and God. Preachers have tended to consider suffering in terms of either Good Friday or Easter, but Holy Saturday can be a way of holding them in tension. Holy Saturday shows the story of God who is present in the deepest and darkest abyss though it has been marked by absence and silence in the liturgy of the church. The language of lament in Holy Saturday neither ends with the destruction and death nor darts off to hope. Pain is preserved on Saturday. B. S. Childs insists on the need to stay: "To pass all too quickly from the threat to the promise can jeopardize the overpowering reality of life under divine judgment."[162] Brown recognizes the place for disconnection between suffering and hope, saying that "news of grace and resurrection rings hollow disconnected from daily realities of loss, dispossession, and yearning for justice."[163] As in Lamentations, God as a listener may let people have time and space to lament and complain, including about God seeming to be remote or silent. The delay of hope may create such a place. This place of lament can also be used as healing to purify negative emotions such as anger, hatred, and frustration.[164] Lament may function as a hinge to link two places. Testifying to eternal hope requires the language of lament. Lament is a multi-layered reflection of suffering and hope that exists in an unsettling space beyond the mere description of suffering and hope. We see a lamenting God in the abyss of Holy Saturday who embraces all of human suffering and sorrow in the place of staying. "The wonders here are not spectacles of strength and power. They are rather manifestations of fidelity that linger in the abyss."[165]

Retelling a detailed painful story in a sermon can be hard, but sometimes it can be necessary. Stephen Ferris argues that "a sermon on lament should reach down toward depths of human suffering," not only because salvation and hope can come from "this moment of utter hopelessness" but because those depths of suffering are valid and deserve our attention and time.[166] Preachers may proclaim a God who forms strong solidarity with humans suffering greatly.

Marie M. Fortune presents the story of a woman named Delia Alaniz who had her husband Roy murdered, a husband who had been both

162. Childs, *Old Testament Theology*, 234.
163. Brown, "When Lament Shapes the Sermon," 28.
164. Hankle, "Therapeutic Implications," 275.
165. Brueggemann, *God*, 17.
166. Farris, *Preaching That Matters*, 57; Tietje, *Toward a Pastoral Theology of Holy Saturday*, 16.

physically and sexually abusing herself and her children for seventeen years. The wife was sentenced to ten years for second-degree murder for hiring a contract killer. Four children who need their mother will now spend ten years without her in pain. Her husband threatened to rape her daughter in front of her and pointed a gun at her son's head. In the reality of their miserable life, Fortune addresses and laments the pain they have suffered and invite people to the place of deep sorrow to face and stay in the reality of injustice, suffering, the fear of death, and hopelessness:

> There are many women facing the choice that Delia faced every day. There are many women who have tried every available means to stop the violence in their lives. . . . [W]here is God's promise to us? Where is God's promise to Delia? Where is God's promise to those who choose to protect themselves in the face of violence? . . . The role that God takes and the role that God expects of all of us is clear: It is to stand with, to be in solidarity with, those who are vulnerable and threatened by violence and harm. It is to provide sanctuary and to seek justice. . . . The killing of Roy Alaniz was not the failure of Delia Alaniz's moral character; it was the failure of our community. We, the community and the legal system, did not protect her from him. Even here, with the Domestic Violence Act, inadequate enforcement and too few social services to support victims mean that we cannot, in fact, guarantee the protection of battered women and their children from their batterers. Until we can, women will choose this last resort to end the violence in their lives.[167]

Note how here Fortune does not rush to hope. Fortune carefully extends Delia's suffering to the fears and pain of all women, and even the pain of racial, religious, and social differences. Nonetheless, I suggest that had she included a reference to Christ's suffering and solidarity, the preaching meaning of Holy Saturday would have been more effectively revealed.[168]

Some characteristics of lament-driven preaching in suffering deal with various layered and depth of suffering in connection with hope. That means the first note of lament song in preaching can be pain, despair, injustice but it has soon a polyphonic dynamic with a note of hope as all the octave notes vibrate when one strikes a note of music.

---

167. Fortune, "Wings of Eagles," 127–31.
168. Fortune, "Wings of Eagles," 131.

The Features of Hope in Lament-Driven Preaching

Lament embraces a sense of suffering. At the same time, it may open a new conversation about hope.[169] Lament shows that when the ashes of Ash Wednesday are applied to the forehead at the beginning of Lent, the gravity of hope from the resurrection is already pulling it.[170] Hope will not be sudden or enforced. Nor will hope be shallow or premature.[171] Hope grows slowly and gradually in the hearts of those who are about to face their pain. As Ellen Davis says, "Honest talk about God and to God in the midst of suffering is the only way to realistic hope. . . . Slowly we add to the almost imperceptibly thin layers of lasting hope each time we turn our hearts honestly and fully toward God."[172] This hope in the deepest heart of the wounded must flow very carefully and genuinely. The scars of Good Friday remain on the body of Christ after Easter. And these scars are a permanent warning against a premature proclamation of hope.[173] In this sense, lament-driven preaching in hope never forgets the sense of suffering.

Envisioning God's Final Promises

When preaching eschatological hope, preachers do well to remember that the final hope and the present hope are intimately linked.[174] Eschatological hope shapes the present life through the Holy Spirit.[175] In the connection between the future and the present, hope is transformed into a more specific word, one that means more than waiting. If the hope of Christianity lies in the cross and resurrection, then waiting can be said to be the mystery of preparing for the coming of Christ and the power of the Holy Spirit based on this hope.[176] The eschatological presupposes God's righteousness, rectifying power, and faithfulness.[177] The faithfulness of God (δικαιοσύνη θεοῦ) can be received as a response to the lament about fallen creation, whatever form that takes.[178] God has a clear goal: the redemption of God's people and the

---

169. Hilkert, "Preaching the Folly of the Cross," 44.
170. Sancken, *Stumbling over the Cross*, 176.
171. Blaine-Wallace, "Politics of Tears," 186.
172. Davis, "Is It Nothing?," para. 11.
173. Brueggemann, *Theology of the Old Testament*, 332.
174. Wright, *Surprised by Hope*, 5.
175. Powery, *Dem Dry Bones*, 84.
176. Pae, "With the Hope to Theology of Waiting," 117.
177. Rutledge, *Crucifixion*, 557, 565.
178. Wright explains the word with three characteristics: covenant language,

ultimate rescue of the entire created world.[179] Grace extends to all creation. The faithfulness of Jesus (πίστεως Χριστοῦ) is how the righteousness of God is revealed.[180] The tension between reality and promise allows us to recognize the promise of the Spirit (τὴν ἐπαγγελίαν τοῦ Πνεύματος, Gal 3:14). Thus, preachers note and claim that the perfect grace revealed through the faithfulness of God is completed through the faithfulness of the Holy Spirit. God not only calls people to enter into a covenant with God: God also helps people to stay in faithful to the covenant (Rom 8:3–4; Gal 4).[181] How does God help them? Through the Holy Spirit, which empowers people to join the time of eschatological approach (Gal 5:23). Thus, *dikaiosyne theou* is expanded by the faithfulness of Jesus and led by the Holy Spirit, who helps the community keep God's covenant. This language recognizes that the God of creation and the God of the covenant are one. People can trust God who is "making all things new" (Rev 21:5). God's justice and love are a response to the fallen creation's lament. When preachers proclaim eschatological hope, it is best conceived as dikaiosyne theou or as a rectifying and faithful power of the triune God who is on the move. Such preaching employs a language that envisions the future and reveals another hidden reality of the world.[182] This provides not only an eschatological picture of the future, but also includes resistance and protest against the present fallen world order.[183]

From Romans 8:18–30, David Jacobson preaches about the present hope of believers who live in the reality of suffering through *dikaiosyne* of the Holy Spirit; the message is based on eschatological hope—the hope of "the Spirit as the down payment of glory in order to help us to hope while we persevere in the suffering of the here and now."[184] Jacobson continues:

---

law-court language, and eschatological language. Wright, *What Saint Paul Really Said*, 104–10, 117–18.

179. Wright, *Justification*, 101.

180. Wright, *What Saint Paul Really Said*, 125. Barclay interprets πίστεως Χριστοῦ (Gal 2:16) as faith in Christ. Barclay says "God considers this 'righteousness' not because faith is a superior disposition, but because faith in Christ is the expression of a life derived from the Christ-event." Barclay, *Paul and the Gift*, 379. It may be controversial to say so, but the Christ-event itself can be understood as the faithfulness of Christ because the action at the apex of God's love is the faithfulness of God in which justice and love are integrated.

181. Wright, *Paul in New Perspective*, 99.

182. Powery, *Dem Dry Bones*, 95; Brueggemann, *Prophetic Imagination*, 7; Campbell, *Word before the Powers*, 104.

183. Powery, *Dem Dry Bones*, 96.

184. Jacobsen, *Preaching in the New Creation*, 100.

We also live in a world groaning for relief. We inhabit a creation sighing for an end to the pain. We Spirit-dwelling church folk also live in a world longing for release.... [W]hen we groan, the Spirit groans with us. We do not sigh alone.... Sure, there is pain. Yet there is also hope—for a new world is coming to birth.... We all remember the news reports a few summers ago about the carnage in Rwanda. The Hutu and Tutsi tribes there were at each other's throats in a Rwandan civil war.... In the meantime, all the Rwandan people suffered. Many died from vicious machete attacks. Others collapsed on the way to refugee camps. Still others languished in exile as the world looked on helplessly. Yet one woman refused to give in. In the midst of her people's pain, she went into labor to give birth to a baby girl: a small newborn swaddled amid clashing tribes and mayhem. Yet with all the old battles over allegiances and identities swirling about her, do you know the name her mother gave the baby? Her mother called her Esperance. Her name means "Hope." Her mother named her hope. Well, this is why God's Spirit has come to our aid, too: to comfort us as the new age is born among us. God's Spirit is here to give hope through the birth pangs—to a new creation."[185]

The eschatological hope is more than an indication of the future.[186] The space in which we are told the word of God is also a place where yesterday, tomorrow, and today meet, and a space that brings us to the day when God will restore everything. Standing in that space and showing what is beyond that space is the job of a preacher. For that, the preacher is dependent on the Holy Spirit. Preachers need to resist "whenever hope no longer lies in the Other, but in the self; whenever this self becomes so introverted that it could be called sin; whenever God-images become so powerful that they contradict the cross; whenever the resurrection is misunderstood as 'power-for-us'; whenever eschatology becomes domesticated."[187] Preachers may act as "agents of eschatological fluidity" who break down fixed identities and maintain s an already-not-yet dynamic.[188]

---

185. Jacobsen, *Preaching in the New Creation*, 135–37.
186. Wright, *Surprised by Hope*, 251, 259; Neal, *Overshadowed Preacher*, 1–23.
187. Campbell and Cilliers, *Preaching Fools*, 168.
188. Campbell and Cilliers, *Preaching Fools*, 168.

Upholding the Vulnerability of Hope

When hope is proclaimed in the place of suffering, preachers have an opportunity to refer not only to a strong and perfect hope but also to the vulnerability of Christ's cross and the vulnerability of the limitation of human understanding about God's acts which bring hope. Jürgen Moltmann says, "Although the Spirit fills Jesus with the divine, living energies through which the sick are healed, it does not turn him into a superman. It participates in his human suffering to the point of his death on the cross."[189] The way of God's salvation is often different from what human beings expect. It is important to recognize the anxiety and incompleteness that are present in hope, and view its imperfection in the fullness of the future.

Fleming Rutledge preaches that the suffering we face is not resolved in a single hopeful event but is constantly present in our lives. She emphasizes that the Exodus, though it may seem like complete salvation, is not the end of suffering; rather, we find ourselves still in Pharaoh's way. In her sermons, the reality of human life appears different from hope that we expect.

> One of the most memorable news stories I ever read in my whole life was a New York Times report of a train ride in South Africa right after the collapse of apartheid. On the day of President Mandela's inauguration, a renowned journalist rode from the Soweto ghetto into Pretoria. During the entire three-hour ride, the black passengers celebrated their liberation by singing and dancing in the aisles. . . . He called it a moment of "historic exultation." . . . Today, several years later, South Africa, as we know, has a whole new set of problems to deal with. Just so, the Exodus was only the beginning of the Israelites' troubles. We still live in a world of bondage to sin, evil, and death. . . . The ways of Pharaoh still rule this age. In this world, the last word for you and the last word for me will be death. All the routes of escape have been closed off.[190]

But later in the sermon, Rutledge once again proclaims hope. "But listen: there is another, greater Way; there is another, greater Life; there is another, greater Power. . . . When all the ways of escape are shut off, when the whole world seems "shut up in the wilderness," . . . listen, listen, people of God."[191] She declares that God's hope continues to operate in the midst of the pervasive reality of suffering. This hope originates from God, not from

---

189. Moltmann, *Spirit of Life*, 62.
190. Rutledge, *And God Spoke to Abraham*, 82.
191. Rutledge, *And God Spoke to Abraham*, 82.

human endeavors or events. It is proclaimed in the midst of suffering, acknowledging its reality rather than denying it. This hope stems from God's ongoing will to set right what is wrong.

Hope can "create feelings of unrest, of knowing that we have not yet arrived at destination.... [L]ament and longing are bound together" in it.[192] In the same vein, Kaethe Weingarten suggests that hope is ongoing, incomplete, and exists with pain.[193] This vulnerable hope is connected to the concept of hope that Campbell and Cilliers name when they write that, "through lament we grieve and learn to relinquish all perceived forms of human restoration, and this grieving opens up the space for hope to be born, a hope that anticipates a new beginning beyond all human endeavors."[194] A preacher who speaks such hope refuses to refine her words, organize her experiences of suffering, give easy answers, or preach as if she knows all the answers. Rather, the preacher invites the congregation to imagine a kind of hope that is vulnerable and that works in a mysterious way.[195]

Presenting the Laments of God

The image of a God who laments with us in our place of pain is crucial to preaching hope in the midst of suffering. This is because this vulnerable and lamenting God, who hears our suffering and joins us in our pain, is a God who responds to that suffering and ultimately brings salvation. God's character in the Bible is diverse, mysterious, and may seem even contradictory, contributing to the view of the "unreadable amalgamation" of many biblical texts.[196] In Jeremiah, Kathleen O'Connor finds a sacred, angry, jealous, and abusive husband (2:1—4:2), a creator of battle, a destroyer of creation, and an army general (4:5—6:30), and a weeping God who constantly mourns over the destruction of people (8:18—9:2).[197] O'Connor gives witness that God, who was separated from Zion's suffering in 8:18-20, dissolves the distance in verse 21.[198] O'Connor captures the message that betrayal, adultery, and evil lead to empathy, weakness, and deep sorrow, not violence, war, and revenge. God's lament overwhelms anger and sympathy replaces

---

192. Campbell and Cilliers, *Preaching Fools*, 48.
193. Weingarten, "Reasonable Hope," 5-25.
194. Campbell and Cilliers, *Preaching Fools*, 145.
195. Sancken, *Words That Heal*, 88.
196. O'Connor "Tears of God," 172-73.
197. O'Connor "Tears of God," 172-85.
198. O'Connor "Tears of God," 182.

anger.[199] God's tears go beyond the meaning of a sign of the loss and tragedy of the world. They unite a ruthless and jealous angry warrior with a weak and helpless God. A lamenting God opens the way to provide an alternative view of the suffering of the exiles, freeing God from the role of a proud male or a cruel warrior.[200]

To be specific, it is intriguing that God's tears precede and lead the women and community mourning in Jeremiah 9.[201] Here God becomes a mourning woman.[202] In the metaphor of God as a weeping woman, God's tears are shed on the reality of the community.[203] The writer sets God within the realities of the community, depicts God as a part of the community, and changes the way people confess God as a liberator. We look at this in relation to the solidarity of God with the community in a reality where no trace of immediate relief is found.[204] The metaphor of the lamenting God challenges the way of divine retribution that has dominated much of the interpretation of the Bible.[205] The metaphor also presents a divine feminine image that balances male images, providing us with an alternative understanding of power, that can give an ethical meaning to a broken world.[206]

In terms of rhetoric and pathos, or emotion, this God "feels intensely: loves, cares, is glad, gets angry over injustice, urges, prods, forgives, is disappointed, becomes frustrated, suffers righteous indignation, weeps, grieves, promises, pours out mercy, rejoices, consoles, wipes away tears, and loves some more."[207] For Moltmann, Jesus' passion was not a passive way; rather it was one in which he actively participated in his own death to demonstrate his solidarity with all those who suffer.[208] "Christ's lament is not merely a commiseration of shared suffering, but instead bears witness to his substitutional and thus redemptive suffering."[209] God responded with compassion to the human plight, especially eagerly caring for the happiness of those who have been sacrificed and who collapsed under historical injustice.[210]

---

199. O'Connor, "Tears of God," 183.
200. O'Connor, "Tears of God," 184.
201. Claassens, *Mourner*, 30.
202. Claassens, *Mourner*, 31.
203. Claassens, *Mourner*, 33.
204. Claassens, *Mourner*, 33.
205. Claassens, *Mourner*, 33.
206. Claassens, *Mourner*, 34.
207. Johnson, *Quest for the Living God*, 57.
208. Moltmann, *Crucified God*, 68–70.
209. Harasta, "Crucified Praise and Resurrected Lament," 211.
210. Johnson, *Quest for the Living God*, 58.

Chi-Seon Kim preaches that God's tears have brought about a final victory.

> The tears of Jesus Christ were tears of love, tears of poignant suffering shed when he saw his people's collapse, and tears of his sacrifice as a Redeemer.... The tears of the Lord accomplished the great work of redemption, which was to save not only the people of Israel but also all of mankind in the past, present, and future.... The tears of Christ brought the final victory, and this is the resurrection of Christ.... We are convinced that great works will appear where the tears of Christ are contained.[211]

Fleming Rutledge likewise preaches that Christ's lamenting brings life and becomes hope. She emphasizes that the message of the resurrection is made of Christ's tears for us:

> Now, as the Messiah at last appears, she [the city] is going to arrest him on a trumped-up charge, try him in the middle of the night, flog him nearly to death, and execute him the way we execute serial killers and terrorist bombers, though in an infinitely worse manner. Yet Jesus does not weep for himself. He weeps for the city. He weeps for those who will soon shout "Crucify him!" In other words, he weeps for us.... All these tears and every tear that has ever been shed by anyone anywhere are rolled up into the tears of Jesus. Jesus weeps for us. The Son of God weeps for you.... Jesus' tears encompass the entire human tragedy.... In the tears of the one man Jesus, God's complete solidarity with human pain, yes, but also with human man sin is shown ... Easter was not "made easy" for Jesus.... Easter cost the greatest price that has ever been paid in the history of the universe.... Your tears and mine are merely sentimental most of the time, but the tears of Jesus are wrung out of God's inmost heart of yearning compassion. The Messiah weeps for the sin that brings him to Jerusalem to die for her redemption. It is our complicity in sin that brings him there; it is our sin that he bears away from us like the scapegoat going into the wilderness. He weeps for you and for me.[212]

Preachers might say that God laments first of all for those who suffer. Preachers neither need to find the reasons for suffering nor seek hasty comfort to offer. Rather, preachers can present the broken heart of God as

---

211. Kim, "Tears of Loving National People," 23–28.
212. Rutledge, "Tears of Palm Sunday," in *Undoing of Death*, 6, 8.

William Coffin preaches in the funeral of his beloved son: "God's heart was the first of all our hearts to break."[213]

The lamenting God can be a good alternative to the negative side of the suffering God. The image of a suffering God may too easily seem to reconcile the fundamental disagreement between God and suffering, and can dissipate the tension that victims feel. Yet, the image of a lamenting God prevents the glorification of human pain by exalting God's suffering.[214] Still, preachers need to defend and uphold the cardinal question of suffering. Without awareness of the lamenting God, the world would be filled with despair and abandonment, or feel compelled to embrace an incomprehensible faith. A lamenting God inspires a hope that respects suffering.

Presenting God as Liberating and Decolonizing

Rutledge argues that the purpose of the cross is "to rescue the oppressed, the imprisoned, and the enslaved" from both "human oppressors and the power of Death and Sin."[215] The biblical testimony claims that God is working to liberate creation from "its bondage to decay" (Rom 8:21). The reality of bondage will exist until the eschaton. This *déjà vu* of pain can be said of any place and any age; all ages are full of the "honest cry of darkest despair."[216] We preachers need to preach the liberating and decolonizing God not just as an event in the future, but rather as an event of love that offers people freedom today.[217]

The idea of a decolonizing God pays specific attention to how "histories and cultures of colonialism/imperialism intrude upon contemporary life."[218] Some scholars project a retaliatory God and may resist minority cultural and political voices.[219] However, it seems closer to the nature of God to say that the triune God seeks to restore and reconstruct human relationships torn by imperialism.[220] The Trinity represents an unconditional love relationship, is mutually considerate, tolerates differences, and is open to the whole creation. The space formed by the Trinity is a creative space where voices speak of new truths and where they are free to refute, reject, change,

---

213. Coffin, "Alex's Death," 262–66.
214. Johnson, *Quest for the Living God*, 65.
215. Rutledge, *Crucifixion*, 451.
216. Swenson, *Living Through Pain*, 140.
217. Moltmann, *Crucified God*, 266.
218. Travis, *Decolonizing Preaching*, 74.
219. Sugirtharajah, "Muddling Along at the Margins," 10.
220. Travis, *Decolonizing Preaching*, 127.

and explain existing truth perceptions.[221] In order to deal with an unjust social illness, it becomes important to rediscover the God of the oppressed. This God laments major aspects of the past, finds the lost, liberates from the structure of dominion and repression, and initiates forgiveness and conciliation.[222]

Minjung theologians understand God in the Old Testament in this way—as the one who responds to the suffering of the oppressed. In their eyes, the New Testament presents a political vision that can make the *minjung* free from suffering and tears, and restore them to their rightful identity as God's people.[223] *Minjung* theology is concerned about what God has done in history.[224] *Minjung* theology values the emancipatory aspects of culture and traditional religion and participates in the historical struggle of suffering and resistance to the ruling class.[225] The language of liberation is linked to God's kin-dom and the good news is closely connected to justice. The ultimate goal of history is the spiritual completion of the kin-dom of God on earth by fighting against sin and structural evil.[226] Nam-Dong Suh considers releasing *han* to be good news and argues that the preachers as priests of *han* need to clarify the history of the sound in *han* and proclaim liberation from the negative accumulation of *han*.[227] In *minjung* theology, God stands on the side of humans who suffer from poverty or oppression and urges human participation in the restoration of the order of creation.[228] The basis for hope is to believe in a God who acts vigorously on behalf of the oppressed.[229]

Susan Bond moves from seeing those who are homeless as those who lack hope and safety to seeing them as the ones who are coming home in keeping with God's promise.[230] Through Isaiah's vision, Bond presents a community of the decolonized and liberated and sees them as having

---

221. Travis, *Decolonizing Preaching*, 127.

222. Travis, *Decolonizing Preaching*, 38, 90, 136; Johnson, *Quest for the Living God*, 80.

223. Park, *Korean Preaching*, 25.

224. Suh, "Historical References for a Theology of *Minjung*," 158.

225. Hyun, "Theological Look at the Mask Dance," 47–54; Suh, *Formulation of Minjung Theology*, 216.

226. Ahn, *Minjung Theology*, 252.

227. Suh, "Towards a Theology of *Han*," 48. In order for the energy of *han* to achieve the practice of social transformation, it must have a qualitative change in its own power, which must be used to end the vicious cycle of violence, which is the negative tendency of *han*. Kim, "Hoffnungs philosophische Interpretation," 332.

228. Lee, "Introductory Search," 53.

229. Powery, *Dem Dry Bones*, 116.

230. Bond, "Coming Home," 67.

security, justice, and inclusion in God's kin-dom. She emphasizes that this vision is concretely and physically realized. Throughout her sermon, God appears as the one who brings people together and fulfills Isaiah's promise: "to bring good news to the oppressed, to bind up the broken-hearted, to proclaim liberty to the captives, and release to the prisoners" (Isa 61:1).

> Isaiah's people . . . are grabbed up and taken into exile in another land. . . . Everybody is on hold and hopeless. There's no safe place anymore. They're convinced that the world is in trouble, but they feel helpless to change things. . . . We think about the growing cliquishness of the world. . . . Colonists came to this country as a pilgrim people wandering in the wilderness to find a freedom home and within 200 years had built up their "sanctuary" into a world-ravaging death machine, wielding power over other countries. The possession of land and wealth or the idea of a "nation for us" can quickly become demonic. But God's nation is not limited to one geographic, or ethnic, or religious, or racial group. . . . The good news is most particularly to those who have been left out, discarded, neglected, orphaned, and forgotten. . . . Do you see Isaiah's vision? In the darkest hour, when all seems hopeless, there is hope. When our children are at risk, when our streets are not safe, when our daily lives are captive to strangers, God's new world still takes shape. God's people gather from all corners of the world, to create a promised land of justice, a promised land of safety, an actual earthly turf where people can be safe and secure.[231]

Preaching God as the one who liberates and decolonizes may help change the essence of colonial discourse, heal the wounds of fear and anger, give oneself to others, create spaces to accept others, proclaim the freedom of the oppressed, destroy the structure of domination and captivity, and teach people to envision a human community formed by a discourse of love and freedom.[232] Where inequality is systemic and structural and violence is rife, action for justice is a concrete expression of belief.[233] Knowing and loving God can align one's life with divine actions, which leads to an experience of God's mysteries as they practice justice and peace for suffering people.[234] However, this is not a human victory, but God's mercy and power working through the human spirit.[235]

231. Bond, "Coming Home," 66–70.
232. Travis, *Decolonizing Preaching*, 90.
233. Johnson, *Quest for the Living God*, 83.
234. Johnson, *Quest for the Living God*, 86.
235. Rutledge, *Crucifixion*, 389.

Introducing People to the Resurrected and Present God

The resurrection of Jesus Christ is the event that ultimately promises that all suffering holds future healing.[236] The resurrection is not just a momentary event. Looking forward to the future, it is about the nation of God that is built in the present time.[237] Proclaiming the resurrected and present God is important in order to deal with suffering in hope because the resurrected and living God is the basis of the act and belief that can use lament to call on God's help and God's inbreaking power to end suffering. However, as Richard Lischer argues, such a sermon "takes death seriously, denying neither death nor the alienation, loneliness, anxiety, sin, and evil which cluster around it."[238] Rather, preachers may confess—as the Psalter does—that God is with us on the day of joy and tears and in heaven and *Sheol* (Ps 139:7–10).

Luke Powery argues that it is necessary to proclaim how the resurrected Lord, the living Lord, is related to human life and circumstance.[239] Proclaiming God who is resurrected, alive, and who is with us is what arouses the possibility of hope.[240] David Buttrick also says that in order to preach the new order of God convincingly, preachers need to be able to see God's action in the world.[241] Preachers do not seek God's presence only within the preacher's individual mind or within the boundaries of a church: they seek God from what happens while reflecting on the image of God in society.[242] Preaching the resurrection in the present tense reveals God's image to the world and participates in the mission toward restoring creation.[243]

Mary Turner's Easter sermon allows her listeners to envision a final day of resurrection without ignoring women's mourning for the suffering of the world, a mourning that will last until the end of time. She ponders the power of staying, finding value in the expression of sorrow through Mary and her willingness to stay and watch at Jesus' grave (John 20:1–18).[244] The "alleluia" which begins slowly at the end of Turner's sermon, lets the congregation overhear and anticipate the loud voice of a great multitude in heaven on the Lord's Day (Rev 19:1). Turner's thoughtful contemplation that we

---

236. Johnson, *Quest for the living God*, 78.
237. Wright, *God in Public*, 11.
238. Lischer, *Theology of Preaching*, 28.
239. Powery, *Dem Dry Bones*, 115.
240. Powery, *Dem Dry Bones*, 102.
241. Buttrick, *Preaching the New and Now*, 132.
242. Buttrick, *Preaching the New and Now*, 132–33.
243. Powery, *Dem Dry Bones*, 84.
244. Hudson and Turner, *Saved from Silence*, 125.

are able to stay in front of the sufferings of the world while recognizing that God is with us embodies God who is resurrected and is present in our lives.

> An invitation to go to those places in the world where there seems to be no hope—only death and despair. An invitation to go straight to the tomb and stay there. Plant ourselves firmly there, and even if the realities are too painful, not to avert our eyes, not to close our ears, and not to move away! Just stay there in the darkness, shivering from the cold, but standing there with whoever is there. Weeping for them, with them. But never, ever running away. Just standing there until the world who is watching cries out: People, why are you weeping? Then we would take the world by the hand and lead the world to the entrance, and we would say, "Look into the tomb." We would show them who is living there. . . . There is a woman there, a vacant look in her eyes. She knows only about a love that is crude and abusive. There is a child with parched, cracking lips and swollen stomach, dying from hunger. There is a person dying alone from a disease that sadly yet has no cure. They are all there; they have given up any hope for life. We would want to turn away. But Mary says to us, "Stay there. Stay and stay and stay. Just stay, until in the midst of the noisy silence of the darkness . . . an alleluia is heard, maybe faint at first, but an alleluia, . . . maybe cold and broken, but an alleluia, a song of survival, a note of hopefulness that in the middle of the grief life brings pouring upon us. . . . [S]tay right there until tears of sadness become tears of joy because then we all know that God is there with us. . . . [W]e must keep our tear stained faces gazing toward all that is seemingly dead and dying until . . . the world hears that melody.[245]

Inviting Participation in the Cruciform Life of the Collective-Self

Until the end of days, the proclamation of hope is drawn into the dynamics between the gravity of suffering and the power of hope because of the real tension between the already and the not-yet. Thus, human life can be shaped by the dynamic that holds suffering and hope. In the Holy Spirit, the dynamics may allow Christians to walk forth toward eschatological hope, forming and reforming Christian identity and community by destroying the fallen old form and recreating one that is new.[246] In particular, it is a place

---

245. Hudson and Turner, *Saved from Silence*, 123–24.
246. Campbell and Cilliers, *Preaching Fools*, 43, 45.

where the communal lament occurs because the power of evil, death, and sin will continue till the end. In this sense, life before the Lord's Day may have a cruciform shape, as a hope that embraces the sorrow of the world.

The act of self-giving that we see in the cross of Christ is compassionate emotional and physical participation with sufferers. In both the Incarnation and the cross, Jesus Christ brings human experience, including that of suffering, betrayal, and death, into the divine life.[247] The cross is a sign of solidarity with sufferers and its power can be unfolded by participation in the cross.[248] The Christian community as a body of Christ has a collective memory in which there are tragedy, struggles, death, and suffering.[249] Thus, the cruciform image teaches us the value of listening and responding to others' pain because "God not only gives us God's word but also lends us God's ear."[250] This perspective indicates that those who listen to another's pain are part of the collective self: "The suffering person is joined by friends who join their tears and prayers in a communal lament. They do not hush up the sound of weeping but augment it. They do not hide the sufferer away from view but bring him or her out into the public square."[251]

To join in the cruciform life can be understood as the conviction that God is always with us, though it may feel like a burden of responsibility or the cost of salvation.[252] The grace manifested in God's unconditional salvation and love does not remove the duty of discipleship; rather grace allows us to embrace the reality of suffering before the cross.[253] The hope of lament has a scope beyond solidarity with those who suffer. Wilson argues that "God's purpose is not merely to make us righteous, but that we extend that righteousness to one another and the created order."[254] Eventually, lament fosters a cruciform life that draws the eschatological *dikaiosyne* into the present. It resonates with the suffering of all creation in the Holy Spirit who laments for the whole creation (cf. Rom 8:22–26). By participating in and responding to the lives of those who suffer, preachers may invite a community to have a sense of collective self with a cruciform life which opens

---

247. Sancken, *Stumbling over the Cross*, 56.
248. Smith, *Preaching as Weeping*, 155.
249. Powery, *Dem Dry Bones*, 44.
250. Bonhoeffer, *Life Together*, 98.
251. Peterson, *Five Smooth Stones*, 143.
252. Sancken, *Stumbling over the Cross*, 18.
253. Wilson, *Four Pages*, 151.
254. Wilson, *Four Pages*, 151.

into "mutual engagement" and a "multiple-subject position," in so doing rejecting a binary choice or way.[255]

Cruciform lament needs to be understood as an act of the resurrected Jesus who is embodied in a community for healing the fallen world. In this regard, the preacher can show God's presence and power, often through the small actions of God's people that restores humanity without trying to solve all of the problems of evil, injustice, and human cruelty.[256] Jesus' story becomes our story, Jesus' mourning becomes our mourning.[257] Congregations can live a life of mourning with others, accepting the pain of others as their own pain, thereby bringing the trace of Jesus' story into their lives.

Ji-Cheol Kim preaches that lament is a mission of the churches. Kim expects that preaching lament can be extended to the listener's missional life and presents the life of Jesus as a model of practicing lament in everyday life.

> Nehemiah heard the news that the people of his country are in great suffering and tribulation, that the walls have all collapsed and burned down, and that the land of his hometown is being assaulted.... As passion arose in Nehemiah's heart, he had to do more than mourn.... He decided to abandon a high-ranking official position in Persia and return to his people who were suffering. Nehemiah does not settle for his comfortable life.... He asked, then heard, and after that, he cried and mourned.... The pain he felt for the community is inherent in the hearts of those with a mission.... Where tears of mourning flow, life takes place. It is because Jesus shed tears of grief for us. Jesus visited the afflicted, healed them, and restored the oppressed. Jesus cried with them, mourned with them, and they shed bitter tears together.... Lament is an expression of pain for yourself, but it is also an expression of pain for our neighbors and for the times. Lament is a feeling of deciding not to live for only ourselves anymore. So, those who know how to mourn become leaders who view lament as the basis of their mission.[258]

To preach participation in a cruciform life of the collective self may seem to be a heavy task for normal preaching, as though it is a burdensome duty for Christians. This is because an invitation to participate in suffering is closely linked to the ethical or moral sense of a text. The purpose of such a sermon can be "to encourage those of different persuasions to make

---

255. Kwok, "Feminist Theology as Intercultural Discourse," 36–37.
256. Sancken, *Words That Heal*, 83.
257. Walsh and Keesmaat, *Colossians Remixed*, 228.
258. Kim, "Leadership of Lament."

responsible decisions for themselves in light of faith."[259] Wilson argues that ethical invitations of this nature may require more firm consideration of God's grace in order to avoid feelings of coercion. Wilson shows that the impossibility of a world full of suffering is turned into a possibility by God's actions and that God is calling believers to do this work.

> If Christmas is up to us there is no hope for the world. There is no Savior who is born.... That is the Christmas where the impossible becomes possible because with God all things are possible.... AIDS would be prevented for thirty million people; everyone would have clean drinking water, food, shelter, schools for their children, and hospitals for their sick. Instead of folks being anxious about the future, they would know the peace of the Prince of Peace, the Son of the Most High. Impossible, some say. Yes, it is impossible. But all things are possible for God. Wait but a little while, and you will see. And while you are waiting say, "Here am I, a servant of the Lord; let it be with me according to your word."[260]

The diversity of the forms of inspiration by God and the mission that God gives to individuals will make it possible for an entire community to participate in the cruciform life of the collective self. God transforms burden into opportunity and privilege.

With the lament features mentioned above, preachers will have ideas about how to preach hope effectively amid suffering. As Nicholas Lash mentions "what was said and done and suffered, then, by Jesus and his disciples [is similar to] what is said and done and suffered, now, by those who seek to share his obedience and hope."[261] Lament-driven preaching embraces both suffering and hope in a dynamic way at an unsettling place and moves them toward eternal hope.

PRACTICAL REFLECTIONS ON LAMENT-DRIVEN PREACHING

Preacher as a Lamenter

Preachers of lament tend to have a high "degree of self-engagement involved in a point of view."[262] This empathy forms a confessional and vulnerable

---

259. Wilson, *Broken Words*, 54.
260. Wilson, *Broken Words*, 57, 62.
261. Lash, "Performing the Scriptures," 42.
262. Buttrick, *Homiletic*, 59.

attitude. They can acknowledge the limitations and failures of the church as well as the wounds caused by concealment, denial, and systems breakdown.[263] Preachers need to acknowledge their lack of answers and inability to heal the wounds, and that the hope they proclaim lies at the border of their will of choice and passivity, the border where they rely on the Holy Spirit.[264] On the other hand, it is essential for preachers to maintain a critical sense of distance as well as sympathy with sufferers so that preachers can critically interpret the Bible and the reality of suffering without being engulfed by others' pain.[265]

Lament can be seen as the people's work empowered and inspired by the Holy Spirit. It is also the action of God who has solidarity with the suffering and who responds to the tears in the world. Preaching God's and humans' lament is "primarily and decisively God's own act" though it includes the willingness of the preacher or congregation.[266] Lament or not, the strong identity of Christian is aligned with God's redemptive action represented by the crucifixion and resurrection. God's work is not a reward for our dedication, and God's plan may be different from ours.[267] Nonetheless, the preacher works with and by the power of the Holy Spirit as God's partner. To God's mourning the preacher responds with all her mind and heart. Only then can the preacher be permeated as Jeremiah was with God's suffering at the state of God's people (Jer 8:18—9:1).[268] When the Spirit moves a preacher to lament, the preacher may lose his or her words and replace the sermon with tears.

A preacher whose lament is filled with the Holy Spirit testifies to all creation's suffering and to God's suffering that is due to the suffering of all creation. Such sermons continue the dialogue between humans and God, and dialogue with the wider society that goes beyond the boundaries of the Christian faith. The preacher cannot stop speaking out because she has gained her authority in her ongoing conversation with God.[269]

---

263. Sancken, *Words That Heal*, 76.
264. Neal, *Overshadowed Preacher*, 182, 184.
265. Eslinger, *Web of Preaching*, 26.
266. Barth, *CD* I/1:93.
267. Taylor, *Gospel Medicine*, 74.
268. Hudson and Turner, *Saved from Silence*, 29.
269. Hudson and Turner, *Saved from Silence*, 52.

The Timing of Hope

Wilson's model of trouble and grace normally presents a 50/50 or 60/40 ratio between suffering and hope. Lowry recommends that four-fifths of the way into a sermon is the place where a "sudden shift" may be made from suffering to hope, but notes that the timing of the gospel message can vary.[270] Lowry says that the reversal can also occur in the last sentence.[271] The liquidity of this reversal plays an important role in lament-driven preaching because moving too quickly to hope can mistakenly prevent giving people enough time to lament, except in situations where there is urgent need of hope—such as worship just before death.[272] Many preachers agree that the resurrection or the cross should not be used as a quick path to hope without probing the text at hand for hope, and developing it first in relation to the situation. When one does make a move to the cross, it is best to respect the depths of the agony on the cross and the sorrow being felt in the human situation.[273] When lament informs preaching, sometimes hope can be deferred. The delayed hope in preaching is not always a problem; rather it may show the relationship between death and life in a more complex way by clearly expressing the theology of God's redemption.[274]

Nonetheless, the ending note needs hope that is founded in God's definitive action. When God seems to be absent, God's word is powerful to give hope, comfort, and healing.[275] Sometimes, proclaiming that God is alive or God is present can of itself provide hope. However, a too-lingering hesitation would be not good for witnessing God's action in response to the suffering. Thus, the timing of hope varies depending on its contexts.

Considering Missing Ones

The majority of lament sermons may deal with the marginalized, the poor, the weak, or the oppressed. However, the gospel is for all. Radically speaking, the gospel includes the privileged, the empowered, the rich, and the oppressors. Not all the rich are oppressors. Preachers may consider that

---

270. Lowry, "Narrative Renewed," 93.

271. Lowry, *Sermon*, 78. The last sentence in Rice's sermon played this role of reversal. Rice, "Theater and Preaching," 23–25.

272. Eslinger, *Web of Preaching*, 52.

273. Wilson, *Practice of Preaching*, 251–52; Hilkert, *Naming Grace*, 42–43; Sancken, *Stumbling over the Cross*, 159; Eslinger, *Web of Preaching*, 38.

274. Rambo, "Spirit and Trauma," 16.

275. O'Connor, *Lamentations and the Tears*, 86.

all people have their own suffering and need the gospel to be addressed to them. In writing about the passage on the prodigal son (Luke 15:11–24), Barbara Brown Taylor raises intriguing questions:

> The church thrives on its ministries to the poor, the broken, the sick and outcast, but what about those of us who are holding our own? What about those of us who are ... trying to serve God and keep up with our other responsibilities, too ... but never seem to get any credit for it, while the homeless and the addicted and the downtrodden get all the attention? Do you have to go off and squander your inheritance before you can come home to be embraced, and kissed, and assured that you belong?[276]

Taylor does not advocate the elder son's sadness and anger, but she raises the matter of the older son's grief as something that also needs to be healed. Although the interpretive conclusions dealing with the grief of the older son in the prodigal son's story of the Bible may vary, the unnamed sorrow that she notices is more revealing of "a love that transcends right and wrong," without downgrading the first son's grief.[277] Considering lament from various angles enables one to find the often overlooked suffering and hidden hope.

Lament as Liturgical Language

The language of lament has been practiced in the liturgy, especially during Holy Week, as a way to remember Christ's crucifixion and to confess our sins. Sufferers commonly face a collapsed language in that pain may make people lose their voice. The role of preachers as leaders of community worship is very important to help people go "from the silence to lament."[278] If a worship space itself is a place of safety and covenant, lament songs draw a faithful God into their situation. The preacher can sustain the lament as a public language by using the word "we" in the public setting. Eastern Orthodox Christians speak of weeping as a second baptism.[279] While this is related to repentance, one of the most important things is that there has been a place in liturgy to practice lament, a place that imbues it with theological value.

---

276. Taylor, *Preaching Life*, 65–66.
277. Taylor, *Preaching Life*, 166.
278. Zylla, *Roots of Sorrow*, 81.
279. Ware, "Obscure Matter," 250.

Lament Prayers

Lament as a prayer has a synergistic effect when it is paired with a lament sermon. Also, as a confessional prayer, it works as a perfect part of the weekly liturgy. When a congregation laments for its own sin, the congregation can also face the wounded world and lament for it. Lament is about the individual and communal prayers of the wounded, confessional prayers, and powerful intercessory prayers for those who are in pain. Prayers of lament provide the space to take part in others' pain, as with the voice of the daughter of Zion, "Is it nothing to you, all you who pass by? Look and see" (Lam 1:12a).

Tonseung prayer (ch. 2) is also one of the strong public lament prayers. This model can be employed in other cultures beyond Korea as a way to include the power of public lament in the liturgy. A versicle prayer based on Lamentations would be a good example for communal lament in the liturgy, a prayer such as the following:

> (The *words in italics* are for all to recite)
> Is it nothing to you, all you who pass by? Look and see if there is any sorrow like my sorrow, which was brought upon me (Lam 1:12ab) I want to invite you to communal lament for the weak, especially for the children and women.
>
> (For Children)
> *My eyes are spent with weeping; my stomach churns; my bile is poured out on the ground because of the destruction of my people, because infants and babes faint in the streets of the city* (Lam 2:11).
>
> Please have pity on the children in the refugee villages of Syria, Myanmar (Rohingya), and South Sudan who have suffered from wars caused by adults.
>
> *My eyes are spent with weeping, Lord.*
>
> Please have pity on children who are abused sexually and mentally.
>
> *My eyes are spent with weeping, Lord.*
>
> Please have pity on children who cannot go to school but must work hard for ten hours a day produce pineapple, coffee, and

shoes in Central America, Southeast Asia, North Korea, and Africa.

My eyes are spent with weeping, Lord.

Please have pity on children who are suffering because they cannot get any help from the social system or from a charity but must live in extreme poverty.

My eyes are spent with weeping, Lord.

Please have pity on little children in Daesh who are being forced to train to kill people.

My eyes are spent with weeping, Lord. O Lord, do not forget how we have suffered and been disgraced (Lam 5:1).

(For Women)
What can I say for you, to what compare you, O daughter Jerusalem? To what can I liken you, that I may comfort you, O virgin daughter of Zion? For vast as the sea is your ruin; who can heal you? (Lam 2:13)

Please have mercy on women who are in danger of being married early, forced to become prostitutes, and forced to endure female circumcision.

My eyes are spent with weeping, Lord.

Please have mercy on Christian women and Yazidi women who are being sold as sex slaves by Boko Haram and Daesh.

My eyes are spent with weeping, Lord.

Please have mercy on women who are subjected to domestic violence.

My eyes are spent with weeping, Lord.

Please have mercy on women who suffer mentally.

My eyes are spent with weeping, Lord because of the sound of pain heard from everywhere. O Lord, do not forget how we have suffered and been disgraced (Lam 5:1)

Amen.

Lament Language in Communion

The language of lament may be a form of Holy Communion or a sacramental act in which Christ is met. Lament-driven preaching is not a series of sermons about the reality of suffering. Rather, it is a theological and communal embodied response to suffering in faith, based on divine and human empathy and participation. Thus, the connectivity of lament language in Communion with lament-driven preaching may create a mutual synergetic effect in a communal and participative sense. It is not necessary that all liturgical components include lament language. Lament may contribute to some part of the celebration of Holy Communion and worship:[280]

> (Invitation) We passed along the path of stories of those who are in pain, both in the Bible and today. The voice of suffering is also resonant on the cross. Jesus hears the pain of the world and laments for it. Jesus has brought the pain of all people in the world into his own life. Now, I invite you all and sufferers into the sacrament. The sacrament that we share with sufferers is to indicate that we are no longer passersby, but we are co-sufferers and we confirm we are not alone in our pain.
>
> (Bread) Our Lord Jesus, on the night before he died, took bread, and after giving thanks to God, broke it, and gave it to his disciples, saying: Take, eat. This is my body, given for you. As there is one loaf, we, different and diverse though we may be, constitute a singular body; for it is one loaf from which we all partake. (Breaking Bread) Now, before we share in it together, please split it apart with both hands. Like the bread we have broken, the heart of our Lord who saw broken people on the earth was broken. Thus, our Lord gladly broke his body like this. Remember the heart of our Lord. Let us share together in eating the bread.
>
> (Cup) In the same way, Jesus took the cup, saying: This cup is the new covenant sealed in my blood. Whenever you drink it, do this in remembrance of me. The land witnesses the blood and tears that have been shed as the result of injustice, terror, hunger, and violence. The blood and tears of Jesus Christ flow over the land. Remember the blood and tears of our Lord for the broken creation. Let us take the cup together.

---

280. The suggested prayer is not an entire Communion prayer, but a sample of language that pastors may consider integrating into their own liturgies.

(Prayer after Communion) We participated in the body and blood of Jesus Christ with those who are in pain. We confess we are one in Christ. Now, all sufferers' pain is our pain, and all sufferers' tears are our tears. May our lives resemble Jesus' life. May our eyes be like the eyes of Jesus, seeing the pain of the world. May our ears be like the ears of Jesus, hearing the voices of sufferers. May our feet be like the feet of Jesus, and go to the places where people are crying. May our hands resemble the hands of Jesus, embracing the wounded. In Jesus' name, Amen.

A language of lament can be applied to many parts of the liturgical setting as a space for suffering and bearing hope. In liturgy, language is important. As Dorothee Sölle argues, "If people are not to remain unchanged in suffering, if they are not to be blind and deaf to the pain of others, if they are to move from purely passive endurance to suffering that can humanize them in a productive way, then one of the things they need is language."[281] However, the language is expressed not only by voice but by movement, liturgical environment, art, gesture, and so forth.[282] Thus, preachers need to collaborate with the worshipers to make space for lament to deal effectively with suffering in hope in various places of worship.

CONCLUSION: LAMENT AS TRANSITIONAL SPACE

Suffering exists everywhere in any era, and seems not to end. This reality makes it unavoidable that preachers deal with suffering. The issues of suffering are intermingled with the powers of sin, death, and evil, all of which have great complexity. Suffering cannot be understood or explained in just one way. In particular, it can be ineffective to preach hope in hasty ways, denying pain, and the dichotomy between pain and hope, or in ways that risk judging people.

There is a need for a language of faith that embraces both suffering and hope but that neither alienates nor slanders anyone. There is a need for an unsettling language that attests to God's presence and God's intervention but does not deny the reality of suffering. There is a need for a safe, open language that can respect and express pain but neither interprets pain from a single angle nor manipulates it into the framework of sin and judgment. Lament language needs to deal with the complex reality of suffering in hope because lament's dual identity continuously crosses over between pain and hope, thus forming a dynamic that refuses to remain on just one side of

281. Sölle, *Suffering*, 75.
282. Hudson and Turner, *Saved from Silence*, 1.

either pain or hope. This dynamic is the way in which the Holy Spirit, given to those who live through the time of already/not yet, works when Christ chooses the cross, stays in the tomb, and finally attains resurrection. The dynamic is a way of *dikaiosyne theou*, our triune God's faithfulness. This is the way of love of our triune God, who weeps with all creatures in suffering, who is willing to be with us even if we are in *Sheol*, who is revealed and affirmed in the resurrection, and who lets people taste the resurrection in today's life. This dynamic is a way of fusing the new heaven and earth through the world of tears. Lament-driven preaching works as a transitional space, constantly moving between suffering and hope, but eventually reaching genuine hope.

The dynamic tension in lament brings it into the liturgy as a language of faith with a communal sense. At the same time, lament contributes to social resilience that goes beyond religious discourse. Preaching as a communal lament uses the collective "I" to participate in the suffering of the world and the suffering of God. It expands the sphere of participation to the public arena by inviting listeners to live with the pathos of lament in their daily lives. Practicing lament-driven preaching is a meaningful and effective way to go beyond the ecclesial community to where there is suffering that awaits the healing tears and touch of Christ.

Conclusion

This work began with the question of how preachers can proclaim hope amid suffering while we face the silence of God. It considered the potential of lament in preaching in Lamentations and in Korean history and culture, and in recent homiletical practices. It showed that lament in preaching can be a practice that draws the faithfulness and hope of God into the present reality of suffering; and that it can do this without neglecting the voices of those suffering. This study verified that lament is critical in preaching to deal with suffering in hope, and that lament-driven sermons can be a useful tool to engage the dynamic between suffering and hope, neither choosing nor staying one side.

Though suffering is pervasive in the current world and in the Bible, many preachers in the world, including in Korea, are largely silent on it. They may have failed to react to collective/individual suffering and may have ignored the importance of speaking out about pain, rage, injustice, and evil power. The incident of the *Sewol* ferry tragedy mirrors the reality of some churches that avoid dealing with suffering in a complex and careful way. Many churches may not have shown that they cared about how people, especially those who live in harsh conditions, were trying to survive and overcome their suffering. Preachers often attempt to solve the suffering from either an overly human-driven or eschatological perspective. This book presented lament as an alternative language and space, suggesting that lament can effectively address suffering based on hope, and that it can resist the tendency to present easy hope that bypasses suffering or denies, or that make a to-do list as a human-driven solution to lament and suffering.

Lament has taught us how to concentrate on suffering itself before hope. Lament provides "a corrective to the euphoric and ecstatic practices of faith which pretend that life is all sweetness and joy."[1] This study has been mostly about the amalgamation of colliding perspectives that seem

---

1. Verhey, *Reading the Bible*, 125.

incompatible, specifically in regard to suffering and hope, victims and victimizers, the oppressed and the oppressors, the future hope and the present hope, *Christus victor* and a lamenting God, the church and outside of the church, and sinners and innocents. It has rejected euphemistic attempts to simplify, explain, and give a single interpretation of the complex nature of pain. Instead, it has provided a safe place for suffering to be expressed, heard, and respected, a place in which to develop firm hope from the fragile and precarious hope without assigning blame. Lament in preaching generates an unsettling and transitional place that serves theological and homiletical dynamics. The Christian gospel is able to be proclaimed between suffering and hope and it also crosses boundaries, and this allows nuanced approaches to suffering rather than presenting a simple dichotomy.

To reveal God's action in suffering, one of the most important parts of this study has been the presentation of lament as part of God's redemptive action—embracing human suffering and hope. It undertook a consideration of how human lament calls on divine lament in the theological review of the value of lament. The instability and tension of life in a world of suffering has inspired Christians to use lament as a language of dependence on God, relying upon hope beyond the language of sorrow and despair. Despite the ubiquity of pain, the causes of suffering are incredibly complex and there is one language that will contain and resolve them all—and that is divine lament, which has been revealed through the crucifixion and resurrection of Jesus Christ. What is revealed to us in the suffering of Christ is neither the image of submissive victims who encourage passivity and obedience, nor the image of coercive power or the power to kill helpless victims.[2] The salvation of humankind came through the one who shared human suffering.[3] The God of lament has borne the sufferings of all the world. God's love descended with humans to the depths of despair. The divine lament is, after all, another language of love, and its action is the achievement of *dikaiosyne*, the faithfulness of God which unites justice and love. A lamenting God embodies God's weakness as God's present way of being in the depths of pain, providing constant comfort to a society that is not easily changed. A lamenting God reveals the force of continuous resistance and transformation.[4] By incorporating our story of sorrow into the story of divine lament and comfort, the Holy Spirit empowers us to live a cruciform life. The Spirit encourages people, fostering within them a willingness to enter and bear the pain of others, share their narratives, and lament with them. Then, the Spirit

---

2. Bond, *Trouble with Jesus*, 126.
3. Lee, "One Woman's Confession of Faith," 215.
4. Kim, "Sewol-ho Disaster and God," 48.

ultimately leads the congregation to be the church "as the community of the cross, the community that suffers with, the community that willingly bears the stigma of the passion in service to others" with firm hope.[5]

Lament may begin in a sermon but goes further into everyday life as a way of being. Lament has moved the human story beyond human moral lessons or inner sorrow; it has comforted people and healed their pain, and has created a language of hope that can be heard as the voice of the gospel. This practice demonstrates that lament has developed as an eschatological posture of waiting; it identifies the true calling of the Christian life, which is to resist injustice and evil, and to participate in and struggle with the suffering in the public square. Many footsteps in the Korean history of *han* have witnessed the power of public lament beyond church boundaries. Lament can be extended to society wherever there is suffering. In this sense, pulpits are at the intersection of faith and culture, and preachers are in a unique position to speak to the wider world beyond the church and, at the same time, to focus clearly on the life of the church.[6] The power of the language spoken in pulpits that is empowered by the Holy Spirit can change our identities by incorporating all our stories into God's story; they fill up our world, and give our world an identity as the home of lamenters who have hope.[7] With the identity of lament empowered by the Holy Spirit, a community may better sustain each other and care for people who suffer in their lives—which is surely all of us!

When we look around, grief is prevalent in the world: "sin, suffering, illness, injustice, violence, sexual abuse, oppression, environmental degradation, hardness of heart, other aspects of human behavior, and natural disaster."[8] In this reality, "without some measure of Godly sorrow, without some deep lament over the condition of our soul, even our nationhood, it is likely that the gospel in our own day will collapse into nothing more than Christian nominality."[9] To deal with suffering effectively in pulpits, therefore, lament needs to be proclaimed and be a part of the Christian gospel. Lament in preaching will contribute to proclaiming God's lament as hope, linking and revealing the gravity of suffering and hope. Lament will persist in the Christian life within the world because the tears of those who lament will continue to be poured out until the kin-dom of God is finally fulfilled, and until God's righteousness is fully realized in the new world. That is the only place without crying, mourning, and pain and death (Rev 21:4).

5. Rutledge, *Crucifixion*, 57.
6. Wogaman, *Speaking the Truth in Love*, 5.
7. Buttrick, *Homiletic*, 11.
8. Wilson, *Setting Words on Fire*, 128.
9. Stackhouse, "Confession and Complaint," 199–200.

Bibliography

Achtemeier, Elizabeth. *Nature, God, and Pulpit*. Grand Rapids: Eerdmans, 1992.
———. *Preaching Hard Texts of the Old Testament*. Peabody, MA: Hendrickson, 1998.
Adorno, Theodor W. *Negative Dialectics*. Translated by E. B. Ashton. New York: Continuum, 1994.
Ahn, Byung-Mu. *Ahn, Byung Mu Collection*. Vol. 2, *Minjung Theology*. Seoul: Hangilsa, 1993.
———. *Minjung Theology Story*. Seoul: Korea Theological Institute, 1988.
Ahn, Kyo-Seong. "A Study on the Construction of the Post-*Sewolho Sinhak* or a Korean Post-disaster Theology: With Special Reference to 911, Tsunami, and Sewolho Events." *Korean Presbyterian Journal of Theology* 48 (2016) 59–83.
Ahn, Suk-Mo. "Pastoral Care for the Korean Souls in Relation to Cultural Issues." *Theology and the World* 9 (2012) 121–71.
Albrektson, Bertil. *Studies in the Text and Theology of the Book of Lamentations: With a Critical Edition of the Peshitta Text*. Lund: CWK Gleerup, 1963.
———. *Text, Translation, Theology: Selected Essays on the Hebrew Bible*. Burlington, VT: Ashgate, 2010.
Allen, Donna E. *Toward a Womanist Homiletic: Katie Cannon, Alice Walker, and Emancipatory Proclamation*. New York: Lang, 2013.
Allen, John L. *The Global War on Christians: Dispatches from the Front Lines of Anti-Christian Persecution*. New York: Image, 2016.
Allen, Leslie. C. *A Liturgy of Grief*. Grand Rapids: Baker Academic, 2011.
Allen, Ronald J. *Preaching and the Other: Studies of Postmodern Insights*. St. Louis: Chalice, 2009.
———. "The Relationship between the Pastoral and the Prophetic in Preaching." *Encounter* 49 (1988) 173–90.
———. *Sermon Tracks: Trailways to Creative Preaching*. Nashville: Abingdon, 2013.
Allen, Ronald J., and Gilbert L. Bartholomew. *Preaching Verse by Verse*. Louisville: Westminster John Knox, 1999.
Allen, O. Wesley, Jr., ed. *The Renewed Homiletic*. Minneapolis: Fortress, 2010.
Andrée, Alexander. *Gilbertus Universalis: Glossa Ordinaria in Lamentationes Ieremie Prophete: Prothemata et Liber I*. Acta Universitatis Stockholmiensis Studia Latina Stockholmiensia. Stockholm: Almquist & WikseInternational, 2005.
Andrews, Molly. "Counter-Narratives and the Power to Oppose." In *Considering Counter-Narratives: Narrating, Resisting, Making Sense*, edited by Michael Bamberg and Molly Andrews, 1–6. Philadelphia: Benjamins, 2004.

Bak, Kyung. "Girls Sold as Nobi in Late Joseon." *Journal of Feminist Theories and Practices* 19 (2008) 186–98.

Bang, Un Kyu. "The Korean Consciousness Structure Found in Woman-Related Proverbs." *Korean Society of Korean National Language and Literature* 32 (2004) 51–83.

Bain, Alexander. *The Emotions and the Will*. New York: Appleton & Company, 1876.

Baird, W. M. "The Spirit among Pyeng Yang Students." *Korean Mission Field* 3 (1907) 65–67.

Balthasar, Hans Urs von. *Mysterium Paschale: The Mystery of Easter*. Translated by Aiden Nichols. San Francisco: Ignatius, 2005.

———. *Theo-Drama: Theological Dramatic Theory*. Vol. 3, *The Dramatis Personae: The Person in Christ*. San Francisco: Ignatius, 1992.

Barclay, John M. G. *Paul and the Gift*. Grand Rapids: Eerdmans, 2015.

Barth, Karl. *Church Dogmatics Study Edition*. Vol. 1, *The Doctrine of the Word of God 1.1*. Edited by G. W. Bromiley and T. F. Torrance. Edinburgh: T. & T. Clark, 1936.

———. *Church Dogmatics*. Vol. 3, *The Doctrine of Creation Part 3*. Edinburgh: T. & T. Clark, 1961.

Bartlett, Anthony W. *Cross-Purposes: The Violent Grammar of Christian Atonement*. Philadelphia: Trinity Press International, 2001.

Bartow, Charles L. "Till God Speaks Light." In *Lament: Reclaiming Practices in Pulpit, Pew, and Public Square*, edited by Sally A. Brown and Patrick D. Miller, 157–67. Louisville: Westminster John Knox, 2005.

Bayer, Oswald. *Martin Luther's Theology: A Contemporary Interpretation*. Grand Rapids: Eerdmans, 2008.

Benjamin, Walter. "Literary History and the Study of Literature." In *Walter Benjamin: Selected Writings*. Vol. 2, Part 2, 459–65. Cambridge: Harvard University Press, 1999.

Berlin, Adele. "Introduction to Hebrew Poetry." In *The New Interpreter's Bible*, edited by Leander E. Keck, 4:301–14. Nashville: Abingdon, 1996.

———. *Lamentations*. Louisville: Westminster John Knox, 2002.

Beverley, John. "Margins at the Center: On Testimonio." *Modern Fiction Studies* 85 (1989) 11–28.

Bhabha, Homi K. "Signs Taken for Wonders: Questions of Ambivalence and Authority under a Tree outside Delhi, May 1817." *Critical Inquiry* 12 (1985) 144–65.

Black, Kathy. *A Healing Homiletic: Preaching and Disability*. Nashville: Abingdon, 1996.

———. "Why Me?" In *Patterns of Preaching: A Sermon Sampler*, edited by Ronald J. Allen, 192–98. St. Louis: Chalice, 1998.

Black, Max. "More about Metaphor." In *Metaphor and Thought*, edited by Andrew Ortony, 19–41. 2nd ed. Cambridge: Cambridge University Press, 1993.

Blaine-Wallace, William. "The Politics of Tears: Lamentation as Justice Making." In *Injustice and the Care of Souls*, edited by Sherly A. Kujawa-Holbrook and Karen B. Montagno, 183–98. Minneapolis: Fortress, 2009.

Blair, William N., and Bruce F. Hunt. *The Korean Pentecost and the Sufferings Which Followed*. Edinburgh: Banner of Truth Trust, 1977.

Bond, Susan L. "Coming Home (Isa 60:1–6)" In *Patterns of Preaching: A Sermon Sampler*, edited by Ronald J. Allen, 65–70. St. Louis: Chalice, 1998.

———. *Trouble with Jesus: Women, Christology, and Preaching*. St. Louis: Chalice, 1999.

Bonhoeffer, Dietrich. *Ethics*. Edited by Clifford J. Green. Translated by Reinhard Krauss et al. Dietrich Bonhoeffer Works 6. Minneapolis: Fortress, 2005.

———. *Life Together; Prayerbook of the Bible*. Edited by Geffrey B. Kelly. Translated by Daniel W. Bloesch and James H. Burtness. Dietrich Bonhoeffer Works 5. Minneapolis: Fortress, 1996.

Borgquist, Alvin. "Crying." *American Journal of Psychology* 17 (1906) 149–205.

Bouer, Jonas. "Enquiring into the Absence of Lament: A Study of Entwining of Suffering and Guilt in Lament." In *Evoking Lament: A Theological Discussion*, edited by Eva Harasta and Brian Brook, 25–43. London: T. & T. Clark, 2009.

Boyd, Gregory A. "Christus Victor View." In *The Nature of the Atonement*, edited by James Beilby and Paul R. Eddy, 23–49. Downers Grove, IL: IVP Academic, 2006.

Bradshaw, Paul F., and Lawrence A. Hoffman. *Passover and Easter: Origin and History to Modern Times*. Notre Dame: University of Notre Dame Press, 1999.

Brenner, Athalya. *The Israelite Woman: Social Role and Literary Type in Biblical Narrative*. Sheffield: JSOT Press, 1985.

Brown, Sally A. *Cross Talk: Preaching Redemption Here and Now*. Louisville: Westminster John Knox, 2008.

———. "When Lament Shapes the Sermon." In *Lament: Reclaiming Practices in Pulpit, Pew, and Public Square*, edited by Sally A. Brown and Patrick D. Miller, 27–37. Louisville: Westminster John Knox, 2005.

Brown, Sally A., and Patrick D. Miller, eds. *Lament: Reclaiming Practices in Pulpit, Pew, and Public Square*. Louisville: Westminster John Knox, 2005.

Brueggemann, Walter. *Cadences of Home: Preaching among Exiles*. Louisville: Westminster John Knox, 1997.

———. *Deep Memory, Exuberant Hope*. Minneapolis: Fortress, 2000.

———. *Disruptive Grace*. Minneapolis: Fortress, 2011.

———. *Finally Comes the Poet: Daring Speech for Proclamation*. Minneapolis: Fortress, 1989.

———. *God, Neighbor, Empire: The Excess of Divine Fidelity and the Command of Common Good*. Waco, TX: Baylor University Press, 2016.

———. *The Message of the Psalms: A Theological Commentary*. Minneapolis: Augsburg, 1984.

———. *Old Testament Theology: Essays on Structure, Theme, and Text*. Minneapolis: Fortress, 1992.

———. "Orphans Come Home (Isaiah 49:8–16a; Psalm 131; 1 Corinthians 4:1–5; Matthew 6:24–34)" In *The Collected Sermons of Walter Brueggemann*, 2:60–65. Louisville: Westminster John Knox, 2015.

———. *A Pathway of Interpretation*. Eugene, OR: Cascade, 2008.

———. *The Prophetic Imagination*. Minneapolis: Fortress, 2018.

———. *Reality, Grief, Hope*. Grand Rapids: Eerdmans, 2014.

———. *Theology of the Old Testament: Testimony, Dispute, Advocacy*. Minneapolis: Fortress, 1997.

Brydon, Diana. "Cross-Talk, Postcolonial Pedagogy, and Transnational Literacy." *Situation Analysis* 4 (2004) 70–87.

Buechner, Frederick. *The Truth: Gospel as Tragedy, Comedy, and Fairytale*. New York: HarperSanFrancisco, 1977.

Burghardt, Walter J. *Preaching the Just Word*. New Haven: Yale University Press, 1996.

Buttrick, David. *A Captive Voice: The Liberation of Preaching.* Louisville: Westminster John Knox, 1994.

———. *Homiletic: Moves and Structures.* London, SCM, 1987.

———. *Preaching the New and Now.* Louisville: Westminster John Knox, 1998.

Byeon, Jong-Ho, ed. *Rev. Lee Yong-Do Collection 6: Yong-Do Faithology (信學).* Seoul: Janganmunwhasa, 1993.

Caemmerer, Richard R. *Preaching for the Church.* St. Louis: Concordia, 1959.

Cahill, Jonathan. "The Descent into Solidarity: Christ's Descent into Hell as Stimulus for Justice." *Journal of Reformed Theology* 9 (2015) 237–48.

Calvin, John. *Commentary on Jeremiah and Lamentations.* Vol. 5. Grand Rapids: Christian Classics Ethereal Library, 2009.

———. *Institutes of the Christian Religion.* Translated by Ford Lewis Battles. 2 vols. Philadelphia: Westminster, 1960.

Campbell, Charles L. "Ethics. Introduction: Ethics and Preaching." In *The New Interpreter's Handbook of Preaching*, edited by Paul Scott Wilson, 115–17. Nashville: Abingdon, 2008.

———. *Preaching Jesus: New Directions for Homiletics in Hans Frei's Postliberal Theology.* Eugene, OR: Wipf & Stock, 2006.

———. *The Word before the Powers: An Ethic of Preaching.* Louisville: Westminster John Knox, 2002.

Campbell, Charles L., and Johan H. Cillier. *Preaching Fools: The Gospel as a Rhetoric of Folly.* Waco, TX: Baylor University Press, 2012.

Capps, Donald. *Pastoral Counseling and Preaching: A Quest for an Integrated Ministry.* Philadelphia: Westminster, 1980.

Caputo, John D. *The Prayers and Tears of Jacques Derrida: Religion without Religions.* Bloomington: Indiana University Press, 1997.

Caraveli, Anna. "The Bitter Wounding: The Lament as Social Protest in Rural Greece." In *Gender and Power in Rural Greece*, edited by Jill Dubisch, 169–94. Princeton: Princeton University Press, 1986.

Cary, Phillip. *Luther: Gospel, Law, and Reformation, Part 1.* Chantilly, VA: Teaching Company, 2004.

Chae, Hee-Wan. "How Would the Alienated Class Be Expressed in Korean Traditional Mask Dance Drama?" *Korean Aesthetics* 5 (2005) 192–233.

Chai, Soo-Il. "The One Who is in God (Acts 3:13–15, 17–19 / 1 John 2:1–6 / Luke 24:44–48)." http://www.kdchurch.or.kr/Board/Detail/39/52470?page=1&searchKind=content&searchKeyword=%25EC%2584%25B8%25EC%259B%2594%25ED%2598%25B8.

———. "The Theological Foundations for the Social Engagement of the Progressive Christians in the 1970s." *Christianity and History in Korea* 18 (2003) 9–35.

Charles, Mark, and Soong-Chan Rah, *Unsettling Truth: The Ongoing, Dehumanizing Legacy of the Doctrine of Discovery.* Downers Grove, IL: InterVarsity, 2019.

Cheon, Yee Doo. "On the Structure of 'Han: 恨.'" *Journal of Modern Literary Theory* 3 (1993) 169–78.

———. "A Study on the Principle of Reconciliation of Korean Han as the Leit-motif of Pansori." *Sunggoknonchong* 24 (1993) 1545–98.

Childs, Brevard S. *Introduction to the Old Testament as Scripture.* Philadelphia: Fortress, 1979.

———. *Old Testament Theology in a Canonical Context.* Philadelphia: Fortress, 1985.

Choi, Seo Yeon. "Controversial Advocacy of a Senior Pastor in a Mega Church." *Asia Economy*, May 23, 2014. http://view.asiae.co.kr/news/view.htm?idxno=201405231 1075282024.
Choi, Young Sil. "Creating a Culture of Reconciliation and Life through Hanpuri and Hanmaji: A Feminist Theological Interpretation of the Miyalhalmi Dance in the Bongsan Talchum (Bongsan Mask Dance)." *Korean Journal of Christian Studies* 56 (2008) 231–56.
Chun, Jin-Sung. "Beyond Politics of Memory toward Cultural History of Memory: A Methodological Critique of Korean Memory Studies." *Critical Review of History* 76 (2006) 451–83.
Chung, Heesung. "Christian Women's Contribution to the Military Comfort Women's Movement." *Korean Journal of Christian Studies* 112 (2019) 293–322.
Chung, Hyun Kyung. *Struggle to Be the Sun Again: Introducing Asian Women's Theology*. Maryknoll, NY: Orbis, 1990.
Claassens, L. Juliana M. *Mourner, Mother, Midwife: Reimagining God's Delivering Presence in the Old Testament*. Louisville: Westminster John Knox, 2012.
Coffin, Henry Sloan. *What to Preach*. New York: Harper and Brothers, 1926.
Coffin, William Sloane. "Alex's Death." In *A Chorus of Witnesses: Model Sermons for Today's Preacher*, edited by Thomas G. Long and Cornelius Plantinga Jr., 262–66. Grand Rapids: Eerdmans, 1994.
Coogan, Michael D. "Acrostic." In *Oxford Companion to the Bible*, edited by Bruce M. Metzger and Michael D. Coogan, 6. Oxford: Oxford University Press, 1993.
Cooper, Jerrold. *The Curse of Agade*. Baltimore: Johns Hopkins University Press, 1983.
Copeland, M. Shawn. "The Cross of Christ and Discipleship." In *Thinking of Christ: Proclamation, Explanation, Meaning*, edited by Tatha Wiley, 177–92. New York: Continuum, 2003.
Cottrill, Amy. "The Articulate Body." In *Lamentations in Ancient and Contemporary Cultural Context*, edited by Nancy Lee and Carleen Mandolfo, 103–14. Atlanta: Society of Biblical Literature, 2008.
Couenhoven, Jesse. "Law and Gospel, or the Law of the Gospel? Karl Barth's Political Theology Compared with Luther and Calvin." *Journal of Religious Ethics* 30 (2002) 181–205.
Cox, James. *Preaching: A Comprehensive Approach to the Design and Delivery of Sermons*. San Francisco: Harper and Row, 1985.
Craddock, Fred B. *As One without Authority*. 2nd ed. Nashville: Abingdon, 1981.
———. *Preaching: 25th Anniversary Edition*. Nashville: Abingdon, 2010.
Crawford, Evans E. *The Hum: Call and Response in African American Preaching*. Nashville: Abingdon, 1995.
Crum, Milton, Jr. *Manual on Preaching*. Valley Forge, PA: Judson, 1977.
Cruz, Gemma Tulud. *Toward a Theology of Migration: Social Justice and Religious Experience*. New York: Palgrave Macmillan, 2014.
Cuéllar, Gregory Lee. "The Collecting Impulse in Lamentations." In *Postcolonial Commentary and the Old Testament*, edited by Hemchand Gossai, 275–89. London: T. & T. Clark, 2018.
Culbertson, Roberta. "Embodied Memory, Transcendence, and Telling: Recounting Trauma, Re-establishing the Self." *New Literary History* 26 (1995) 169–95.
Davies, Eryl W. *The Immoral Bible: Approaches to Biblical Ethics*. London: T. & T. Clark, 2010.

Davis, Ellen F. "Is It Nothing? (Apr. 18, 2014)." https://chapel.duke.edu/sites/default/files/EllenDavis--GoodFri.pdf.

———. *Preaching the Luminous Word: Biblical Sermons and Homiletical Essays*. Grand Rapids: Eerdmans, 2016.

Davis, Kenneth G. "Cross-Cultural Preaching." In *Preaching and Culture in Latino Congregations*, edited by Kenneth G. Davis and Jorge L. Presmanes, 41–61. Chicago: Liturgy Training, 2000.

De La Torre, Miguel A. *Reading the Bible from the Margins*. Maryknoll, NY: Orbis, 2002.

Deutsch, Helene, and Edith Jackson. "Absence of Grief." *Psychoanalytic Quarterly* 6 (1937) 12–22.

A Diary of Gwanghaegun. Vol. 40. April 14, 1611. http://sillok.history.go.kr/id/kob_10304014_002.

Dijk-Hemmes, Fokkelien van. "Traces of Women's Text in the Hebrew Bible." In *On Gendering Texts: Female and Male Voices in the Hebrew Bible*, edited by Athalya Brenner and Fokkelien van Dijk-Hemmes, 17–109. New York: Brill, 1996.

Dobbs-Allsopp, F. W. "The Enjambing Line in Lamentations: A Taxonomy (Part 1)." *Zeitschrift für die alttestamentliche Wissenschaft* 113 (2001) 219–39.

———. *Lamentations*. Interpretation: A Bible Commentary for Teaching and Preaching. Louisville: Knox, 2002.

———. *On Biblical Poetry*. Oxford: Oxford University Press, 2015.

———. "R(az/ais)ing Zion in Lamentations 2." In *David and Zion*, edited by Bernard F. Batto and Kathryn L. Roberts, 21–68. Winona Lake, IN: Eisenbrauns, 2004.

———. "Tragedy, Tradition, and Theology in the Book of Lamentations." *Journal for the Study of the Old Testament* 22 (1997) 29–60.

Doka, Kenneth. *Disenfranchised Grief: New Directions, Challenges, and Strategies for Practice*. Champaign, IL: Research, 2002.

Duff, Nancy J. "Recovering Lamentation as a Practice in the Church." In *Lament: Reclaiming Practices in Pulpit, Pew, and Public Square*, edited by Sally A Brown and Patrick D. Miller, 3–14. Louisville: Westminster John Knox, 2005.

Dykstra, Robert C. "Rending the Curtain: Lament as an Act of Vulnerable Aggression." In *Lament: Reclaiming Practices in Pulpit, Pew, and Public Square*, edited by Sally A. Brown and Patrick D. Miller, 59–69. Louisville: Westminster John Knox, 2005.

Eliot, Thomas. "Bereavement: Inevitable but Not Insurmountable." In *Family, Marriage, and Parenthood*, edited by Howard Becker and Reuben Hill, 641–68. Boston: Heath, 1948.

Elizondo, Virgilio P. *A God of Incredible Surprises: Jesus of Galilee*. Lanham, MD: Rowman & Littlefield, 2003.

Ellacuría, Ignacio. *Filosofía de la realidad histórica*. San Salvador: UCA Editores, 1990.

Encyclopedia of Korean Culture. https://encykorea.aks.ac.kr/.

Eslinger, Richard L. *The Web of Preaching: New Options in Homiletic Method*. Nashville: Abingdon, 2002.

Farhadian, Charles E. "Emerging Theology on an Asian Frontier: History and the Future of Memories in West Papua, Indonesia." In *Asian and Oceanic Christianities in Conversation: Exploring Theological Identities at Home and in Diaspora*, edited by Hŭb-yŏng Kim et al., 185–202. Amsterdam: Rodopi, 2011.

Farley, Wendy. *Tragic Vision and Divine Compassion: A Contemporary Theodicy*. Louisville: Westminster/John Knox, 1990.

Farris, Stephen. "Hermeneutics." In *The New Interpreter's Handbook of Preaching*, edited by Paul Scott Wilson, 31–37. Nashville: Abingdon, 2008.
———. *Preaching That Matters: The Bible and Our Lives*. Louisville: Westminster John Knox, 1998.
Fernandez, Eleazar S. *Toward a Theology of Struggle*. Maryknoll, NY: Orbis, 1994.
Ferris, Paul, Jr. *The Genre of Communal Lament in the Bible and the Ancient Near East*. Atlanta: Scholars, 1992.
Flowers, Elizabeth H. *Into the Pulpit: Southern Baptist Women & Power Since World War II*. Chapel Hill, NC: University of North Carolina Press, 2012.
Forbes, James. *The Holy Spirit and Preaching*. Nashville: Abingdon, 1989.
Fortune, Marie M. "Wings of Eagles and Holes in the Earth." In *Telling the Truth: Preaching about Sexual and Domestic Violence*, edited by John S. McClure and Nancy J. Ramsay, 127–32. Cleveland: United Church, 1998.
Fosdick, Harry Emerson. *The Living of These Days*. New York: Harper & Brothers, 1956.
———. "What Is the Matter with Preaching?" *Harper's Magazine*, July 1928.
Freed, Edwin D. "The Parable of the Judge and the Widow." *New Testament Study* 33 (1987) 38–60.
Fry Brown, Teresa L. *Weary Throats and New Songs: Black Women Proclaiming God's Word*. Nashville: Abingdon, 2003.
Gafney, Wilda. *Womanist Midrash: A Reintroduction to the Women of the Torah and the Throne*. Louisville: Westminster John Knox, 2017.
Gibson, Scott M. "Point Form." In *The New Interpreter's Handbook of Preaching*, edited by Paul Wilson, 401–4. Nashville: Abingdon, 2008.
Galchinsky, Michael. "Lament as Transitional Justice." *Human Rights Review* 15 (2014) 259–81.
Gerstenberger, Erhard. *Psalms, Part 2, and Lamentations*. Grand Rapids: Eerdmans, 2001.
Gil, Hye-Min. "The Possibility of Ghost Life and Mourning of the Comfort Women: In Kim Soom's One Person and Nora Okja Keller's Comfort Women." *Journal of History* 33 (2017) 185–217.
González, Justo L., and Catherine Gunsalus González. *Liberation Preaching: The Pulpit and the Oppressed*. Nashville: Abingdon, 1980.
Gottwald, Norman K. *Studies in the Book of Lamentations*. Eugene, OR: Wipf & Stock, 1954.
Graetz, Naomi. "Jerusalem the Widow." *Shofar* 17 (1999) 16–24.
Grant, Jacquelyn. *White Women's Christ and Black Women's Jesus: Feminist Christology and Womanist Response*. Atlanta: Scholars, 1989.
Grey, Mary. *Beyond the Dark Night: A Way Forward for the Church*. London: Cassell, 1997.
Griffiths, Gareth. "The Myth of Authenticity: Representation, Discourse, and Social Practice." In *De-scribing Empire: Post-colonialism and Textuality* edited by Alan Lawson and Chris Tiffin, 70–85. New York: Routledge, 1994.
Groody, Daniel G. *Border of Death, Valley of Life: An Immigrant Journey of Heart and Spirit*. Lanham, MD: Rowman & Littlefield, 2002.
Guest, Deryn. "Hiding behind the Naked Women in Lamentations." *Biblical Interpretation* 7 (1999) 413–48.
Gutiérrez, Gustavo. *On Job: God-Talk and the Suffering of the Innocent*. Maryknoll, NY: Orbis, 1987.

Gwon, Jung Ja. "Military Sexual Slavery's Secret History 3." *Naver* (blog), August 15, 2012. https://blog.naver.com/dramo23/164171497.

Halbwachs, Maurice. *The Collective Memory*. New York: Harper & Row, 1980.

Hall, Delroy. "The Middle Passage as Existential Crucifixion." *Black Theology* 7 (2009) 45–63.

Hall, Douglas John. *God and Human Suffering: An Exercise in the Theology of the Cross*. Minneapolis: Augsburg, 1986.

Han, Kyung Chik. "For Our Nation (Apr. 24, 1960)." In *Rev. Han, Kyung Chik Sermon Collection*, 4 (1959-60): 341–46. Seoul: Kyung Chik Han Foundation, 2009.

Han, Suk-Won. "True Tears." In *Baekmokkanyeon*, edited by Ik-Hwan Yang, 107–9. Gyeongseong: Parkmoon, 1920.

Hankle, Dominik D. "The Therapeutic Implications of the Imprecatory Psalms in the Christian Counseling Setting." *Journal of Psychology and Theology* 38 (2010) 275–80.

Harasta, Eva. "Crucified Praise and Resurrected Lament." In *Evoking Lament: A Theological Discussion*, edited by Eva Harasta and Brian Brook, 204–17. London: T. & T. Clark, 2009.

Harris, Beau, and Carleen Mandolfo. "The Silent God in Lamentations." *Interpretation* 67 (2013) 133–43.

Harris, James Henry. *Preaching Liberation*. Minneapolis: Fortress, 1995.

Hauerwas, Stanley. "The Pastor as Prophet: Ethical Reflections on an Improbable Mission." In *Christian Existence Today: Essays on Church, World, and Living in Between*, 149–70. Durham, NC: Labyrinth, 1988.

Hauerwas, Stanley, and David Burrell. "From System to Story: An Alternative Pattern for Rationality in Ethics." In *What's the Shape of Narrative Preaching?*, edited by Mike Graves and David J. Schlafer, 158–90. St. Louis: Chalice, 2008.

Herman, Judith L. *Trauma and Recovery: The Aftermath of Violence—From Domestic Abuse to Political Terror*. New York: Basic, 2015.

Heschel, Abraham J. *The Prophets: An Introduction*. New York: Harper & Row, 1962.

Hilkert, Mary Catherine. *Naming Grace: Preaching and the Sacramental Imagination*. New York: Continuum, 1997.

———. "Preaching the Folly of the Cross." *Word and World* 19 (1999) 39–48.

Hillers, Delbert. *Lamentations*. New York: Doubleday, 1992.

Hinze, Bradford E. "Ecclesial Impasse: What Can We Learn from Our Laments?" *Theological Studies* 72 (2011) 470–95.

Hirsch, Marianne. *Family Frames: Photography, Narrative, and Postmemory*. Cambridge: Harvard University Press, 1997.

Hogg, David S. "Christian Interpretation of Lamentations in the Middle Ages." In *Great Is Thy Faithfulness? Reading Lamentations as Sacred Scripture*, edited by Robin A. Parry and Heath A. Thomas, 120–24. Eugene, OR: Pickwick, 2011.

Holbert, John C. *Preaching Creation: The Environment and the Pulpit*. Eugene, OR: Cascade, 2011.

Holmes, Barbara A. *Joy Unspeakable: Contemplative Practices of the Black Church*. Minneapolis: Fortress, 2017.

Hong, Chi-Ho. "The Problem of *Han* in *Minjung* Theology." *Presbyterian Theological Quarterly* 51 (1990) 136–51.

Hong, Seong-Phil. "The Saga of the Japanese Wartime Sexual Slavery: A Noble Search for Human Dignity by the Korean Female Victims." *Justice* 102 (2008) 216–54.

Horsley, Richard A. *Jesus and Empire: The Kingdom of God and the New World Disorder*. Minneapolis: Fortress, 2003.

House, Paul R. *Lamentations*. Nashville: Nelson, 2004.

———. "Outrageous Demonstrations of Grace: The Theology of Lamentations." In *Great Is Thy Faithfulness? Reading Lamentations as Sacred Scripture*, edited by Robin A. Parry and Heath A. Thomas, 26–54. Eugene, OR: Pickwick, 2012.

Hudson, Mary Lin, and Mary Donovan Turner. *Saved from Silence: Finding Women's Voice in Preaching*. St. Louis: Chalice, 1999.

Hughes, Richard A. *Lament, Death, and Destiny*. New York: Lang, 2004.

Human Right Commission of The National Council of Churches in Korea. *Democratic Movement in the 1970s*. Vol. 1, *Focused on Christian Human Right Movements*. Seoul: The National Council of Churches in Korea, 1987.

Hunsinger, Deborah van Deusen. *Bearing the Unbearable: Trauma, Gospel, and Pastoral Care*. Grand Rapids: Eerdmans, 2015.

Hunsinger, George. *Disruptive Grace: Studies in the Theology of Karl Barth*. Grand Rapids: Eerdmans, 2000.

Hwang, Cheol-Hwan, and Ji-Hoon Han. "The Bereaved of Sewol Ferry Accused Pastor Jung-Hyun and Gwang-Jak Jo." *Yonhapnews*, June 10, 2014. https://www.yna.co.kr/view/AKR20140610166900004.

Hwang, Jihye. "The 'Han' Ethos and Releasing of 'Han': Toni Morrison's Beloved." *Journal of East-West Comparative Literature* 40 (2017) 295–315.

Hyde, Lewis. *Trickster Makes This World: Mischief, Myth, and Art*. New York: Farrar, Straus, and Giroux, 1998.

Hyun, Young-Hak. "A Theological Look at the Mask Dance in Korea." In *Minjung Theology: People as the Subjects of History*, edited by Commission on Theological Concerns of Christian Conference of Asia, 47–54. Maryknoll, NY: Orbis, 1981.

The Institute of the History of Christianity in Korea, *The History of Korean Christianity*. Vol. 3, *Until the End of the 20th Century after Liberation*. Seoul: PUTS, 2013.

Irenaeus. *The Demonstration of the Apostolic Preaching*. London: SPCK, 1920. Kindle.

Jacobsen, David Schnasa. *Preaching in the New Creation: The Promise of New Testament Apocalyptic Texts*. Louisville: Westminster John Knox, 1999.

Jakobson, Roman. "The Metaphoric and Metonymic Poles." In *Metaphor and Metonymy in Comparison and Contrast*, edited by René Dirven and Ralf Pörings, 41–48. Berlin: de Gruyter, 2002.

Jang, Il-Gu. "A Study of the Historical Trauma and the Narrative Therapy in the Novels with May 18 Motif." *Korean Literary Theory and Criticism* 20 (2003) 262–82.

Jang, Yoon Jae. "The Power of Lament (Isa 61:1–3, 1 Pet 3:8–12, and Luke 6:20–21)." http://veritas.kr/articles/33067/20190318/%EC%8A%AC%ED%94%94%EC%9D%98-%ED%9E%98.htm.

Jeon, Kwang-don. *In the Beginning, There Was Han*. Seoul: Christian Literature Society of Korea, 2007.

Jeong, Jin Seong. "The Formation of Depressed Women's Subjectivity and the Mobilization of 'Comfort Women' for Military." *Society and History* 54 (1998) 74–96.

Jeong, Young-geun. "Korean Philosophy: Expansion of Silla Buddhism Horizon and Development of Education and Scholarship." *Korean Thought and Culture* 22 (2003) 245–62.

Jimenez, Pablo A. "Liberation Criticism." In *The New Interpreter's Handbook of Preaching*, edited by Paul Scott Wilson, 45–49. Nashville: Abingdon, 2008.

———. "Toward a Postcolonial Homiletic: Justo L. Gonzalez's Contribution to Hispanic Preaching." In *Hispanic Christian Thought at the Dawn of the 21st Century*, edited by Alvin Padilla et al., 159–67. Nashville: Abingdon, 2005.

Jin, Jae Hyuk. "Lamenting Community (Matt 5:4)." https://www.jiguchon.or.kr/bbs/board.php?bo_table=C01&wr_id=1557&sfl=wr_subject%7C%7Cwr_content&stx=%EC%95%A0%ED%86%B5&sop=and&page=2.

Joh, Wonhee Anne. *Heart of the Cross: A Postcolonial Christology*. Louisville: Westminster John Knox, 2006.

Johnson, Elizabeth A. *Quest for the Living God: Mapping Frontiers in the Theology of God*. New York: Continuum, 2007.

Johnson, Kimberly P. *The Womanist Preacher: Proclaiming Womanist Rhetoric from the Pulpit*. London: Lexington, 2017.

Joo, Kyo Don. "A Homiletic Geared towards Ethical Living: An Examination of Gospel and the Third Use of the Law with Relation to the Divine and Human Roles in Sanctification." PhD diss., St. Michael's College, University of Toronto, 2014.

Joyce, Paul M., and Diana Lipton. *Lamentations through the Centuries*. Chichester: Wiley-Blackwell, 2013.

Ju, Hyun Shik. "A Study about the Theater Therapeutic Quality of The Talchum." *Drama Research* 40 (2013) 173–202.

Julien, Isaac, and Kobena Mercer. "De Margin and De Centre." In *Stuart Hall: Critical Dialogues in Cultural Studies*, edited by David Morley and Kuan-Hsing Chen, 452–67. New York: Routledge, 1996.

Jung, Dae-ha. "A High School Student Who Was Raped by Soldiers during the May 18 Movement Became a Monk." *Hankyoreh*, May 9, 2018. http://www.hani.co.kr/arti/society/area/843817.html.

Jung, Hae Seung. *Entertainment Economics*. Paju: Human Business, 2006.

Jung, Kum-Chul. "The Poetics of Korean Traditional Emotion 'Han(恨).'" *Studies in Humanities* 21 (2009) 107–31.

Jung, Kyung Il. "Lament, Remember, Resistance—Minjung Theology in Sewol Ferry." *Christian Thought* 668 (2014) 172–88.

Jung, Sung-Mi. "Metaphor, Language of Emotion, and Humanities Therapy." *Studies in Humanities* 17 (2010) 201–20.

Jung, Tae-Ki. "An Approach of Pastoral Care and Counseling for "Han-Pu-Rie."" *Theological Studies* 37 (1996) 245–60.

Jüngel, Eberhard. *God as the Mystery of the World: On the Foundation of the Theology of the Crucified One in the Dispute between Theism and Atheism*. London: T. & T. Clark, 2014.

Kang, Han Young. ed. *Jaehyo Shin Pansori Editorial Collection*. Seoul: Minjungseokwan, 1971.

Kang, Young-Ok. "Understanding of Suffering with Shamanistic Perspective." *Catholic Theology and Thought* 19 (1997) 57–73.

Katongole, Emmanuel. *Born from Lament: The Theology and Politics of Hope in Africa*. Grand Rapids: Eerdmans, 2017.

Kaveny, M. Cathleen. "Anger, Lamentation, and Common Ground." *Theological Studies* 82 (2021) 663–85.

Keller, Nora Okja. *Comfort Woman*. New York: Penguin, 1997.

Kim, Byung Oh. "Psychological-Social understanding about Korean Chemyon and Shame." *Christian Thought* 42 (1998) 234–47.
Kim, Byung-Suk. "A Study on the Principle of Preaching in the Korean Early Presbyterian Church Based on the Adaptive Scheme of Herrick Johnson." *Theology and Praxis* 51 (2016) 111–39.
Kim, Chai Choon. "The Reminiscence and Prospects of 4.19." *Christian Thought* 6 (1962) 16–22.
Kim, Chang-Hoon. "Prophetic Preaching: Its Meaning and Significance." *Bible and Theology* 52 (2009) 193–223.
Kim, Chi-Seon. "Tears of Loving National People (Matt. 23:37–38 and Luke 19:41–44)." In *Sermons of Korean Christian Leaders*, edited by KIATS, 10:21–28. Seoul: Hongseongsa, 2018.
Kim, Chung-Choon. "The People of God." In *The Heaven Buried in the Earth*, 577–84. Seoul: The Christian Literature Society of Korea, 1969.
Kim, Eun Mi, and Byung Oh Kim. "A Study on Experience of Bereaved Family Members Who Lost Children in the Sewol Ferry Disaster." *Korean Journal of Christian Counseling* 29 (2018) 89–129.
Kim, Gwang Dong, ed. *32nd Annual Mission Education Conference Source Book*. Seoul: Presbyterian Church of Korea Youth, 1982.
Kim, Haengsik, ed. *A Shortened History of 3.1 Movement: This Is Curious*. Incheon: Korean Independence Movement Spirit and Thought Research Group, 2003.
Kim, Heung Soo. "Kibok Faith: Christian Change after the Korean War." *Journal of The Church History Society in Korea* 9 (2000) 9–30.
Kim, Ho Gui. "Fidelity Types and Buddhist Roles from Fables of Samgukyusa." *Studies of Seon Culture* 14 (2013) 257–95.
Kim, Hye Jin. "A Study of Education for Understanding Koreans' Emotion of Han—With a Focus on Pansori Novels." *Journal of Yeongju Language & Literature* 27 (2014) 297–333.
Kim, I-Gon. "The Theology of Lament of the Abandoned." In *Minjung Theology in the Transitional Period*, edited by Editorial Committee of the Memorial Papers of Rev. Jukje Seo Nam-Dong, 311–25. Seoul: Korea Theological Institute, 1992.
Kim, Ji-Cheol. "Blessing of Lamenter (Matt 5:1–4)." Sermon preached at Somang Presbyterian Church, January 13, 2018.
———. "Eloi, Eloi Lama? (Ps 22:1–4)." Sermon preached at Somang Presbyterian Church, March 25, 2018.
———. "The Leadership of Lament, Nehemiah (Neh 1:1–5)." Sermon preached at Somang Presbyterian Church, June 24, 2018.
Kim, Jin. "Die hoffnungs philosophische Interpretation zu dem Begriff Han." *Korean Journal of Philosophy* 78 (2004) 319–45.
Kim, Ji Su. "Confucianism and Feminism." *Culture and Covergence* 39 (2017) 399–428.
Kim, Jung Ho, and Beom Doo Moon. "Study on Funeral Culture and Funeral-Rite Folk Songs of Namhae Goon." *Korean Language* 52 (2013) 75–103.
Kim, Matthew D. *Preaching with Cultural Intelligence: Understanding the People Who Hear Our Sermons*. Grand Rapids: Baker Academic, 2017.
Kim, Myung Hye. "Incomplete Stories: Experience and Memory of 'Comfort Women.'" *Korea Cultural Anthropology* 37 (2004) 3–22.
Kim, Myungsil. "*Tongsunggido* as a Communal Lament Prayer: A Search for the Theological Identity of *Tongsunggido* and a suggestion for the Appropriate

Practices for the Future of Korean Church." *Theology and Praxis* 24 (2010) 299–335.

Kim, Se Kwang. "History Buried in the Triple-Time Salvation of the Five-Folds Gospel." *Christian Thought* 48 (2004) 44–57.

Kim, Seunghwan. "The Cry of Justice Resonated in 37 Places around the World." *SegyeIlbo*, August 15, 2020. http://www.segye.com/newsView/20190814510528.

Kim, Soo-Youn. "The Sewol-ho Disaster and God (the Moved Mover): A Study on the Weakness of God from a Feminist Theological Perspective." *Theological Forum* 79 (2015) 48.

Kim, So-wol. "Invocation of the Dead." https://cardiacslaves.wordpress.com/2017/01/06/invocation-of-the-dead-by-kim-so-wol/.

Kim, Unyong. *A History of Preaching in Korea: Preachers' Story in the Perspective of Story Innovativeness*. Seoul: Saemulgyeol Plus, 2018.

―――. "A Homiletical Evaluation and Suggestion on 'Counseling Preaching.'" *Theology and Praxis* 30 (2012) 291–319.

Kim, Young-Ju. "A Study on *Keundang* and *Kongkwan* of Sungkyunkwan Yuseng in Joseon Dynasty." *Journal of Communication Science* 8 (2008) 253–98.

Kim, Young-seok. "The Folk Imagination of Modern Korean Poetry: The Structure of Complaining and the Principle of Sowol Kim's Poetry." *Study of Korean Language and Literature* 11 (1997) 115–69.

Kim, Yung Jae. "Eschatology of the Korean Church." *Hapshin Theological Journal* 11 (1993) 261–87.

Kim, Yu-Soon. "Give Us Enthusiasm." In *Joseon Pulpit: 35 People's Sermons*, edited by Yi-Young Ha and Choon Bae Kim, 32–33. Gyeongseong: Sungmoondang, 1928.

King, Martin Luther, Jr. "I Have a Dream." In *The Speech: The Story behind Dr. Martin Luther King Jr's Dream*, edited by Gery Younge, xi–xvii. Chicago: Haymarket, 2013.

Kitamori, Kazoh. *Theology of the Pain of God*. Richmond: Knox, 1965.

Knight. Carolyn Ann. "If Thou Be a Great People." In *Patterns of Preaching: A Sermon Sampler*, edited by Ronald J. Allen, 225–30. St. Louis: Chalice, 1998.

Kübler-Ross, Elisabeth, and David Kessler. *On Grief and Grieving: Finding the Meaning of Grief through the Five Stages of Loss*. New York: Scribner, 2005.

Ku, Eliana Ah-Rum. "Lament as Resistance and Rage: An Asian Woman Immigrant's Reading of Psalm 137 in the Light of Anti-Asian Hate Crimes of North America." *Asian American Theological Forum* 8 (2021) 7–12.

―――. "Resisting Apathy and Amnesia: The Significance of Preaching Lament." *Conrad Grebel Review* (forthcoming).

Kwak, Shin-Hwan. "Confucian Philosophical Interpretation of Pain." In *What Is Evil?*, edited by Academy of Korean Studies, 289–308. Seoul: Chang, 1992.

Kwok, Pui-Lan. "Feminist Theology as Intercultural Discourse." In *The Cambridge Companion to Feminist Theology*, edited by Susan Frank Parsons, 23–39. Cambridge: Cambridge University Press, 2002.

―――. "God Weeps with Our Pain." In *New Eyes for Reading: Biblical and Theological Reflection by Women from the Third World*, edited by John S. Pobee and Barbel von Wartenberg-Potter, 90–95. Geneva: World Council of Churches, 1986.

Kwon, Teck Young. "The Mode of Remembering in Keller's *Comfort Woman*." *Studies in Hawthorne & the American Novel* 12 (2005) 215–36.

Kye, Seung-Bum. "Birth and Diffusion of the Concept of Yangban Society: Its Historical Consideration." *Korean Journal of History of Historiography* 41 (2020) 75–114.

Lakkis, Stephen. "Have You Any Right to Be Angry?" In *Evoking Lament: A Theological Discussion*, edited by Eva Harasta and Brian Brook, 168–82. London: T. & T. Clark, 2009.

Lakoff, George, and Mark Johnson. *Metaphors We Live By*. Chicago: University of Chicago Press, 2003.

LaRue, Cleophus J. *The Heart of Black Preaching*. Louisville: Westminster John Knox, 2000.

———. *Rethinking Celebration: From Rhetoric to Praise in African American Preaching*. Louisville: Westminster John Knox, 2016.

Lasalle-Klein, Robert. "A Postcolonial Christ." In *Thinking of Christ: Proclamation, Explanation, Meaning*, edited by Tatha Wiley, 135–53. New York: Continuum, 2003.

Lash, Nicholas. "Performing the Scriptures." In *Theology on the Way to Emmaus*, 37–46. London: SCM, 1986.

Lathrop, Gordon W. *The Pastor: A Spirituality*. Minneapolis: Fortress, 2006.

Lauber, David. *Barth on the Descent into Hell: God, Atonement, and the Christian Life*. New York: Routledge, 2017.

Lee, Byoung-Tak. "Adorno's Negative Dialectic." *Journal of East-West Humanities* 13 (2020) 69–97.

Lee, Cheong-jun. "Namdo People 5." In *Seopyeonje*, 140–87. Seoul: Yeolrimwon, 1998.

Lee, Dae-Ung. "Pastor Lee, Clarification the Dispute about His Preaching." *Christian Today*, April 25, 2014. http://www.christiantoday.co.kr/news/271771.

Lee, Dong Chun. "A Christian Ethics Reflection on an Attitude of the Korean Church toward Pain of Others." *Mission and Theology* 37 (2015) 233–61.

Lee, Doo-Hyun. *Korean Mask Paly*. Seoul: Iljisa, 1979.

Lee, Eun-Seun. *Sewol Ferry and Korean Feminist Theology: In the Conversation with Hanna Arendt*. Seoul: Dongyeon, 2018.

Lee, Gyutae. *Essay on Koreanology*. Vol. 1, *Grafting Tradition onto Life*. Seoul: Shinwon, 1995.

Lee, Hee-kwon. "A Study on *Keundang* and *Kongkwan* in Late Joseon Dynasty." *Sahak Yonku* 30 (1980) 31–64.

Lee, Hoon Ku. "Syncretism Ideology of Buddhism, Confucianism, and Christianity." *Korean Society of Mission Studies* 21 (2009) 233–54.

Lee, Hoon-seok. *Korean Woman's Lessons*. Seoul: Daehoonsa, 1990.

Lee, Hyo-Jea. "Korean Patriarchy and Women." *Women and Society* 7 (1996) 160–76.

Lee, Jie Sung. "A Study on Suffering Narrative for Sympathy." *Christian Social Ethics* 30 (2014) 69–98.

Lee, Jung Bae. "Sewol Tragedy Second Anniversary Memorial Prayer Meeting." *Newnjoy*, April 12, 2016. http://www.newsnjoy.or.kr/news/articleView.html?idxno=202931.

Lee, Jung Ho. "The Life of Korean Minjung at the Early Period of Park Jung-hee's Yushin." *ChamSesang*, April 12, 2013. http://www.newscham.net/news/view.php?board=news&nid=69981.

Lee, Jung-hwan. "Comfort from the Christmas Message of 1971." *OhMyNews*, December 25, 2015. http://www.ohmynews.com/NWS_Web/View/at_pg.aspx?CNTN_CD=A0002170837&PAGE_CD=N0004&CMPT_CD=E0018M.

Lee, Jung Young. *Korean Preaching: An Interpretation*. Nashville: Abingdon, 1997.

———. *Marginality: The Key to Multicultural Theology*. Minneapolis: Fortress, 2015.

Lee, Kyung Hee. "The Therapeutic Aspects of Korean Mask Dance." *Korean Journal of Dance Studies* 37 (2012) 27–44.

Lee, Mehye. "Punish Doo-Hwan Chun Who Is a Principal Offender of the Genocide of 5.18 Movement." *Cheonjiilbo*, March 11, 2019. http://www.newscj.com/news/articleView.html?idxno=610309.

Lee, Nancy. "Lamentations and Polemic." *Interpretation* 67 (2013) 155–83.

———. *Lyrics of Lament*. Minneapolis: Fortress, 2010.

Lee, Oo Chung. "One Woman's Confession of Faith." In *New Eyes for Reading: Biblical and Theological Reflection by Women from the Third World*, edited by John S. Pobee and Bärbel von Wartenberg-Potter, 18–20. Geneva: World Council of Churches, 1986.

Lee, Sang Hyun. *From a Liminal Place: An Asian American Theology*. Minneapolis: Fortress, 2010.

Lee, Sarye. *Lee, Gi-Pung: Korea's First Missionary to End Life with Martyrdom*. Seoul: Christian Literature, 2008.

Lee, Seong-Bong. "God's Beloved Son (Matt. 3:17)." In *Korean Christian Leaders Series*, edited by KIATS, 106–10. Seoul: KIATS, 2008.

Lee, Susanna. "What I Have." In *Baekmokkanyeon*, edited by Ik-Hwan Yang, 153–61. Gyeongseong: Parkmoon, 1920.

Lee, Yoo Hyeok. "Traveling or Troubling Memories: On the Transnational Movement of Korean Comfort Women's Trauma, Its Literary Representation, and Colonial Amnesia." *Humanities Research* 64 (2012) 267–300.

LeFever, Perry D. *Understanding Prayers*. Philadelphia: Westminster, 1981.

Levenson, Jon D. *Creation and the Persistence of Evil: The Jewish Drama of Divine Omnipotence*. Princeton: Princeton University Press, 1988.

Lewis, Alan E. *Between Cross and Resurrection: A Theology of Holy Saturday*. Grand Rapids: Eerdmans, 2001.

Lewis, C. S. *A Grief Observed*. London: Faber & Faber, 1961.

Lim, Hee-Kuk. "Political Participation of the Korean Presbyterian Church during the First Republic (1948–1960)." *Korean Presbyterian Journal of Theology* 44 (2012) 13–39.

Linafelt, Tod. *Surviving Lamentations*. Chicago: University of Chicago Press, 2000.

Lischer, Richard. *A Theology of Preaching: The Dynamics of the Gospel*. Eugene, OR: Wipf & Stock, 1992.

Long, Thomas G. "Funeral." In *The New Interpreter's Handbook of Preaching*, edited by Paul Scott Wilson, 385–90. Nashville: Abingdon, 2008.

———. *What Shall We Say? Evil, Suffering, and the Crisis of Faith*. Grand Rapids: Eerdmans, 2011.

Longman, Tremper, III. *Jeremiah, Lamentations*. New Interpretation Biblical Commentary. Milton Keynes: Paternoster, 2008.

Lowry, Eugene L. *The Homiletical Plot: The Sermon as Narrative Art Form*. Atlanta: Knox, 1980.

———. "Narrative Renewed." In *The Renewed Homiletic*, edited by O. Wesley Allen Jr., 81–104. Minneapolis: Fortress, 2010.

———. *The Sermon: Dancing the Edge of Mystery*. Nashville: Abingdon, 1997.

Lubac, Henri de. *Medieval Exegesis*. Grand Rapids: Eerdmans, 2000.

Luccock, Halford. *In the Minister's Workshop*. New York: Abingdon, 1944.

Lundblad, Barbara K. *Transforming the Stone: Preaching through Resistance to Change*. Nashville: Abingdon, 2001.

Luther, Martin. *Lectures on Psalms II*. Edited by Hilton C. Oswald. Luther's Works 11. St. Louis: Concordia, 1976. Kindle.

———. *Lectures on Minor Prophets I*. Edited by Hilton C. Oswald. Luther's Works 18. St. Louis: Concordia, 1975.

———. *Church Postils I*. Edited by Benjamin T. G. Mayes and James L. Langebartels. Luther's Works 75. St. Louis: Concordia, 2013.

Lutz, Tom. *Crying: The Natural and Cultural History of Tears*. New York: Norton, 1999.

MaCann, J. Clinton. *A Theological Introduction to the Book of Psalms: The Psalms as Torah*. Nashville: Abingdon, 1993.

MacIntyre, Alasdair. "The Virtues, the Unity of a Human Life, and the Concept of a Tradition." In *Why Narrative? Readings in Narrative Theology*, edited by Stanley Hauerwas and L. Gregory Jones, 89–111. Grand Rapids: Eerdmans, 1989.

Macquarrie, John. *Martin Heidegger*. Richmond: Knox, 1968.

Macvaugh, Gillbert Stillman. "A Structural Analysis of the Sermon of Dr. Harry Emerson Fosdick." *Quarterly Journal of Speech* 18 (1932) 531–46.

Mandolfo, Carleen. *Daughter Zion Talks Back to the Prophets*. Atlanta: Society of Biblical Literature, 2007.

Marshall, Chris. *Little Book of Biblical Justice: A Fresh Approach to the Bible's Teachings on Justice*. Intercourse, PA: Good, 2005.

Matter, E. Ann. "The Lamentations Commentaries of Hrabanus Maurus and Paschasius Radbertus." *Traditio* 38 (1982) 137–63.

McCarroll, Pamela. *Waiting at the Foot of the Cross: Toward a Theology of Hope for Today*. Eugene, OR: Pickwick, 2014.

McClure, John. "Alienation > Emptying > Compassion (Phil 2:5–11)." In *Patterns of Preaching: A Sermon Sampler*, edited by Ronald J. Allen, 248–51. St. Louis: Chalice, 1998.

———. *Other-Wise Preaching: A Postmodern Ethic for Homiletics*. St. Louis: Chalice, 2001.

———, ed. *The Roundtable Pulpit: Where Leadership and Preaching Meet*. Nashville: Abingdon, 1995.

McKenzie, Alyce M. "Popular Psychology and Preaching." In *The New Interpreter's Handbook of Preaching*, edited by Paul Scott Wilson, 404–6. Nashville: Abingdon, 2008.

The Meeting of Investigators in Working Party on Sewol Ferry, Avoided and Disregarded. Seoul: Book Comma, 2017.

Meier, John P. "The Bible as a Source for Theology." In *Catholic Theological Society of America: Proceedings of the Forty-Third Annual Convention*, 1–14. https://ejournals.bc.edu/index.php/ctsa/article/view/3473/3068.

Metz, Johann Baptist. "A Short Apology of Narrative." In *Why Narrative? Readings in Narrative Theology*, edited by Stanley Hauerwas and L. Gregory Jones, 251–62. Grand Rapids: Eerdmans, 1989.

Middlemas, Jill Anne. *Lamentations: An Introduction and Study Guide*. London: T. & T. Clark, 2021.

———. *The Templeless Age: An Introduction to the History, Literature, and Theology of the "Exile."* Louisville: Westminster John Knox, 2007.

———. *The Troubles of Templeless Judah*. Oxford: Oxford University Press, 2005.

———. "War, Comfort, and Compassion in Lamentations." *Expository Times* 130 (2019) 345–56.
Miller, Patrick D. *Deuteronomy*. Louisville: Knox, 1990.
Min, Anselm. "Migration and Christian Hope." In *Faith on the Move: Towards a Theology of Migration in Asia*, edited by Fabio Baggio and Agnes Brazal, 177–202. Quezon City: Ateneo de Manila University Press, 2008.
Min, Gyeong-bae. *A History of Christian Churches in Korea*. Seoul: Christian Literature Society of Korea, 1982.
———. *Korean Christian Church History*. Seoul: Christian Literature Society of Korea, 1992.
Mintz, Alan. "The Rhetoric of Lamentations and the Representation of Catastrophe." *Prooftexts* 2 (1982) 1–17.
Mitchell, Henry H. *Celebration and Experience in Preaching*. Nashville: Abingdon, 2008.
———. *The Recovery of Preaching*. San Francisco: Harper & Row, 1977.
Moltmann, Jürgen. *The Crucified God: The Cross of Christ as the Foundation and Criticism of Christian Theology*. Minneapolis: Fortress, 1993.
———. *Ethics of Hope*. Minneapolis: Fortress, 2012.
———. *The Spirit of Life: A Universal Affirmation*. Minneapolis: Fortress, 1992.
———. *The Way of Jesus Christ*. Minneapolis: Fortress, 1993.
Moltmann-Wendel, Elisabeth. "Zur Kreuzestheologie Heute Gibt es eine Feministische Kreuzestheologie?" *Evangelische Theologie* 50 (1990) 546–57. https://doi.org/10.14315/evth-1990-1-656.
Moon, Ik-hwan. "Will Democracy Succeed in Korea? (Rom 7:14–25, 1961)." In *Moon Ik-hwan Collected Works*. Vol. 12, *Sermons*, edited by Young-Joon Joe, 267–71. Seoul: Sakyejul, 1999. Kindle.
Moon, Moo-Byung. "Crossing Relationship of Aesthetic Category between Poongyooh Boundary and Sitgim Boundary: Haehak and Han in the Myth and Gut of Jeju." *Korean Aesthetics* 6 (2007) 65–103.
Morrison, Toni. *Beloved*. New York: Vintage, 2004.
Morrow, Lance. *Evil: An Investigation*. New York: Basic, 2003.
Moss, Otis, III. *Blue Note Preaching in a Post-Soul World*. Louisville: Westminster John Knox, 2015.
Myers, Ched. *Who Will Roll Away the Stone? Discipleship Queries for First World Christians*. Maryknoll, NY: Orbis, 1994.
Nam, Dongshin. "Medieval Korean Society and Buddhism." *Journal of Humanities* 8 (2003) 95–113.
Nam, Heung Seok. "Confucian View of Women and the Issue of Modern Women's Leadership." *Tongbanghak* 14 (2008) 275–97.
Neal, Jerusha Matsen. *The Overshadowed Preacher: Mary, the Spirit, and the Labor of Proclamation*. Grand Rapids: Eerdmans, 2020.
Nieman, James R., and Thomas G. Rogers. *Preaching to Every Pew: Cross-Cultural Strategies*. Minneapolis: Fortress, 2001.
Noh, Jong-Hae. "Church and Policy." *Dangdang News*, February 14, 2017. http://www.dangdangnews.com/news/articleView.html?idxno=27983.
Norén, Carol M. *The Woman in the Pulpit*. Nashville: Abingdon, 1991.
Novello, Henry L. "Jesus' Cry of Lament." *Irish Theological Quarterly* 78 (2013) 38–60.

O, Yang-jin. "The Korean War and a Matter of Mourning—On Lee, Ho-cheol's *Na-Sang* (*A Naked Image*) and Hwang, Sun-won's *Bibary* (*A Woman Diver*)." *Journal of Korean Studies* 42 (2012) 227–49.
Oates, Wayne E. *The Christian Pastor*. Philadelphia: Westminster, 1951.
O'Connor, Kathleen M. "Lamentations." In *The New Interpreter's Bible*, edited by Leander E. Keck, 6:1011–72. Nashville: Abingdon, 2001.
———. *Lamentations and the Tears of the World*. Maryknoll, NY: Orbis, 2002.
———. "Stammering toward the Unsayable: Old Testament Theology, Trauma Theory, and Genesis." *Interpretation* 70 (2016) 301–13.
———. "Tears of God and Divine Character." In *God in the Fray*, edited by Tod Linafelt and Timothy K. Beal, 172–85. Minneapolis: Fortress, 1998.
———. "Voice Arguing about Meaning." In *Lamentations in Ancient and Contemporary Context*, edited by Nancy C. Lee and Carleen Mandolfo, 27–32. Atlanta: Society of Biblical Literature, 2008.
Oh, Deok-Kyo. "Calvin's View on Schismatic Movement of Korean Church." *Hapshin Theological Journal* 20 (2002) 194–224.
Öhler, Markus. "To Mourn, Weep, Lament and Groan: On the Heterogeneity of the New Testament's Statement on Lament." In *Evoking Lament: A Theological Discussion*, edited by Eva Harasta and Brian Brook, 149–65. London: T. & T. Clark, 2009.
Orlansky, Harold. "Reactions to the Death of President Roosevelt." *Journal of Social Psychology* 26 (1947) 235–66.
Pae, Kyung-Sik. "With the Hope to Theology of Waiting." *Theological Forum* 57 (2009) 85–122.
Palais, James B. "Confucianism and the Aristocratic/Bureaucratic Balance in Korea." *Harvard Journal of Asiatic Studies* 44 (1984) 427–68.
Park, Andrew Sung. *From Hurt to Healing: A Theology of the Wounded*. Nashville: Abingdon, 2004.
———. *The Wounded Heart of God: The Asian Concept of Han and the Christian Doctrine of Sin*. Nashville: Abingdon, 1993.
Park, Chang Hyon "A Theology of the Post-Sewolho (*Sewol* Ship) Calamity: How Will the Korean Church Be a Witness of the Resurrection of Jesus Who Died with the Sewolho?" *Korean Journal of Christian Studies* 103 (2017) 345–72.
Park, Choong Gu. "Christian Social Ethics Korean Indigenous Theology." *Christian Thought* 35 (1991) 109–35.
Park, Jae Soon. "Critical Review of Christology and Hamartiology." In *Minjung Theology in Transitional Period: Focused on Theological Thoughts of Jukje Nam Dong Seo*, edited by Editorial Committee of the Memorial Papers of Rev. Jukje Seo Nam-Dong, 180–202. Seoul: Korea Theological Institute, 1992.
Park, Jong Hwha. "Resurrected! (1 Sam 2:6–10, 1 Cor 15:51–57, and Mark 16:1–8)." http://www.kdchurch.or.kr/Board/Detail/38/46490?page=19.
Park, Qu-Hwan. "Christian Faith and National Consciousness in Protestant Sermons during the Japanese Occupation." *Christianity and History in Korea* 39 (2013) 251–80.
Park, Sangyil. *Korean Preaching, Han, and Narrative*. New York: Lang, 2008.
Park, Yong-Kyu. *Korean Christian History 2*. Seoul: Korean Institution of Church History, 2017.

Parry, Robin A. "Jesus and Jerusalem: Christological Interpretation of Lamentations in the Church." In *Reading Lamentations Intertextually*, edited by Heath A. Thomas and Brittany N. Melton, 252–65. London: T. & T. Clark, 2021.

———. *Lamentations*. Two Horizons. Grand Rapids: Eerdmans, 2010.

Pearce, Susan M. *On Collecting: An Investigation into Collecting in the European Tradition*. New York: Routledge, 2005.

Pembroke, Neil. "Theocentric Therapeutic Preaching: A Sample Sermon with Commentary." *Practical Theology* 5 (2014) 237–58.

Pesch, Otto Hermann. "Law and Gospel: Luther's Teaching in the Light of the Disintegration of Normative Morality." *Speculative Quarterly Review* 34 (1970) 84–113.

Peterson, Eugene. *Five Smooth Stones for Pastoral Work*. Grand Rapids: Eerdmans, 1992.

Phan, Peter C. "The Experience of Migration as Source of Intercultural Theology." In *Contemporary Issues of Migration and Theology*, edited by Elaine Padilla and Peter C. Phan, 179–209. New York: Palgrave Macmillan, 2013.

Pleins, J. David. *The Psalms: Songs of Tragedy, Hope, and Justice*. Maryknoll, NY: Orbis, 1993.

Powery, Luke A. *Dem Dry Bones: Preaching, Death, and Hope*. Minneapolis: Fortress, 2012.

———. "Holy Spirit/Passion." In *The New Interpreter's Handbook of Preaching*, edited by Paul Wilson, 308–10. Nashville: Abingdon, 2008.

———. "My God, My God, Why?" https://chapel.duke.edu/sites/default/files/My%20God%20My%20God%20Why%203-29-13.pdf.

———. *Spirit Speech: Lament and Celebration in Preaching*. Nashville: Abingdon, 2009.

Provan, Iain W. *Lamentations*. Grand Rapids: Eerdmans, 1991.

Punt, Jeremy. *Postcolonial Biblical Interpretation: Reframing Paul*. Leiden: Brill, 2015.

Raboteau, Albert. *A Sorrowful Joy*. New York: Paulist, 2002.

Rambo, Shelly. "Spirit and Trauma." *Interpretation* 69 (2015) 7–19.

———. *Spirit and Trauma: A Theology of Remaining*. Louisville: Westminster John Knox, 2010.

Ramsey, G. Lee. *Care-Full Preaching: From Sermon to Caring Community*. St. Louis: Chalice, 2000.

Raphael, Melissa. *The Female Face of God in Auschwitz: A Jewish Feminist Theology of the Holocaust*. London: Routledge, 2003.

Ray, Darby Kathleen. *Deceiving the Devil: Atonement, Abuse, and Ransom*. Cleveland: Pilgrim, 1998.

Re'emi, S. Paul. "The Theology of Hope: A Commentary on the Book of Lamentations." In *God's People in Crisis*, edited by Robert Martin-Achard, 73–134. Grand Rapids: Eerdmans, 1984.

Reid, Barbara E. "Beyond Petty Pursuits and Wearisome Widows." *Interpretation* 56 (2002) 284–94.

Renkema, Johan. *Lamentations*. Leuven: Peeters, 1998.

———. "The Meaning of the Parallel Acrostics in Lamentations." *Vetus Testamentum* 45 (1995) 379–83.

Rha, Soong-Chan. *Prophetic Lament: A Call for Justice in Troubled Times*. Downers Grove, IL: InterVarsity, 2015.

Rhie, Deok-Joo. "Early Korean Indigenous Church Formation and Religious Culture: Historical-theological Approach to the Nativization Theology." *Journal of Korean Cultural Theological Society* 8 (2005) 35–70.

Rhodes, Harry A., ed. *History of the Korea Mission, PCUSA*. Vol. 1, *1884–1934*. Seoul: Chosen Mission Presbyterian Church USA, 1934.

Rhodes, Lisa D. "It's Time to Break the Silence (Esth 4:14)." In *Those Preaching Women*, edited by Ella Pearson Mitchell and Jacqueline B. Class, 4:11–20. Valley Forge, PA: Judson, 2004.

Rice, Charles L. *Interpretation and Imagination*. Philadelphia: Fortress, 1970.

———. "The Theater and Preaching." *Journal for Preachers* 8 (1984) 19–25.

Roberts, Jonathan. "Introduction." In *The Oxford Handbook of the Reception History of the Bible*, edited by Michael Lieb et al., 1–8. Oxford: Oxford University Press, 2011.

Rohls, Jan. *Reformed Confessions: Theology from Zurich to Barmen*. Louisville: Westminster John Knox, 1998.

Rong, Lina. *Forgotten and Forsaken by God*. Eugene, OR: Pickwick, 2013.

Rose, Lucy Atkinson. *Sharing the Word: Preaching in the Roundtable Church*. Louisville: Westminster John Knox, 1997.

Rosenberg, Ruth Emily. "A Voice Like Thunder: Corsican Women's Lament as Cultural Work." *Current Musicology* 78 (2004) 31–51.

Russell, Letty. *Church in the Round: Feminist Interpretation of the Church*. Louisville: Westminster John Knox, 1993.

Rutledge, Fleming. *And God Spoke to Abraham: Preaching from the Old Testament*. Grand Rapids: Eerdmans, 2011.

———. *The Bible and the New York Times*. Grand Rapids: Eerdmans, 1998.

———. *The Crucifixion: Understanding the Death of Jesus Christ*. Grand Rapids: Eerdmans, 2015.

———. *The Seven Last Words from the Cross*. Grand Rapids: Eerdmans, 2005.

———. *The Undoing of Death: Sermons for Holy Week and Easter*. Grand Rapids: Eerdmans, 2002.

Ryoo, Jang-Hyun. "A Theological Critique of the Prosperity Theology." *Theological Forum* 61 (2010) 7–30.

Sancken, Joni S. *Stumbling over the Cross: Preaching the Cross and Resurrection Today*. Eugene, OR: Cascade, 2016.

———. *Words That Heal: Preaching Hope to Wounded Souls*. Nashville: Abingdon, 2019.

Schaff, Philip, ed. *A Select Library of the Nicene and Post-Nicene Fathers of the Christian Church*. New York: Christian Literature, 1887–94.

Schapp, Wilhelm. *In Geschichten verstrickt: Zum Sein von Mensch und Ding*. Hamburg: Meiner, 1953.

Schlafer, David J. *What Makes This Day Different? Preaching Grace on Special Occasions*. Cambridge: Cowley, 1998.

Schüssler Fiorenza, Elisabeth. *Bread Not Stone: The Challenge of Feminist Biblical Interpretation*. Boston: Beacon, 1984.

———. *Jesus: Miriam's Child, Sophia's Prophet: Critical Issues in Feminist Christology*. 2nd ed. London: Bloomsbury T. & T. Clark, 2015.

———. "Jesus of Nazareth in Historical Research." In *Thinking of Christ: Proclamation, Explanation, Meaning*, edited by Tatha Wiley, 29–48. New York: Continuum, 2003.

———. *Rhetoric and Ethic: The Politics of Biblical Studies*. Minneapolis: Fortress, 1999.

Schwager, Raymund. *Must There Be Scapegoats? Violence and Redemption in the Bible.* Translated by Maria L. Assad. New York: Crossroad, 2000.

Seibert, Eric A. "Recent Research on Divine Violence in the Old Testament (with Special Attention to Christian Theological Perspectives)." *Currents in Biblical Research* 15 (2016) 8–40.

Sewol Ferry Tragedy Countermeasure Committee in The National Council of Churches in Korea. *To Be With.* Seoul: The Christian Literature Society of Korea, 2014.

Sewol Special Investigative Committee Investigators Association. *Turned Away and Avoided.* Seoul: Book Comma, 2017.

Shea, William H. "The Qinah Structure of the Book of Lamentations." *Biblica* 60 (1979) 103–7.

Shin, Eun-kyung. *Pungryu: The Source of East Asian Aesthetics.* Paju: Bogosa, 1999.

Smith, Christine M. *Preaching as Weeping, Confession, and Resistance: Radical Responses to Radical Evil.* Louisville: Westminster/John Knox, 1992.

———. *Risking the Terror: Resurrection in This Life.* Eugene, OR: Wipf & Stock, 2010.

———. "Unspeakable Loss (Jud 11:29–40)." In *Preaching as Weeping, Confession, and Resistance: Radical Responses to Radical Evil,* 164–72. Louisville: Westminster/John Knox, 1992.

———. *Weaving the Sermon: Preaching in a Feminist Perspective.* Louisville: Westminster John Knox, 1989.

Snider, Phil. "Introduction." In *Preaching as Resistance: Voices of Hope, Justice, and Solidarity,* edited by Phil Snider, 1–10. St. Louis: Chalice, 2018.

Sobrino, Jon. *Christ the Liberator: A View from the Victims.* Maryknoll, NY: Orbis, 2001.

———. *Jesus the Liberator: A Historical-Theological Reading of Jesus of Nazareth.* Maryknoll, NY: Orbis, 1993.

———. "The Significance of Puebla for the Catholic Church in Latin America." In *Reflections on Puebla,* by John Paul II, 22–43. London: Catholic Institute for International Relations, 1980.

Sohn, Hohyun. "Yoon Dong-Ju and Theology of Sorrow: Yoon's Theodicy in the 'Beatitudes.'" *Theological Forum* 81 (2015) 107–38.

Sölle, Dorothee. *Suffering.* Philadelphia: Fortress, 1975.

Son, Jae-Seo. "A Study on the 'Yunsan' Structure of Korean Mask Dance through the Theory of 'Shinmyung.'" *Korean Aesthetics* 14 (2015) 75–106.

Son, Kyu Tae. "Blessed Are Those Who Mourn (Matt 5:4)." http://veritas.kr/archive/bbs/board.php?bo_table=drson_1&wr_id=32&page=2.

Song, Choan-Seng. *Jesus, the Crucified People.* New York: Crossroad, 1990.

Song, Ju Yol. "Fourth Anniversary of Sewol Disaster, Was Korean Church a Neighbor of Those Who Suffer?" *CBS Nocut News,* April 11, 2018. https://www.nocutnews.co.kr/news/4953243.

Stackhouse, Ian. "Confession and Complaint: Christian Pastoral Reflections on Lamentations." In *Great Is Thy Faithfulness? Reading Lamentations as Sacred Scripture,* edited by Robin A. Parry and Heath A. Thomas, 198–210. Eugene, OR: Pickwick, 2011.

St. Clair, Raquel A. "Womanist Criticism." In *The New Interpreter's Handbook of Preaching,* edited by Paul Scott Wilson, 170–72. Nashville: Abingdon, 2008.

Stears, Karen. "Death Becomes Her: Gender and Athenian Death Ritual." In *Lament: Studies in the Ancient Mediterranean and Beyond,* edited by Ann Suter, 139–55. Oxford: Oxford University Press, 2008.

Steimle, Edmund A. "Preaching and the Biblical Story of Good and Evil." *Preaching* 31 (1976) 198–211.
Stern, Elsie R. "Lamentations in Jewish Liturgy." In *Great Is Thy Faithfulness? Reading Lamentations as Sacred Scripture*, edited by Robin A. Parry and Heath A. Thomas, 88–91. Eugene, OR: Pickwick, 2011.
Stuempfle, Herman G., Jr. *Preaching Law and Gospel*. Philadelphia: Fortress, 1978.
Sugirtharajah, Rasiah. S. "Muddling Along at the Margins." In *Still at the Margins: Biblical Scholarship Fifteen Years after Voices from the Margin*, edited by R. S. Sugirtharajah, 8–21. London: T. & T. Clark, 2008.
———. *Postcolonial Criticism and Biblical Interpretation*. Oxford: Oxford University Press, 2002.
Suh, Changwon. *A Formulation of Minjung Theology: Toward a Socio-Historical Theology of Asia*. Seoul: Nathan, 1990.
Suh, Nam-Dong. "The Formation of Han and Its Theological Reflection." In *Inquiry of Minjung Theology*, 108–45. Seoul: Hangilsa, 1983.
———. "Historical References for a Theology of Minjung." In *Minjung Theology: People as the Subjects of History*, edited by Commission on Theological Concerns of Christian Conference of Asia, 155–84. Maryknoll, NY: Orbis, 1981.
———. *The Study of Minjung Theology*. Seoul: Dongyeon, 2018.
Suter, Ann. "Introduction." In *Lament: Studies in the Ancient Mediterranean and Beyond*, edited by Ann Suter, 3–17. Oxford: Oxford University Press, 2008.
Swenson, Kristine M. *Living Through Pain*. Waco, TX: Baylor University Press, 2005.
Swinton, John. *Raging with Compassion*. Grand Rapids: Eerdmans, 2007.
Switzer, David K. *The Dynamics of Grief*. Nashville: Abingdon, 1970.
Talley, Thomas J. *The Origins of the Liturgical Year*. New York: Pueblo, 1986.
Taylor, Barbara Brown. *Gospel Medicine*. Cambridge: Cowley, 1995.
———. *The Preaching Life*. Cambridge: Cowley, 1993.
Taylor, John R. "Category Extension by Metonymy and Metaphor." In *Metaphor and Metonymy in Comparison and Contrast*, edited by Rene Dirven and Ralf Parings, 323–48. Berlin: de Gruyter, 2002.
Taylor, Mark Lewis. *The Executed God: The Way of the Cross in Lockdown America*. 2nd ed. Minneapolis: Fortress, 2015.
Terrien, Samuel. *The Elusive Presence*. New York: Harper & Row, 1978.
Theissen, Gerd. *The Sign Language of Faith*. London: SCM, 1995.
Thomas, Frank A. *They Like to Never Quit Praisin' God: The Role of Celebration in Preaching*. Cleveland: United Church, 1997.
Thomas, Heath A. "Feminist Interpretation(s) and Lamentations." In *Great Is Thy Faithfulness? Reading Lamentations as Sacred Scripture*, edited by Robin A. Parry and Heath A. Thomas, 166–74. Eugene, OR: Pickwick, 2011.
———. "Holy Scripture and Hermeneutics: Lamentations in Critical and Theological Reflection." In *Great Is Thy Faithfulness? Reading Lamentations as Sacred Scripture*, edited by Robin A. Parry and Heath A. Thomas, 1–25. Eugene, OR: Pickwick, 2011.
———. "Lamentations in the Patristic Period." In *Great Is Thy Faithfulness? Reading Lamentations as Sacred Scripture*, edited by Robin A. Parry and Heath A. Thomas, 113–9. Eugene, OR: Pickwick, 2011.
———. *Poetry and Theology in the Book of Lamentations: The Aesthetics of an Open Text*. Sheffield: Sheffield Phoenix, 2013.

———. "The Rabbis Talk Back through the Prophets: Intertextuality, Lamentations, and Divine Mourning." In *Reading Lamentations Intertextually*, edited by Heath A. Thomas and Brittany N. Melton, 266–78. London T. & T. Clark, 2021.

Tiemeyer, Lena-Sofia. "Lamentations in Isaiah 40–55." In *Great Is Thy Faithfulness? Reading Lamentations as Sacred Scripture*, edited by Robin A. Parry and Heath A. Thomas, 55–63. Eugene, OR: Pickwick, 2011.

Tietje, Adam D. *Toward a Pastoral Theology of Holy Saturday: Providing Spiritual Care for War Wounded Souls*. Eugene, OR: Wipf & Stock, 2018.

Tisdale, Leonora Tubbs. "God's No and Ours (Esther 1:1–22; Gal 5:1)." In *Patterns of Preaching: A Sermon Sampler*, edited by Ronald J. Allen, 201–6. St. Louis: Chalice, 1998.

———. *Prophetic Preaching: A Pastoral Approach*. Louisville: Westminster John Knox, 2010.

Tolbert, Elizabeth. "Women Cry with Words: Symbolization of Affect in the Karelian Lament." *Yearbook for Traditional Music* 22 (1990) 80–105.

Travis, Sarah. *Decolonizing Preaching: The Pulpit as Postcolonial Space*. Eugene, OR: Cascade, 2014.

Trigg, Joseph W. *Origen*. New York: Rutledge, 1998.

Turner, Mary Donovan. "Prophetic Preaching." In *The New Interpreter's Handbook of Preaching*, edited by Paul Scott Wilson, 101–3. Nashville: Abingdon, 2008.

Tyler, J. Jeffrey, ed. *Jeremiah, Lamentations*. Reformation Commentary on Scripture OT 11. Downers Grove, IL: IVP Academic, 2018.

Um, Yo Seop. "Morphology of Contemporary Korean Church Sermons II." *Christian Thought* 16 (1972) 126–31.

Verhey, Allen. *Reading the Bible in the Strange World of Medicine*. Grand Rapids: Eerdmans, 2003.

The Veritable Records of the Joseon Dynasty. *Veritable Records of King Jungjon*. Vol. 37. http://sillok.history.go.kr/id/kka_11411016_013.

———. *Veritable Records of King Jungjong*. Vol. 43. http://sillok.history.go.kr/id/kka_11610023_003.

———. *Veritable Records of King Sejong*. Series 1, chapter 1. http://sillok.history.go.kr/id/kda_000.

———. *Veritable Records of King Seonjo*. Vol. 34. http://sillok.history.go.kr/id/kna_12601018_001.

Volf, Miroslav. *The End of Memory: Remembering Rightly in a Violent World*. Grand Rapids: Eerdmans, 2006.

———. *Exclusion and Embrace: A Theological Exploration of Identity, Otherness, and Reconciliation*. Nashville: Abingdon, 1996.

Walker, Alice. *In Search of Our Mothers' Gardens: Womanist Prose*. San Diego: Harcourt Brace Jovanovich, 1983.

Walsh, Brian J., and Sylvia C. Keesmaat. *Colossians Remixed: Subverting the Empire*. Downers Grove, IL: InterVarsity, 2004.

Walton, John H. *Ancient Israelite Literature in Its Cultural Context: A Survey of Parallels between Biblical and Ancient Near Eastern Texts*. Grand Rapids: Regency Reference Library, 1989.

Ware, Kallistos. "An Obscure Matter: The Mystery of Tears in Orthodox Spirituality." In *Holy Tears: Weeping in the Religious Imagination*, edited by Kimberley Christine

Patton and John Stratton Hawley, 242–54. Princeton: Princeton University Press, 2005.
Warnock, Mary. *Imagination*. Berkeley: University of California Press, 1976.
Webb, Stephen H. "Why von Balthasar Was Wrong about Holy Saturday." *First Things*, August 27, 2013. https://www.firstthings.com/web-exclusives/2013/08/why-von-balthasar-was-wrong-about-holy-saturday.
Weems, Renita J. *Battered Love: Marriage, Sex, and Violence in the Hebrew Prophets*. Minneapolis: Fortress.
Weingarten, Kaethe. "Reasonable Hope: Construct, Clinical Applications, and Supports." *Family Process* 49 (2010) 5–25.
Wendland, Kristin J. "Naming Jerusalem: Poetry and the Identity of the Personified City in Lamentations 1–2." *Journal for the Study of the Old Testament* 46 (2021) 64–78.
Wenthe, Dean O., ed. *Jeremiah, Lamentations*. Ancient Christian Commentary on Scripture OT 12. Downers Grove, IL: InterVarsity, 2009.
Wesley, John. "Sermon 43: The Scripture Way of Salvation (Ephesians 2:8)." In *Sermons on Several Occasions*, 1:384–91. New York: Lane & Scott, 1852.
Westermann, Claus. *Lamentations*. Minneapolis: Fortress, 1994.
———. *Praise and Lament in the Psalms*. Edinburgh: T. & T. Clark, 1981.
Whybray, R. N. "'Shall Not the Judge of All the Earth Do What Is Just?' God's Oppression of the Innocent in the Old Testament." In *Shall Not the Judge of All the Earth Do What Is Right? Studies on the Nature of God in Tribute to James L. Crenshaw*, edited by D. Penchansky and P. L. Redditt, 1–19. Winona Lake, IN: Eisenbrauns, 2000.
Wiersbe, Warren W. *Preaching and Teaching with Imagination: The Quest for Biblical Ministry*. Grand Rapids: Baker, 1994.
Willey, Patricia. *Remember the Former Things*. Atlanta: Scholars, 1997.
Williams, Delores S. "Black Women's Surrogate Experience and the Christian Notion of Redemption." In *After Patriarchy: Feminist Transformations of the World Religions*, edited by Paula M. Cooey et al., 1–14. Maryknoll, NY: Orbis, 1990.
Willimon, William H. "Religious Rage." In *The Collected Sermons of William H. Willimon*, 103–8. Louisville: Westminster John Knox, 2010.
Wilson, Paul Scott. *Broken Words: Reflections on the Craft of Preaching*. Nashville: Abingdon, 2004.
———. *A Concise History of Preaching*. Nashville: Abingdon, 1992.
———. *The Four Pages of the Sermon: A Guide to Biblical Preaching*. Nashville: Abingdon, 2018.
———. *Imagination of the Heart*. Nashville: Abingdon, 1988.
———. *The Practice of Preaching*. Nashville: Abingdon, 1995.
———. *Preaching and Homiletical Theory*. St. Louis: Chalice, 2004.
———. *Setting Words on Fire: Putting God at the Center of the Sermon*. Nashville: Abingdon, 2008.
Wimberly, Edward P. *Moving from Shame to Self-Worth: Preaching and Pastoral Care*. Nashville: Abingdon, 1999.
Wogaman, J. Philip. *Speaking the Truth in Love: Prophetic Preaching to a Broken World*. Louisville: Westminster John Knox, 1998.
Women's Division in Institute for National Democracy Movement. "Humiliated Diplomacy with Japan, Weeping Revengeful Spirits of 'Comfort Women.'" *Situation Research* 30 (1992) 131–40.

Wright, N. T. *Evil and the Justice of God*. Downers Grove, IL: InterVarsity, 2006.
———. *God in Public: How the Bible Speaks Truth to Power Today*. London: SPCK, 2016.
———. *Justification: God's Plan & Paul's Vision*. Downers Grove, IL: IVP Academic, 2009.
———. *Paul in New Perspective*. Minneapolis: Fortress, 2009.
———. *Surprised by Hope: Rethinking Heaven, the Resurrection, and the Mission of the Church*. New York: HarperOne, 2008.
———. *What Saint Paul Really Said*. Grand Rapids: Eerdmans, 1997.
Yang, Hyun Ah. "Testimony and Writing History: Representation of Korean Military Comfort Women's Subjectivities." *Society and History* 60 (2001) 60–98.
Yang, Xiaoli. "Towards a Chinese Theology of Displacement: The Poetic Journey of a Chinese Migrant." *Mission Studies* 37 (2020) 193–217.
Yi, Jungyeon. "Modern Man with Premodern Religiosity: Ideology of Growth in the 1970s and Yoido Full Gospel Church." *Korean Journal of Sociology* 52 (2018) 207–24.
Yi, Mahn Yol. *Korean Christianity and National Consciousness*. Paju: Jisik-Sanup, 2000.
Yim, Jeong-A. "A Study on the Korean Women's Shame from the Perspective of Pastoral Care and Counseling: Focusing on the Psychological and Theological Aspects and Strategies for Pastoral Care." *Pastoral Care and Counseling* 32 (2019) 263–95.
Yoo, Chang Hyung. "3.1 Movement from the Perspective on Christian Participation in Political Issues." *Journal of Systematic Theology* 32 (2019) 88–121.
Yoo, Sun-hee. "I Wish You Shared Sadness and Are Comforted through a Yellow Handkerchief." *Ohmynews*, May 7, 2014. http://www.ohmynews.com/NWS_Web/View/at_pg.aspx?CNTN_CD=A0001988528.
You, Eunho. "Spirituality of Prayer in the Gospel of Luke." *Theology and Praxis* 32 (2012) 571–606.
Yu, Dong Sik. *The Vein of Korean Theology*. Seoul: Junmangsa, 1984.
Yu, Jeboon. "Ethics of Representation: Memory and Mourning of the 'Comfort' Women in *A Gesture Life*." *Modern English Novel* 13 (2006) 77–95.
Yum, Phil Hyung. "A Theological Analysis of the Historical Development of Preaching in Korea." *Theology and the World* 11 (1985) 217–51.
Zehr, Howard. *Changing Lenses: A New Focus for Crime and Justice*. Scottdale, PA: Herald, 2005.
Zylla, Phil C. *The Roots of Sorrow*. Waco, TX: Baylor University Press, 2012.

Subject Index

absence, God, xviii, 81, 85, 90, 101, 132, 149, 165, 177–79, 181
act of hope. See hope, act.
Asians, 98, 121, 138, 192
apocalyptic, xv, 3, 53, 88, 89, 95, 96, 106, 107, 150
apocalyptic hope. See hope, apocalyptic.
atonement, 94, 95, 99, 100, 108, 120

Bansang system, 51
biblical lament, xvi, xvii, 2, 3, 27, 38, 40
black preaching. See preaching, black.
Blacks, xiii, 4, 99, 120, 129, 138, 140, 144–47, 172, 189, 192

Christ's suffering. See suffering, Christ.
Christ's victory, xv, 96, 113, 219
Christus Victor. See Christ's victory.
city lament. See lament, city.
collective-self, 38, 87, 188, 206–9, 217
"Comfort Women", 49, 50, 58, 60–62, 68, 188, 191,
communal lament. See lament, communal.
community mourning. See lament, communal.
counter-testimony, xvi, 24, 28, 29, 83
crisis, public, xvii, 130, 143
cross-cultural preaching. See preaching, cross-cultural.
crucifixion, x, xvii, 5, 35, 37, 77, 79, 80, 83, 93, 95, 97–100, 103, 108–10, 118–21, 123, 134, 145, 157, 158, 170, 180, 210, 212, 219
cry of suffering. See suffering, expression.

Daesungtonggok, 65
Dikaiosyne, 110, 111, 113, 124, 188, 196, 207, 217, 219
divine-human reconciliation, 95, 109, 187
divine lament. See lament, God.
divine suffering. See suffering, God.

Easter, 37, 78, 80, 107, 108, 116, 117, 163, 193, 195, 201, 205
enjambment, 21, 22
envisioning, xiv, xvi, xvii, xix, 33, 81, 101, 147, 162, 195, 196, 204, 205
epic chant, Korea. See Pansori
eschatological, 24, 52, 53, 81, 82, 85, 89, 96, 104, 109–13, 120, 157, 162, 167, 195–97, 206, 207, 218, 220
eschatological hope. See hope, eschatological.
eternal life, 108, 109, 147, 163
ethics-driven preaching. See preaching, ethics-driven.

faith community, 24, 40
feminist/womanist preaching. See preaching, feminist/womanist.
fragmentary hope. See hope, fragmentary.

frame of the law-gospel. See law and gospel.
funeral dirge. See lament, funeral. (Burial)

Good Friday, 38, 98, 99, 102, 116, 117, 193, 195
God's absence. See absence, God.
God's presence. See presence, God.
God's transcendence. See transcendence.
God's triumph, 122
gospel
    gospel communication, 151, 168
    gospel experience, 144, 165, 173
    gospel, language, 148, 220
    gospel, preaching, xiii, 127, 145, 157, 161, 162, 180, 219, 220
grace, assurance, 132, 145
grace, God, 8, 9, 82, 86, 114, 159–61, 163, 170, 187, 209
grace and trouble. See trouble and grace.
Gut, 42, 62, 64, 66, 67

Han, x, xvii, 40–43, 50–52, 56–59, 61–70, 72, 74, 75, 78, 99, 117, 118, 165, 180, 184, 203, 220
Hanpuri, xvii, 40–42, 57, 62–64, 66, 67, 72, 78, 79
Holy Saturday, xviii, 24, 105–7, 113, 117, 132, 165, 183, 184, 193, 194
Holy Spirit, x, xv, xviii, 3, 8, 47, 55, 70, 77, 107, 109, 110, 113, 115, 135, 143–46, 164, 170, 180, 195–97, 206, 107, 210, 217, 219, 220
honor-shame culture. See Korean culture.
Hope
    hope, act, 38
    hope against hope, 112, 123–25
    hope, apocalyptic, 88
    hope, eschatological, 52, 157, 195–197, 206
    hope, fragmentary, 31
    hope in God, 24, 32, 116
    hope in Lamentations, 9, 36

hopelessness, xiv, 102, 104, 140, 165, 187, 193, 194
hope, proclamation, 26, 38, 130, 195, 206
hope, suffering, See suffering and hope.
hope, timing, xix, 211

imagination, xviii, 92, 102, 127, 129, 153–56, 158
incarnation, 115–17, 207
Ingwauengbo, 48
I-voice, See voice, I.

Japanese oppression, 44, 54, 59–61, 68, 191
Japanese Colonial period, See Japanese imperialism.
Japanese colonialism, See Japanise imperialism.
Japanese imperialism, 42, 45, 49, 53, 67, 68, 69, 70
Jesus' suffering. See suffering, Christ.

Korean Christianity, See Korean church.
Korean church, 42–47, 52, 53, 55, 56, 70, 73–76
Korean culture, xvii, 39–41, 47, 48, 50, 72, 180
Korean honor-shame culture. See Korean culture.
Korean literature, 41, 67
Korean people (Koreans), xvii, 43–49, 53, 54, 72–74
Korean poet. See Korean literature.
Korean preachers, 48, 52, 53, 70, 76
Korean pulpit. See Korean preachers.
Korean theologians, 75
Korean thought. See Korean culture.
Korean War, 44–46, 49, 69, 71, 73

Lament
    lament, Bible. See biblical lament. (lament in the Bible)
    lament, city, 14, 16, 18
    lament, communal, xiv, xvi, xvii, xix, 4, 14–17, 24–26, 32, 38, 40,

62, 69, 78, 79, 82, 88, 126, 143, 147, 183, 207, 200, 213, 217
lament, funeral, xiv, 2, 14, 15, 18, 65, 202
lament, God (divine lament, lamenting God, God lamenting, God laments), xv, xvii, xviii, xix, 3, 26, 78–81, 91, 92, 97, 100, 101, 106, 107, 109, 119, 123, 124, 126, 132, 144, 169, 189, 193, 199, 200–203, 219
lament, human, xv, xvii, xix, 81, 82, 91, 106, 126, 144, 169, 219
lament, language, xvii, 67, 181, 184, 193, 212, 215–19
lament preaching. See lament-driven preaching.
lament psalms, 2, 3, 15, 16, 18, 147, 186
lament, public, 27, 40, 59, 75, 188, 213, 220
lament and celebration, xi, 145, 146, 163
lament-driven preaching, xv, xviii, xix, 35, 79, 126, 168, 169, 183, 189, 192, 194, 195, 209, 211, 215, 217
lament theology, 12, 29, 78, 80, 81, 123, 124
lamenting women, 27, 181
law and gospel, xviii, 159–62
law-gospel movement. See law and gospel.
lectionaries, xviii, 147
liberation preaching. See preaching, liberation.
liturgy, xvi, 7, 17, 38, 193, 212, 213, 216, 217

mask dancing, Korea. See Talchum.
metaphor, xviii, 20, 25, 37, 41, 53, 64, 95, 103, 127, 135, 137, 148, 151–53, 156, 158, 159, 173, 175, 179, 185, 200
Minjung theology, 56, 57, 123, 203
mourning, 3, 5, 7, 15, 36, 38, 69, 75, 76, 92, 99, 106, 113, 131, 132, 136, 143, 156, 157, 178, 179, 181, 183, 185, 186, 200, 205, 208, 210, 220
narrative preaching. See preaching, narrative.

New Homiletic, 126, 127, 148, 149, 151

pain and hope. See hope, suffering.
Pansori, 41, 62, 63
Paschal Triduum narratives, 80, 81, 91, 115, 117, 120, 124, 125
pastoral consciousness in preaching. See preaching, pastoral.
postcolonial preaching. See preaching, postcolonial.
pray together loudly, Korea. See Tongseong prayer.
preaching
  preaching, black, (black preacher, black preaching, black tradition) 144–47
  preaching, cross-cultural, 136, 141, 142
  preaching, ethics-driven, 130
  preaching, feminist/womanist, 136–39, 141, 142
  preaching, imagination 127, 148, 153–156, 158
  preaching, lament-driven. See lament-driven preaching.
  preaching, liberation, 139–42
  preaching, narrative, 127, 151
  preaching, pastoral, 133, 134
  preaching, postcolonial, 129
  preaching, social justice, 133, 136, 143, 153
  preaching, trauma-aware, 164
  preaching about suffering. See suffering, preaching.
  preaching on social justice. See preaching, social justice.
  preaching with pastoral awareness. See preaching, pastoral.
presence, God, xv, 31, 90, 105, 119, 124, 132, 135, 161, 177–80, 205, 208, 216

proclamation of hope. See hope, proclamation.
prophetic preaching. See preaching, ethics-driven.
providence, 108
psychological, xviii, 13, 31, 32, 47, 56, 62, 181, 183, 190
public crisis. See crisis, public.
public lament. See lament, public.
public lament prayer. See lament, public.

reality of suffering. See suffering, reality.
redemptive, xvi, xvii, 44, 72, 81, 88, 91, 100, 108, 109, 114, 120, 137, 161, 165–67, 178, 200, 210, 219
Reformed Church, 102, 159
resilience, xvii, 18, 39, 40, 64, 75, 78, 79, 114, 172, 181, 183, 217
response to suffering. See suffering, expression.
retributive justice. See Ingwauengbo.
ritual of shamanism, Korea. See Gut.

salvation, 7, 10, 30, 31, 43, 53, 57, 69, 71, 79, 87, 95, 98, 105, 107, 108, 110, 114, 119, 130, 135, 143, 147, 150, 151, 157–160, 165, 167, 173, 177, 180, 181, 186, 193, 198, 199, 207, 219
Sewol ferry, 40, 66, 73, 74, 78, 186, 188, 190, 191, 218
shamanism ritual, Korea. See Gut.
silence of God, xiii, 1, 23, 27, 29, 30, 33, 88–91, 106, 107, 177–79, 186, 218
social justice, xvii, 71, 111, 133, 136, 143, 153, 185
social injustice, xiii, xiv, xvi, xviii, 3, 59, 63, 72, 78, 83, 85, 118, 121, 130, 132, 133, 135, 142, 167, 170
social movement, xvii, 57–59, 140
solidarity, xv, 31, 35, 81, 94, 102, 104–7, 113, 115, 116, 122–25, 132, 133, 137, 139, 142, 144, 147, 169–71, 187, 188, 191, 193, 194, 200, 201, 207, 210

status system, Korea. See Bansang system.
storytelling in preaching. See preaching, narrative.
suffering
  suffering and hope (pain and hope, suffering and salvation, suffering-hope frames) xiv, xv, xvii–xix, 13, 24, 35, 40, 81, 87, 116, 126, 127, 130, 148, 153, 156–158, 168, 169, 180, 186, 193, 206, 209, 211, 216–20
  suffering and salvation. See suffering and hope.
  suffering, Christ, xv, 6–8, 38, 84, 98, 100, 106, 138, 147, 164, 121, 170, 173, 194, 219
  suffering, expression (response to suffering, cry of suffering) 89, 91, 215
  suffering, faith, xvi, 39, 215
  suffering-hope frame. See suffering and hope
  suffering, God, 117, 119, 147, 202, 210, 217
  suffering in faith. See suffering, faith.
  suffering of Jesus. See suffering, Christ.
  suffering, preaching, 126, 173, 177, 194
  suffering, reality, xiii, xiv, xix, 6, 12, 13, 22, 29, 63, 76, 81, 84, 113, 124, 130, 156–58, 161, 196, 198, 207, 210, 215, 216, 218
  suffering servant, 54, 91, 122, 173
  suffering, unbearable, 16, 25, 40, 81, 189
  suffering, unjust, 85, 120
sympathy, xvii, 32, 35, 36, 61, 175, 199, 210

Talchum, 35, 62, 64, 65, 180
tears, xiv, 1, 4, 6, 22, 36, 67, 71, 91, 92, 94, 113, 114, 143, 175, 180, 184, 200, 201, 203, 205–8, 210, 215–17, 220

theodicy, xviii, 10, 75, 106, 123, 146, 147, 151
theological concept of trouble-grace. See trouble and grace.
threat of Japan. See Japanese oppression.
timing of hope. See hope, timing.
Tongseong prayer, 69, 70
transcendence, 57, 69, 72
transitional, xiv, xv, xvii, xviii, 81, 127, 146, 156, 157, 168, 216, 217, 219
trauma and healing, 164
trauma-aware preaching. See preaching, trauma-aware.
trouble and grace, 127, 157, 158, 162–68, 180, 211
trouble-grace dynamics/structure/frame/form. See trouble and grace.
truth telling, 24, 36, 61, 187–90

unbearable suffering. See suffering, unbearable.
unjust suffering. See suffering, unjust.

violence, xiii, xviii, 20, 23, 27, 34, 46, 49–51, 60, 68, 83, 95, 96, 99, 100, 107, 110, 120–22, 133, 136–38, 141, 156, 163, 166, 167, 172, 174–77, 179, 191, 194, 199, 203, 204, 214, 215, 220
voice
 voice, I, 31
 voice(s) in Lamentations, xiii, xvi, xvii, 1, 11, 22–24, 26, 28–36, 69, 70, 86, 91, 124, 171, 179, 186, 213
 voiceless, 34, 84, 88, 111, 117, 130
 voice of Christ/God/Jesus, 6, 7, 131, 162, 177
 voice of complaint/sufferers/survivors/victims, xv, 4, 7, 13, 36, 65, 73, 90, 114, 129, 170, 171, 172, 184, 185, 188, 190, 192, 215, 216, 218
 voice, We, 30–33
vulnerability, 33, 34, 98, 165, 184, 198
wailing out together loudly, Korea. See Daesungtonggok.

We-voice, See voice, We.
Weeping, xiv, 58, 85, 92, 101, 124, 132, 138, 157, 166, 181, 199, 200, 206, 207, 212–14
Woe oracles, 3

www.ingramcontent.com/pod-product-compliance
Lightning Source LLC
Chambersburg PA
CBHW050346230426
43663CB00010B/2008